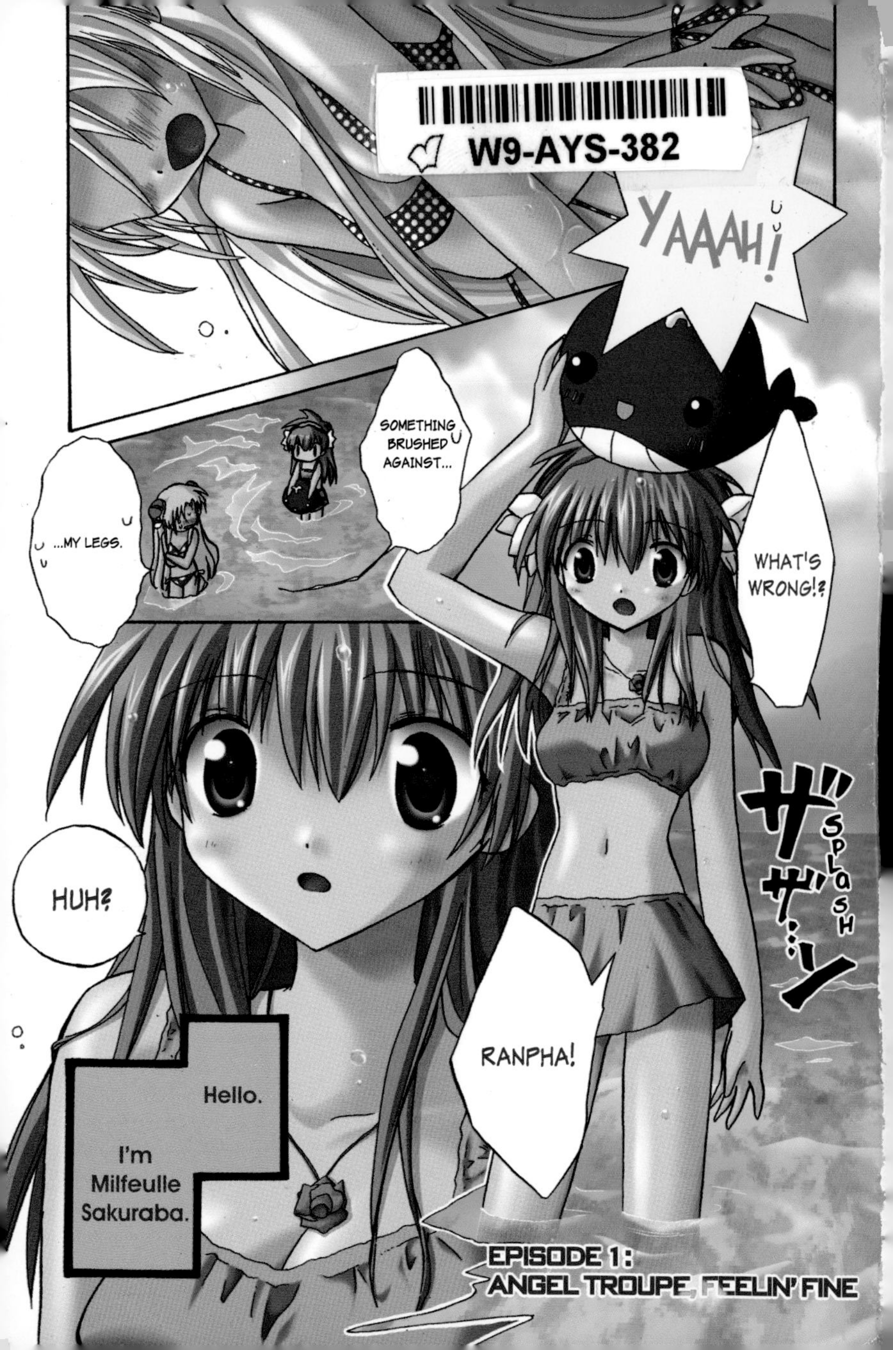
YAAAH!
WHAT'S WRONG!?
SOMETHING BRUSHED AGAINST...
...MY LEGS.
ザザ…ン
SPLASH
RANPHA!
HUH?
Hello.
I'm Milfeulle Sakuraba.
EPISODE 1:
ANGEL TROUPE, FEELIN' FINE

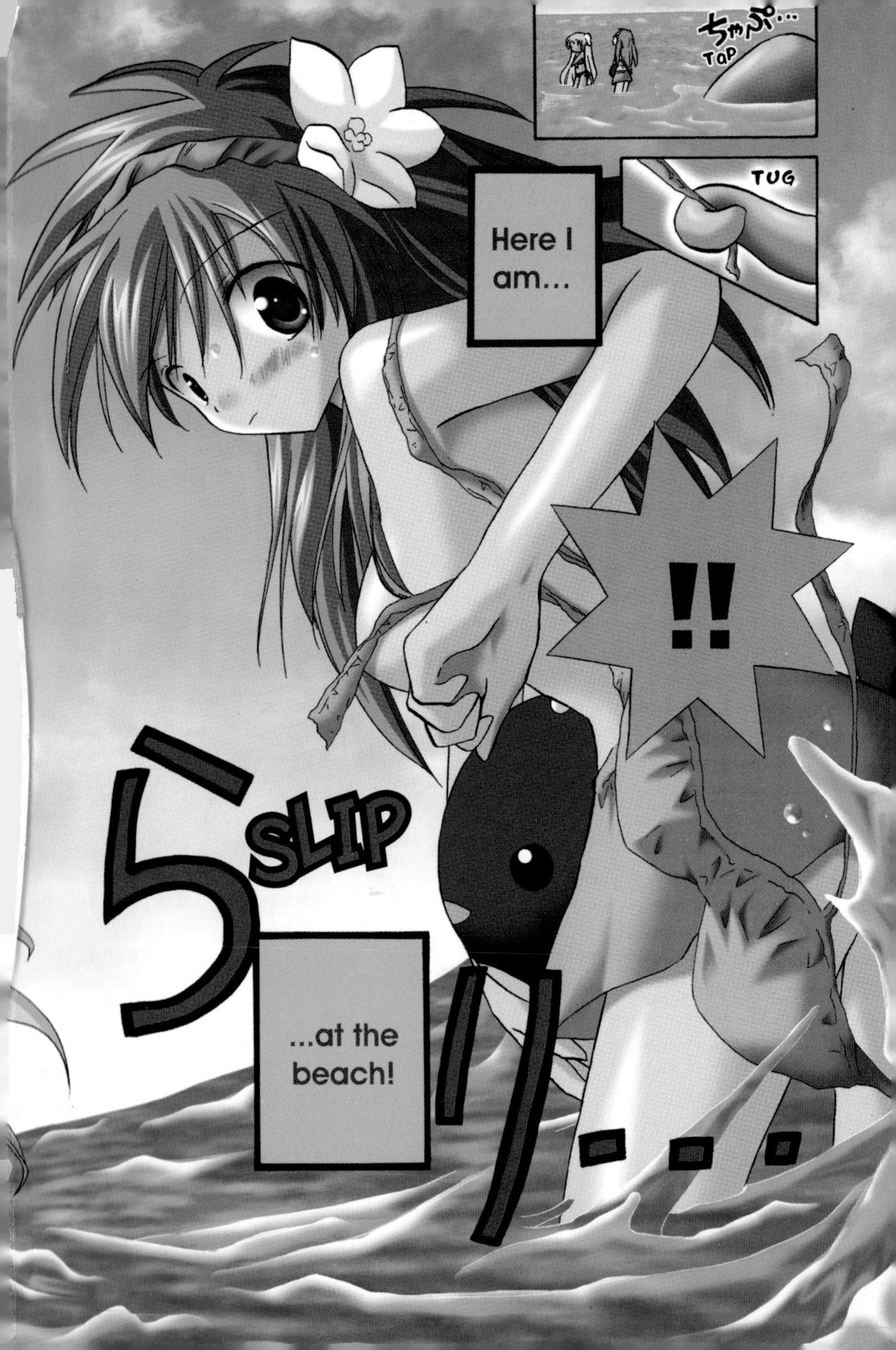
ちゃぷ…
TAP
TUG
Here I am…
!!
SLIP
...at the beach!

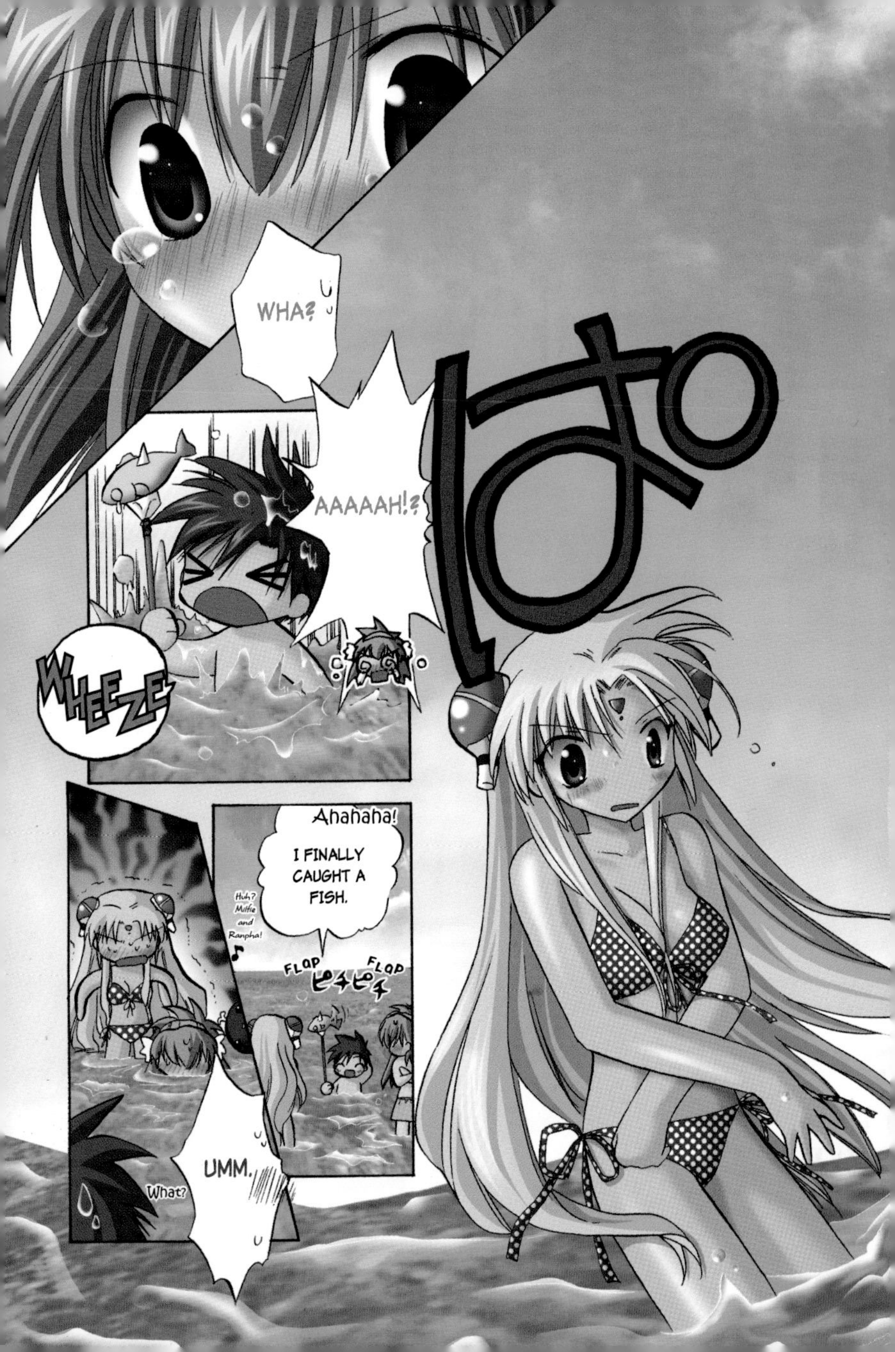
ぱ
WHA?
AAAAAH!?
WHEEZE
Ahahaha!
I FINALLY CAUGHT A FISH.
Huh? Milfie and Ranpha!
FLAP ピチピチ FLAP
UMM.
What?

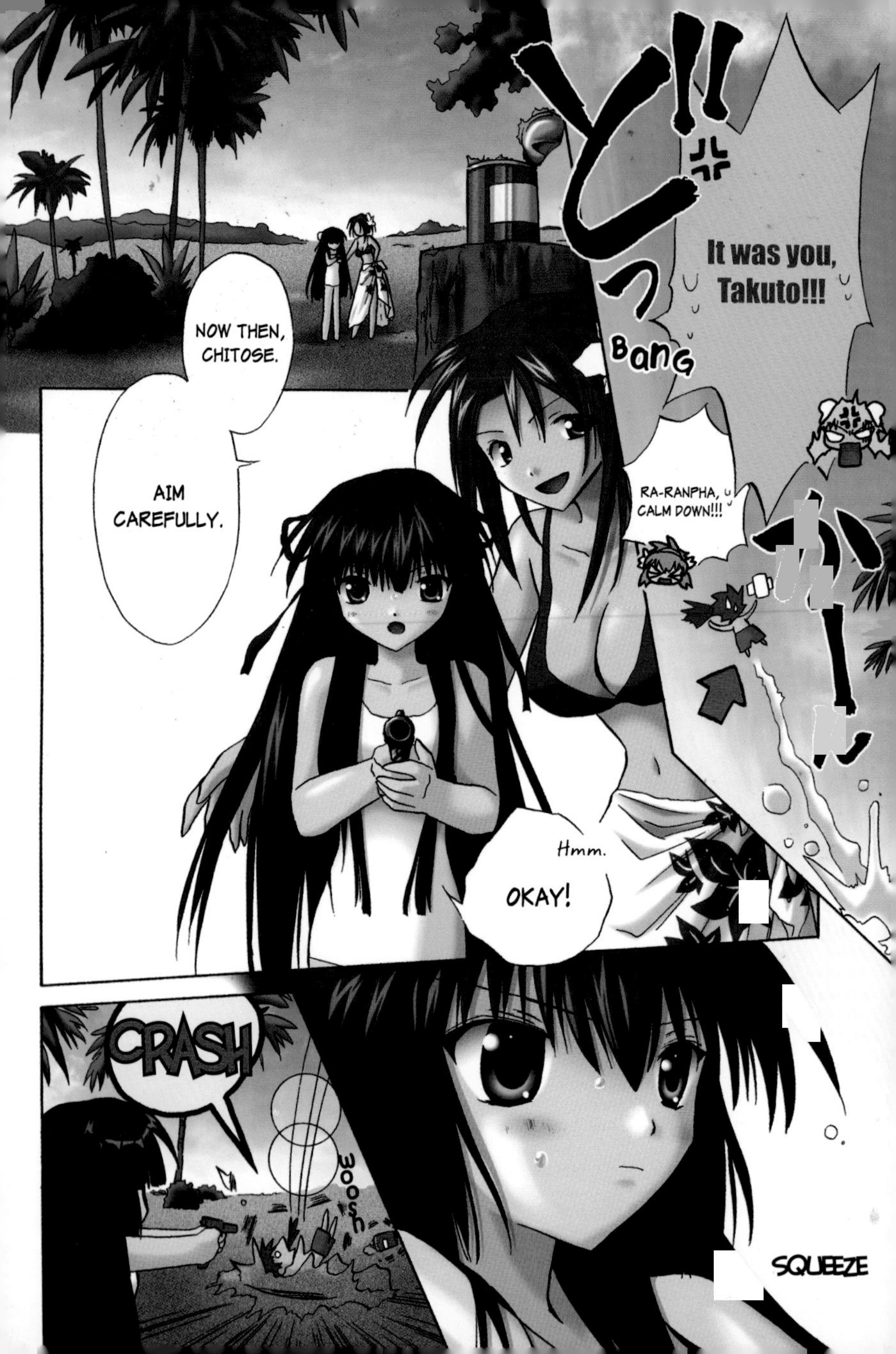
どっ!!
It was you, Takuto!!!
Bang
RA-RANPHA, CALM DOWN!!!
NOW THEN, CHITOSE.
AIM CAREFULLY.
Hmm.
OKAY!
SQUEEZE
CRASH
Woosh

Galaxy Angel β

BETA

1

Other titles available from Broccoli Books

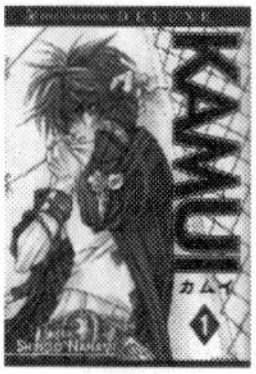
KAMUI

KAMUI

Infused with the spirit of an ancient sword, young Atsuma must leave his village to reclaim the stolen sacred spirit Okikurumi. His quest leads him to NOA, an organization of gifted youths similarly empowered by spirits, which may hold the key to Okikurumi. It is up to Atsuma to save the world before Okikurumi can be turned into a weapon of destruction.

Story & Art by Shingo Nanami
Suggested Retail Price: $9.99 each
Volume 1 Coming Fall 2005!

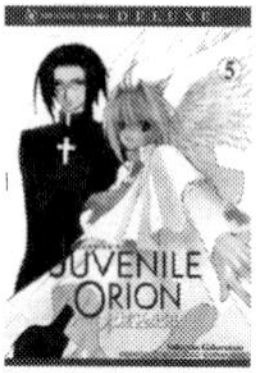
ORION

Aquarian Age – Juvenile Orion

Sixteen-year-old Mana returns to her hometown and reunites with her childhood friend Kaname after 7 years. But he seems to have changed during their years apart. They soon discover that they are part of the Aquarian Age—a secret war raging for thousands of years—and Mana just might hold the key to end it!

Story & Art by Sakurako Gokurakuin
Suggested Retail Price: $9.99 each

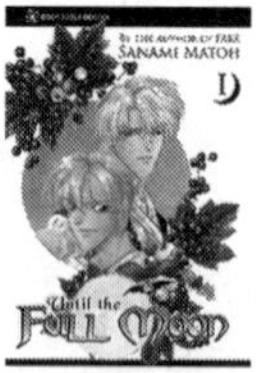
SANAMI MATOH

Until the Full Moon

Marlo is half-vampire, half-werewolf with a problem. On nights when the full moon shines, Marlo undergoes a mysterious transformation... he turns into a girl.

Story & Art by Sanami Matoh
Suggested Retail Price: $9.99 each

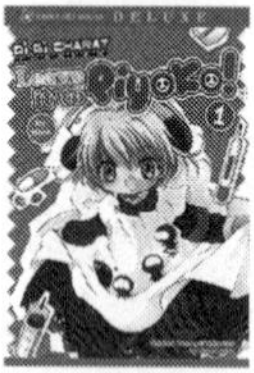

Di Gi Charat Theater – Leave it to Piyoko!

Follow the daily adventures of the Black Gema Gema Gang, as they continue their road to evil.

Story & Art by Hina.
Suggested Retail Price: $9.99
Volume 2 Coming Soon!

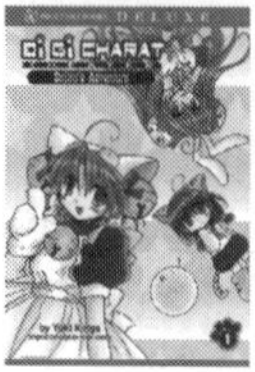

Di Gi Charat Theater – Dejiko's Adventure

Dejiko has destroyed the Gamers retail store! Now it's up to her and the rest of the gang as they search for the secret treasure that will save Gamers.

Story & Art by Yuki Kiriga
Suggested Retail Price: $9.99
Volumes 2-3 Coming Soon!

For more information about Broccoli Books titles,
check out **bro-usa.com!**

Galaxy Angel Beta™ Volume 1

English Adaptation Staff
Translation: Koji Tajii
English Adaptation: Jason R. Grissom
Touch-Up, & Lettering: Fawn "tails" Lau
Cover & Graphic Supervision: Chris McDougall

Editor: Dietrich Seto
Sales Manager: Ardith D. Santiago
Managing Editor: Shizuki Yamashita
Publisher: Kaname Tezuka

Email: editor@broccolibooks.com
Website: www.broccolibooks.com

A ⓑ BROCCOLI BOOKS Manga
Broccoli Books is a division of Broccoli International USA, Inc.
P.O. Box 66078 Los Angeles, CA 90066

ISBN-13: 978-1-5974-1021-2
ISBN-10: 1-5974-1021-7

Published by Broccoli International USA, Inc.
First printing, September 2005

www.bro-usa.com

10 9 8 7 6 5 4 3 2 1
Printed in the United States

CONTENTS

Episode 01: Angel Troupe, Feelin' Fine! 5
Episode 02: Ranpha's Dreams....................................35
Episode 03: Memories and Emotions 67
Episode 04: The Key of Happiness
               Opens the Locked Heart 99
Episode 05: Why I Fight....................................131
Afterword 163
Author's Note 163
Preview of Next Volume....................................167
The Universe of GA part 5....................................170
Translation Notes 172

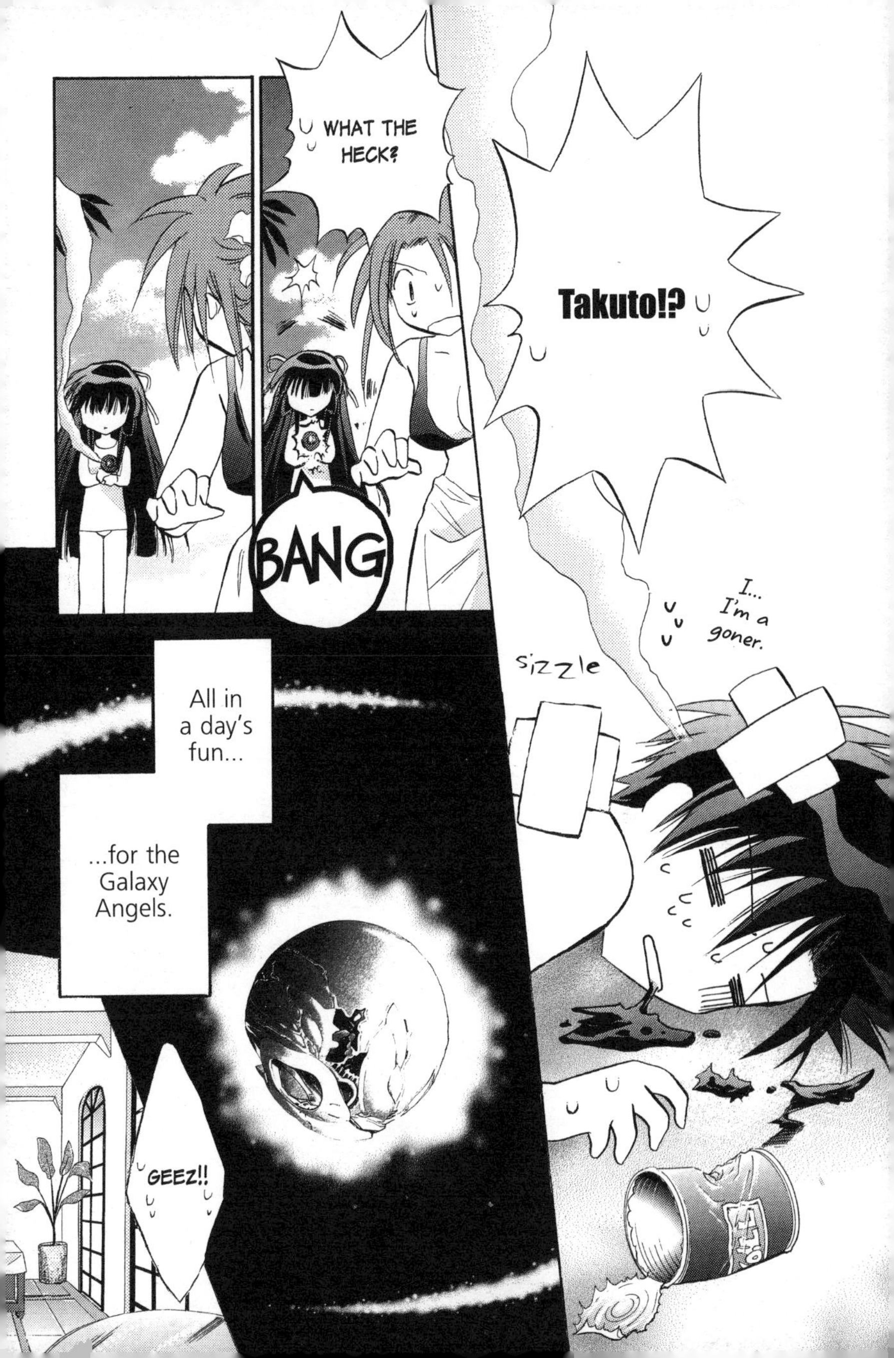

Takuto!?
sizzle
I... I'm a goner.
WHAT THE HECK?
BANG
All in a day's fun...
...for the Galaxy Angels.
GEEZ!!

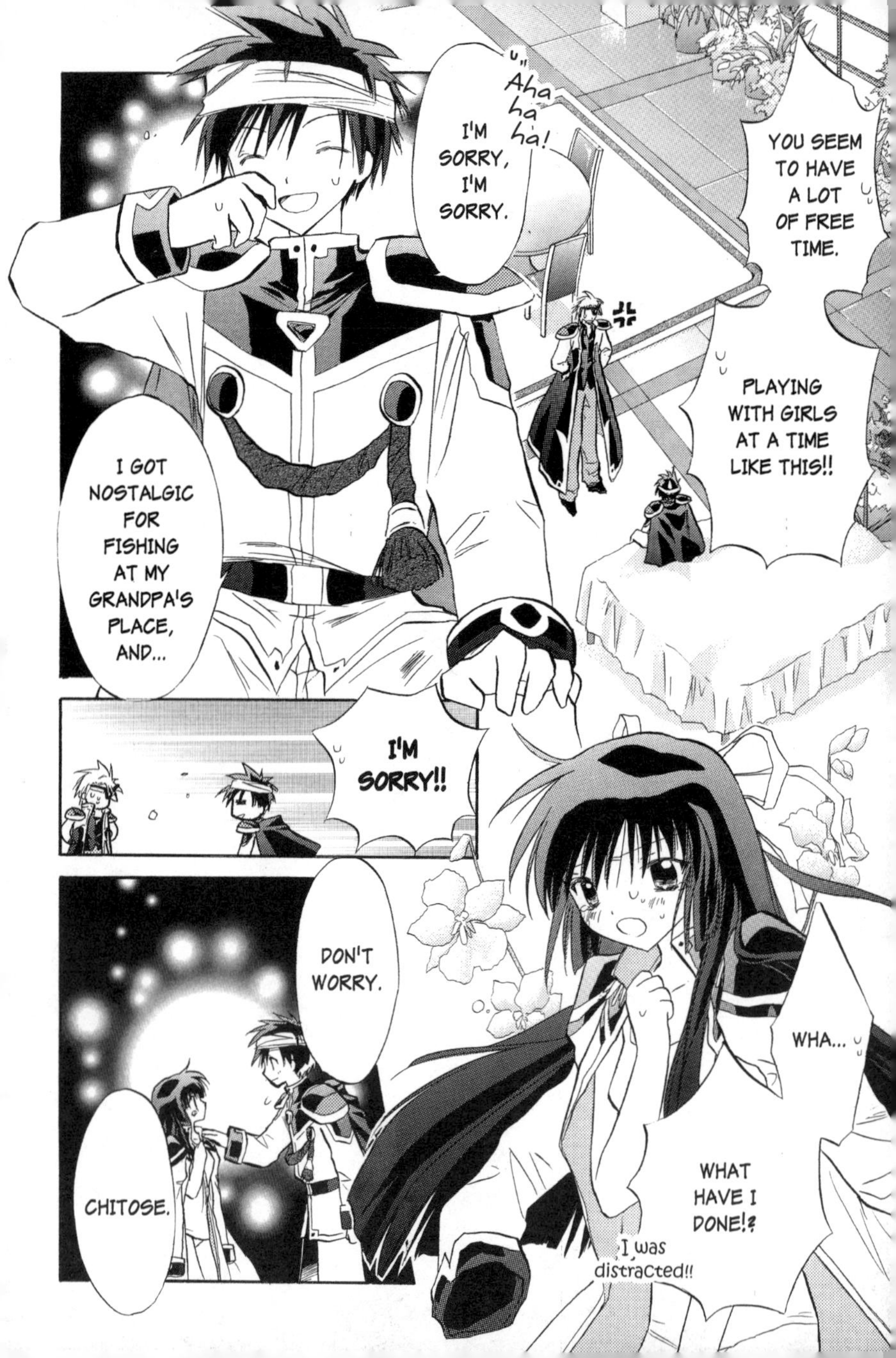
YOU SEEM TO HAVE A LOT OF FREE TIME.
PLAYING WITH GIRLS AT A TIME LIKE THIS!!
Aha ha ha!
I'M SORRY, I'M SORRY.
I GOT NOSTALGIC FOR FISHING AT MY GRANDPA'S PLACE, AND...
WHA...
WHAT HAVE I DONE!?
I was distracted!!
I'M SORRY!!
DON'T WORRY.
CHITOSE.

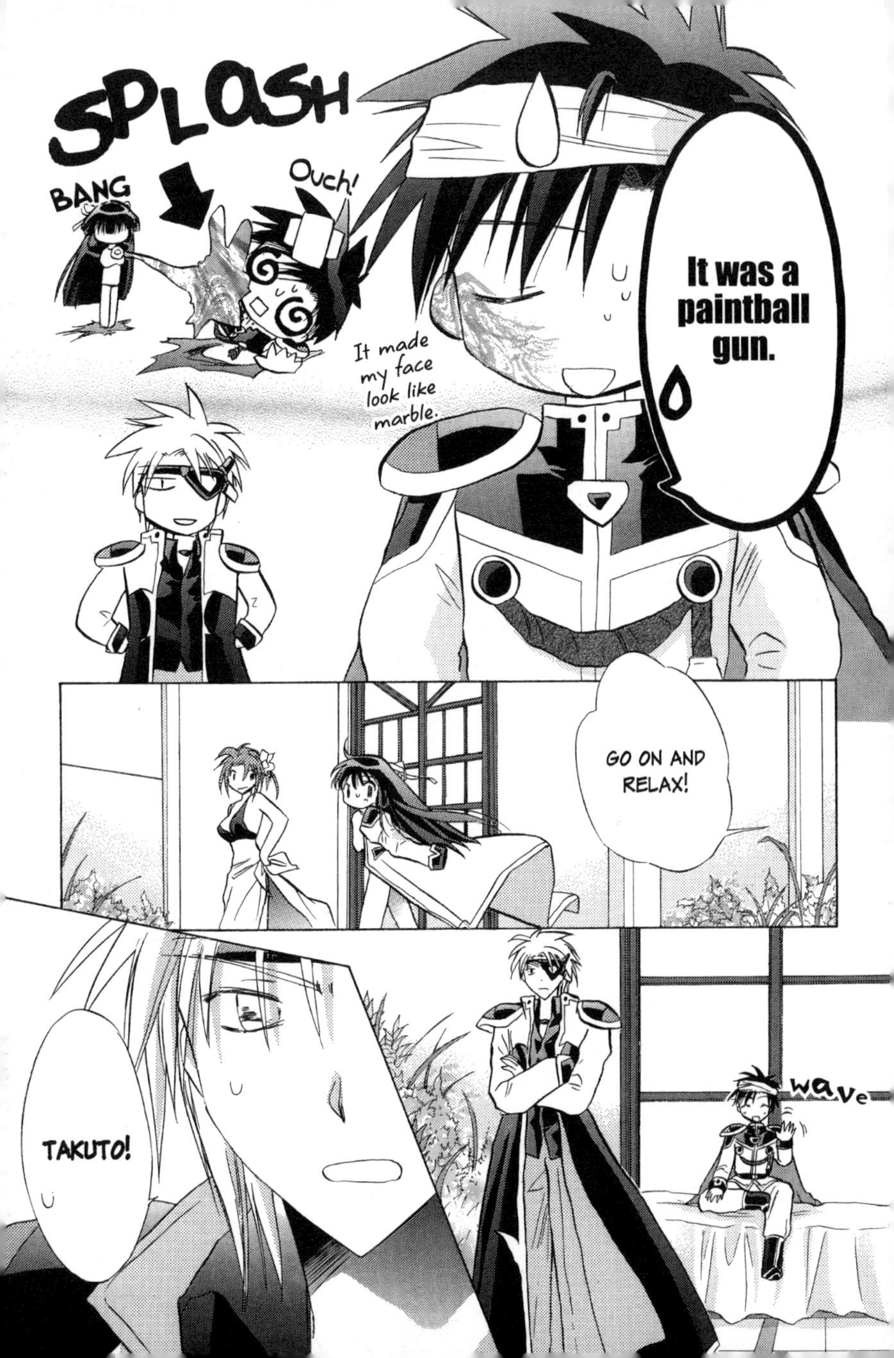
It was a paintball gun.
It made my face look like marble.
SPLASH
Ouch!
BANG
GO ON AND RELAX!
wave
TAKUTO!

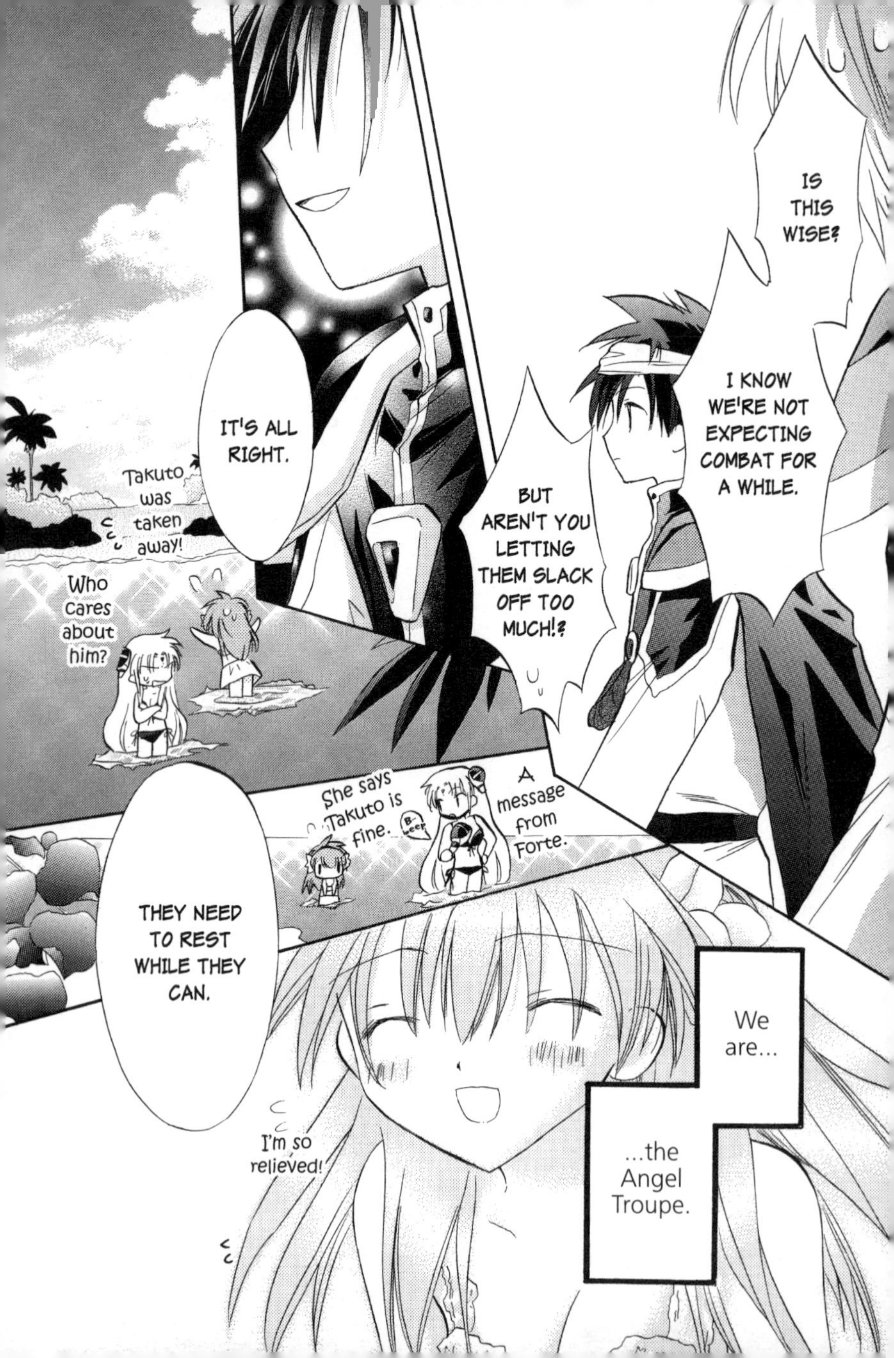
IS THIS WISE?
I KNOW WE'RE NOT EXPECTING COMBAT FOR A WHILE.
BUT AREN'T YOU LETTING THEM SLACK OFF TOO MUCH!?
IT'S ALL RIGHT.
Takuto was taken away!
Who cares about him?
A message from Forte.
She says Takuto is fine.
B-beep
THEY NEED TO REST WHILE THEY CAN.
I'm so relieved!
We are...
...the Angel Troupe.

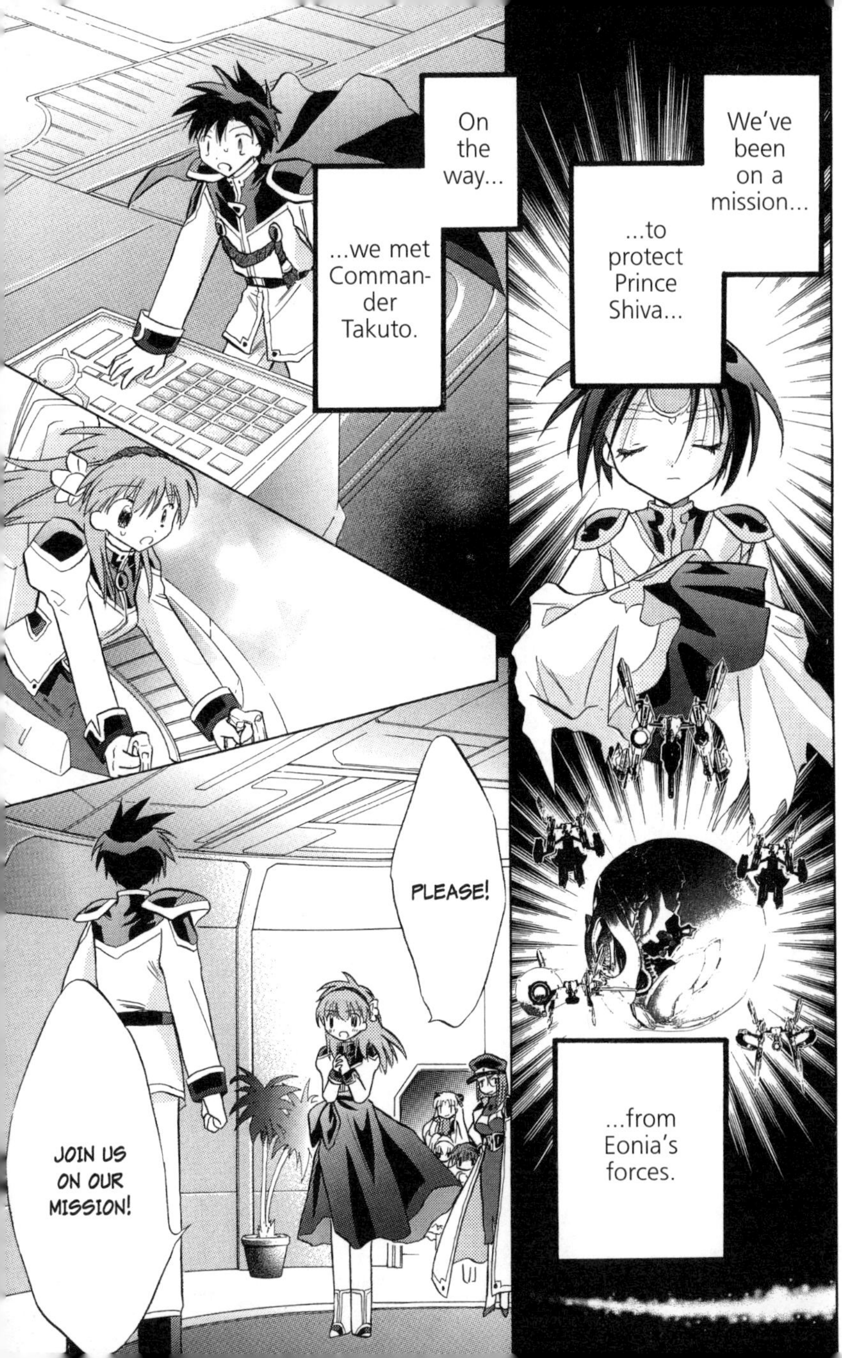
We've been on a mission...
...to protect Prince Shiva...
...from Eonia's forces.
On the way...
...we met Commander Takuto.
PLEASE!
JOIN US ON OUR MISSION!

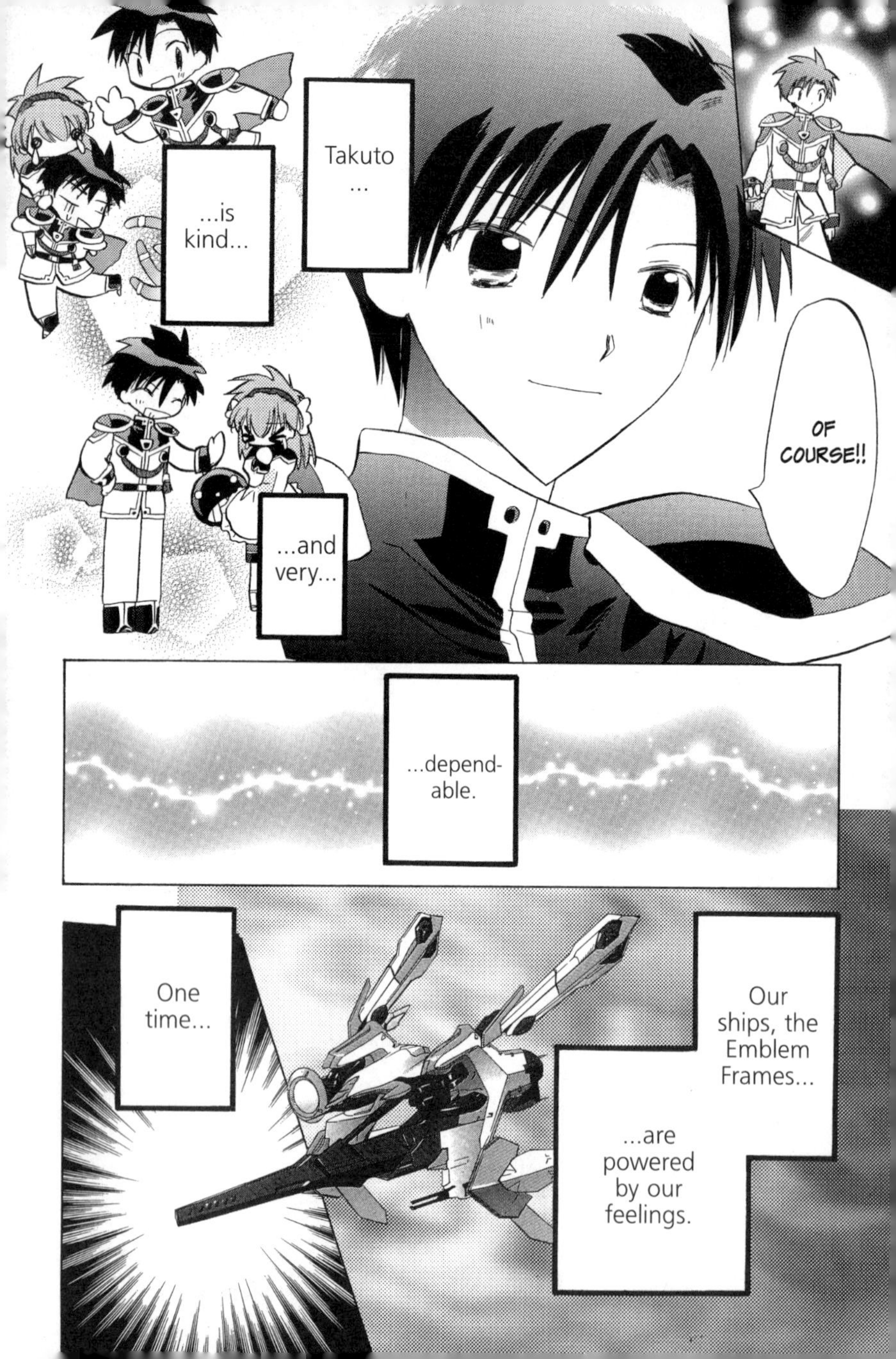
Takuto
...
...is kind...
OF COURSE!!
...and very...
...depend-able.
Our ships, the Emblem Frames...
...are powered by our feelings.
One time...

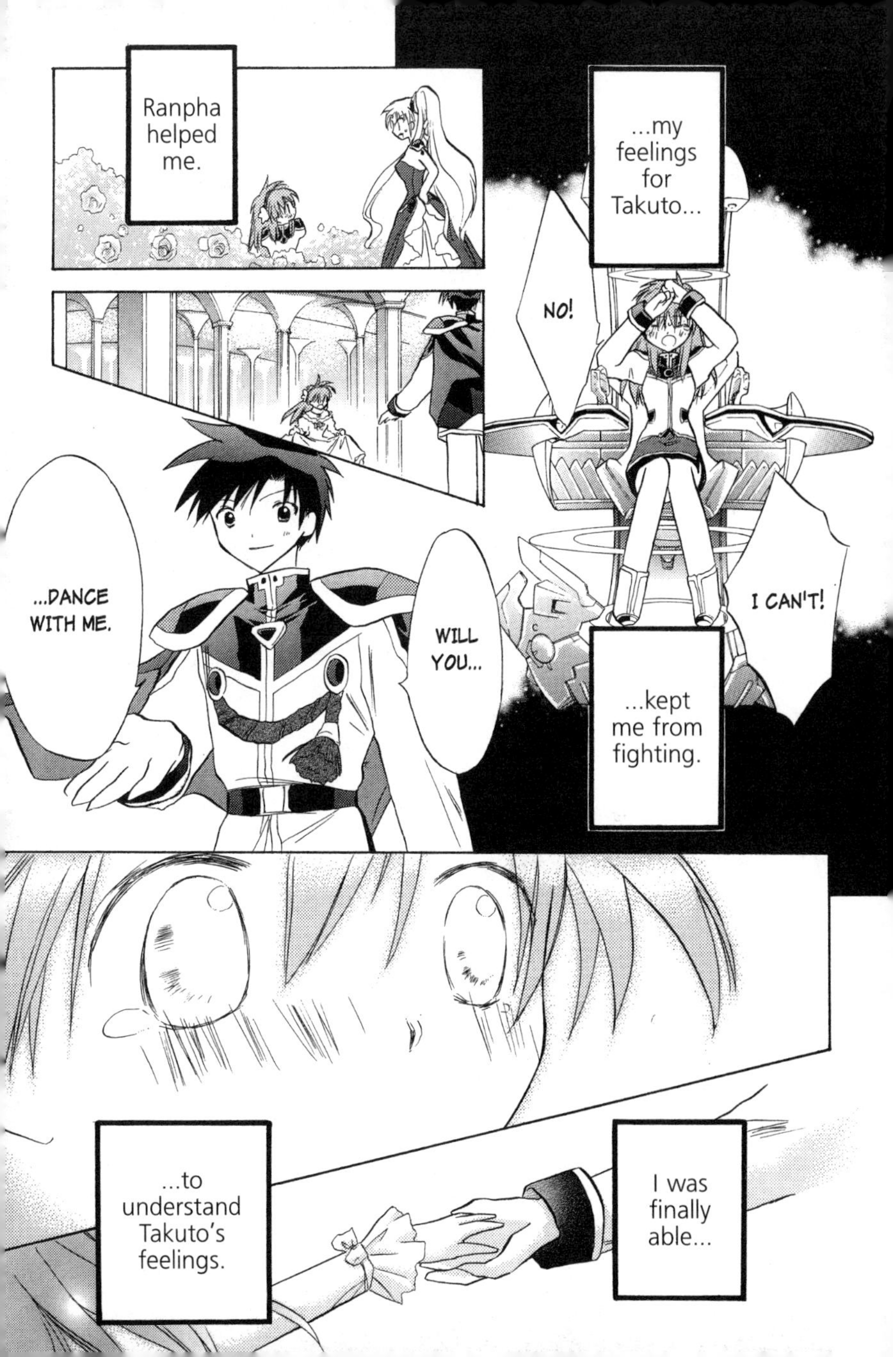
...my feelings for Takuto...
NO!
I CAN'T!
...kept me from fighting.
Ranpha helped me.
WILL YOU...
...DANCE WITH ME.
I was finally able...
...to understand Takuto's feelings.

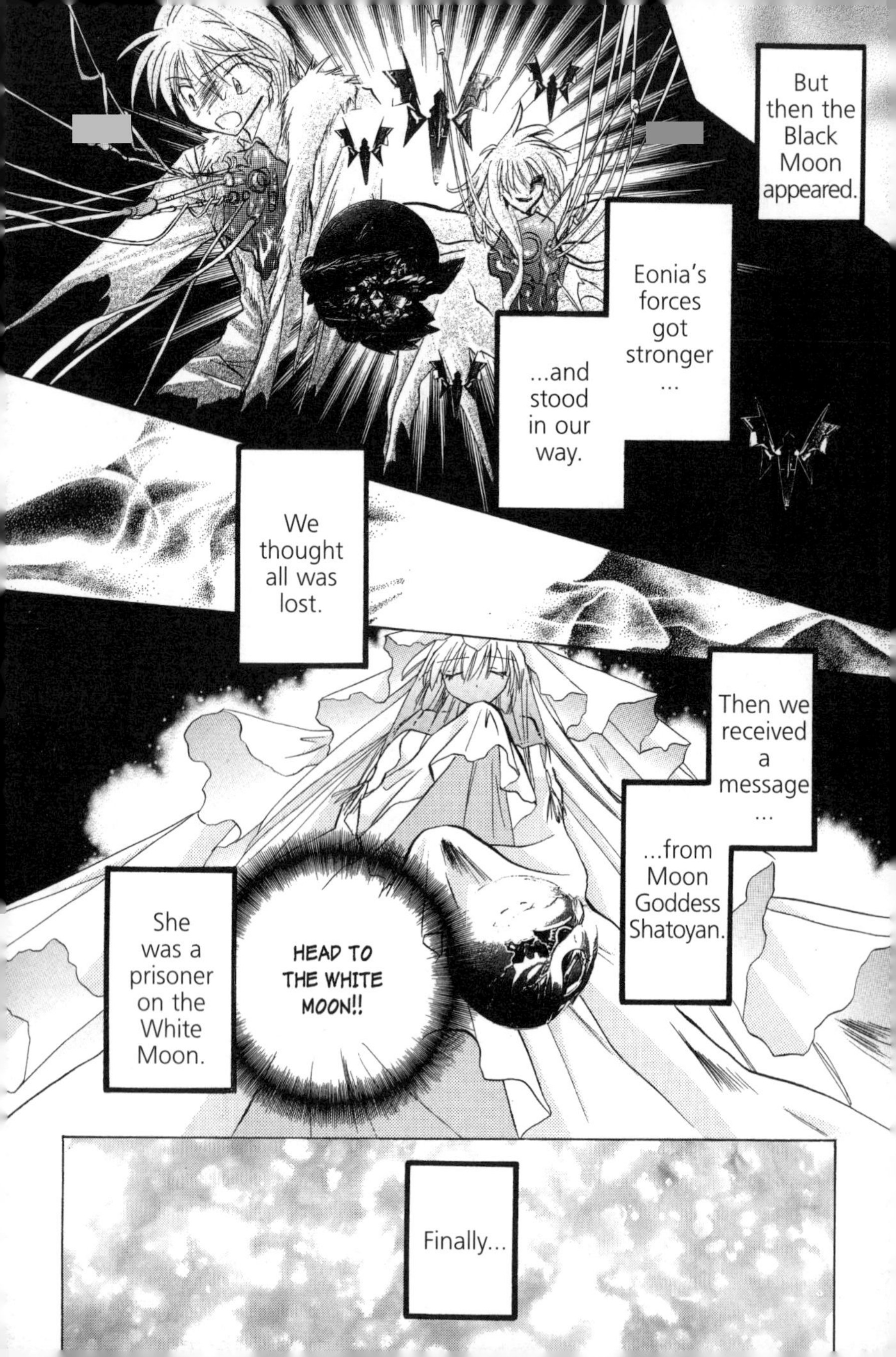
But then the Black Moon appeared.
Eonia's forces got stronger...
...and stood in our way.
We thought all was lost.
Then we received a message...
...from Moon Goddess Shatoyan.
HEAD TO THE WHITE MOON!!
She was a prisoner on the White Moon.
Finally...

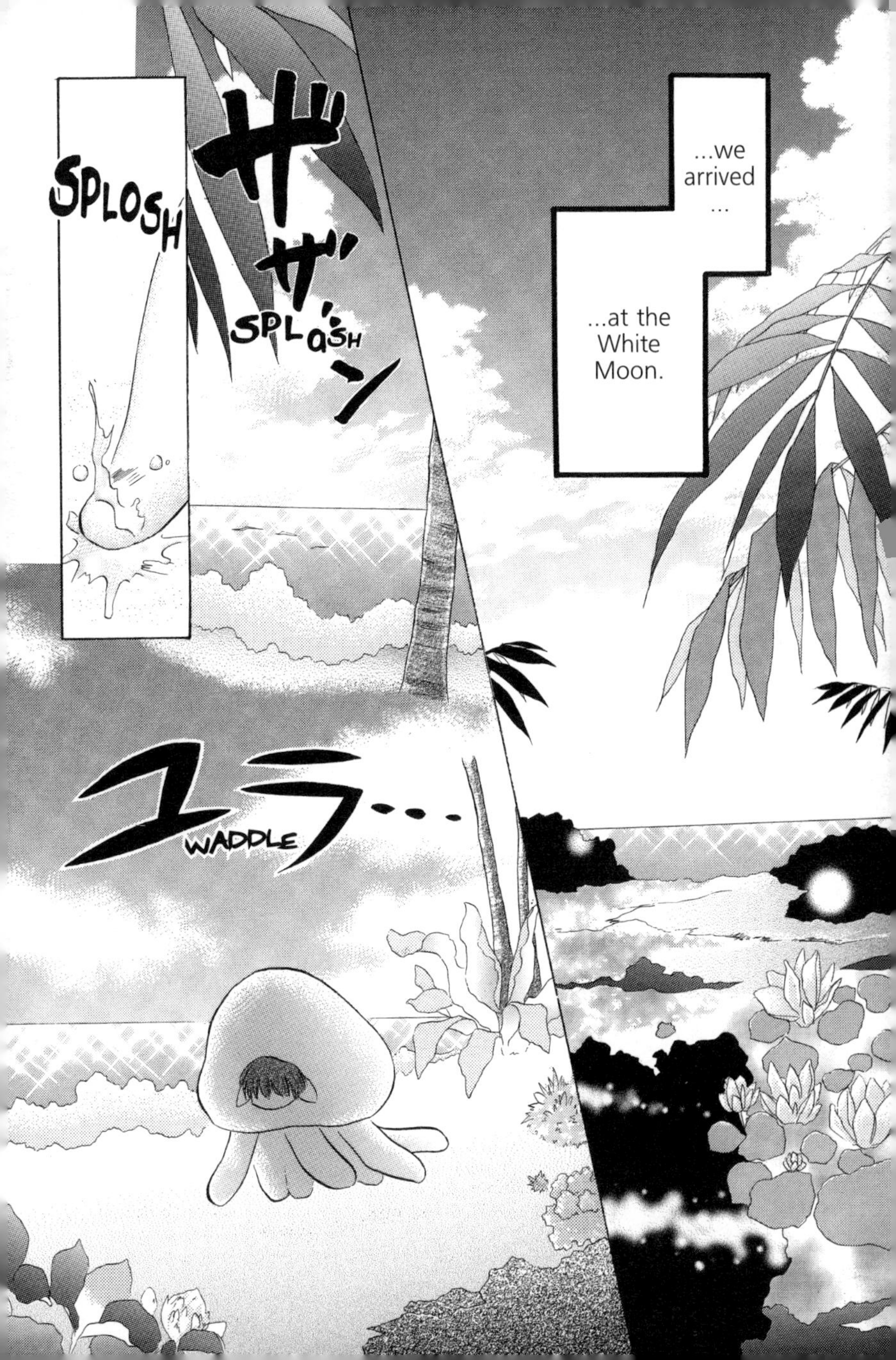
...we arrived ...
...at the White Moon.
SPLOSH
ザザン
SPLASH
ユラ...
WADDLE

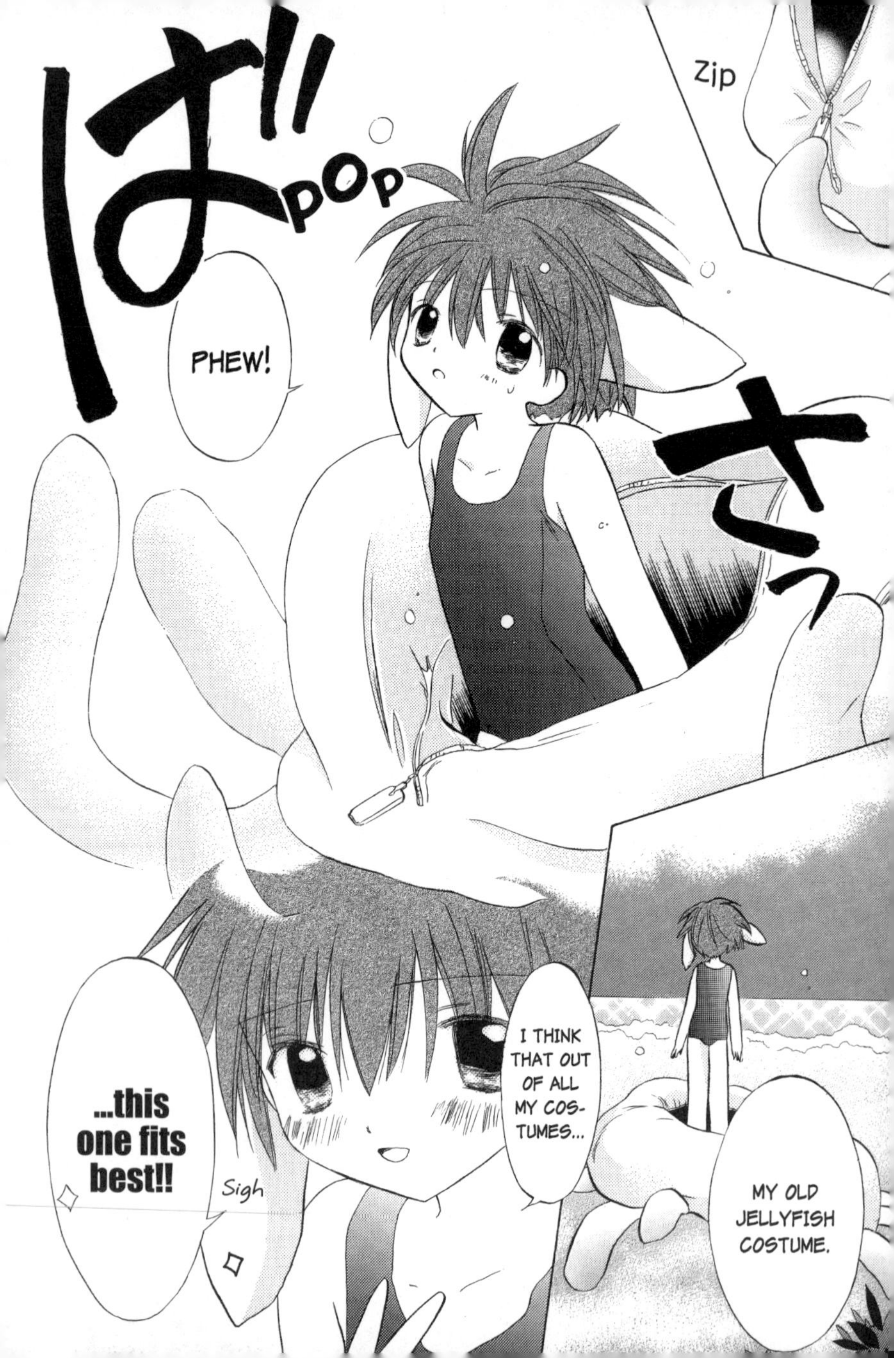
Zip
ぱっ
pop
PHEW!
さっ
MY OLD JELLYFISH COSTUME.
I THINK THAT OUT OF ALL MY COS-TUMES...
...this one fits best!!
Sigh

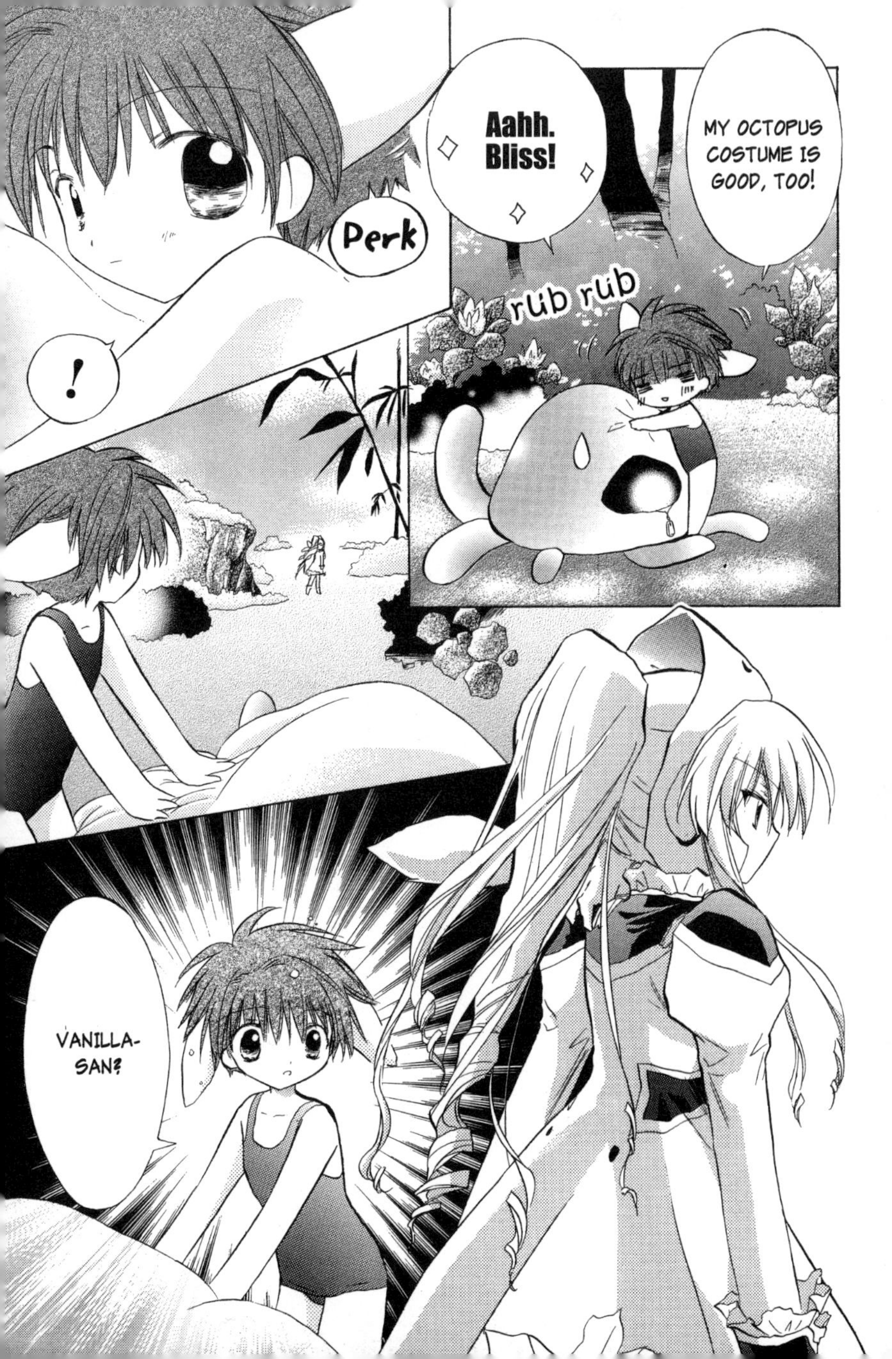
MY OCTOPUS COSTUME IS GOOD, TOO!
Aahh. Bliss!
rub rub
Perk
!
VANILLA-SAN?

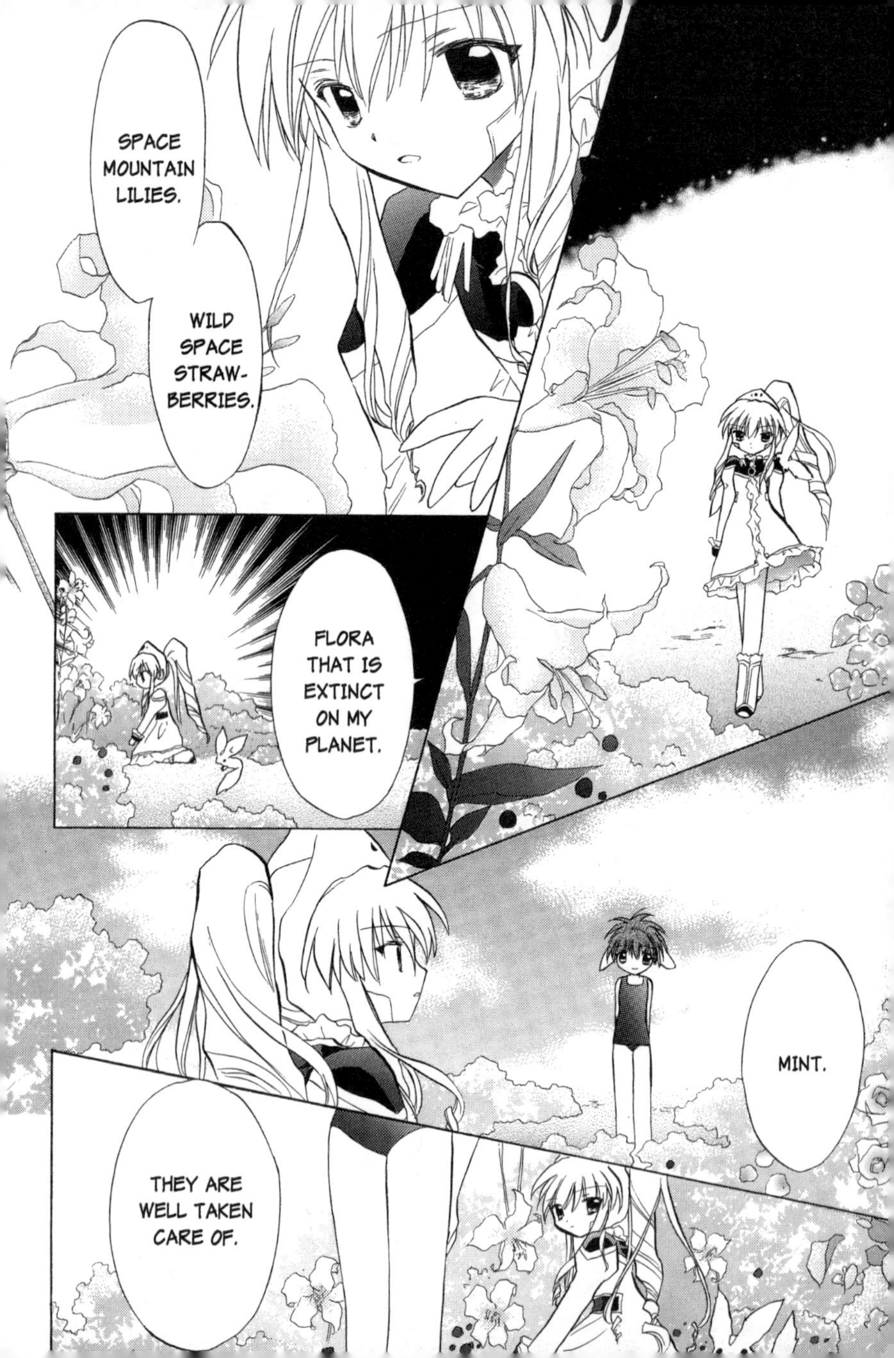
SPACE MOUNTAIN LILIES.
WILD SPACE STRAW-BERRIES.
FLORA THAT IS EXTINCT ON MY PLANET.
MINT.
THEY ARE WELL TAKEN CARE OF.

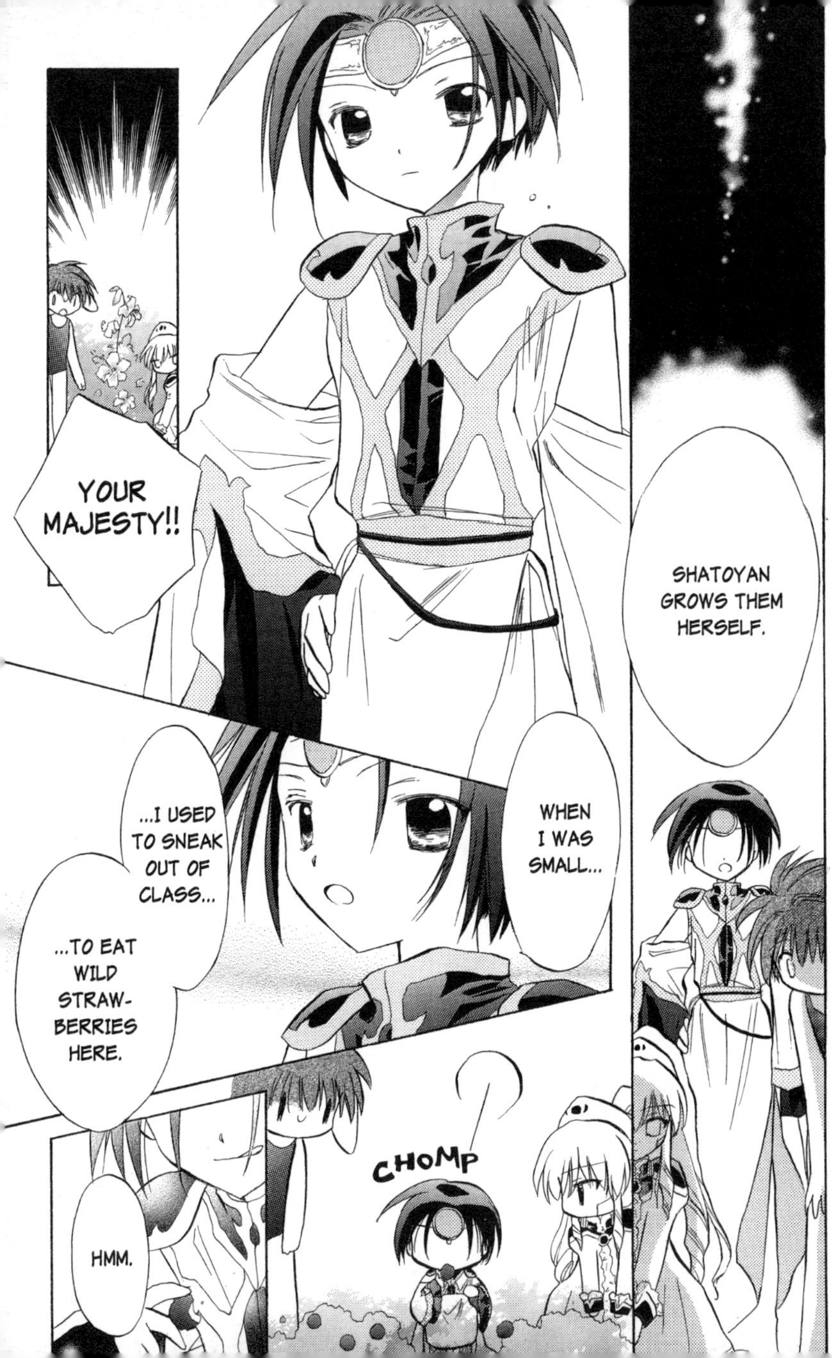

SHATOYAN GROWS THEM HERSELF.
YOUR MAJESTY!!
WHEN I WAS SMALL...
...I USED TO SNEAK OUT OF CLASS...
...TO EAT WILD STRAW-BERRIES HERE.
?
CHOMP
HMM.

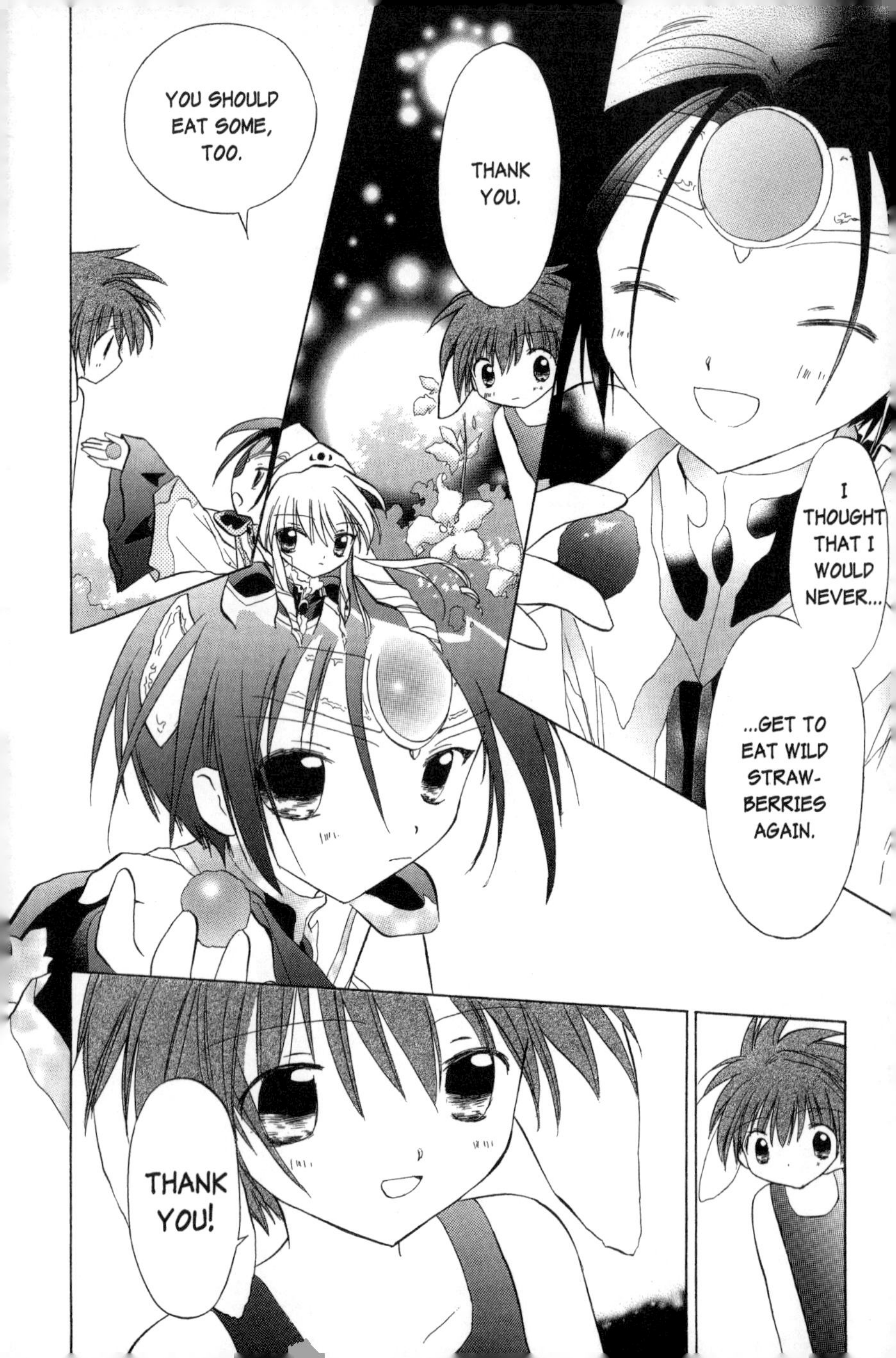
I THOUGHT THAT I WOULD NEVER...
...GET TO EAT WILD STRAW-BERRIES AGAIN.
THANK YOU.
YOU SHOULD EAT SOME, TOO.
THANK YOU!

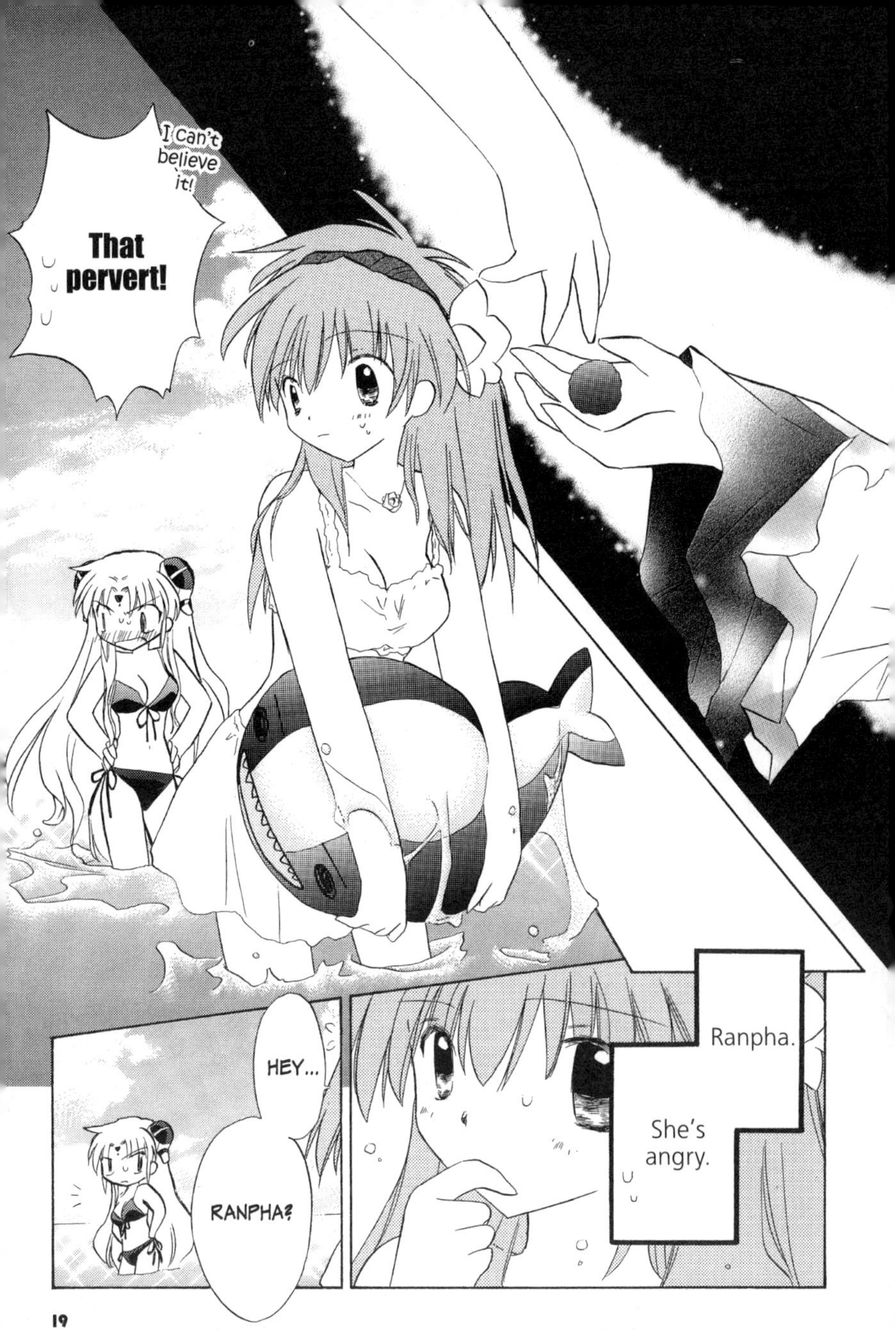

I can't believe it!
That pervert!
Ranpha.
She's angry.
HEY...
RANPHA?

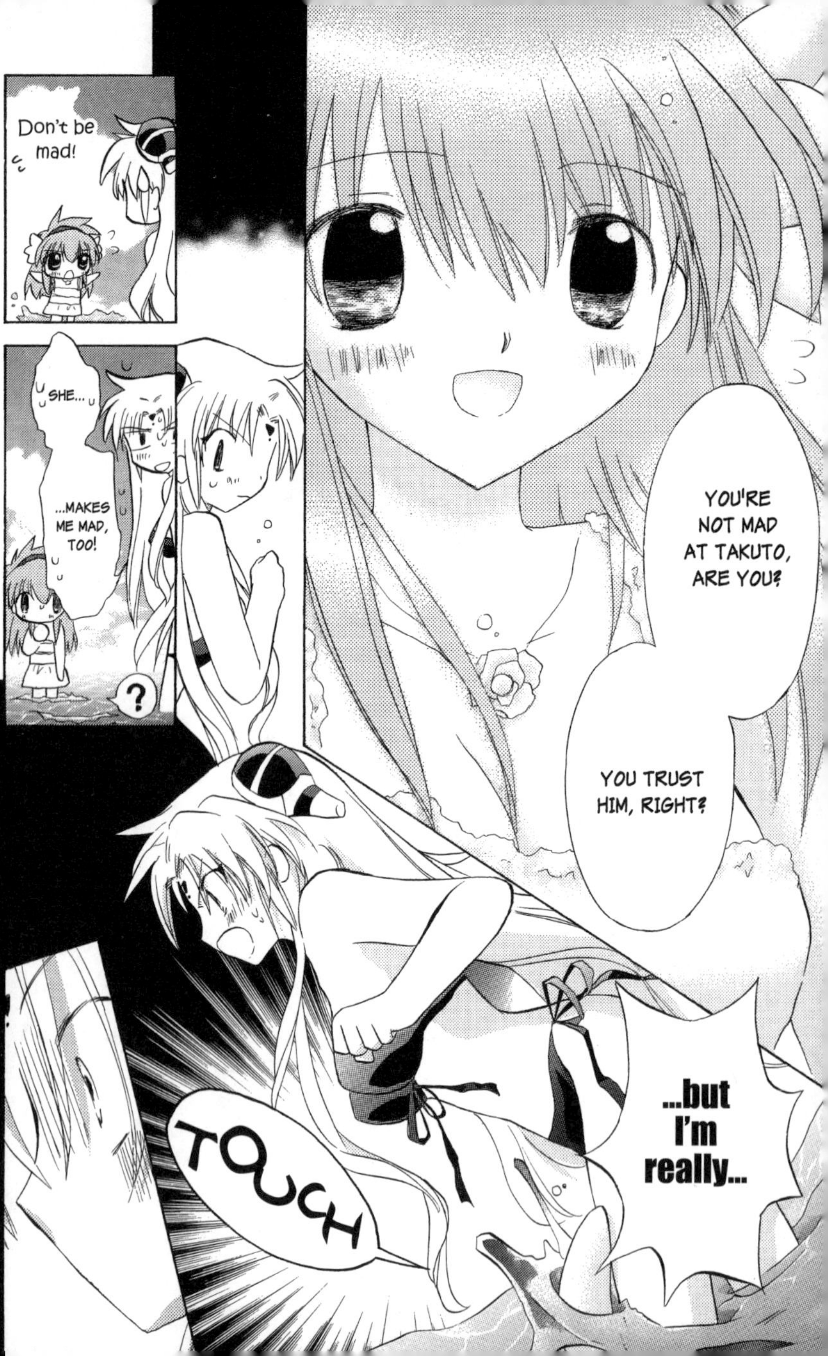
YOU'RE NOT MAD AT TAKUTO, ARE YOU?
YOU TRUST HIM, RIGHT?
...but I'm really...
Don't be mad!
SHE...
...MAKES ME MAD, TOO!
?
TOUCH

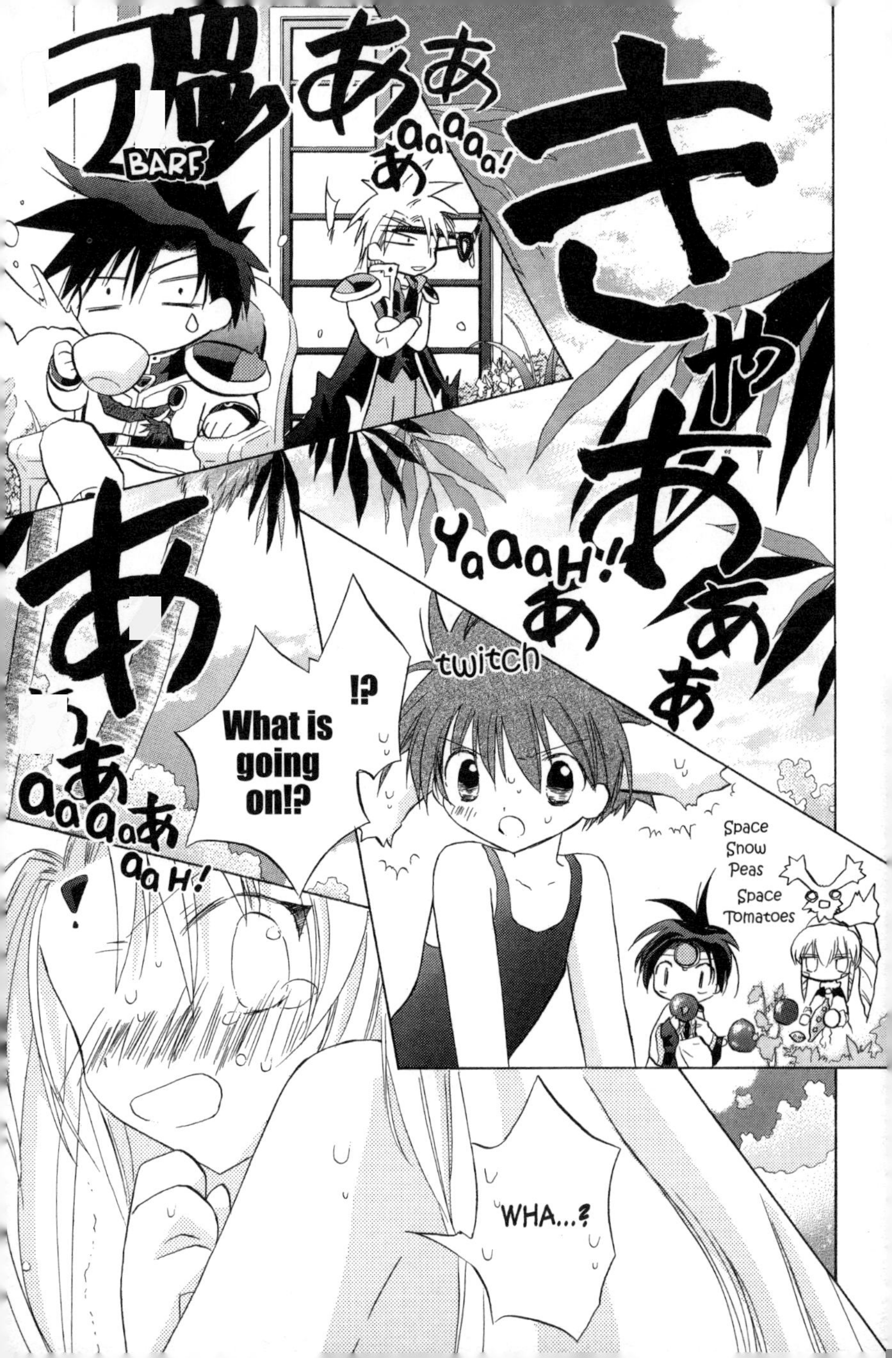
YaaaH!!
BARF
aaaaa!
twitch
!?
What is going on!?
Space Snow Peas
Space Tomatoes
aaaaaaH!
WHA...?

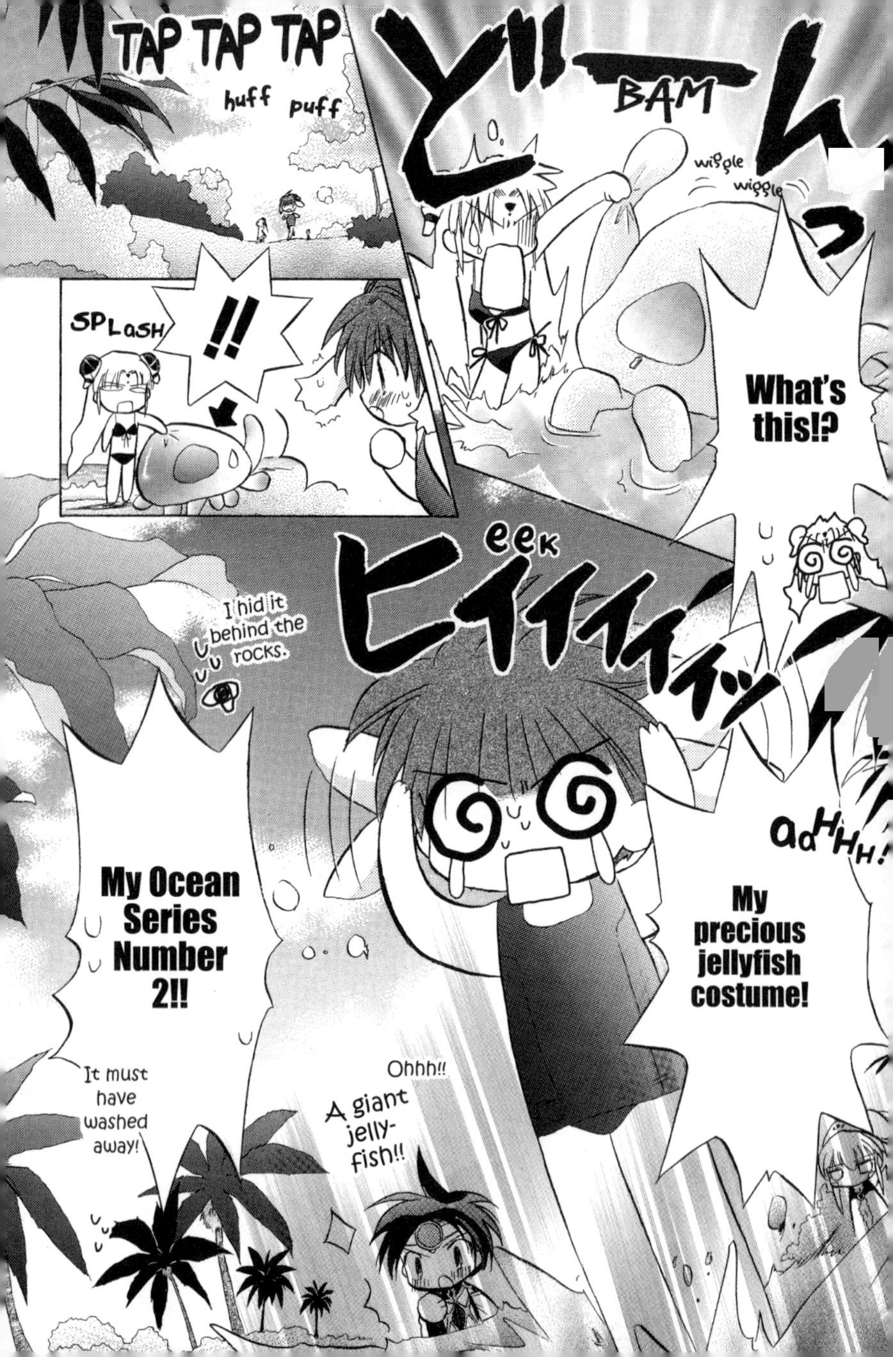

BAM
wiggle wiggle
TAP TAP TAP
huff puff
SPLASH
!!
What's this!?
eek
aaHHHH!
My precious jellyfish costume!
I hid it behind the rocks.
My Ocean Series Number 2!!
Ohhh!!
A giant jelly-fish!!
It must have washed away!

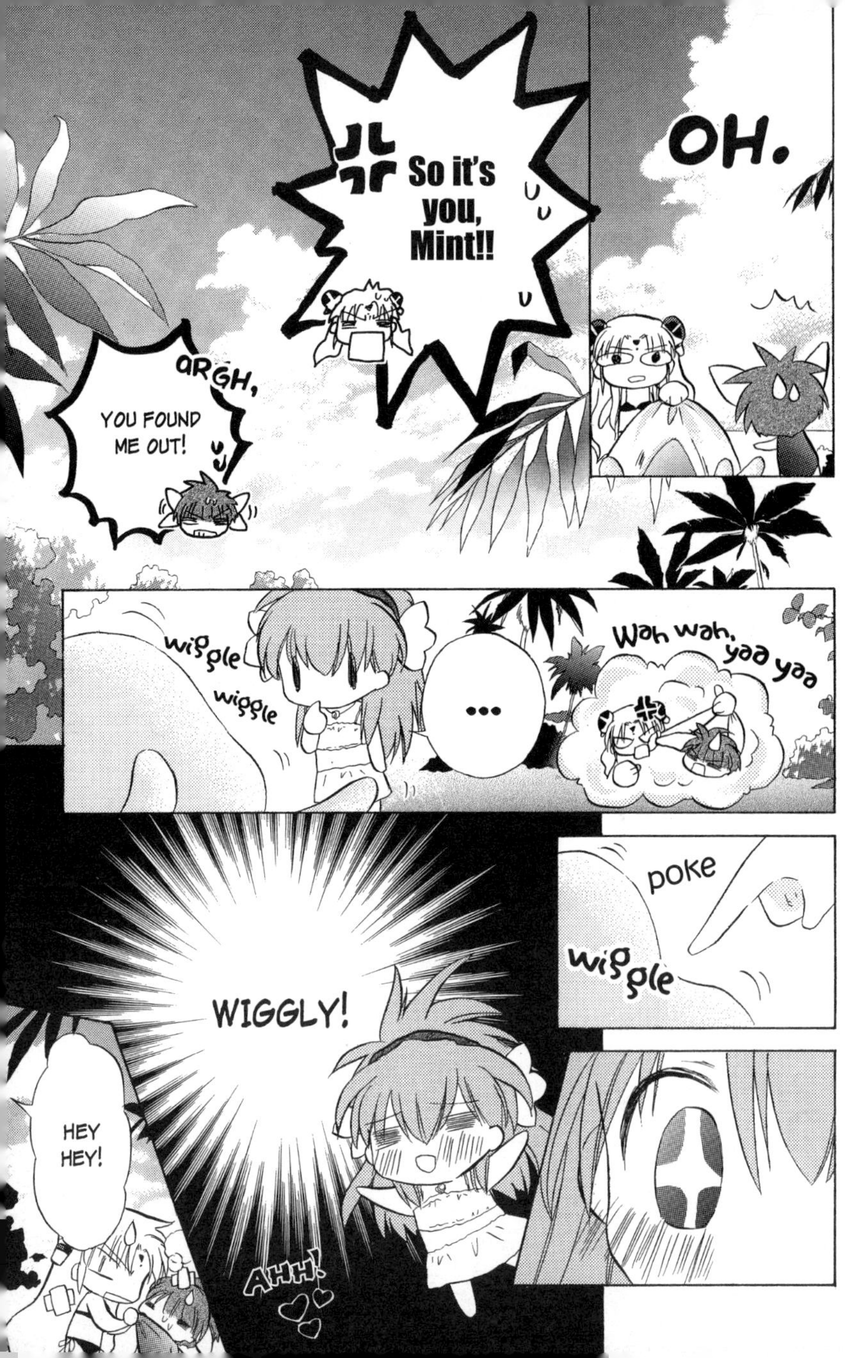
OH.
So it's you, Mint!!
ARGH, YOU FOUND ME OUT!
Wah wah, yaa yaa
...
wiggle wiggle
poke
wiggle
WIGGLY!
AHH!
HEY HEY!

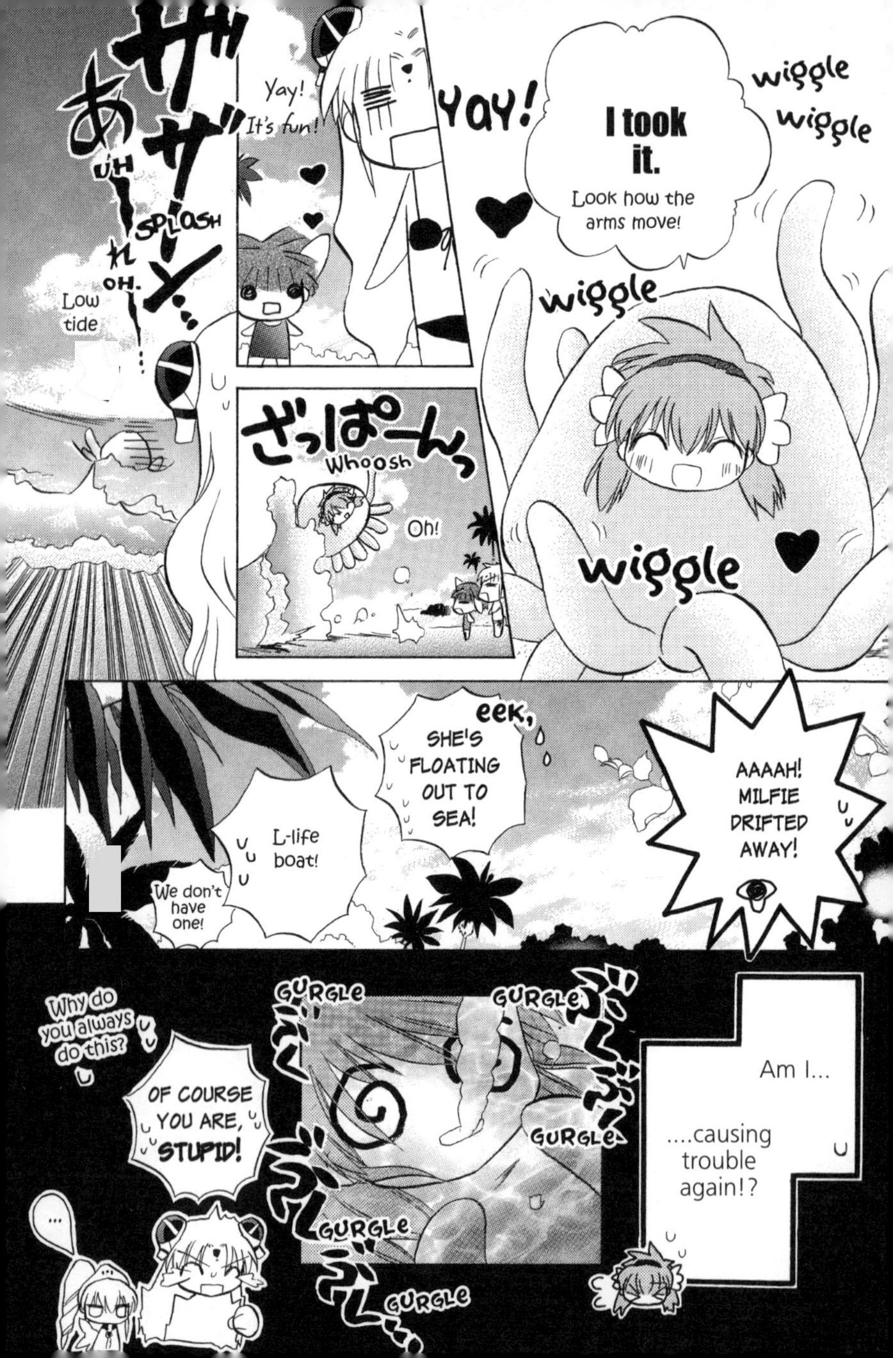

I took it.
Look how the arms move!
wiggle wiggle
wiggle
wiggle
Yay! It's fun!
YAY!
ざっぱーん
Whoosh
Oh!
ザザーン…
SPLASH
あれ…
UH OH.
Low tide
AAAAH! MILFIE DRIFTED AWAY!
eek,
SHE'S FLOATING OUT TO SEA!
L-life boat!
We don't have one!
Am I...
....causing trouble again!?
ぶくぶく
GURGLE
GURGLE
OF COURSE YOU ARE, STUPID!
Why do you always do this?
ぶくぶく…
GURGLE
GURGLE
GURGLE
...

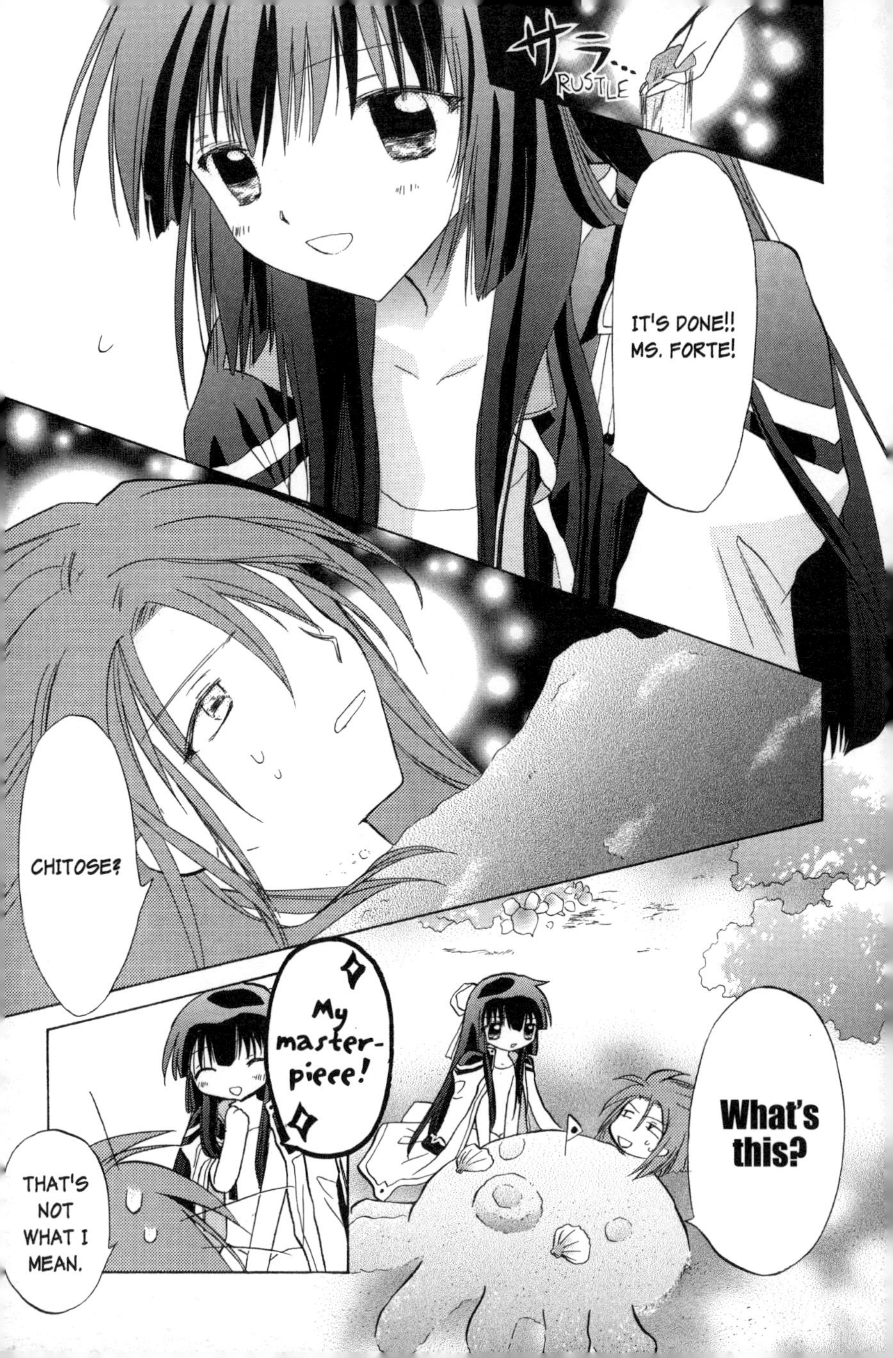
サラ...
RUSTLE
IT'S DONE!! MS. FORTE!
CHITOSE?
What's this?
My master-piece!
THAT'S NOT WHAT I MEAN.

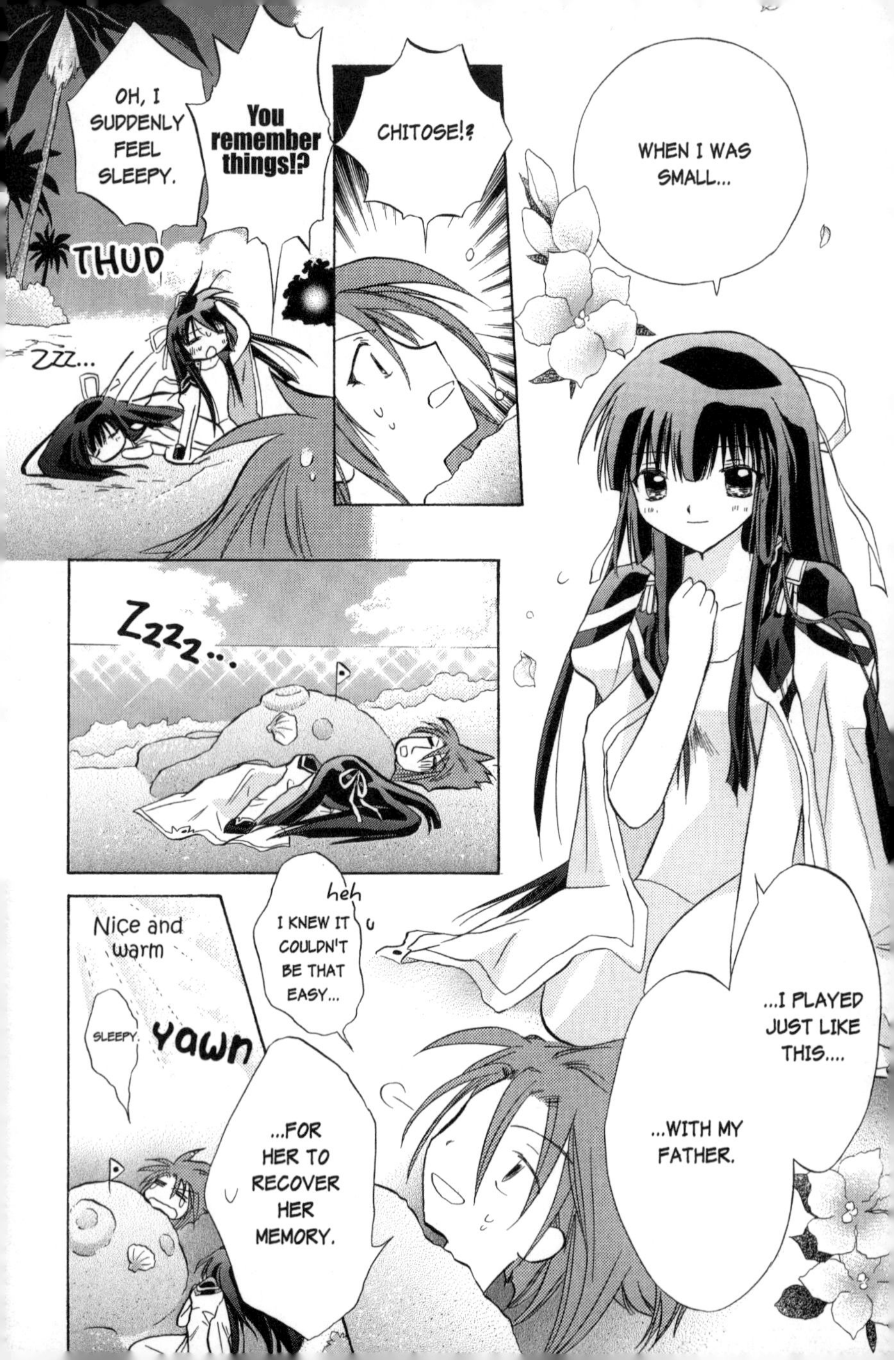

WHEN I WAS SMALL...
...I PLAYED JUST LIKE THIS....
...WITH MY FATHER.
CHITOSE!?
You remember things!?
OH, I SUDDENLY FEEL SLEEPY.
THUD
ZZZ...
Zzzz...
heh
I KNEW IT COULDN'T BE THAT EASY...
...FOR HER TO RECOVER HER MEMORY.
Nice and warm
SLEEPY.
yawn

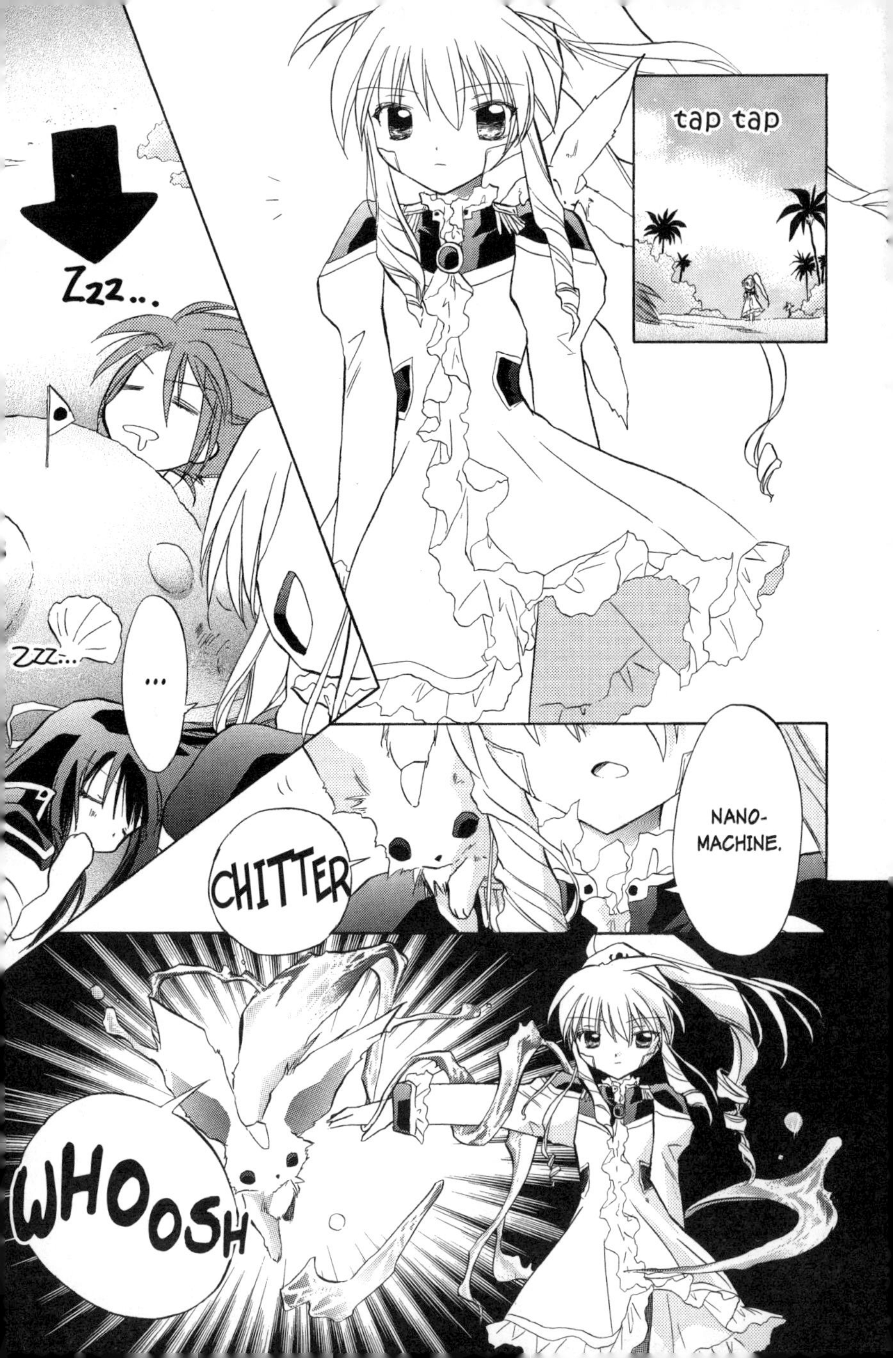

tap tap
Zzz...
zzz...
...
NANO-MACHINE.
CHITTER
WHOOSH

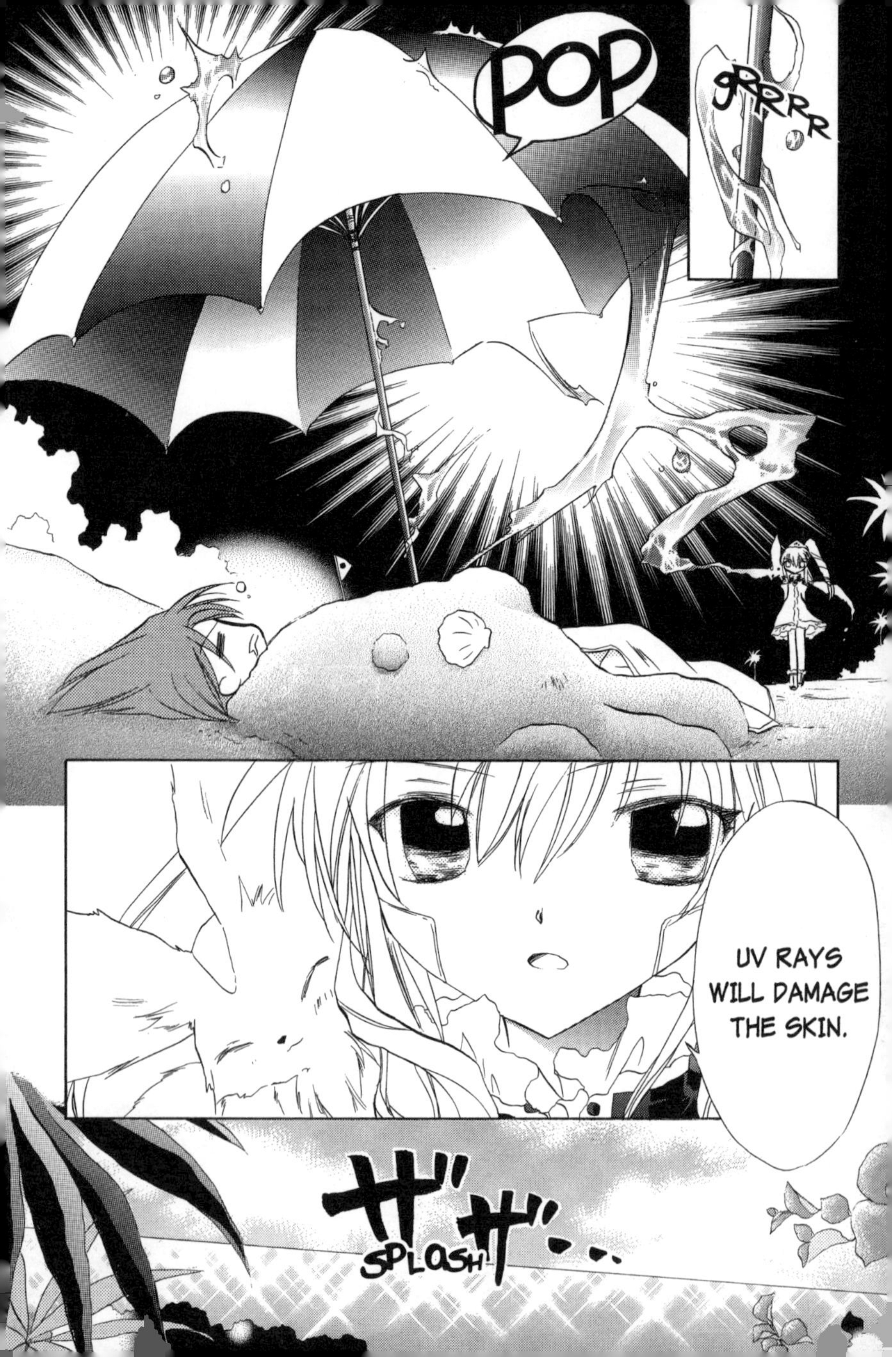
gRRRR
POP
UV RAYS WILL DAMAGE THE SKIN.
ザザ...
SPLASH

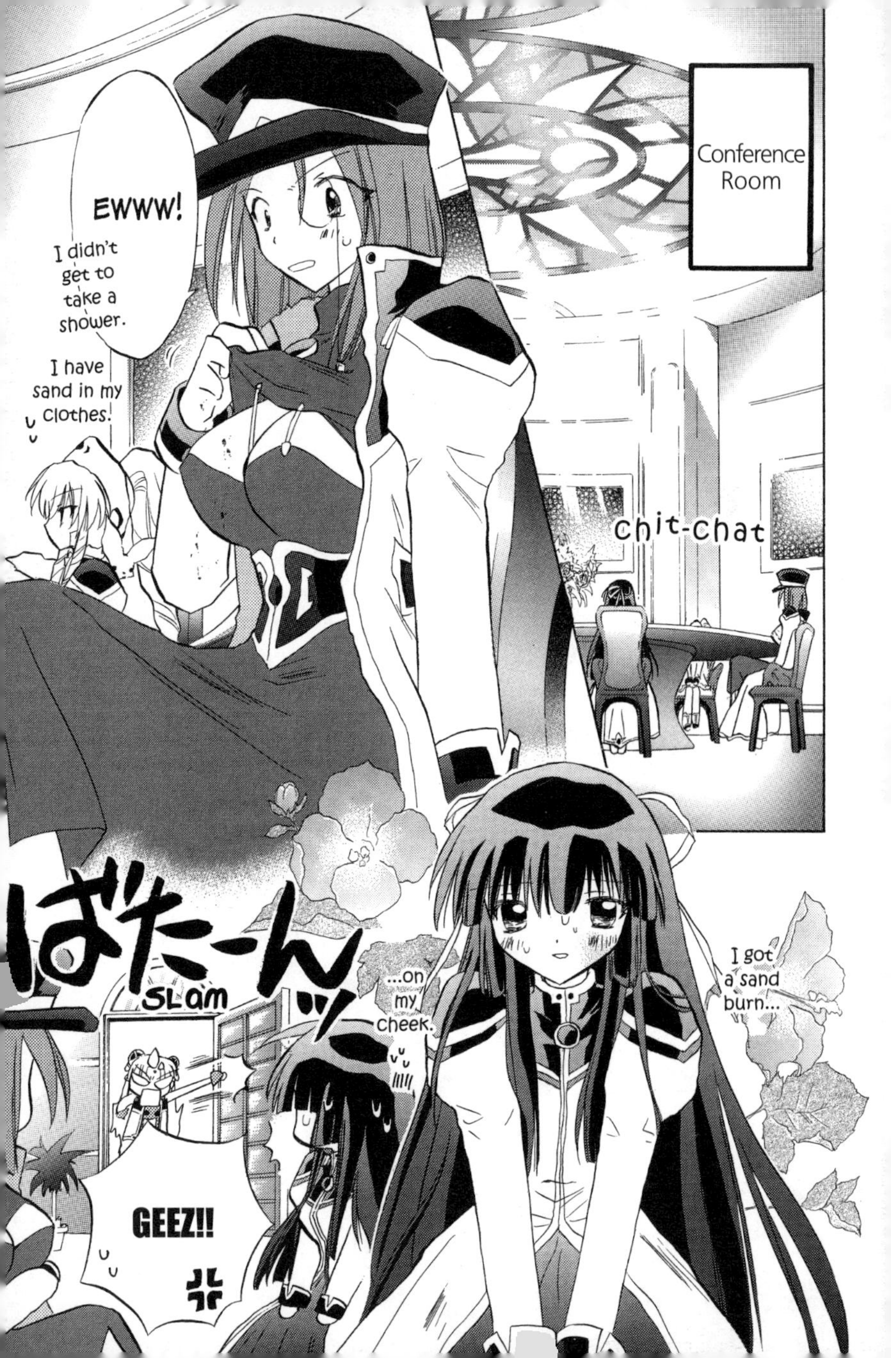

Conference Room
chit-chat
EWWW!
I didn't get to take a shower.
I have sand in my clothes.
I got a sand burn...
...on my cheek.
ばたーんッ
SLAM
GEEZ!!

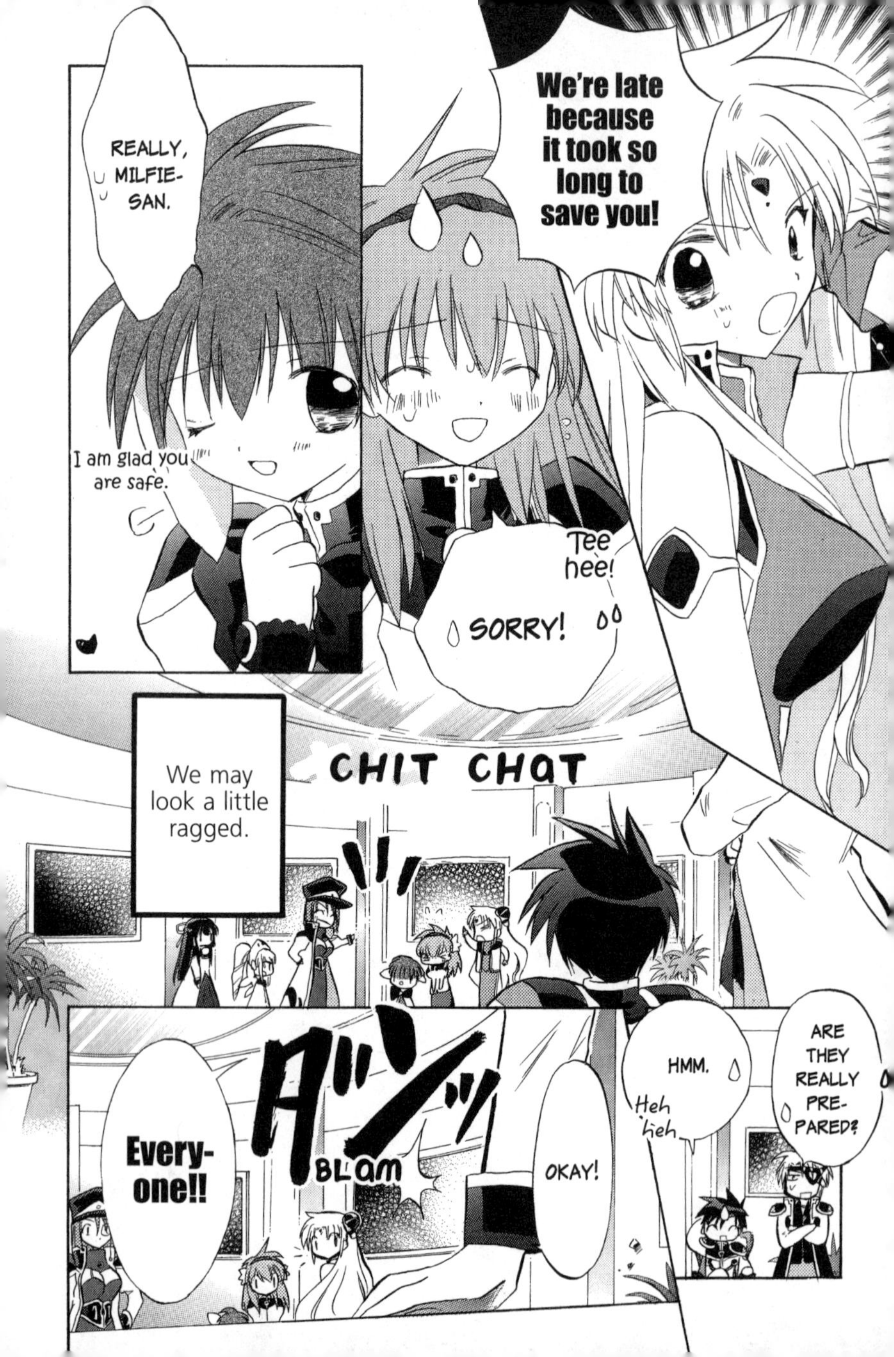

We're late because it took so long to save you!
Tee hee!
SORRY!
REALLY, MILFIE-SAN.
I am glad you are safe.
We may look a little ragged.
CHIT CHAT
ARE THEY REALLY PRE-PARED?
HMM.
Heh heh
OKAY!
BLAM
Every-one!!

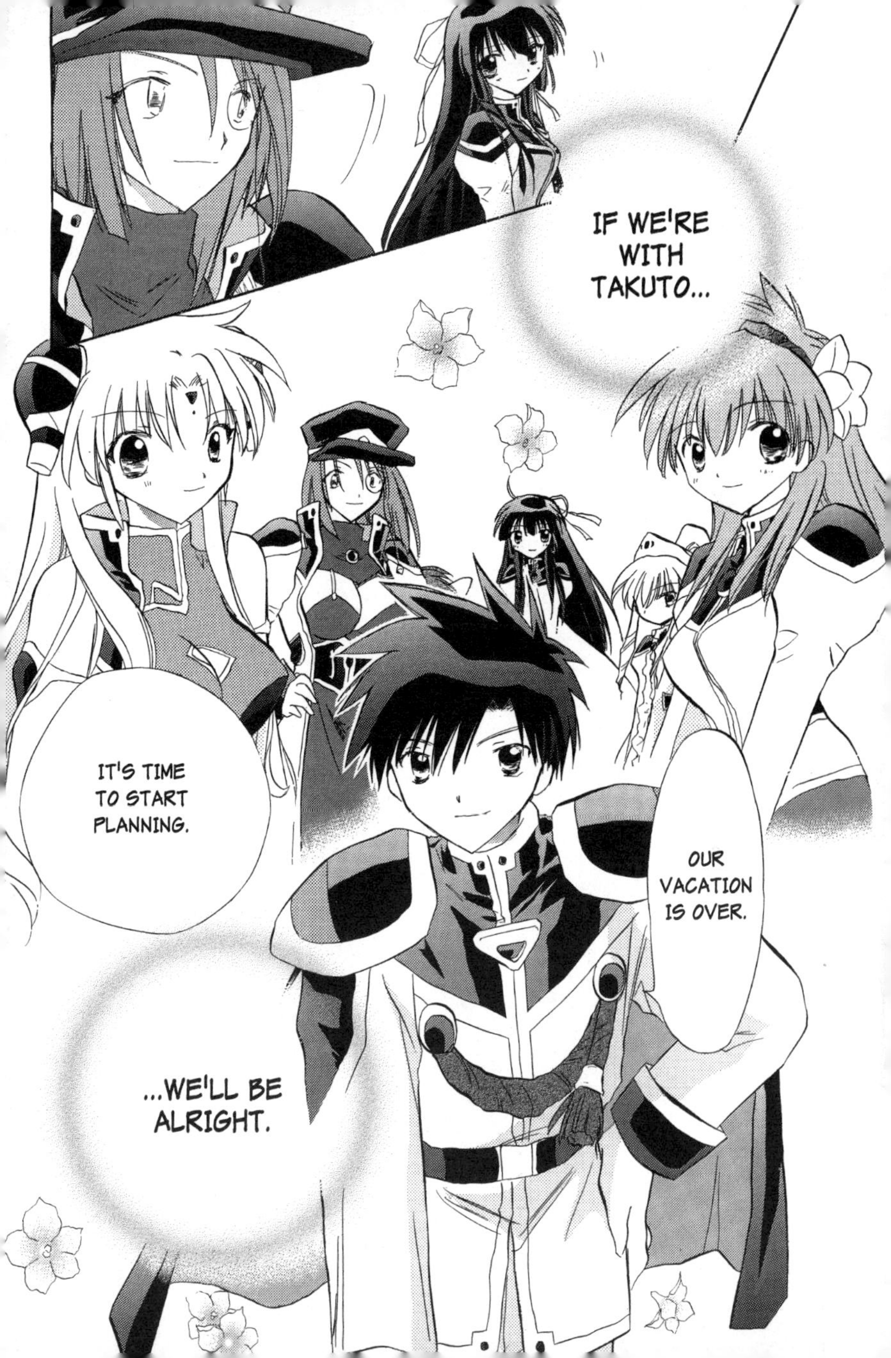
IF WE'RE WITH TAKUTO...
OUR VACATION IS OVER.
IT'S TIME TO START PLANNING.
...WE'LL BE ALRIGHT.

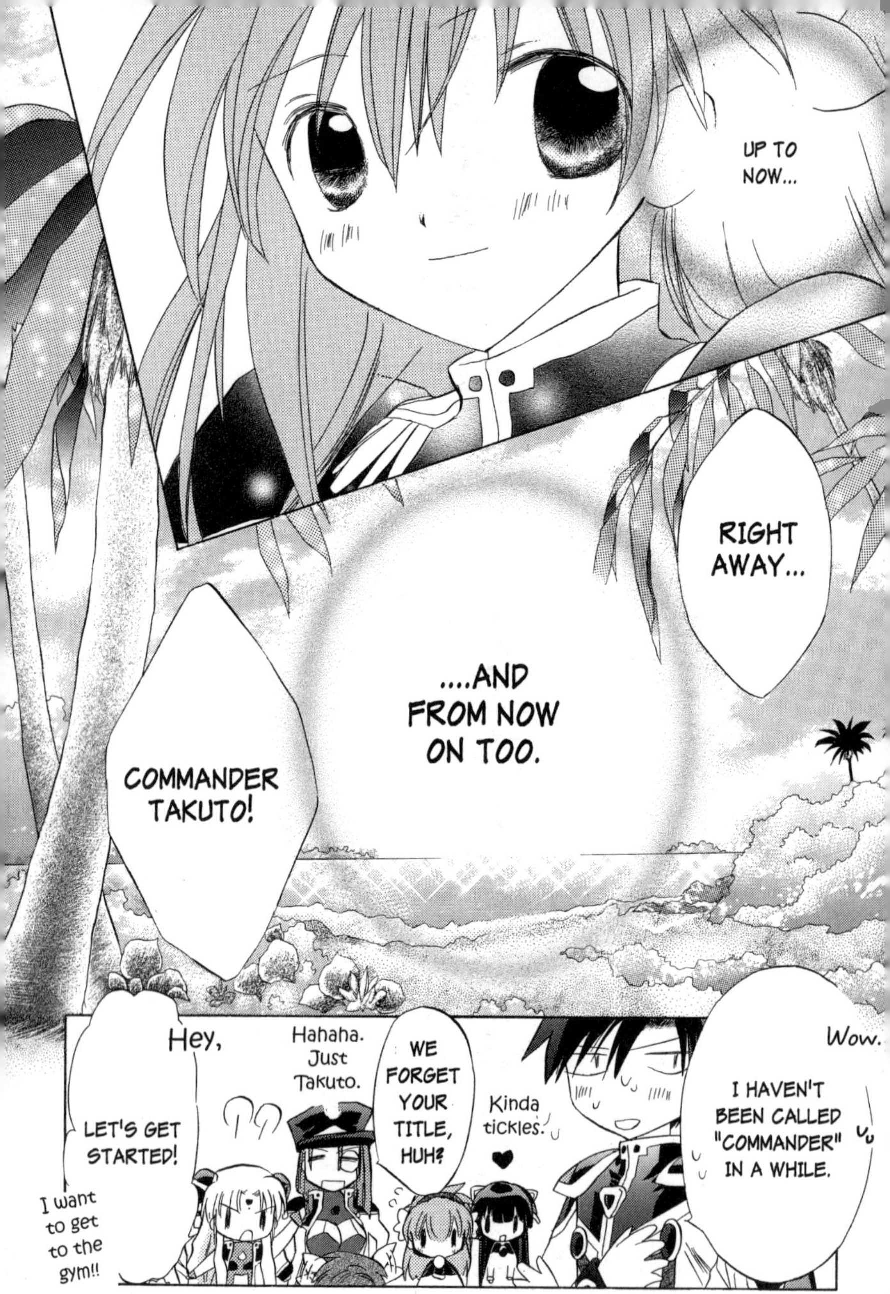
UP TO NOW...
RIGHT AWAY...
....AND FROM NOW ON TOO.
COMMANDER TAKUTO!
Wow.
I HAVEN'T BEEN CALLED "COMMANDER" IN A WHILE.
Kinda tickles.
WE FORGET YOUR TITLE, HUH?
Hahaha. Just Takuto.
Hey,
LET'S GET STARTED!
I want to get to the gym!!

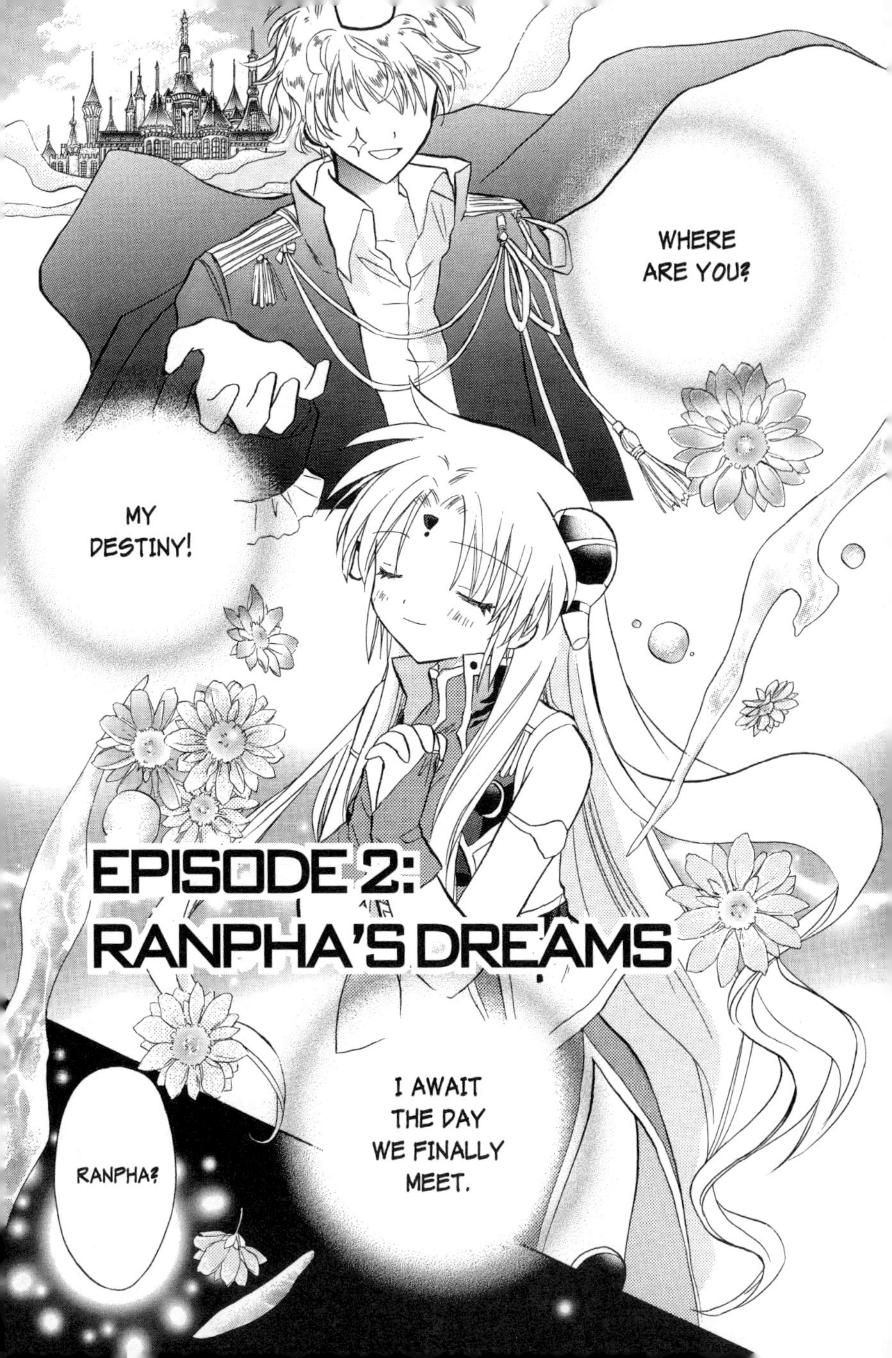
WHERE ARE YOU?
MY DESTINY!
EPISODE 2: RANPHA'S DREAMS
I AWAIT THE DAY WE FINALLY MEET.
RANPHA?

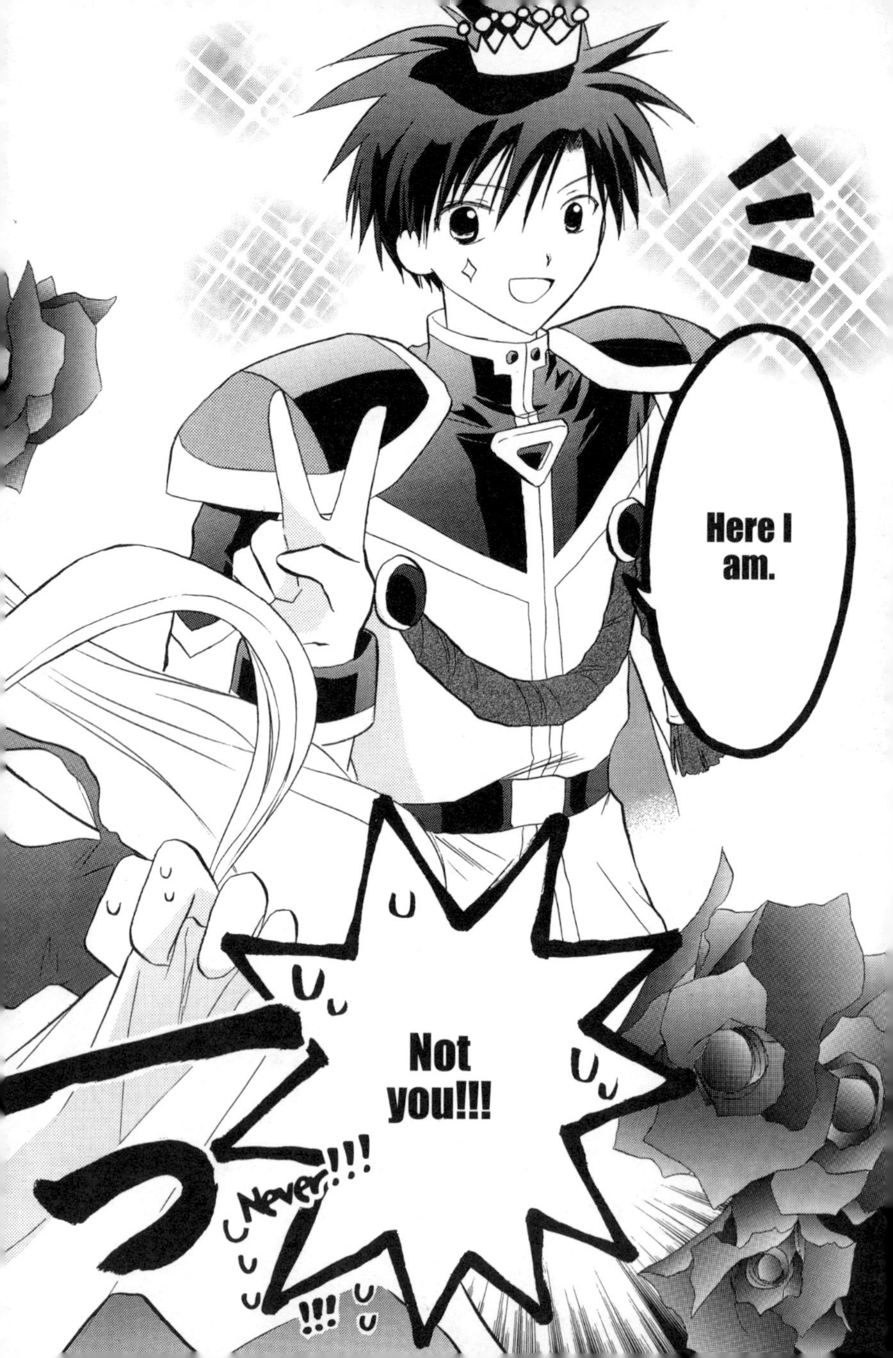
Here I am.
Not you!!!
Never!!!
!!!

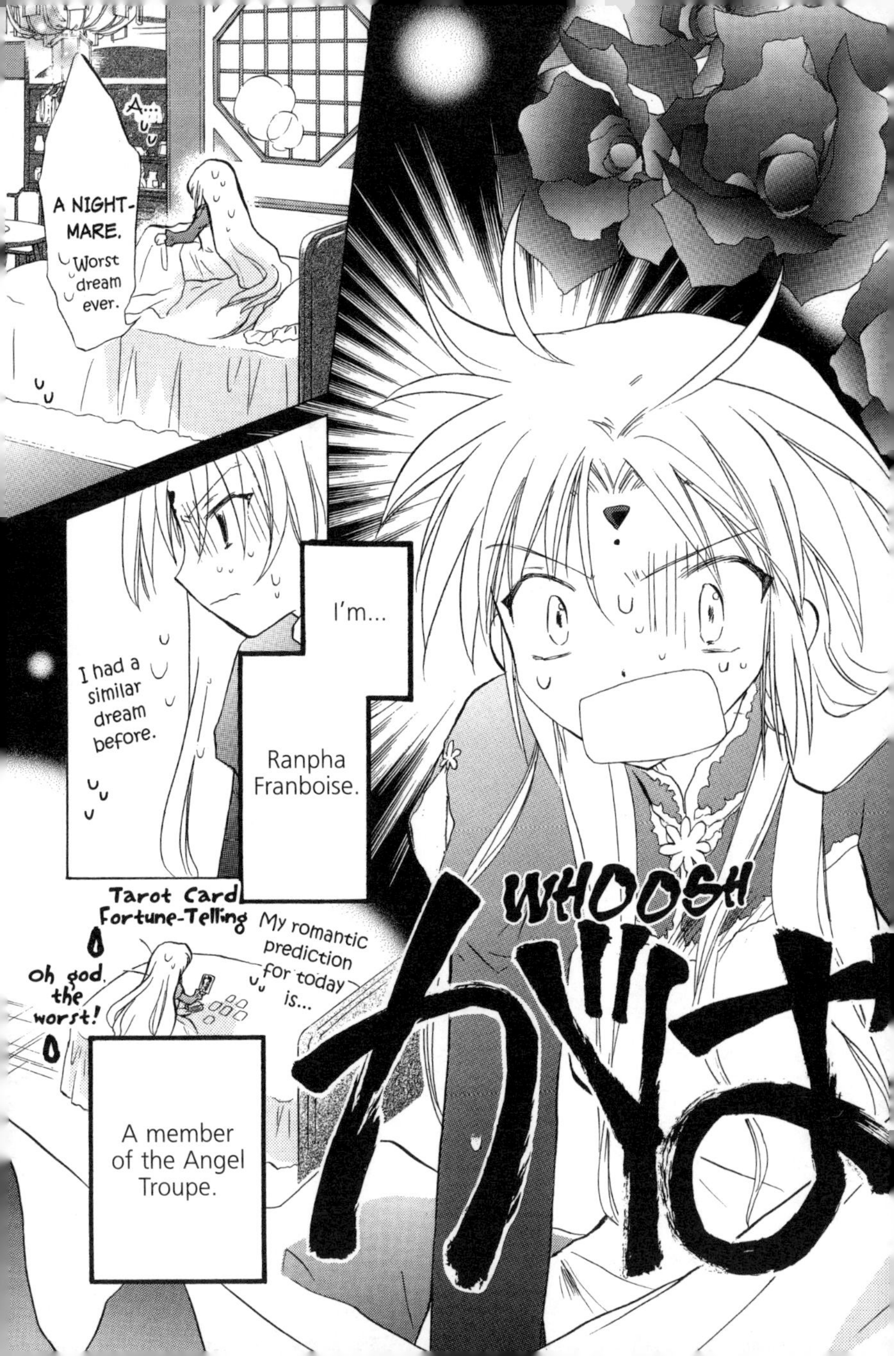
WHOOSH
A...
A NIGHT-MARE.
Worst dream ever.
I'm...
Ranpha Franboise.
I had a similar dream before.
My romantic prediction for today is...
Tarot Card Fortune-Telling
Oh god, the worst!
A member of the Angel Troupe.

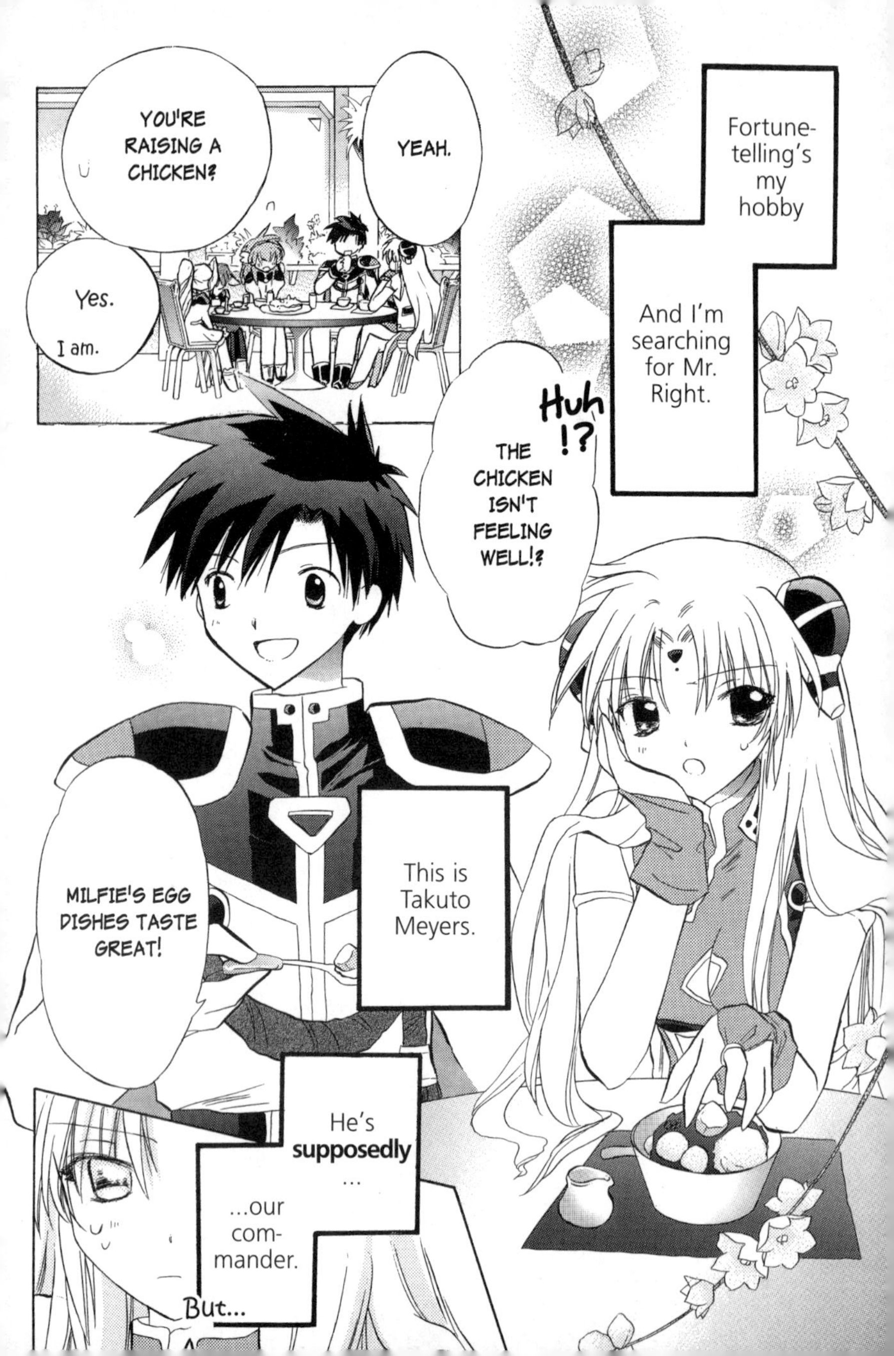
Fortune-telling's my hobby
And I'm searching for Mr. Right.
YOU'RE RAISING A CHICKEN?
YEAH.
Yes. I am.
Huh!?
THE CHICKEN ISN'T FEELING WELL!?
This is Takuto Meyers.
MILFIE'S EGG DISHES TASTE GREAT!
He's supposedly ...
...our commander.
But...

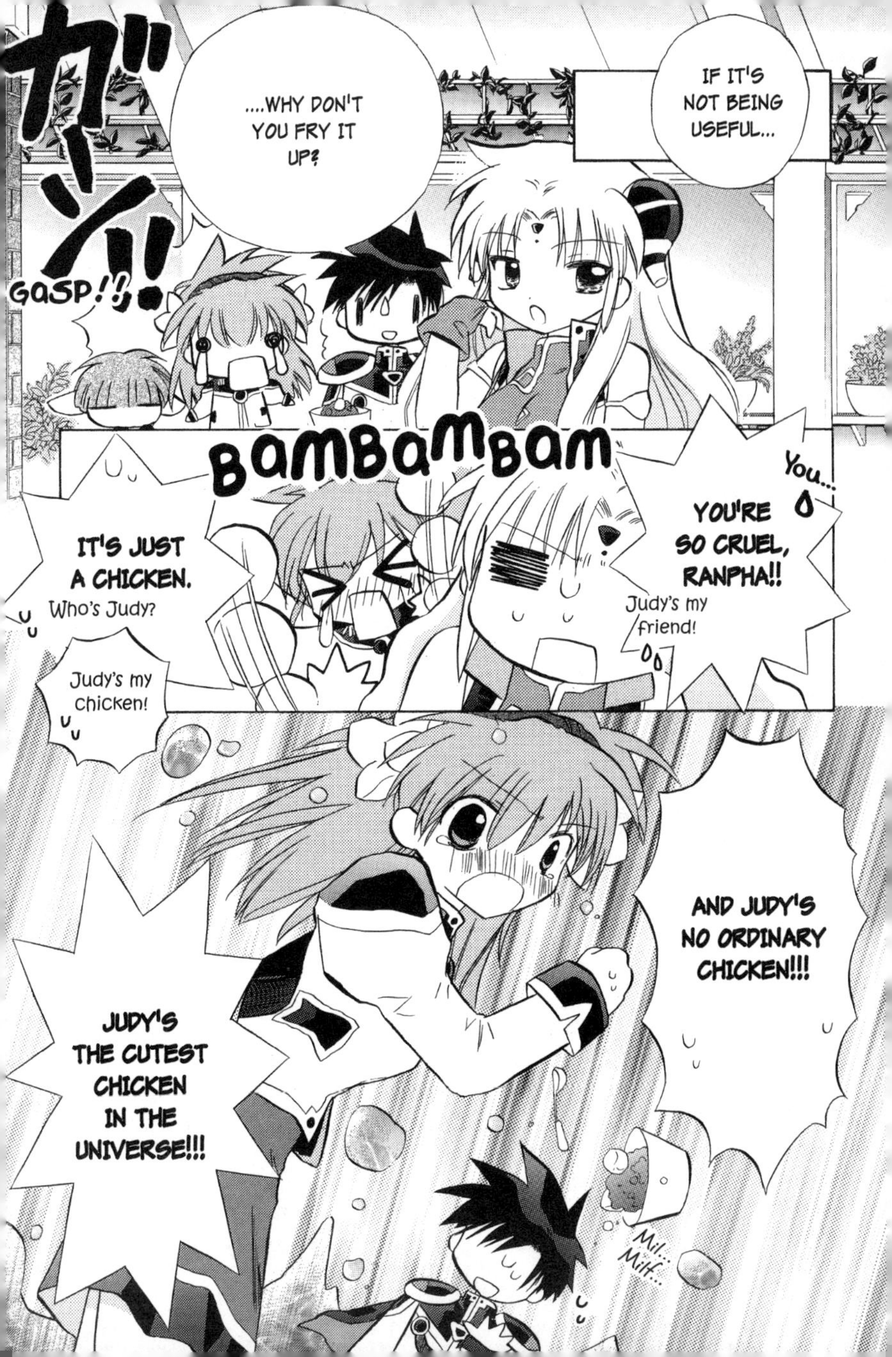

IF IT'S NOT BEING USEFUL...
....WHY DON'T YOU FRY IT UP?
ガッ!!
GASP!!
BAMBAMBAM
You...
YOU'RE SO CRUEL, RANPHA!!
Judy's my friend!
IT'S JUST A CHICKEN.
Who's Judy?
Judy's my chicken!
AND JUDY'S NO ORDINARY CHICKEN!!!
JUDY'S THE CUTEST CHICKEN IN THE UNIVERSE!!!
Mil... Milf...

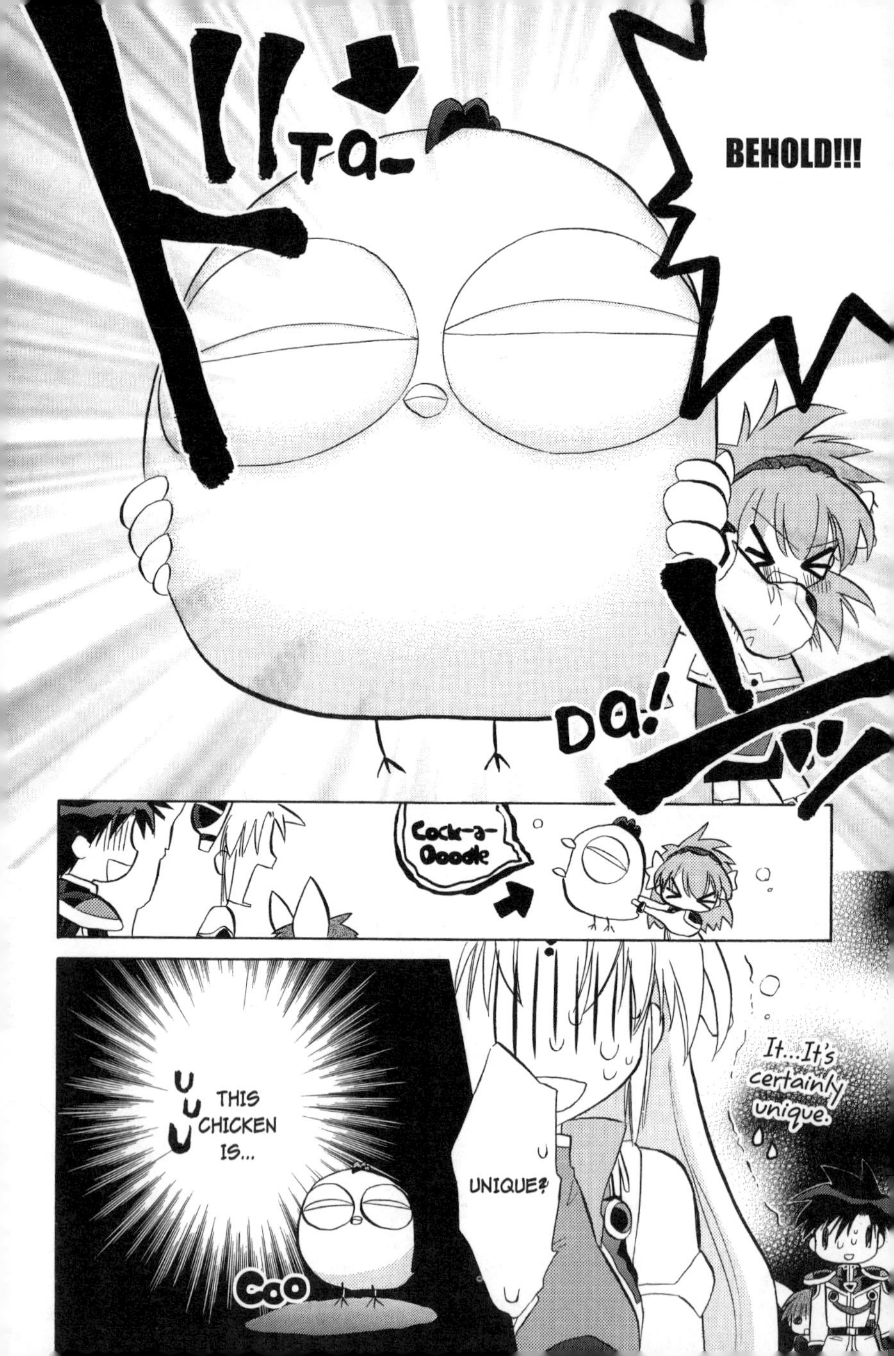
BEHOLD!!!
Ta-
Da!
Cock-a-Doodle
It...It's certainly unique.
UNIQUE?
THIS CHICKEN IS...
Coo

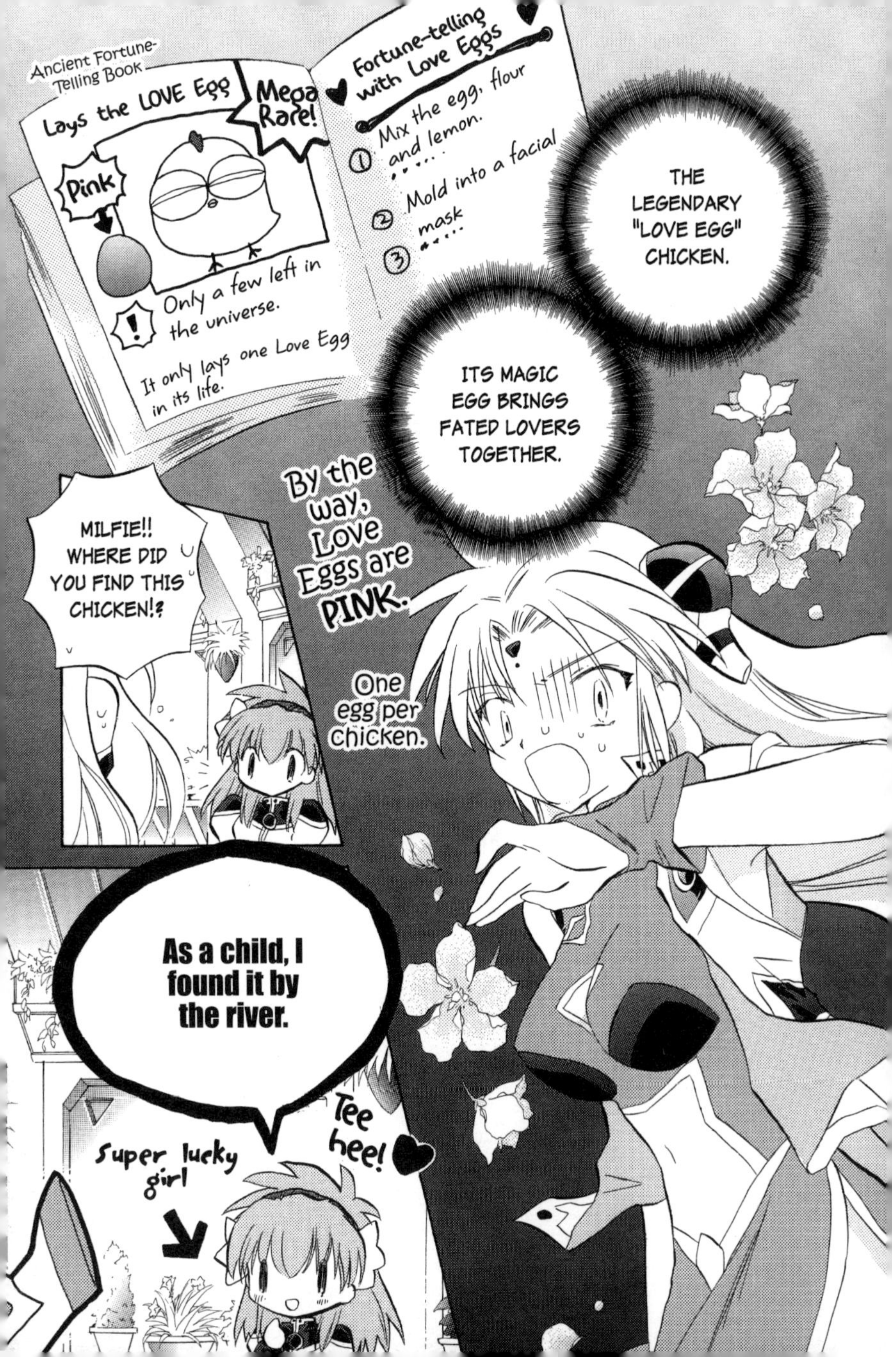
THE LEGENDARY "LOVE EGG" CHICKEN.
ITS MAGIC EGG BRINGS FATED LOVERS TOGETHER.
Ancient Fortune-Telling Book
Lays the LOVE Egg
Mega Rare!
Pink
Only a few left in the universe.
It only lays one Love Egg in its life.
Fortune-telling with Love Eggs
① Mix the egg, flour and lemon......
② Mold into a facial mask......
③ ......
By the way, Love Eggs are PINK.
One egg per chicken.
MILFIE!! WHERE DID YOU FIND THIS CHICKEN!?
As a child, I found it by the river.
Tee hee!
Super lucky girl

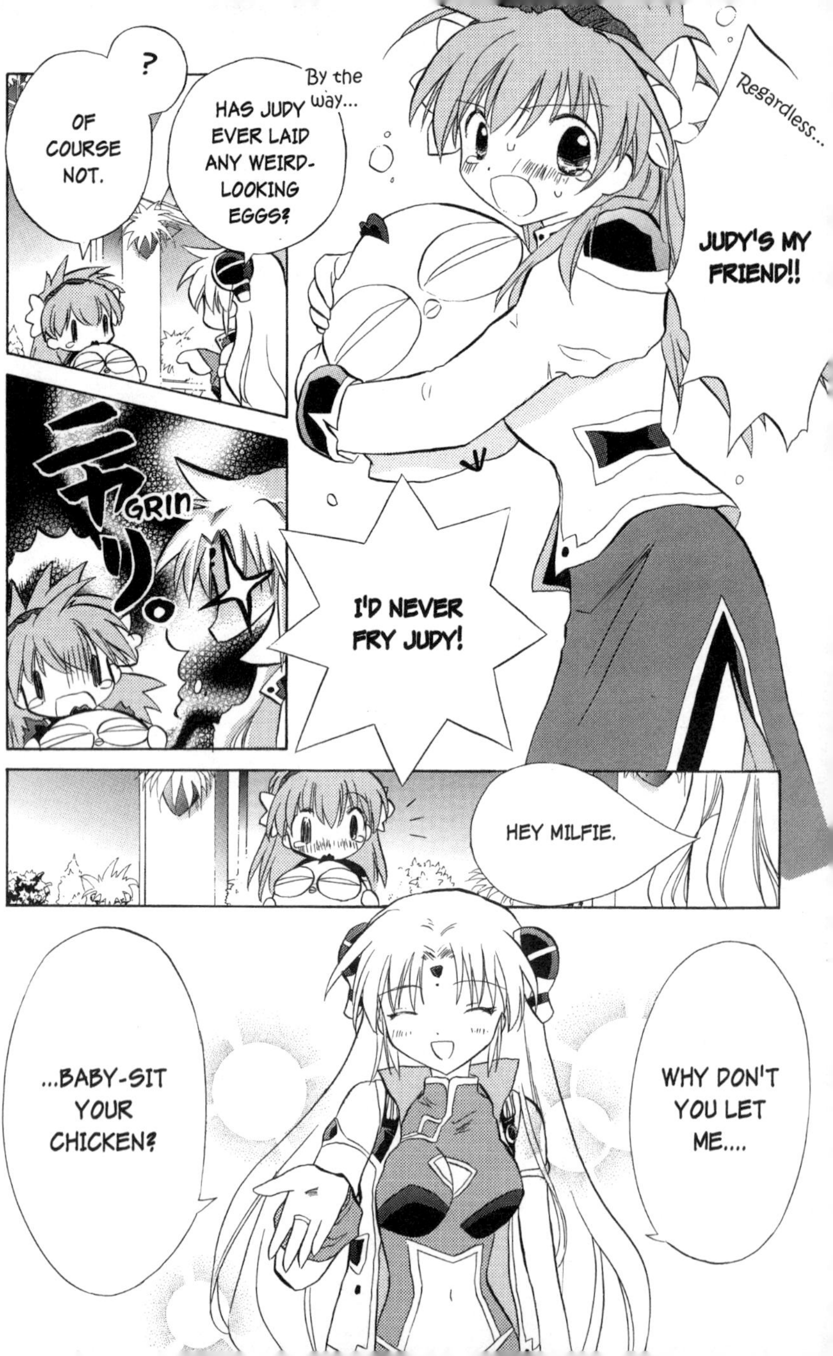
Regardless...
JUDY'S MY FRIEND!!
I'D NEVER FRY JUDY!
By the way...
HAS JUDY EVER LAID ANY WEIRD-LOOKING EGGS?
?
OF COURSE NOT.
GRIN
HEY MILFIE.
WHY DON'T YOU LET ME....
...BABY-SIT YOUR CHICKEN?

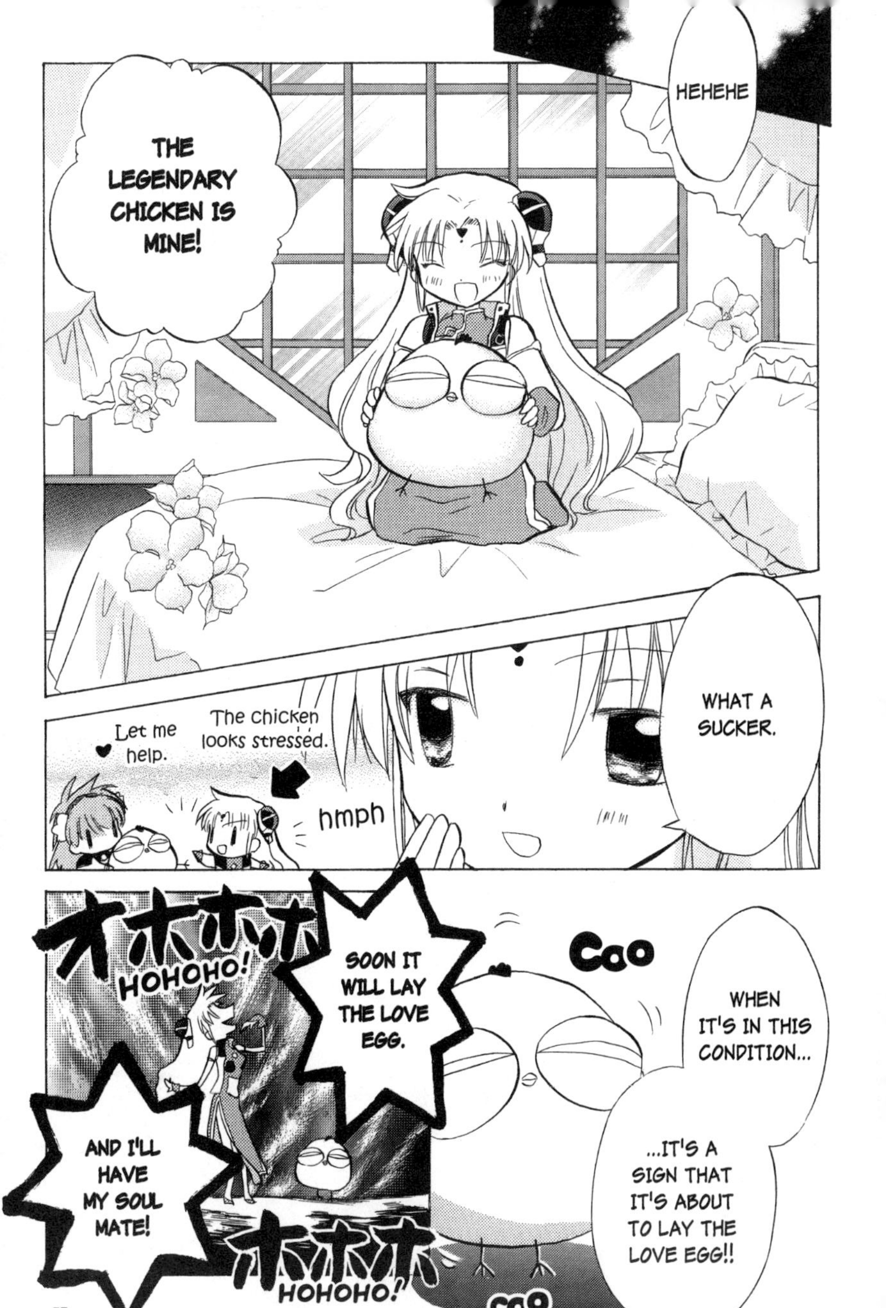
HEHEHE
THE LEGENDARY CHICKEN IS MINE!
WHAT A SUCKER.
hmph
The chicken looks stressed.
Let me help.
Cao
WHEN IT'S IN THIS CONDITION...
...IT'S A SIGN THAT IT'S ABOUT TO LAY THE LOVE EGG!!
cao
SOON IT WILL LAY THE LOVE EGG.
HOHOHO!
AND I'LL HAVE MY SOUL MATE!
HOHOHO!

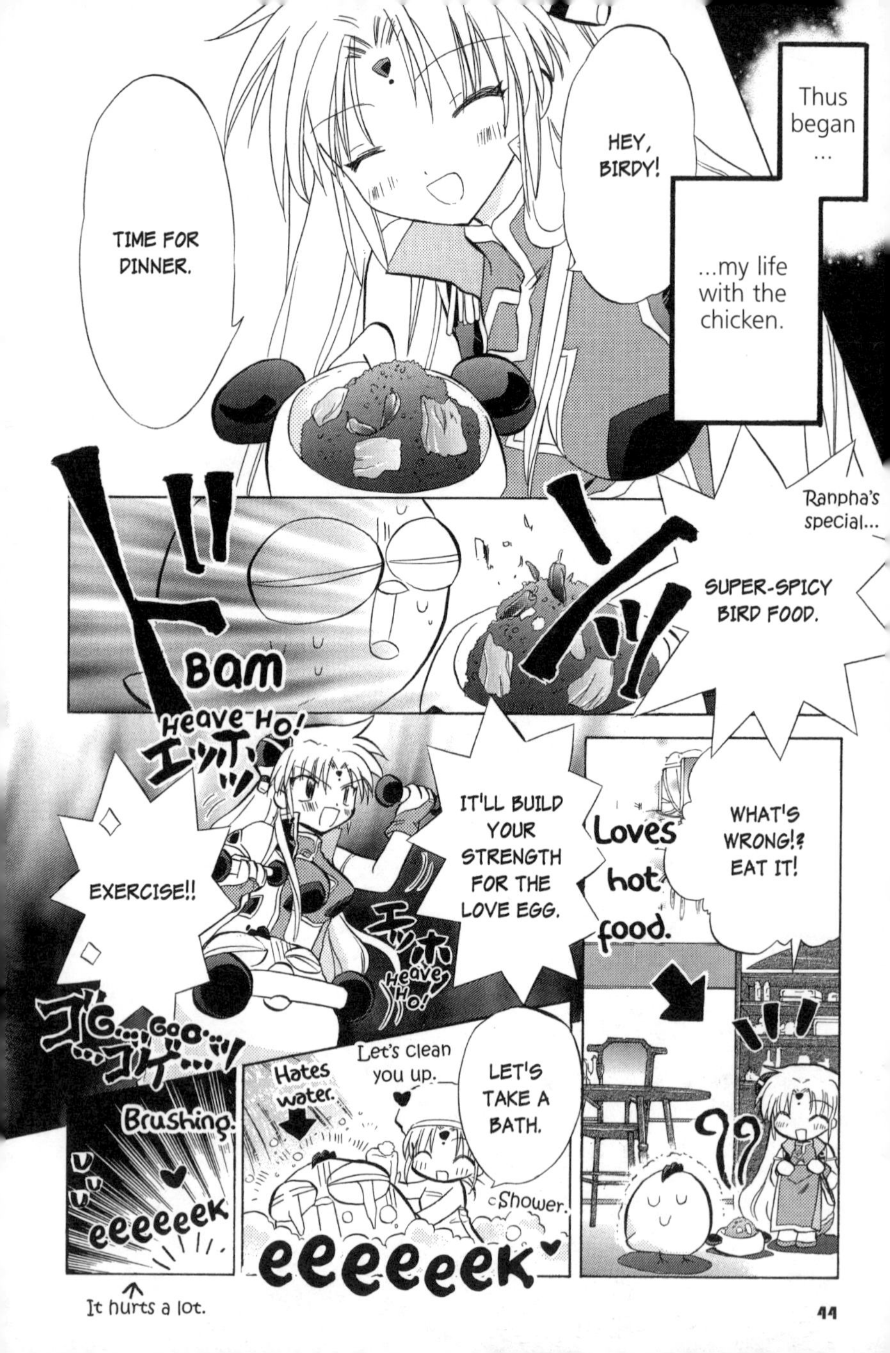
Thus began ...
...my life with the chicken.
HEY, BIRDY!
TIME FOR DINNER.
Ranpha's special...
SUPER-SPICY BIRD FOOD.
Bam
WHAT'S WRONG!? EAT IT!
Loves hot food.
IT'LL BUILD YOUR STRENGTH FOR THE LOVE EGG.
Heave-Ho!
EXERCISE!!
Heave Ho!
LET'S TAKE A BATH.
Let's clean you up.
Hates water.
Shower.
eeeeeek
G... GOO...
Brushing.
eeeeeek
It hurts a lot.

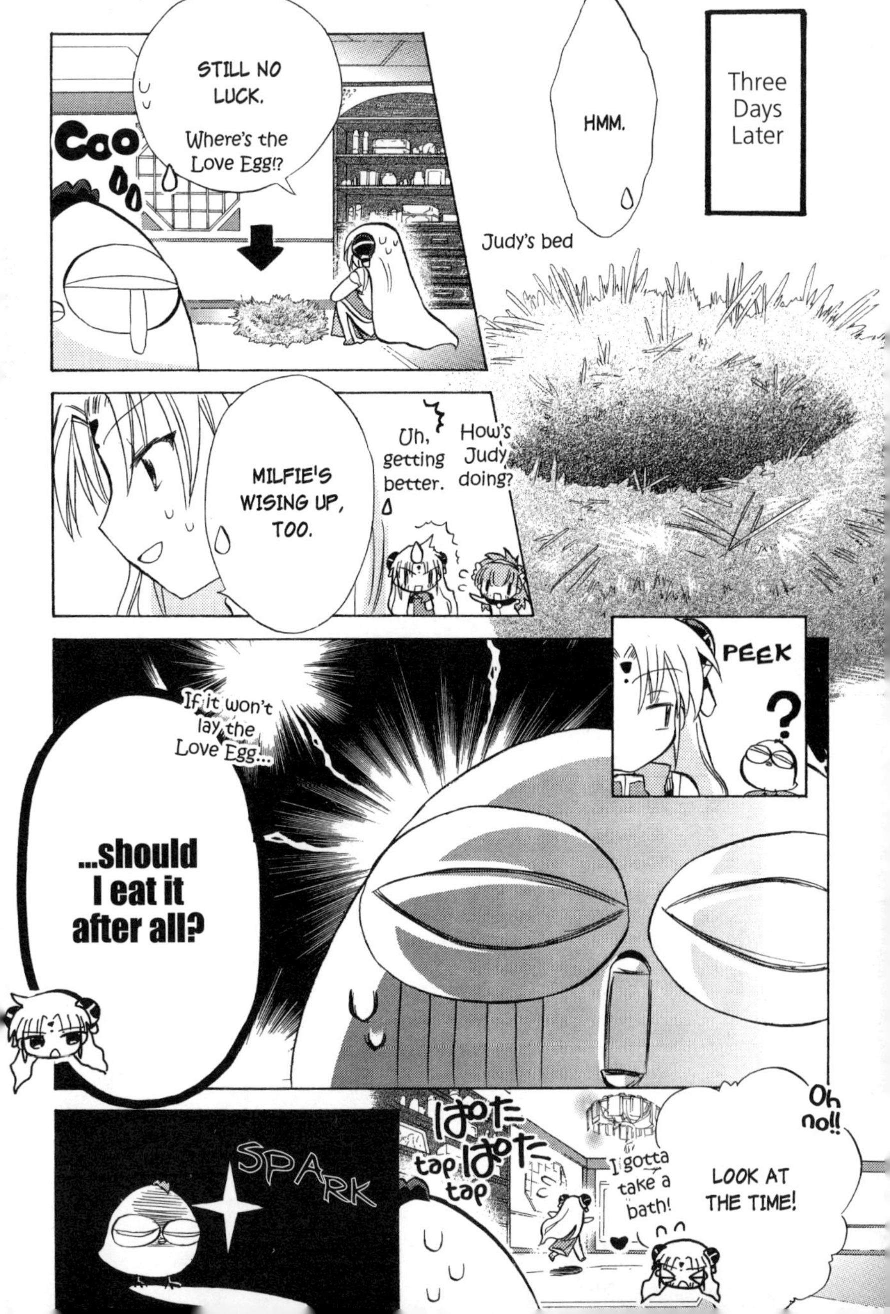
Three Days Later
HMM.
Judy's bed
STILL NO LUCK. Where's the Love Egg!?
COO DO
How's Judy doing?
Uh, getting better.
MILFIE'S WISING UP, TOO.
PEEK
?
If it won't lay the Love Egg...
...should I eat it after all?
Oh no!! LOOK AT THE TIME!
I gotta take a bath!
ぽたぽた
tap tap
SPARK

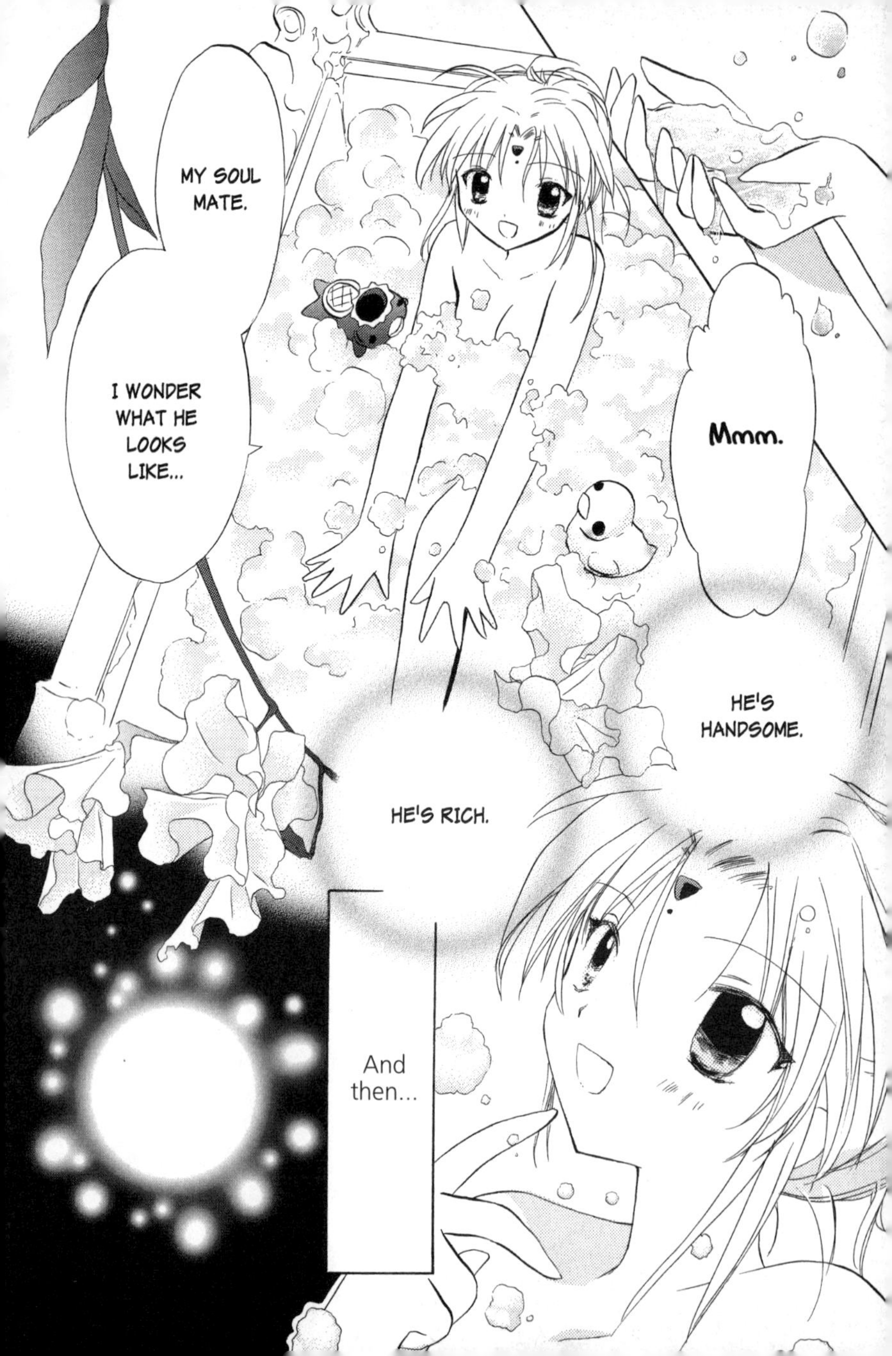
MY SOUL MATE.
I WONDER WHAT HE LOOKS LIKE...
Mmm.
HE'S HANDSOME.
HE'S RICH.
And then...

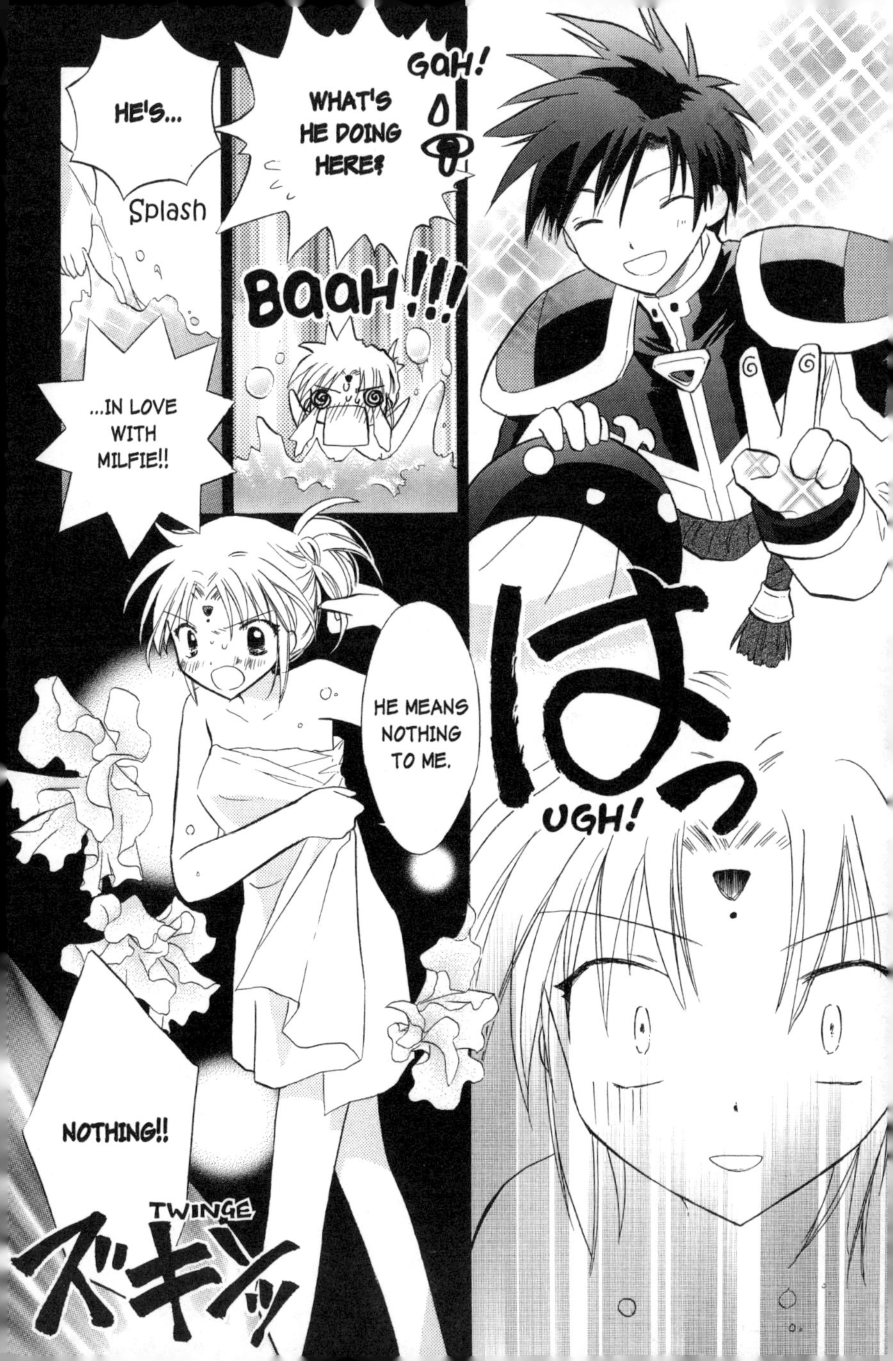

はっ
UGH!
GAH!
WHAT'S HE DOING HERE?
BAAH!!!
HE'S...
Splash
...IN LOVE WITH MILFIE!!
HE MEANS NOTHING TO ME.
NOTHING!!
TWINGE
ズキッ

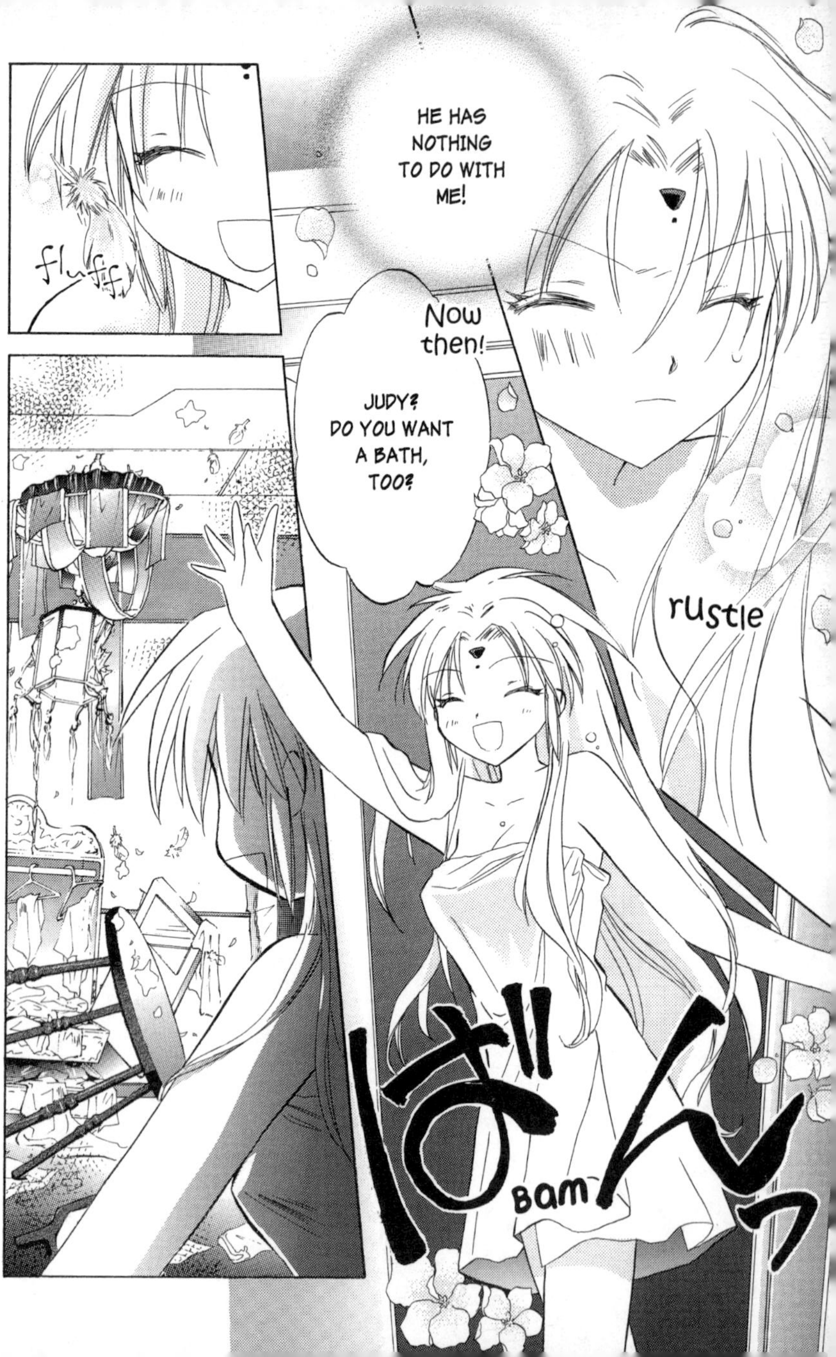
HE HAS NOTHING TO DO WITH ME!
rustle
fluff
Now then!
JUDY? DO YOU WANT A BATH, TOO?
Bam

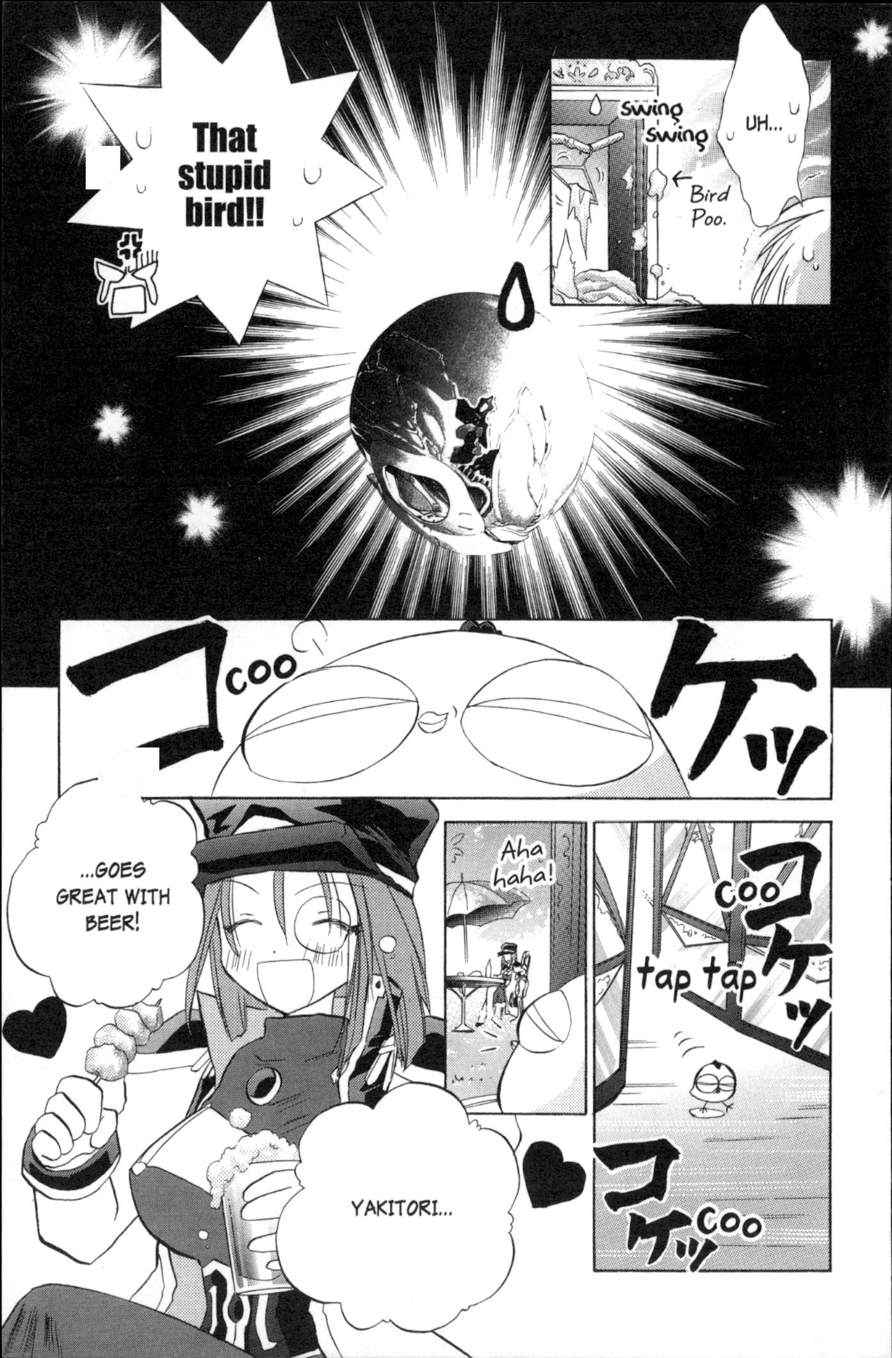
UH...
swing swing
Bird Poo.
That stupid bird!!
コ COO ケッ
COO コケッ
tap tap
コケッ COO
Aha haha!
YAKITORI...
...GOES GREAT WITH BEER!

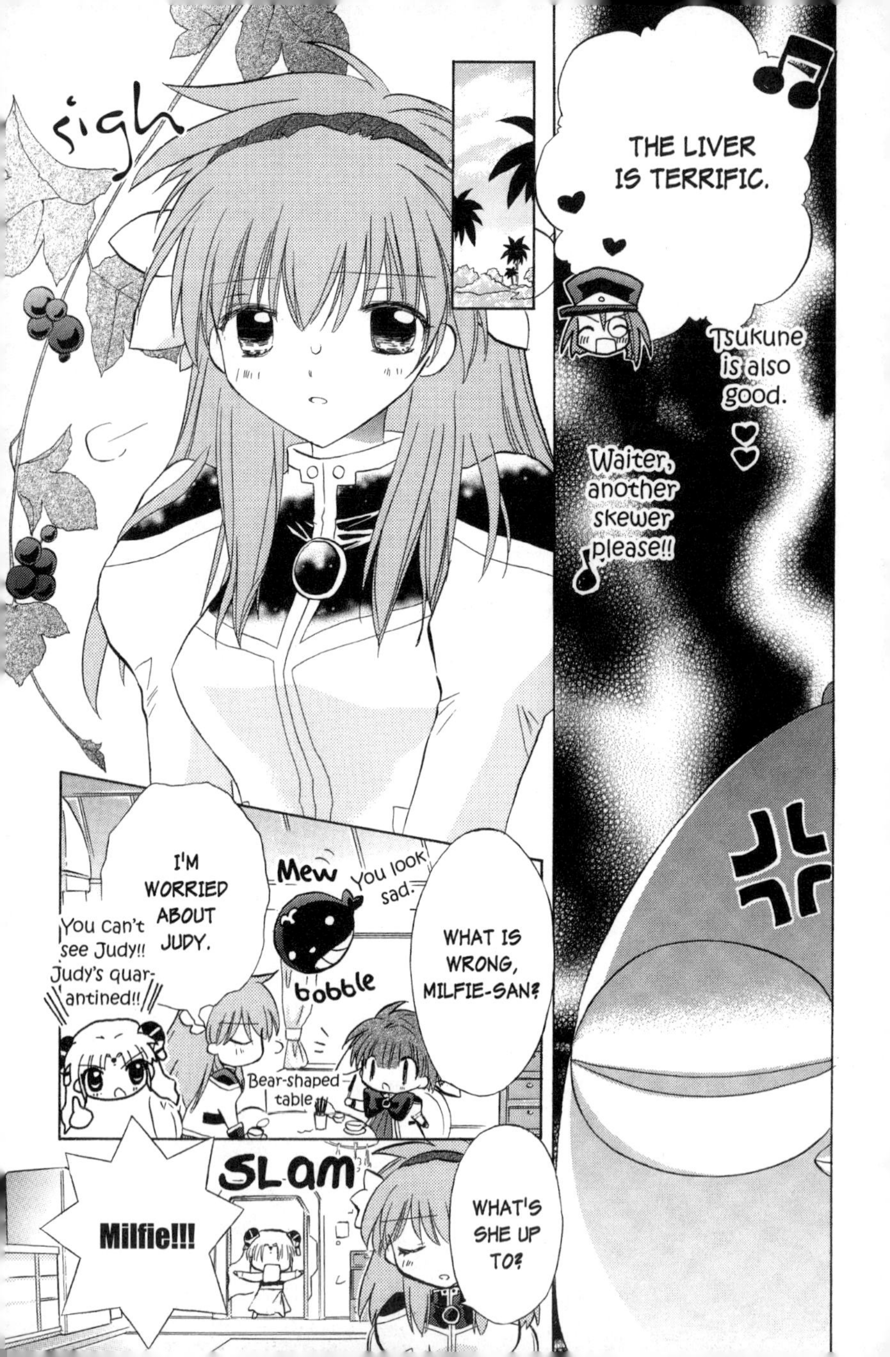
THE LIVER IS TERRIFIC.
Tsukune is also good.
Waiter, another skewer please!!
sigh
WHAT IS WRONG, MILFIE-SAN?
You look sad.
Mew
bobble
I'M WORRIED ABOUT JUDY.
You can't see Judy!! Judy's quar-antined!!
Bear-shaped table
WHAT'S SHE UP TO?
SLAM
Milfie!!!

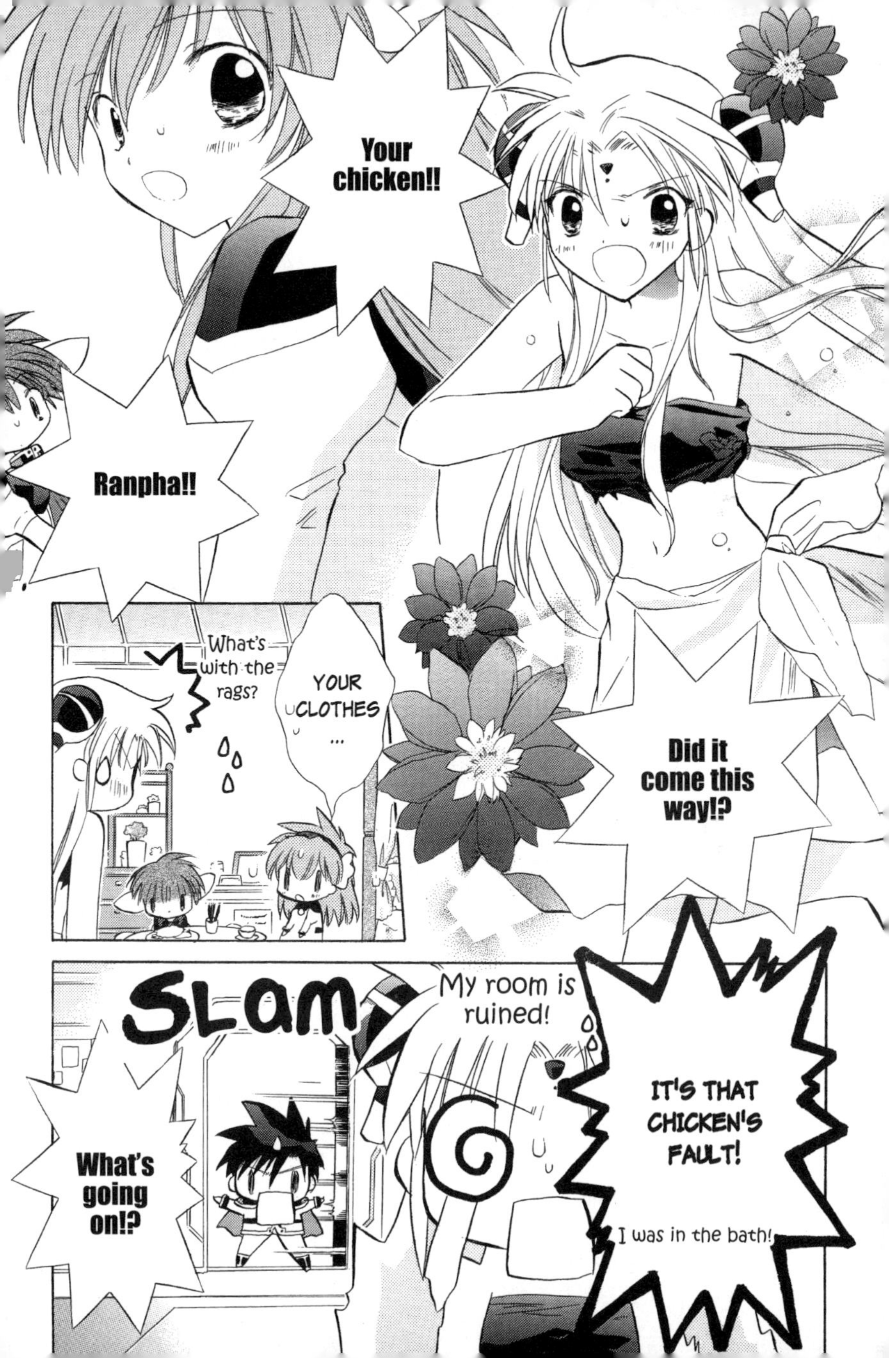

Your chicken!!
Ranpha!!
Did it come this way!?
YOUR CLOTHES ...
What's with the rags?
My room is ruined!
IT'S THAT CHICKEN'S FAULT!
I was in the bath!
SLAM
What's going on!?

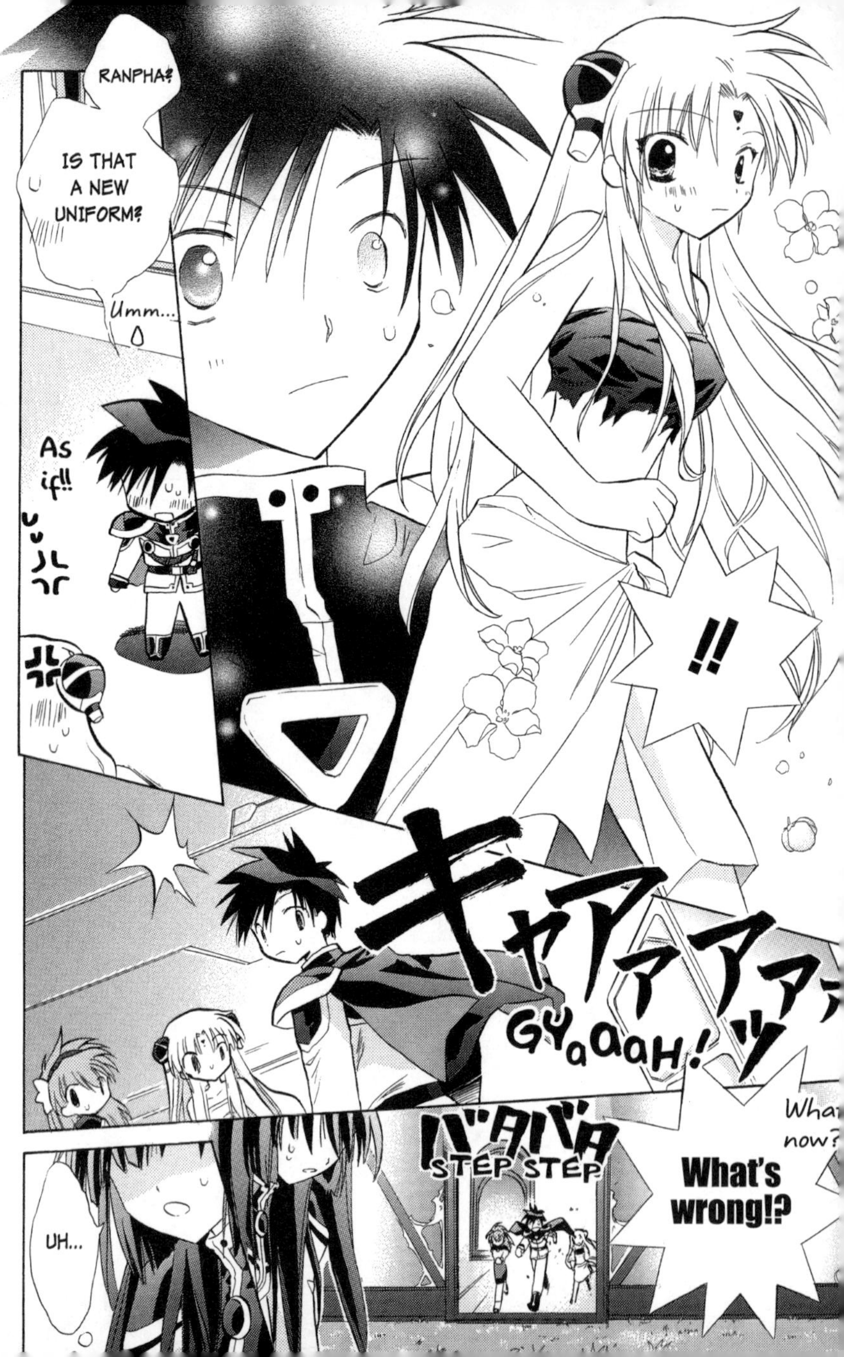
!!
RANPHA?
IS THAT A NEW UNIFORM?
Umm...
As if!!
キャアァアァッ
GYaaaH!
What now?
What's wrong!?
バタバタ
STEP STEP
UH...

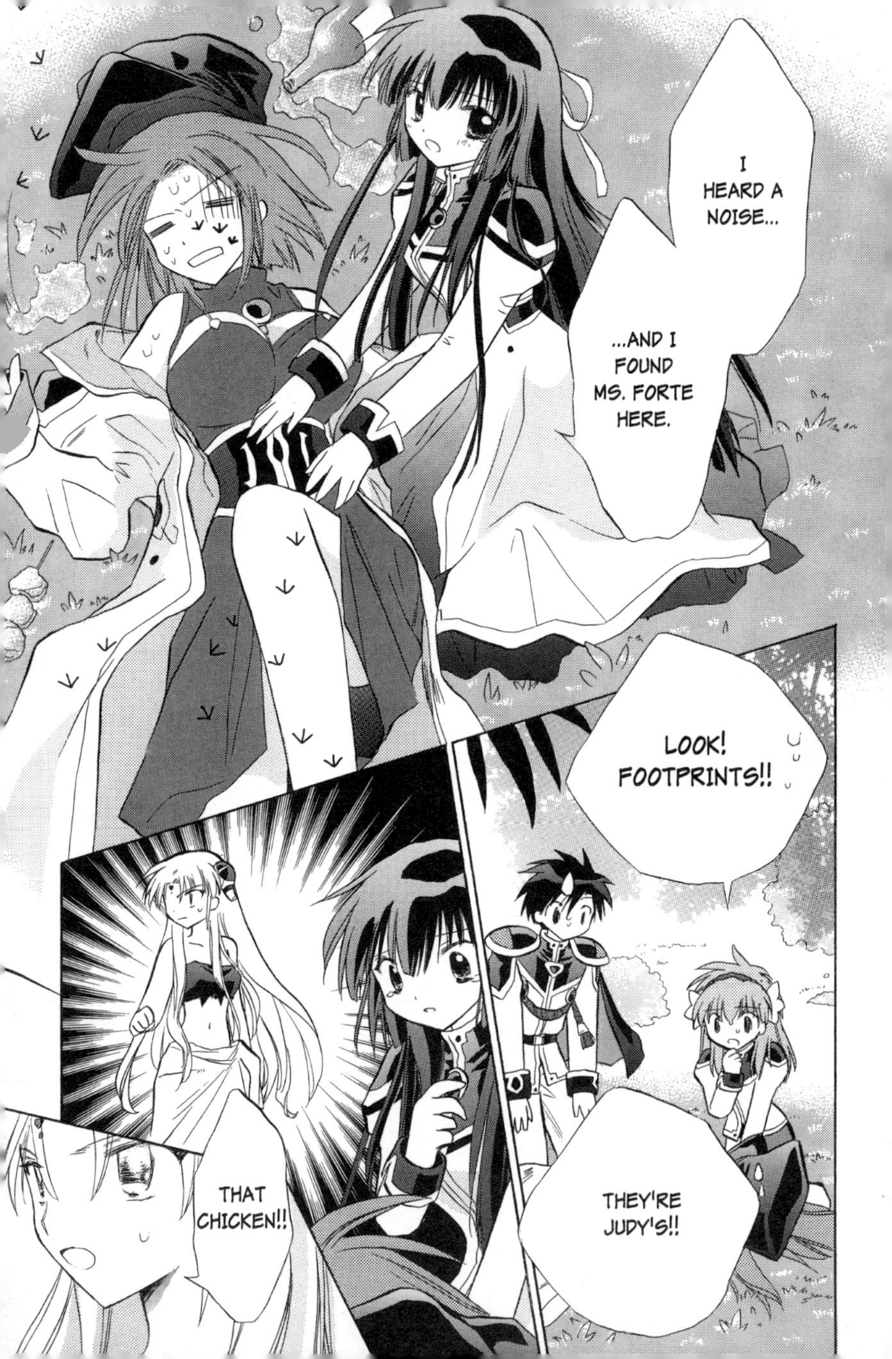
I HEARD A NOISE...
...AND I FOUND MS. FORTE HERE.
LOOK! FOOTPRINTS!!
THEY'RE JUDY'S!!
THAT CHICKEN!!

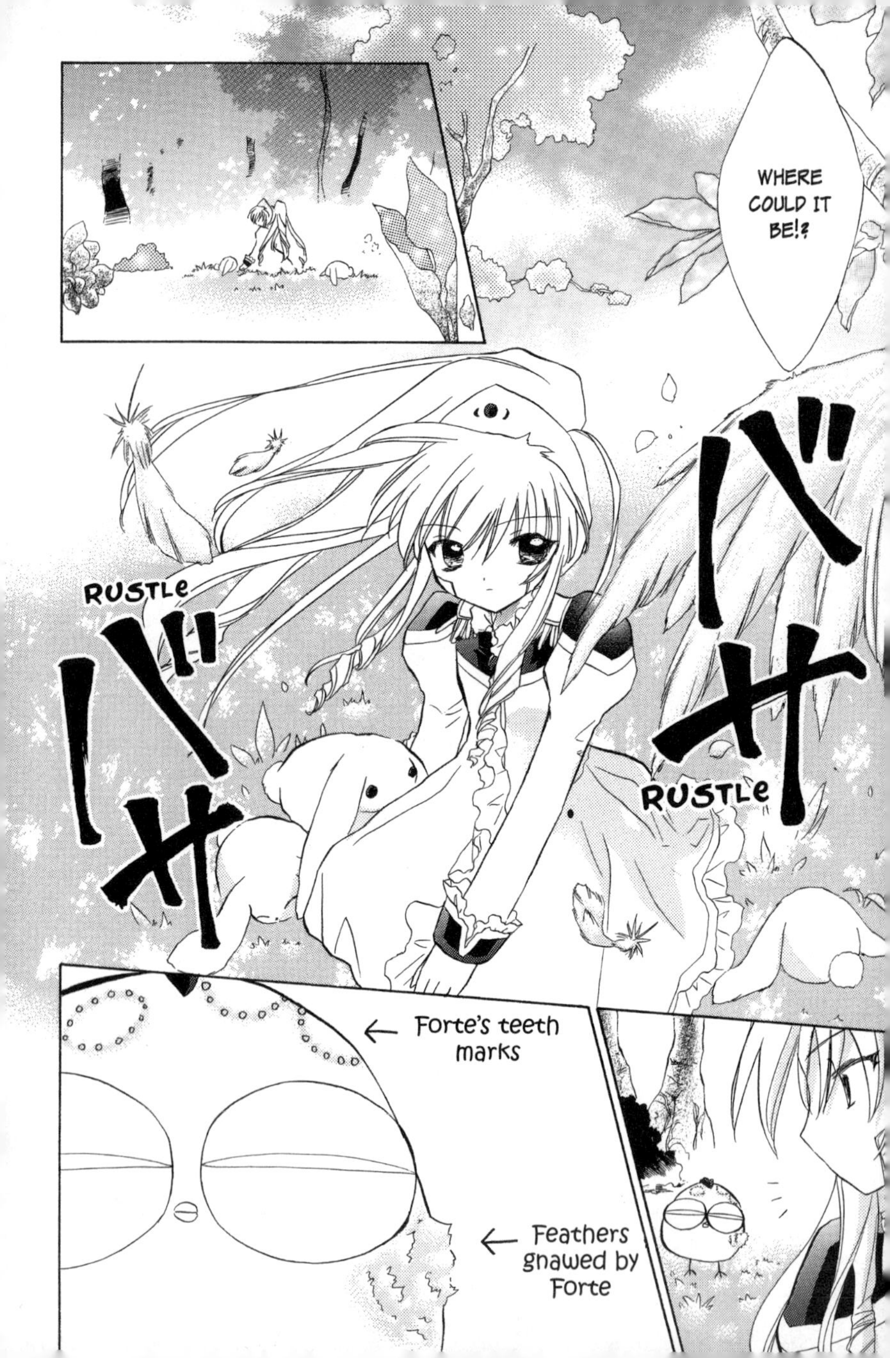
WHERE COULD IT BE!?
バサ
RUSTLE
バサ
RUSTLE
← Forte's teeth marks
← Feathers gnawed by Forte

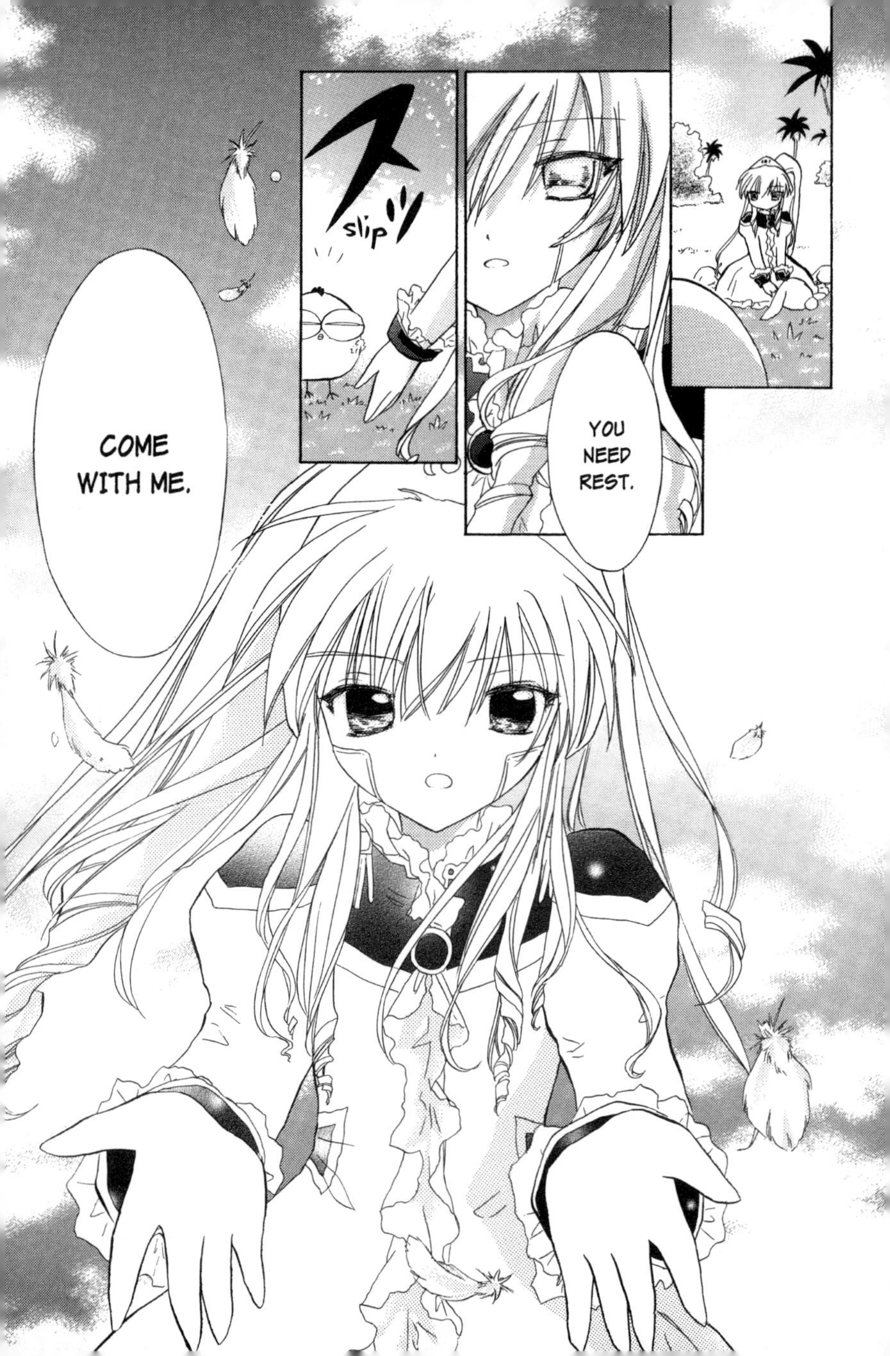
YOU NEED REST.
slip
COME WITH ME.

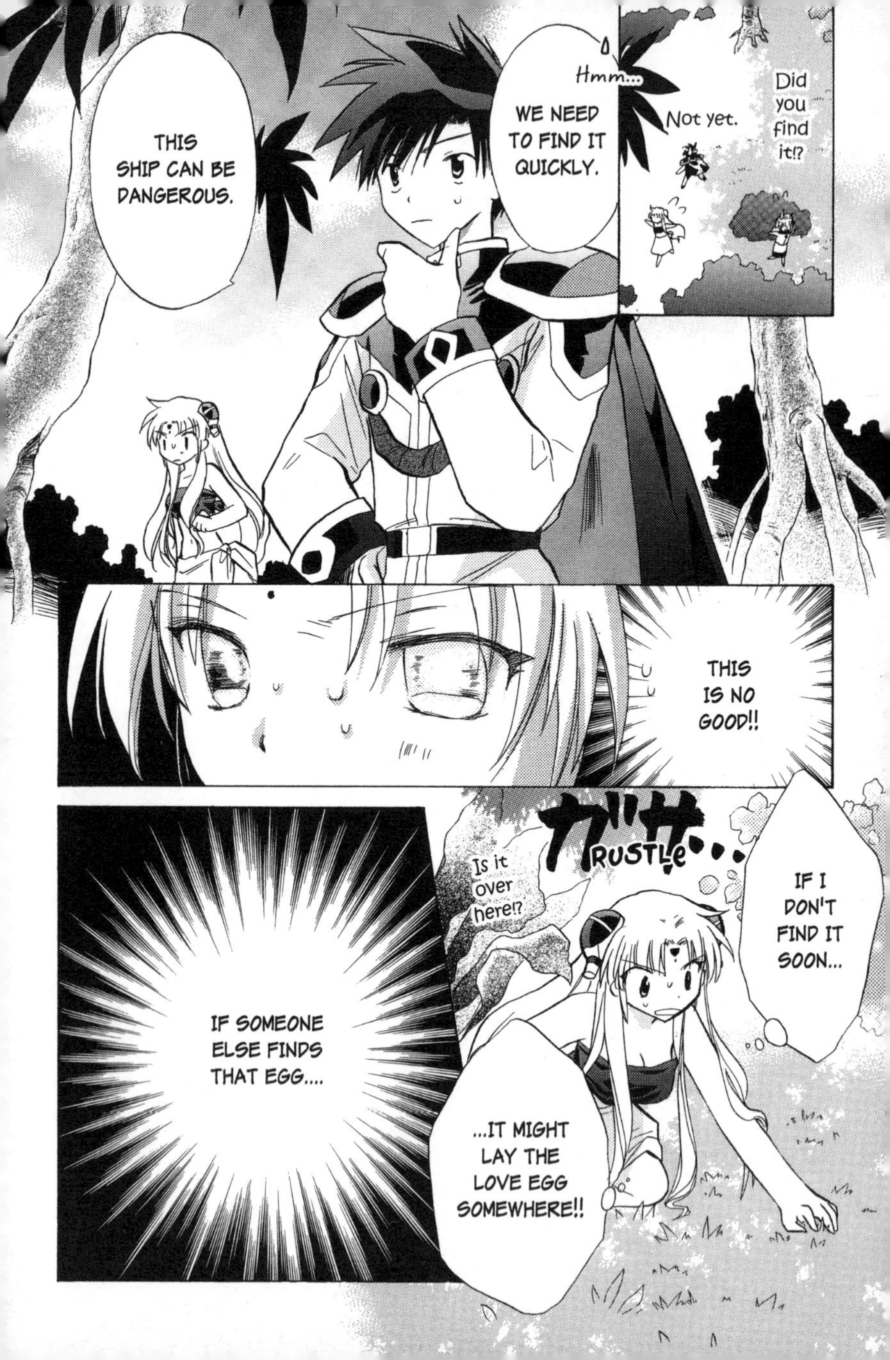
Did you find it!?
Not yet.
Hmm...
WE NEED TO FIND IT QUICKLY.
THIS SHIP CAN BE DANGEROUS.
THIS IS NO GOOD!!
RUSTLE...
IF I DON'T FIND IT SOON...
Is it over here!?
IF SOMEONE ELSE FINDS THAT EGG....
...IT MIGHT LAY THE LOVE EGG SOMEWHERE!!

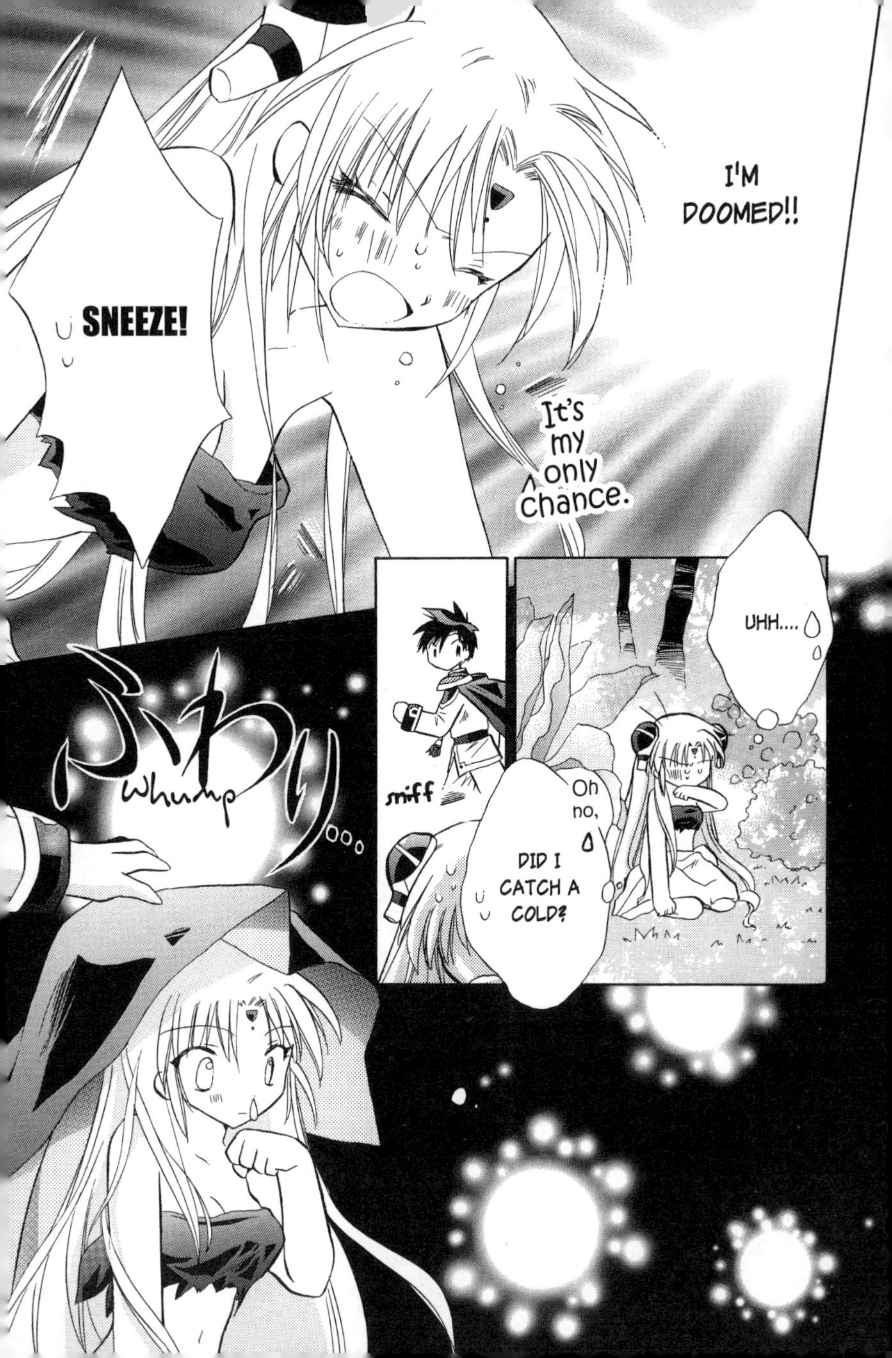
I'M DOOMED!!
It's my only chance.
SNEEZE!
UHH....
Oh no,
DID I CATCH A COLD?
sniff
ふわり
Whump

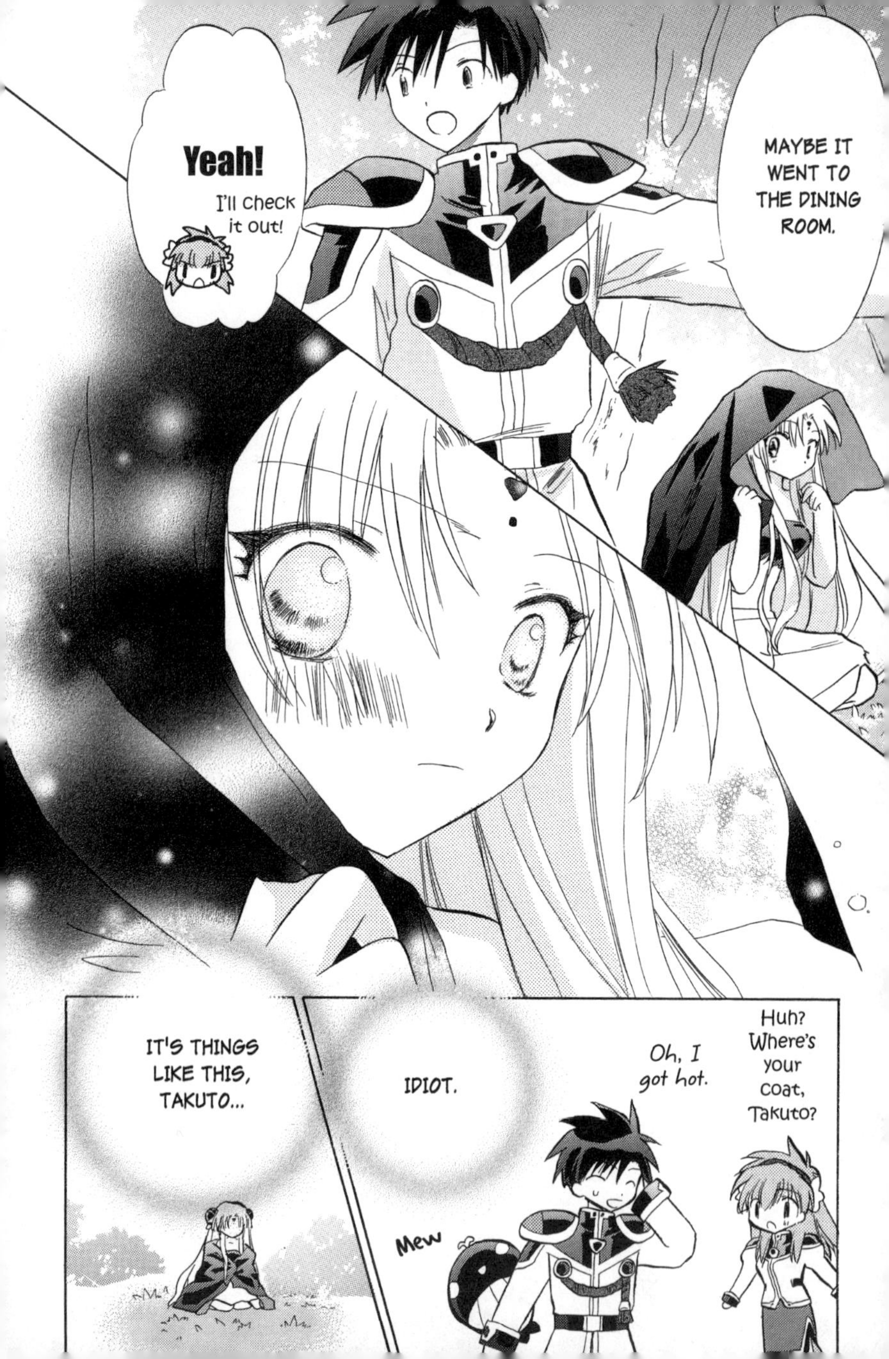
MAYBE IT WENT TO THE DINING ROOM.
Yeah!
I'll check it out!
Huh? Where's your coat, Takuto?
Oh, I got hot.
Mew
IDIOT.
IT'S THINGS LIKE THIS, TAKUTO...

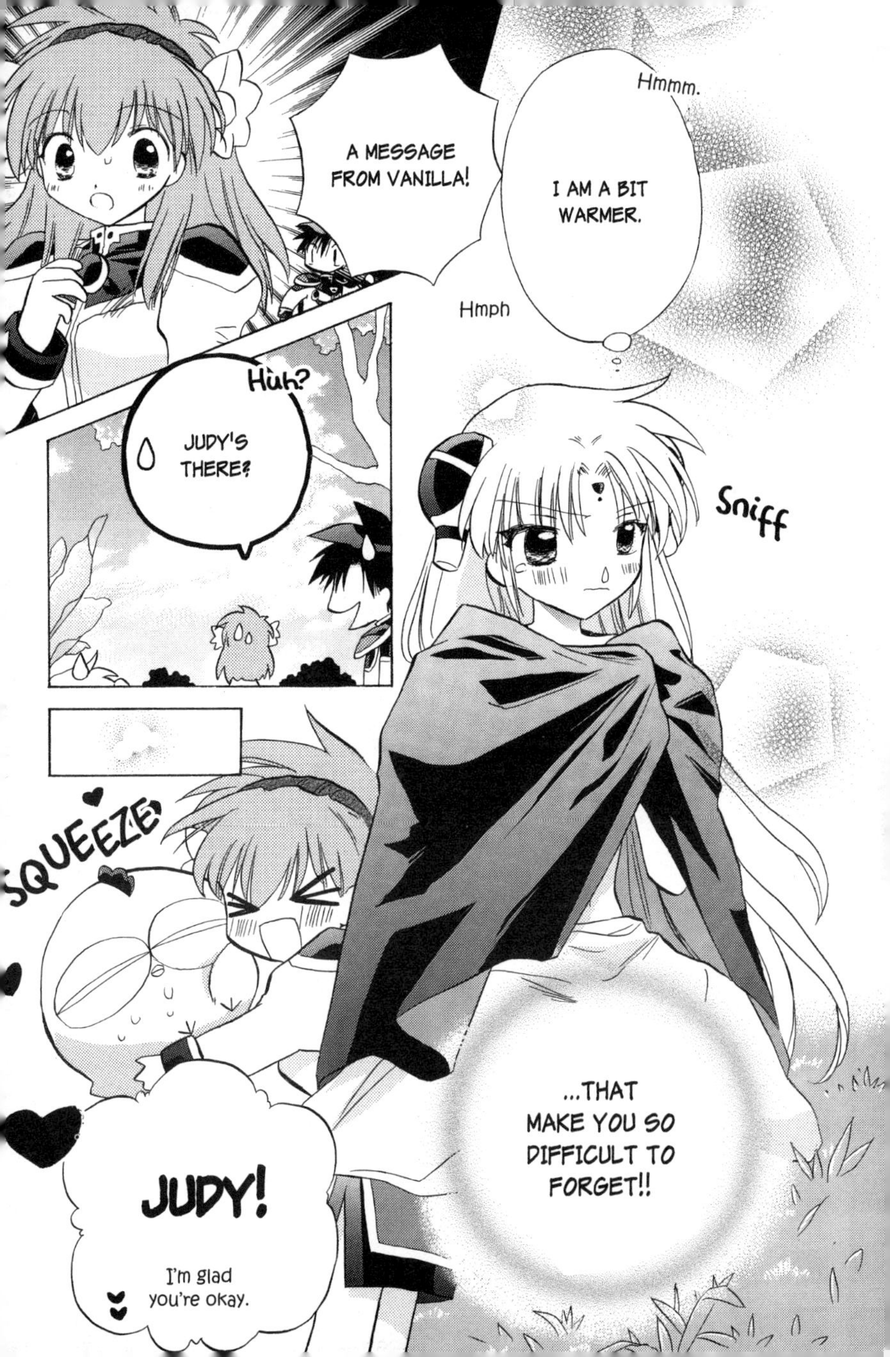
Hmmm.
I AM A BIT WARMER.
Hmph
Sniff
...THAT MAKE YOU SO DIFFICULT TO FORGET!!
A MESSAGE FROM VANILLA!
Huh?
JUDY'S THERE?
SQUEEZE
JUDY!
I'm glad you're okay.

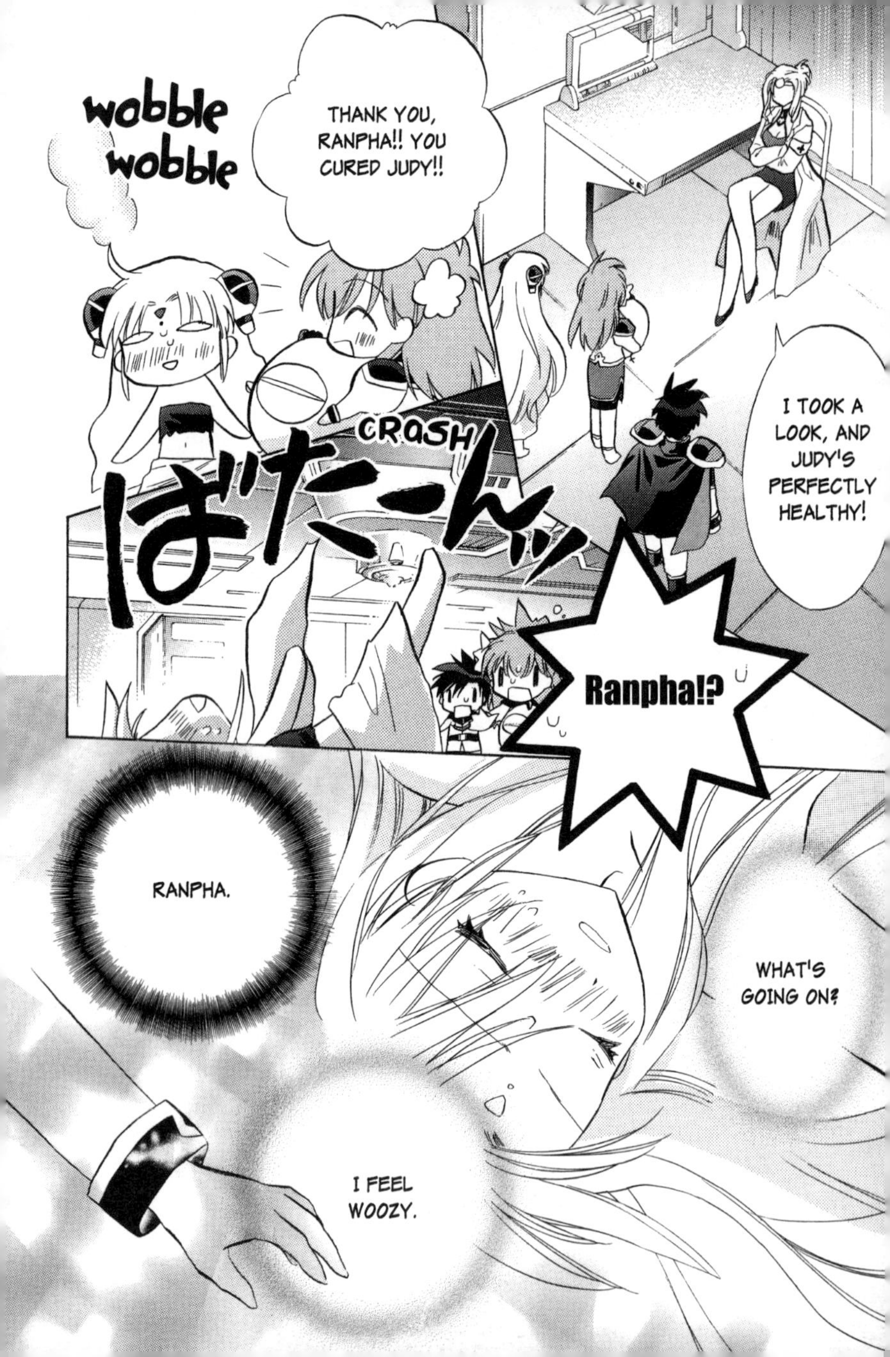
I TOOK A LOOK, AND JUDY'S PERFECTLY HEALTHY!
wobble wobble
THANK YOU, RANPHA!! YOU CURED JUDY!!
CRASH
ばたーん
Ranpha!?
RANPHA.
WHAT'S GOING ON?
I FEEL WOOZY.

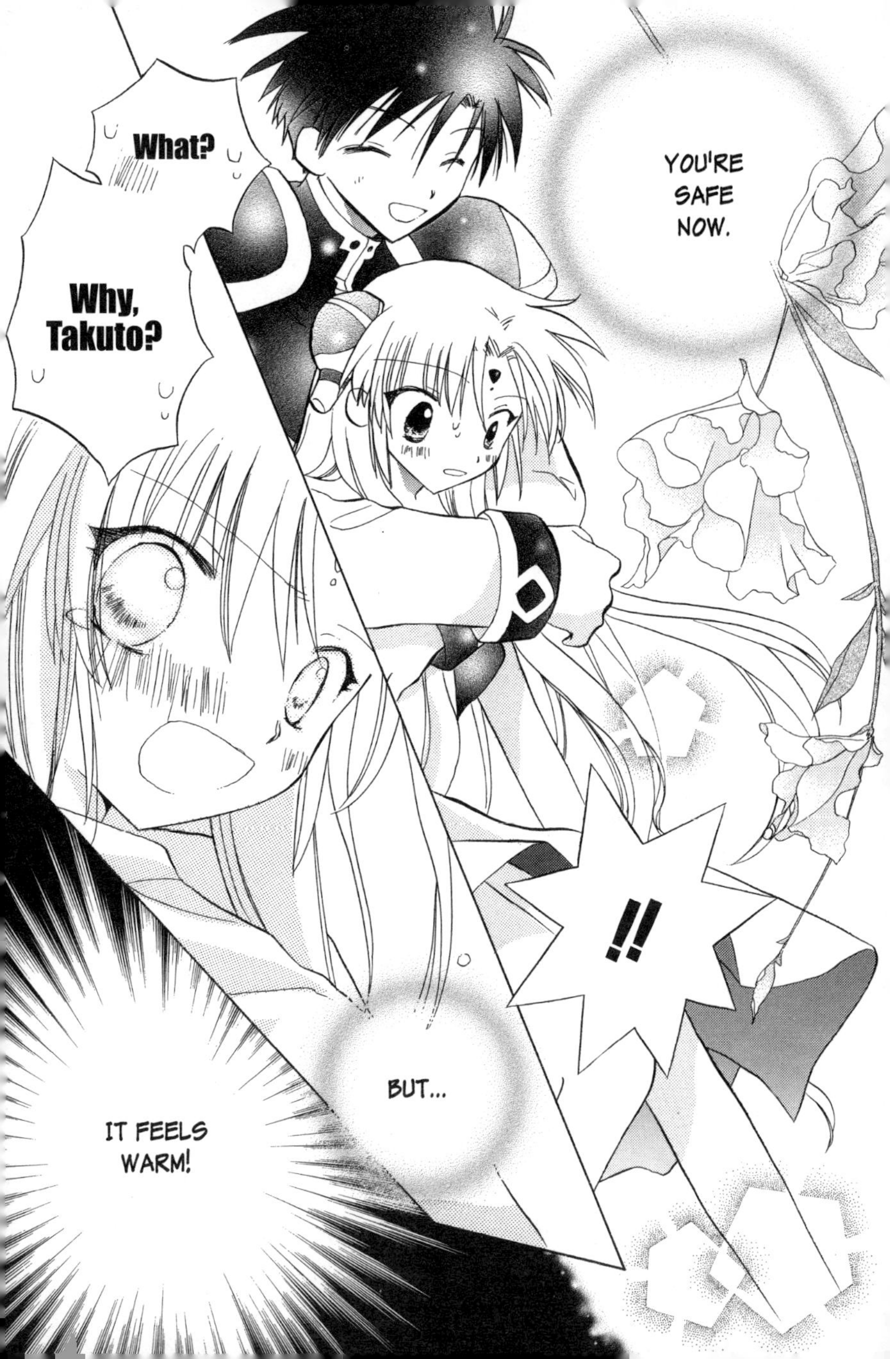
YOU'RE SAFE NOW.
What?
Why, Takuto?
!!
BUT...
IT FEELS WARM!

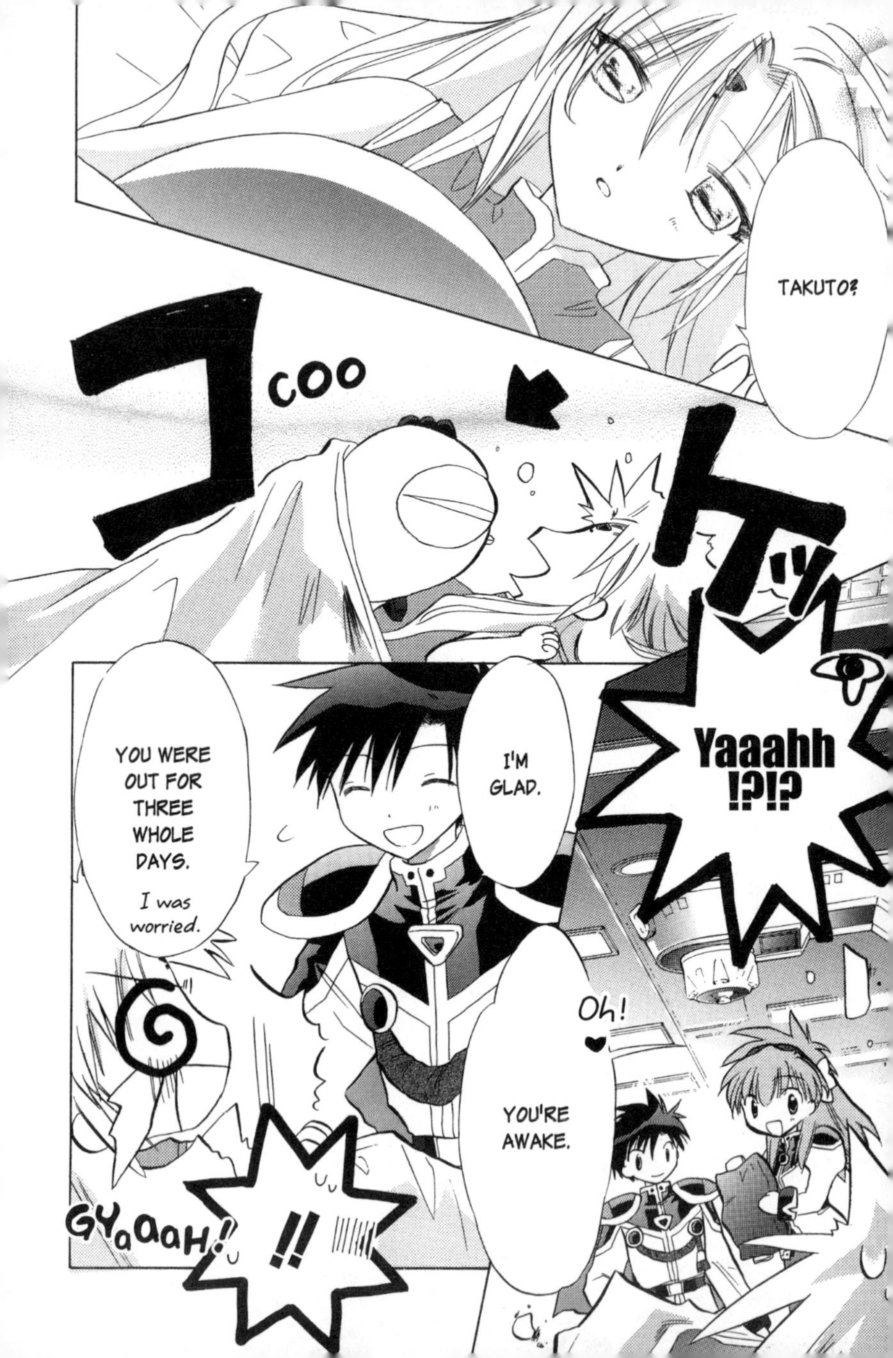
TAKUTO?
コトッ
COO
Yaaahh !?!?
I'M GLAD.
YOU WERE OUT FOR THREE WHOLE DAYS.
I was worried.
Oh!
YOU'RE AWAKE.
GYaaaH!
!!

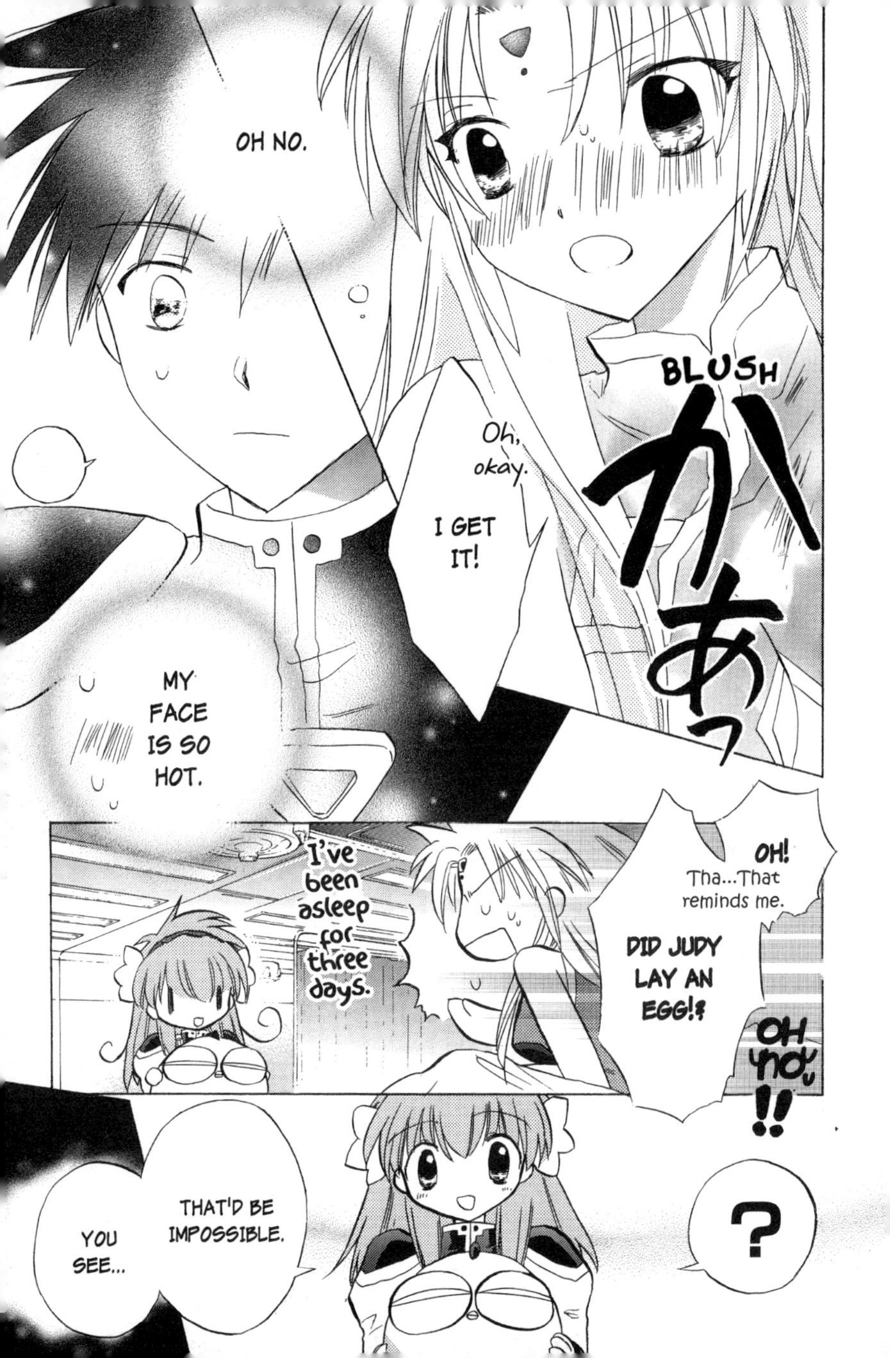

BLUSH
かあっ
Oh, okay.
I GET IT!
OH NO.
MY FACE IS SO HOT.
OH! Tha...That reminds me.
DID JUDY LAY AN EGG!?
OH NO!!
I've been asleep for three days.
?
THAT'D BE IMPOSSIBLE.
YOU SEE...

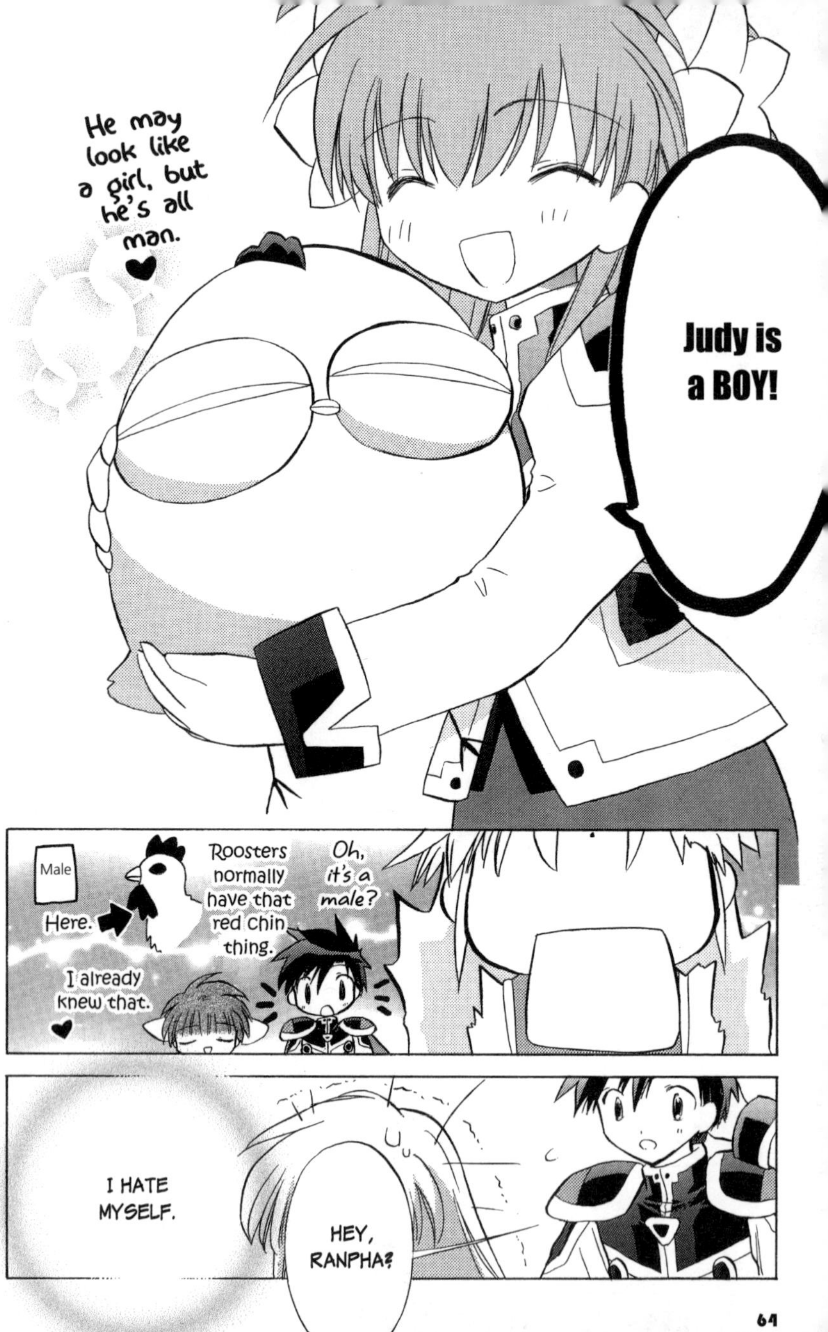
Judy is a BOY!
He may look like a girl, but he's all man. ♥
Oh, it's a male?
Roosters normally have that red chin thing.
Male
Here.
I already knew that. ♥
HEY, RANPHA?
I HATE MYSELF.

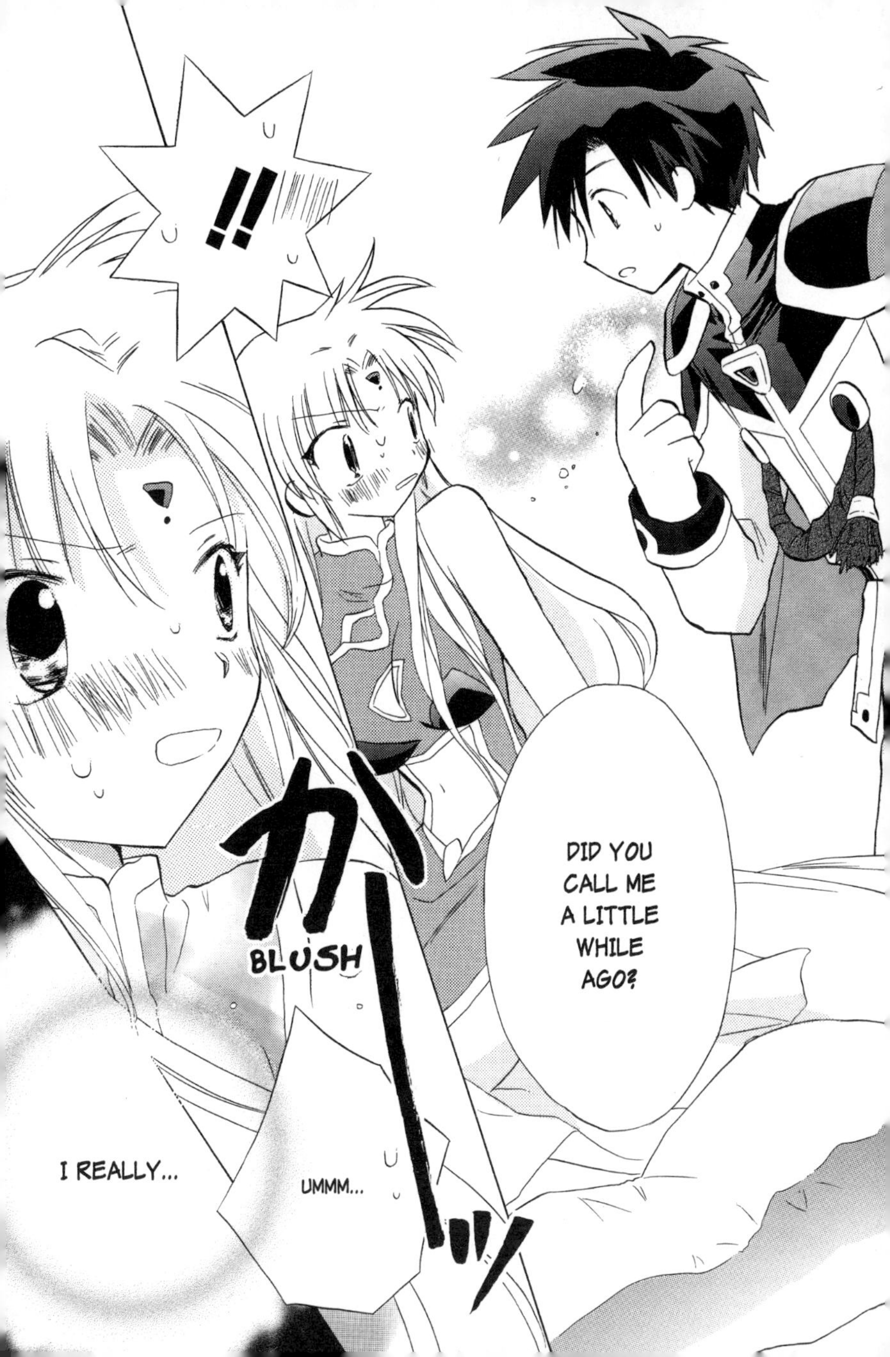
!!
DID YOU CALL ME A LITTLE WHILE AGO?
かーッ
BLUSH
UMMM...
I REALLY...

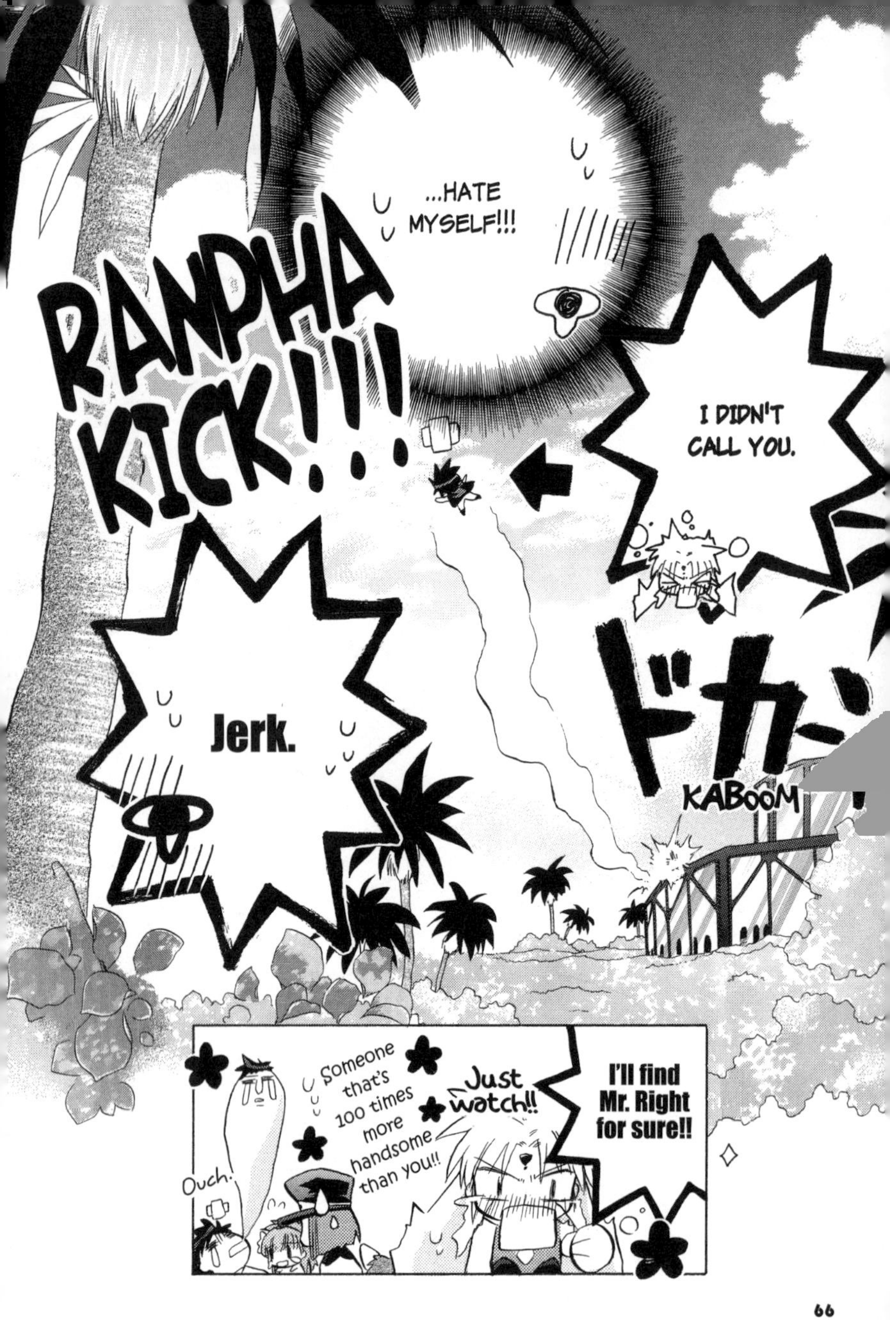
...HATE MYSELF!!!
I DIDN'T CALL YOU.
RANPHA KICK!!!!
ドカー
KABOOM
Jerk.
I'll find Mr. Right for sure!!
Just watch!!
Someone that's 100 times more handsome than you!!
Ouch!

EPISODE 3: MEMORIES AND EMOTIONS

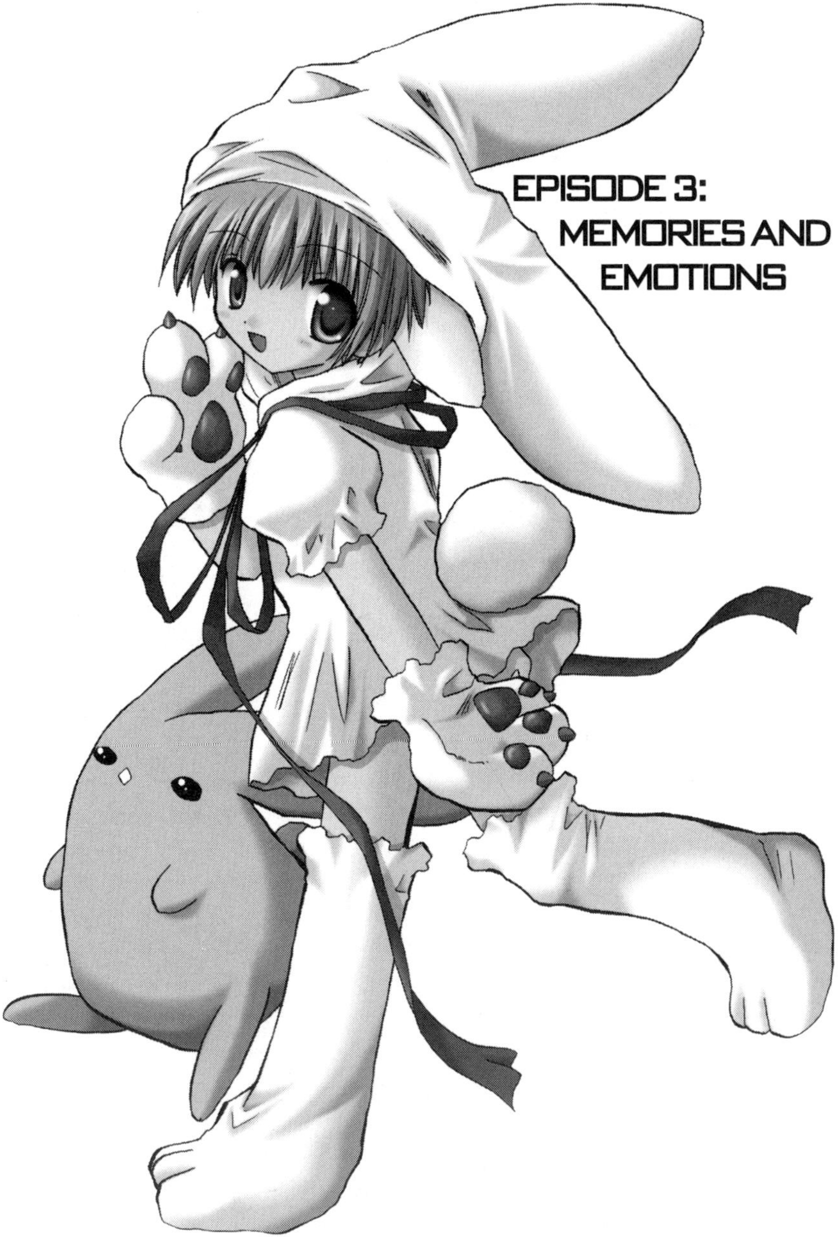

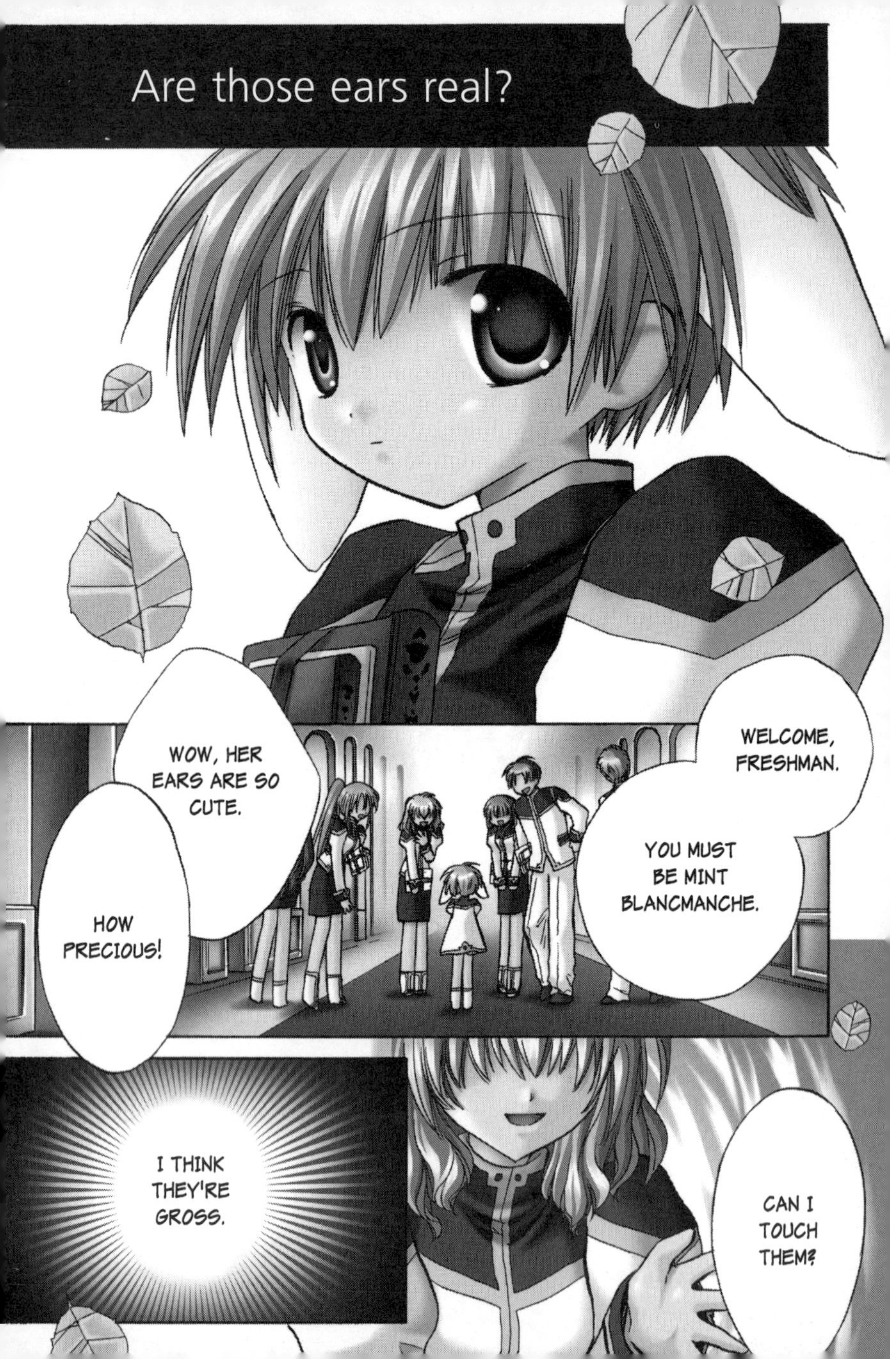
Are those ears real?
WELCOME, FRESHMAN.
YOU MUST BE MINT BLANCMANCHE.
WOW, HER EARS ARE SO CUTE.
HOW PRECIOUS!
CAN I TOUCH THEM?
I THINK THEY'RE GROSS.

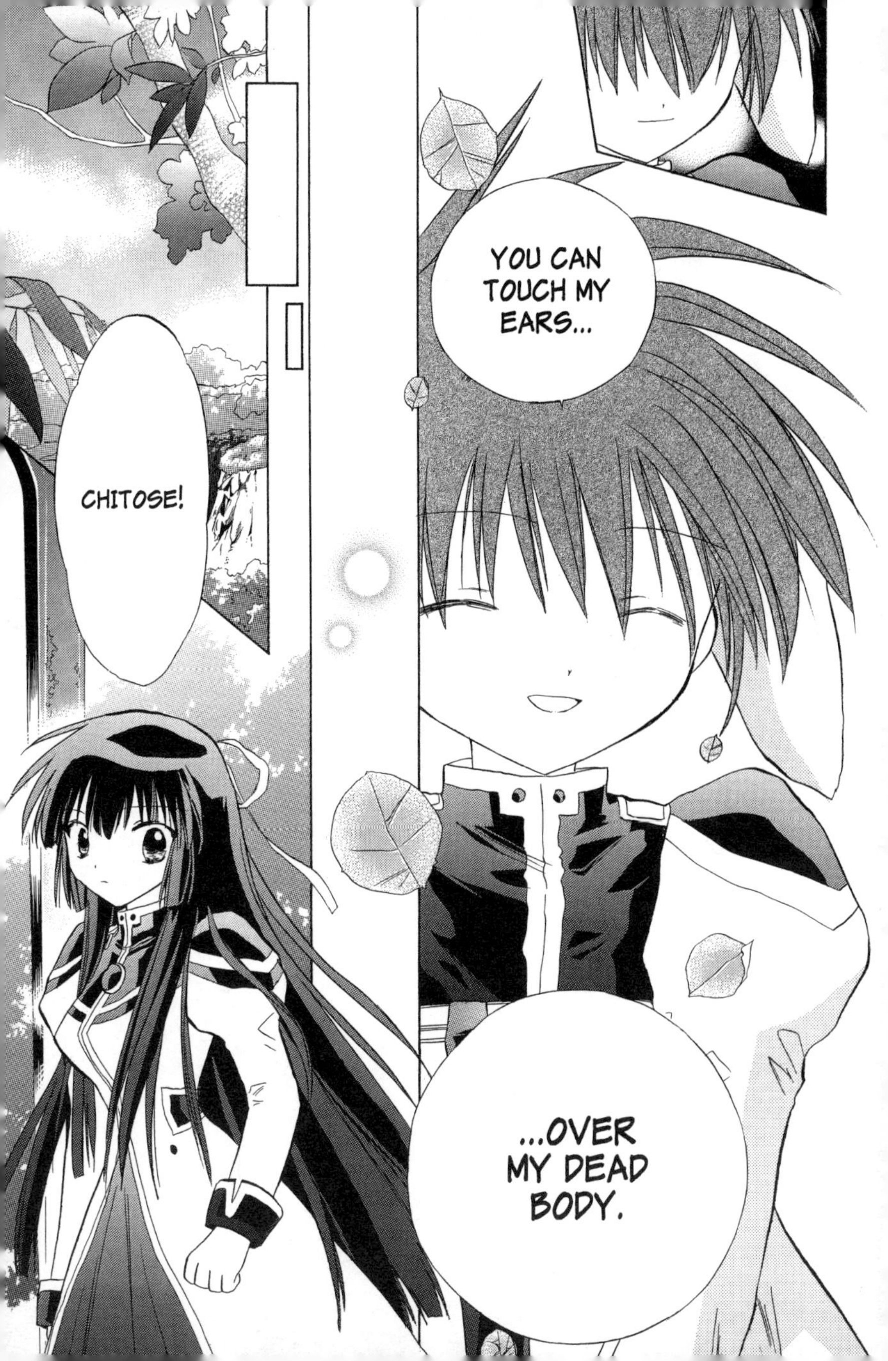
YOU CAN TOUCH MY EARS...
...OVER MY DEAD BODY.
CHITOSE!

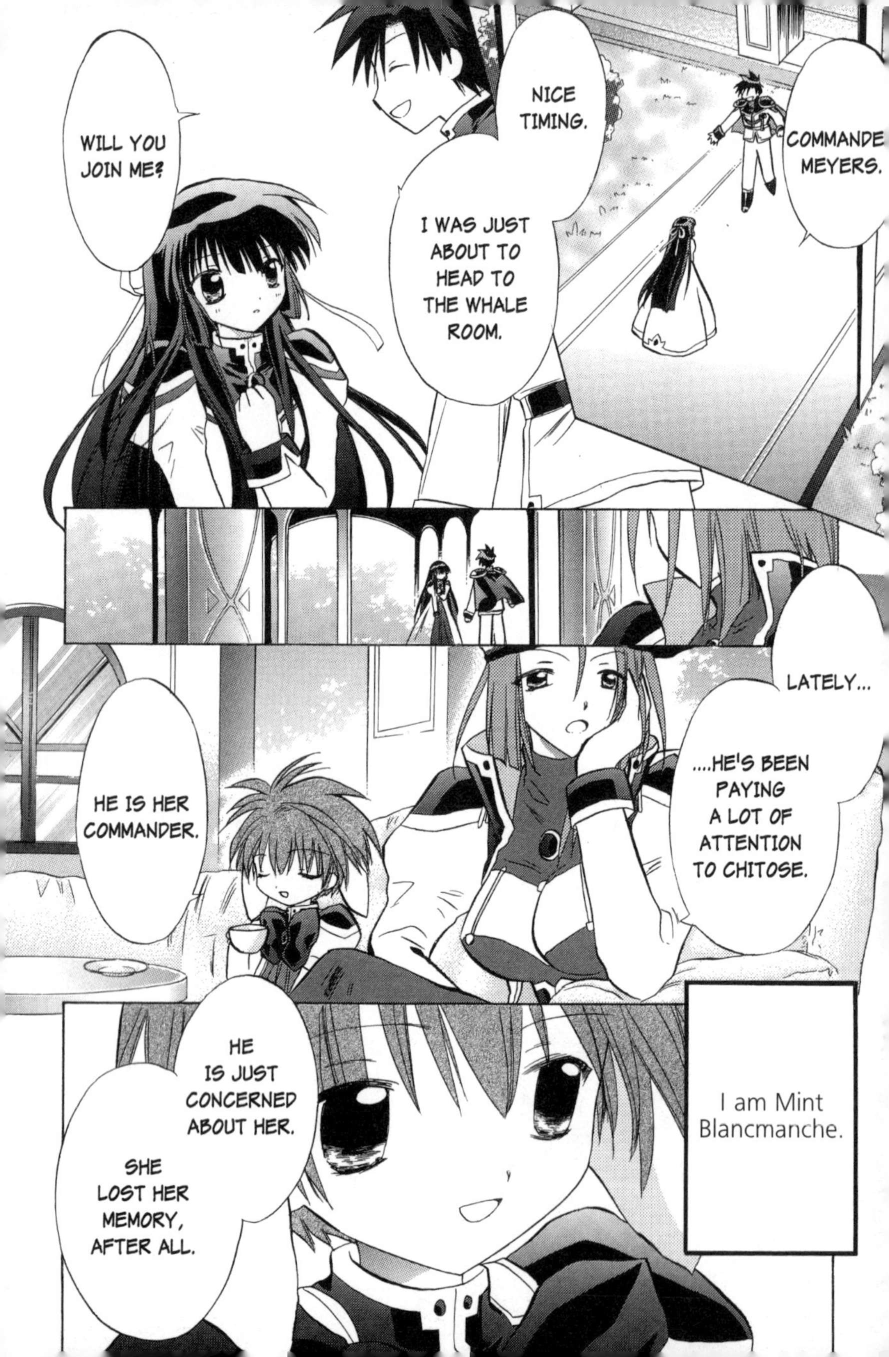
COMMANDE MEYERS.
NICE TIMING.
I WAS JUST ABOUT TO HEAD TO THE WHALE ROOM.
WILL YOU JOIN ME?
LATELY...
....HE'S BEEN PAYING A LOT OF ATTENTION TO CHITOSE.
HE IS HER COMMANDER.
I am Mint Blancmanche.
HE IS JUST CONCERNED ABOUT HER.
SHE LOST HER MEMORY, AFTER ALL.

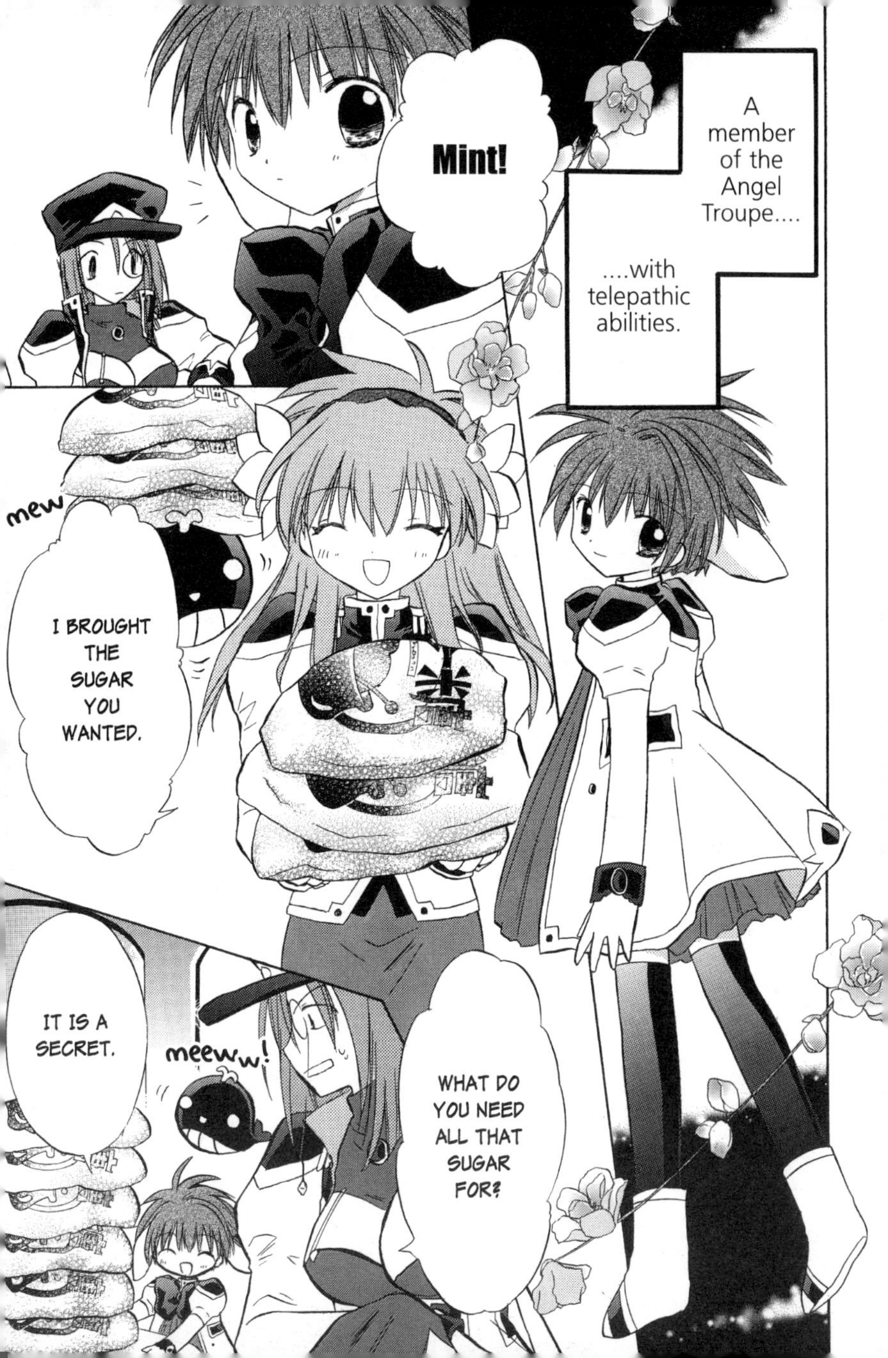
Mint!
A member of the Angel Troupe....
....with telepathic abilities.
mew
I BROUGHT THE SUGAR YOU WANTED.
WHAT DO YOU NEED ALL THAT SUGAR FOR?
meewww!
IT IS A SECRET.

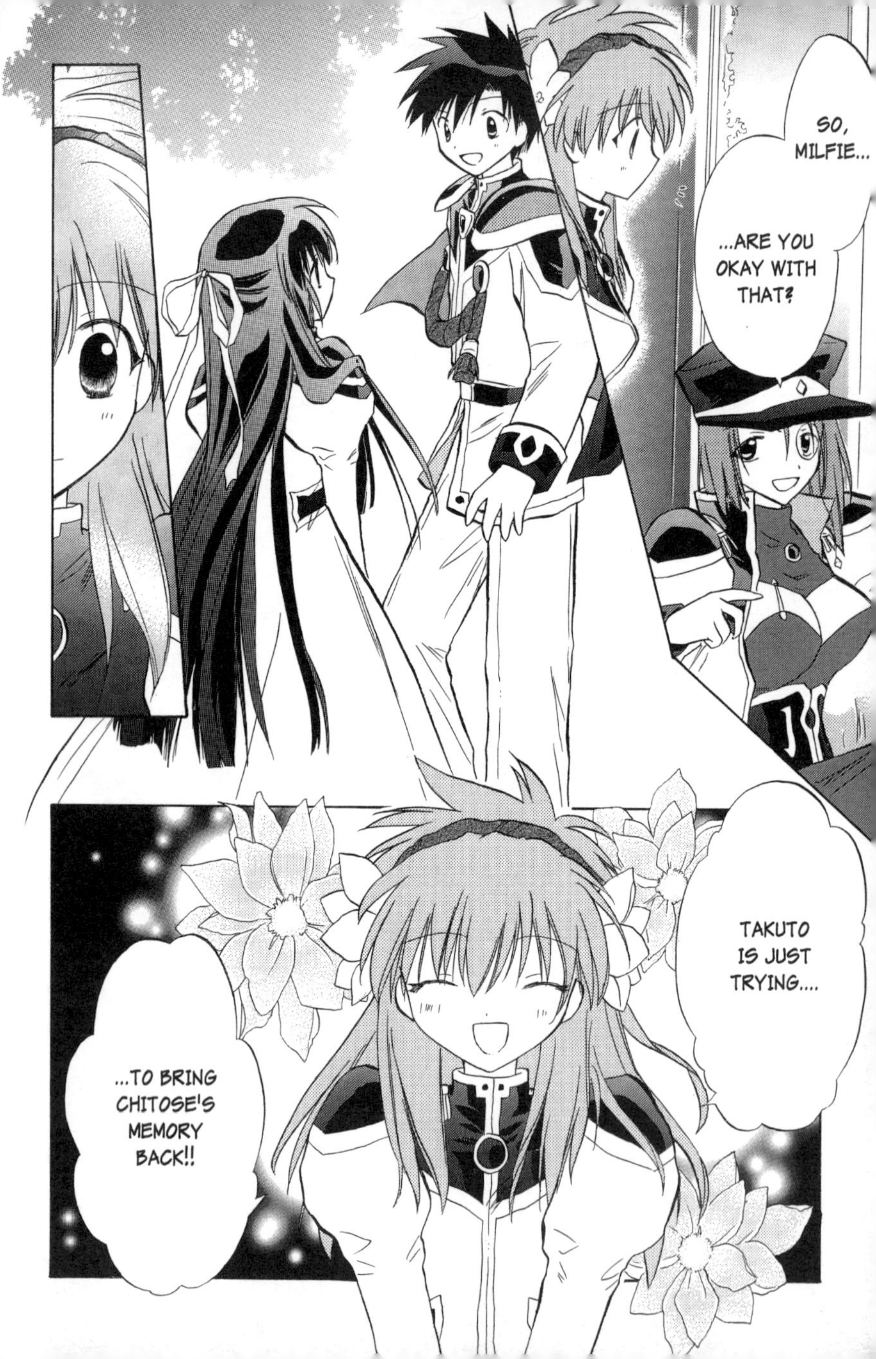
SO, MILFIE...
...ARE YOU OKAY WITH THAT?
TAKUTO IS JUST TRYING....
...TO BRING CHITOSE'S MEMORY BACK!!

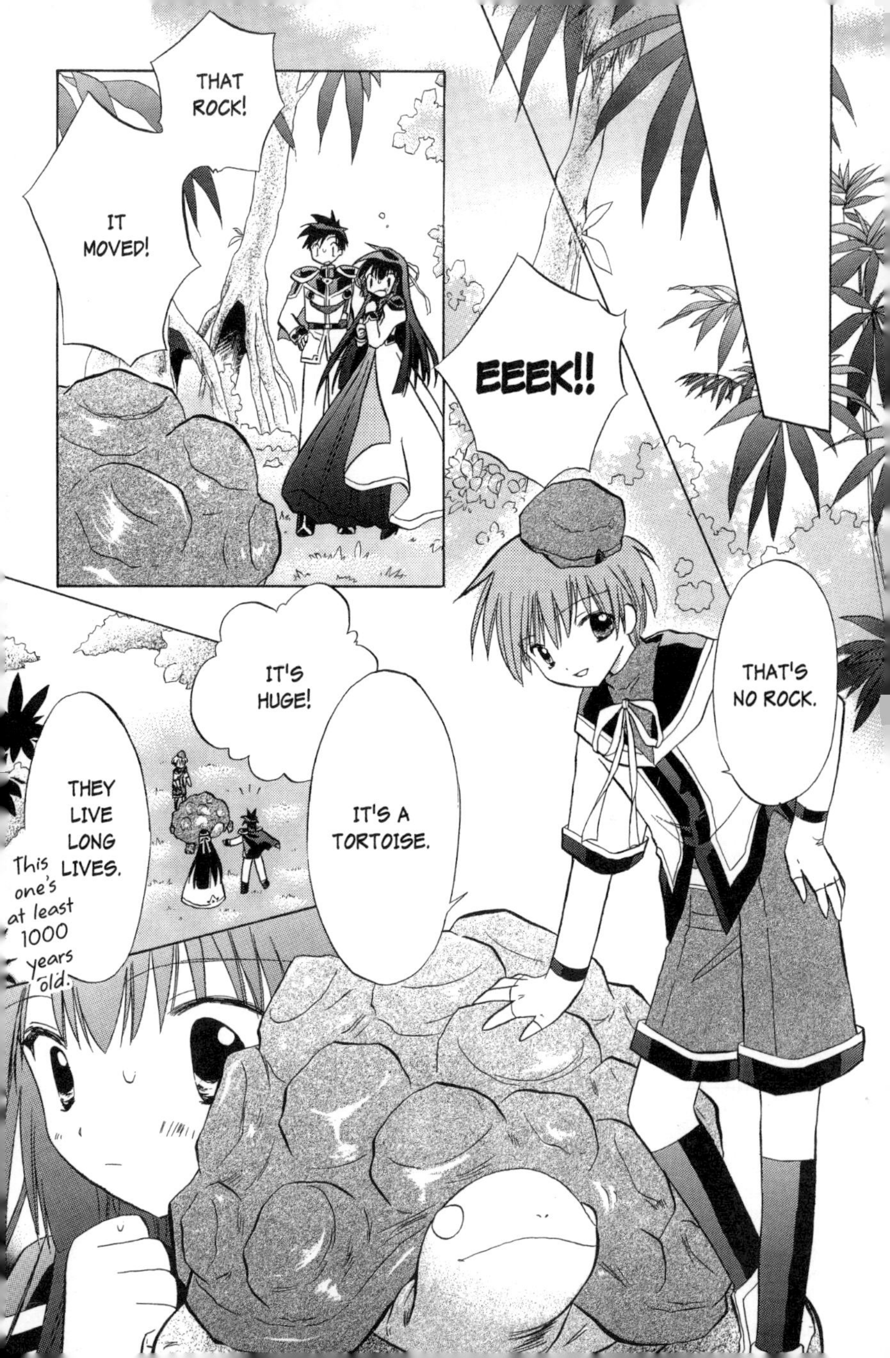
THAT ROCK!
IT MOVED!
EEEK!!
THAT'S NO ROCK.
IT'S HUGE!
IT'S A TORTOISE.
THEY LIVE LONG LIVES.
This one's at least 1000 years old.

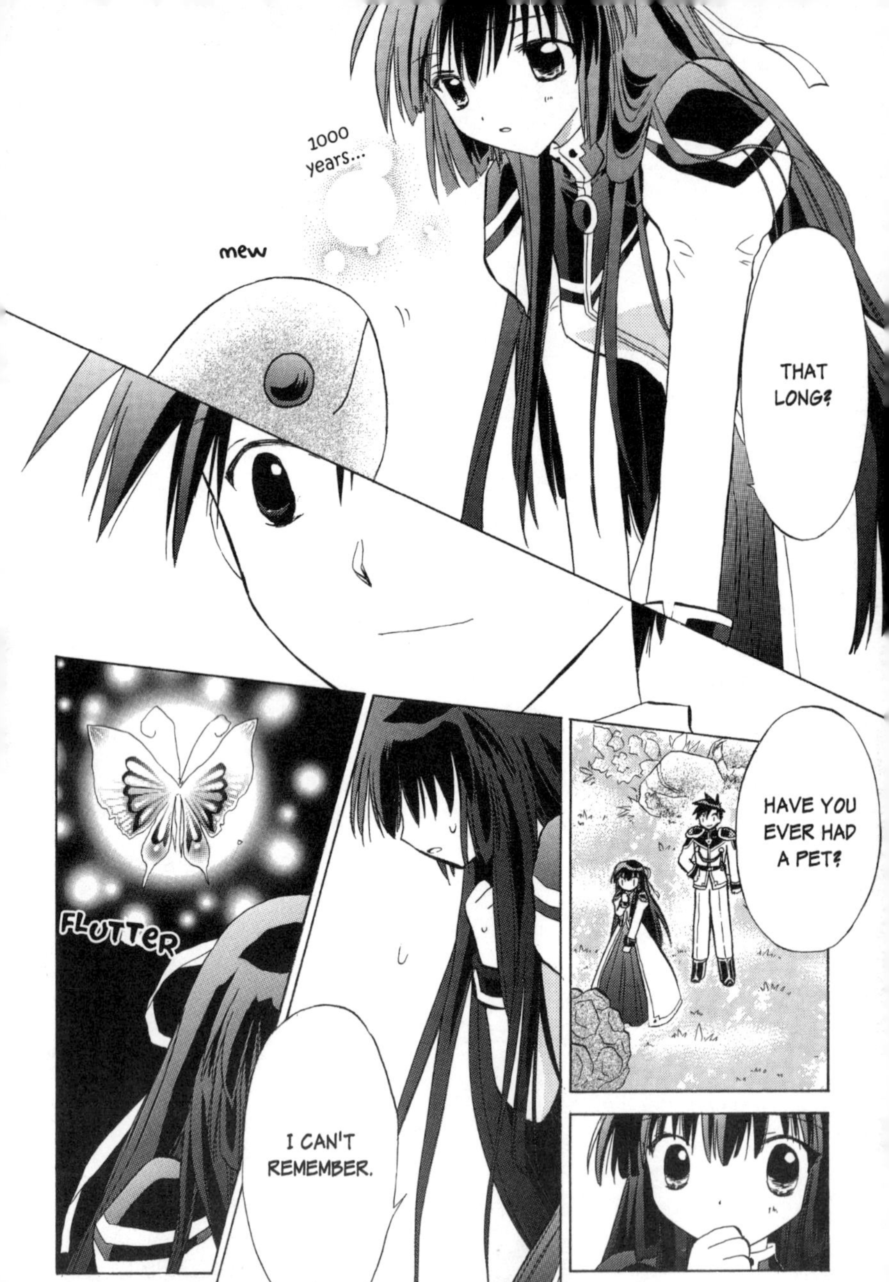
1000 years...
THAT LONG?
mew
HAVE YOU EVER HAD A PET?
I CAN'T REMEMBER.
FLUTTER

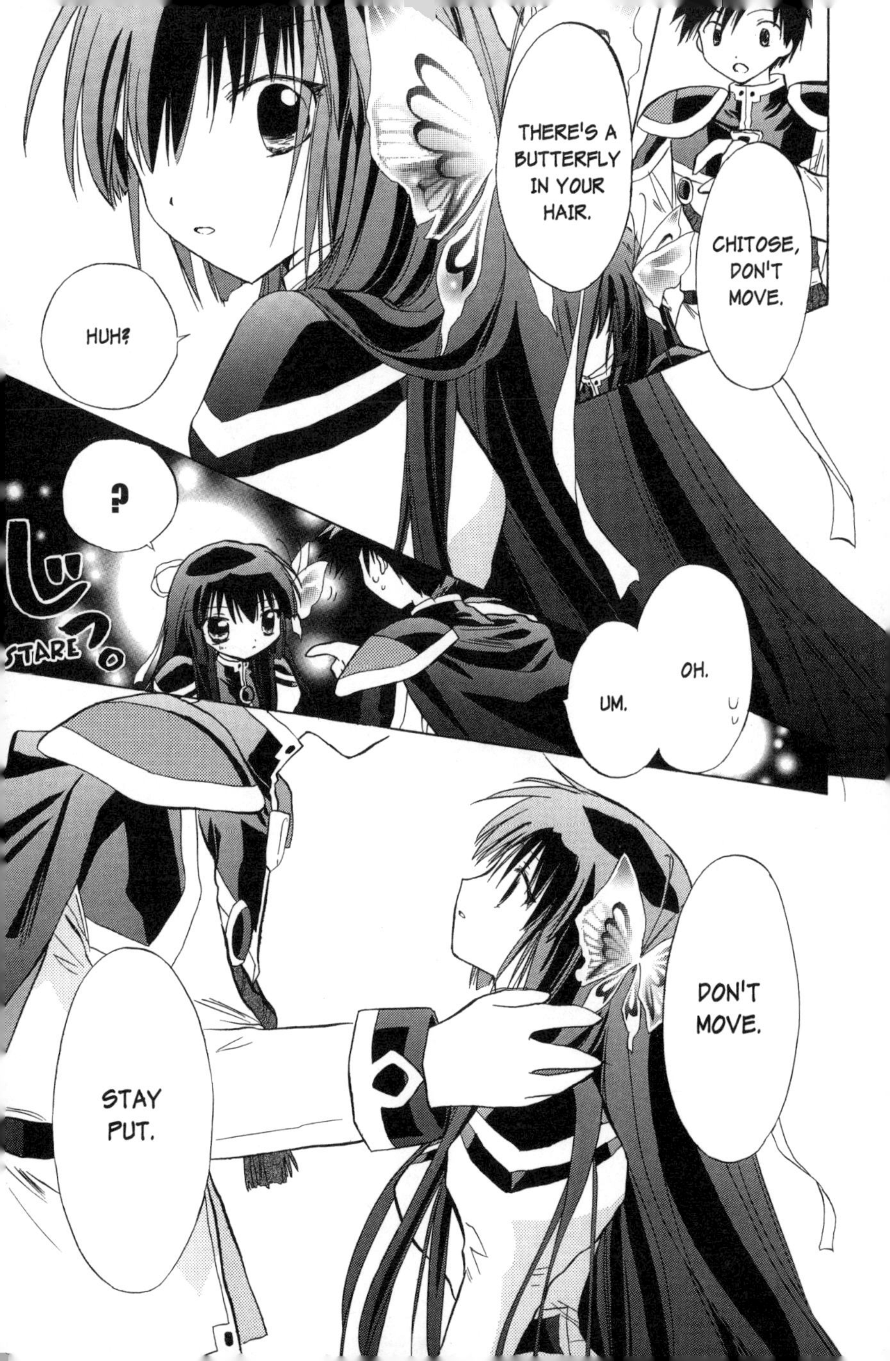
CHITOSE, DON'T MOVE.
THERE'S A BUTTERFLY IN YOUR HAIR.
HUH?
OH.
UM.
?
STARE
DON'T MOVE.
STAY PUT.

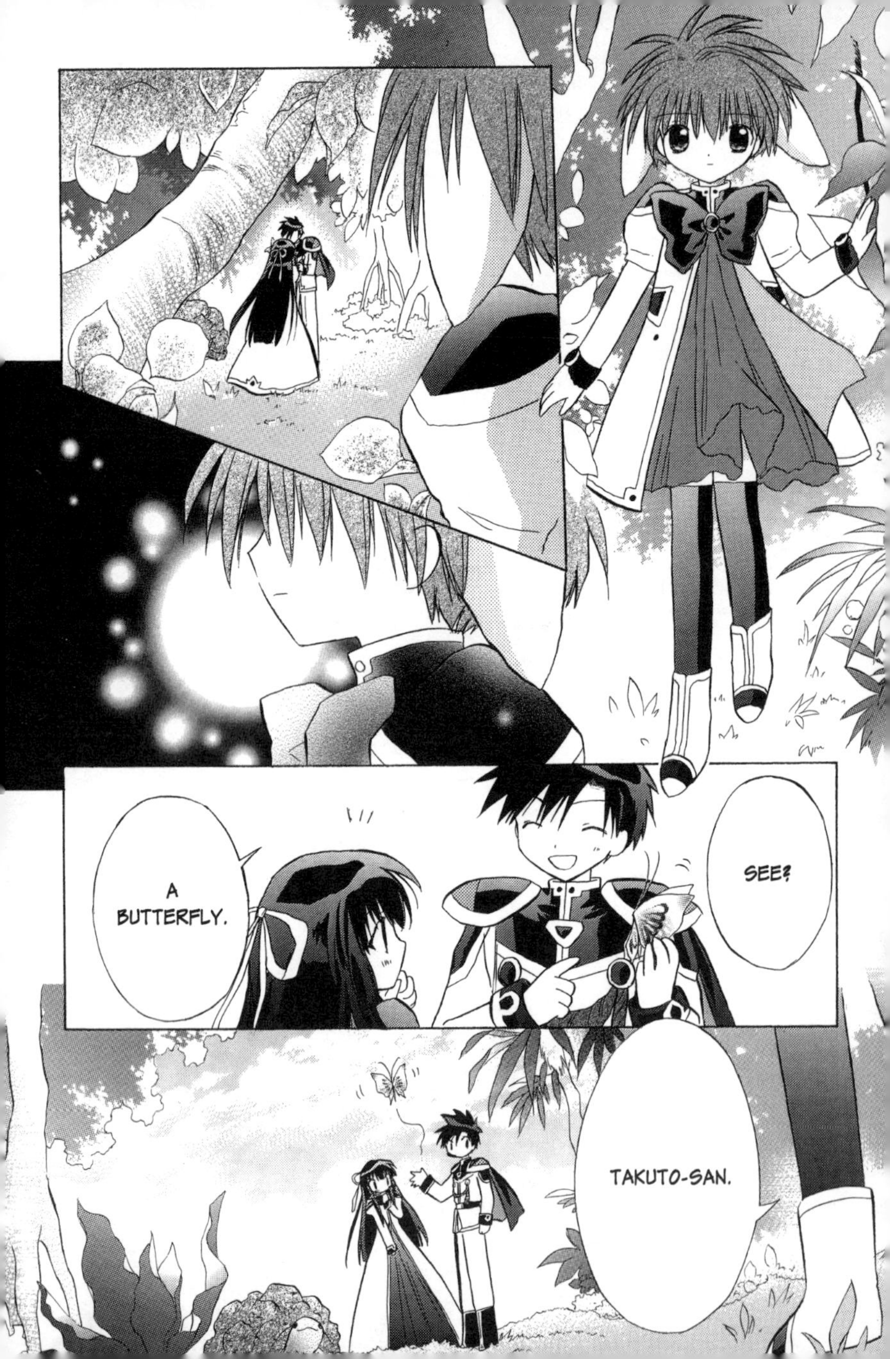
SEE?
A BUTTERFLY.
TAKUTO-SAN.

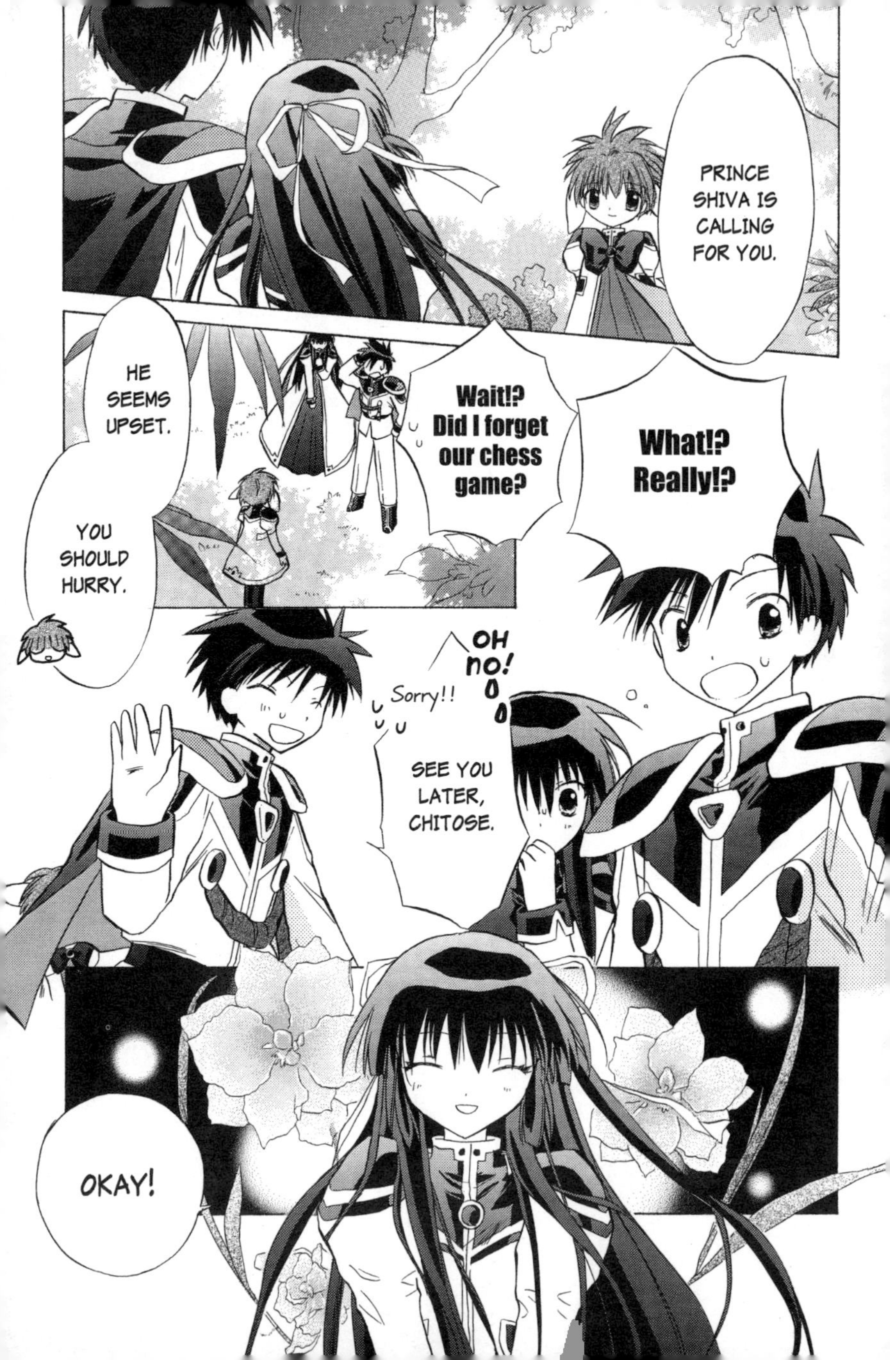
PRINCE SHIVA IS CALLING FOR YOU.
What!? Really!?
Wait!? Did I forget our chess game?
HE SEEMS UPSET.
YOU SHOULD HURRY.
OH no!
Sorry!!
SEE YOU LATER, CHITOSE.
OKAY!

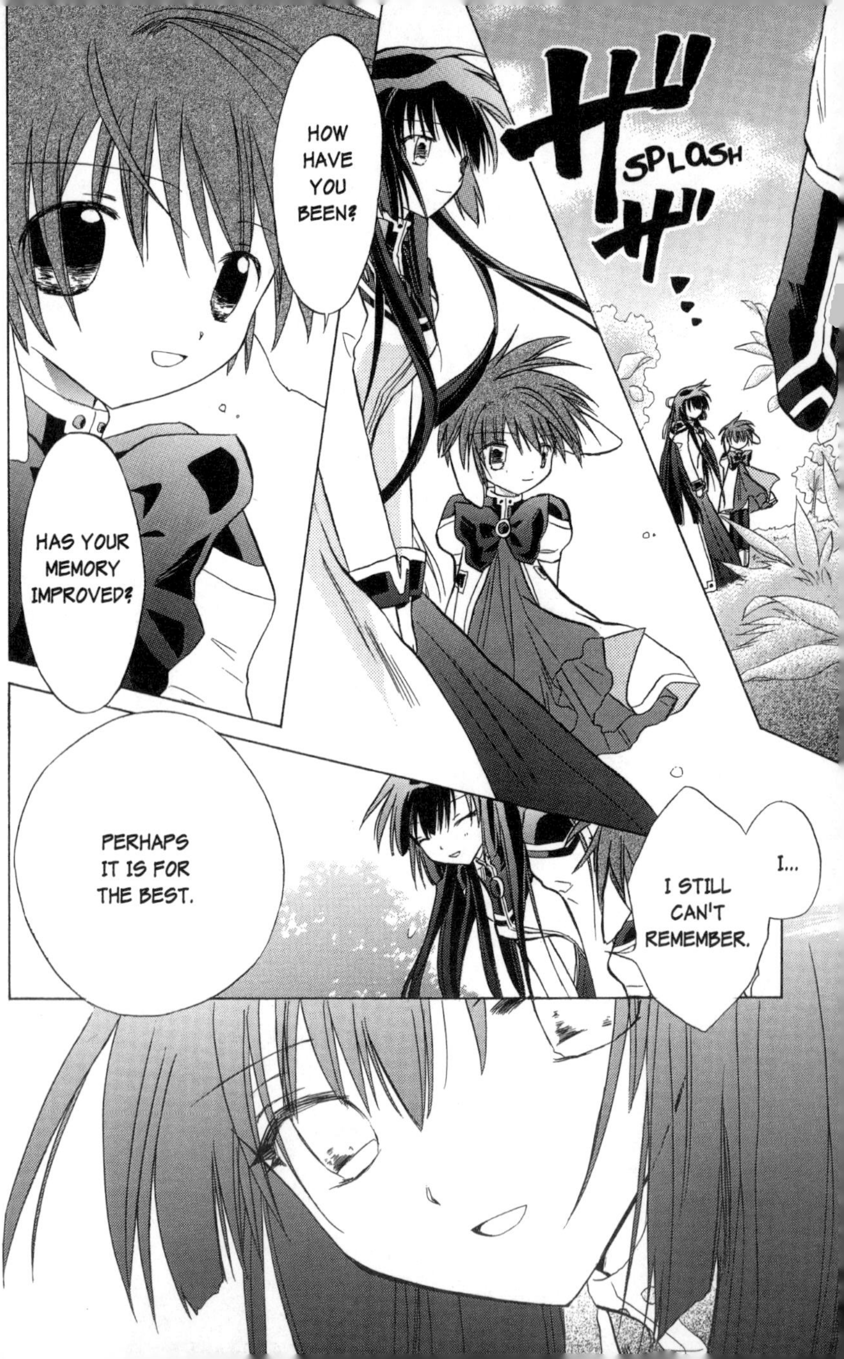
ザザ
SPLASH
HOW HAVE YOU BEEN?
HAS YOUR MEMORY IMPROVED?
I...
I STILL CAN'T REMEMBER.
PERHAPS IT IS FOR THE BEST.

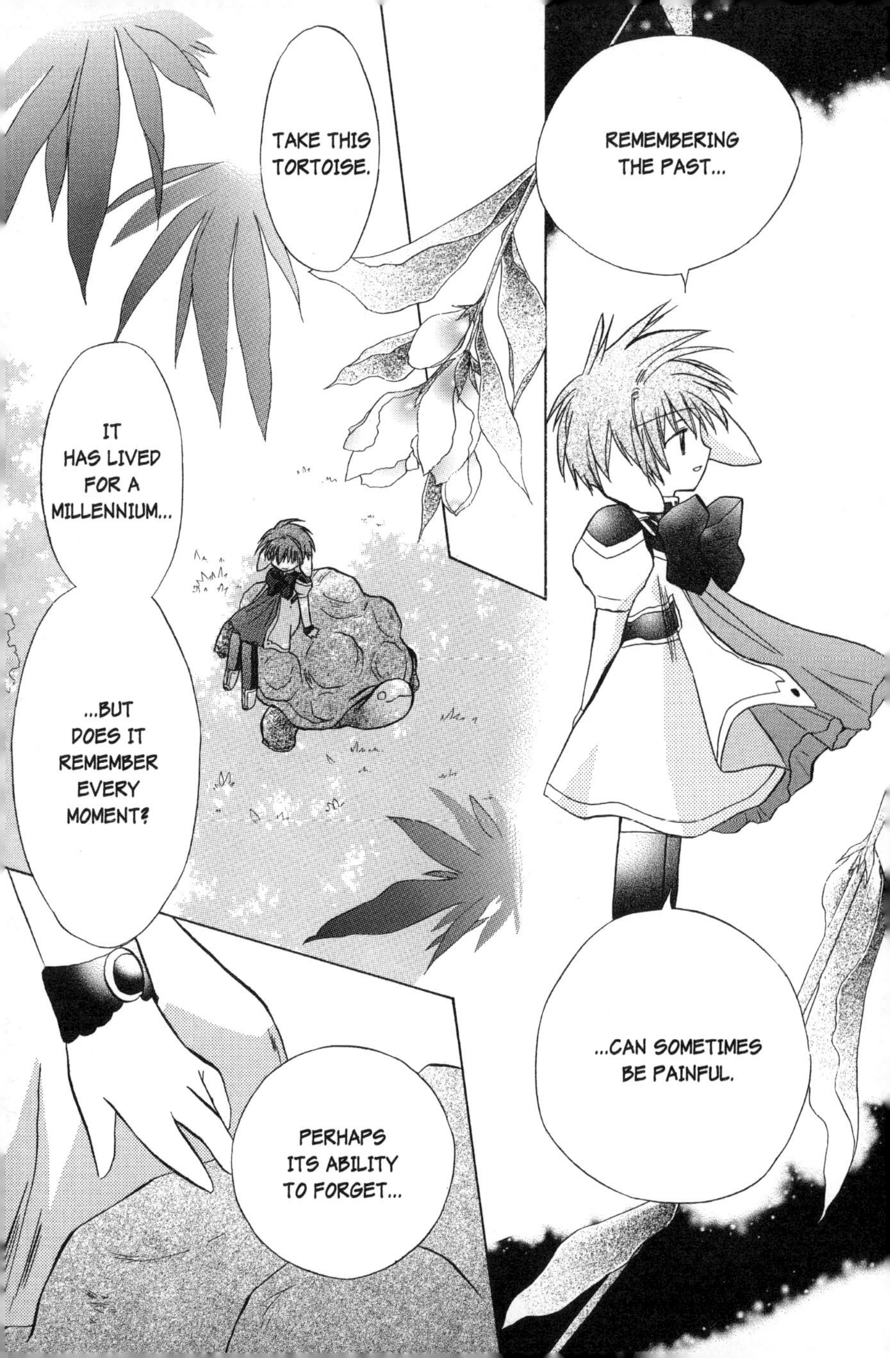
REMEMBERING THE PAST...
...CAN SOMETIMES BE PAINFUL.
TAKE THIS TORTOISE.
IT HAS LIVED FOR A MILLENNIUM...
...BUT DOES IT REMEMBER EVERY MOMENT?
PERHAPS ITS ABILITY TO FORGET...

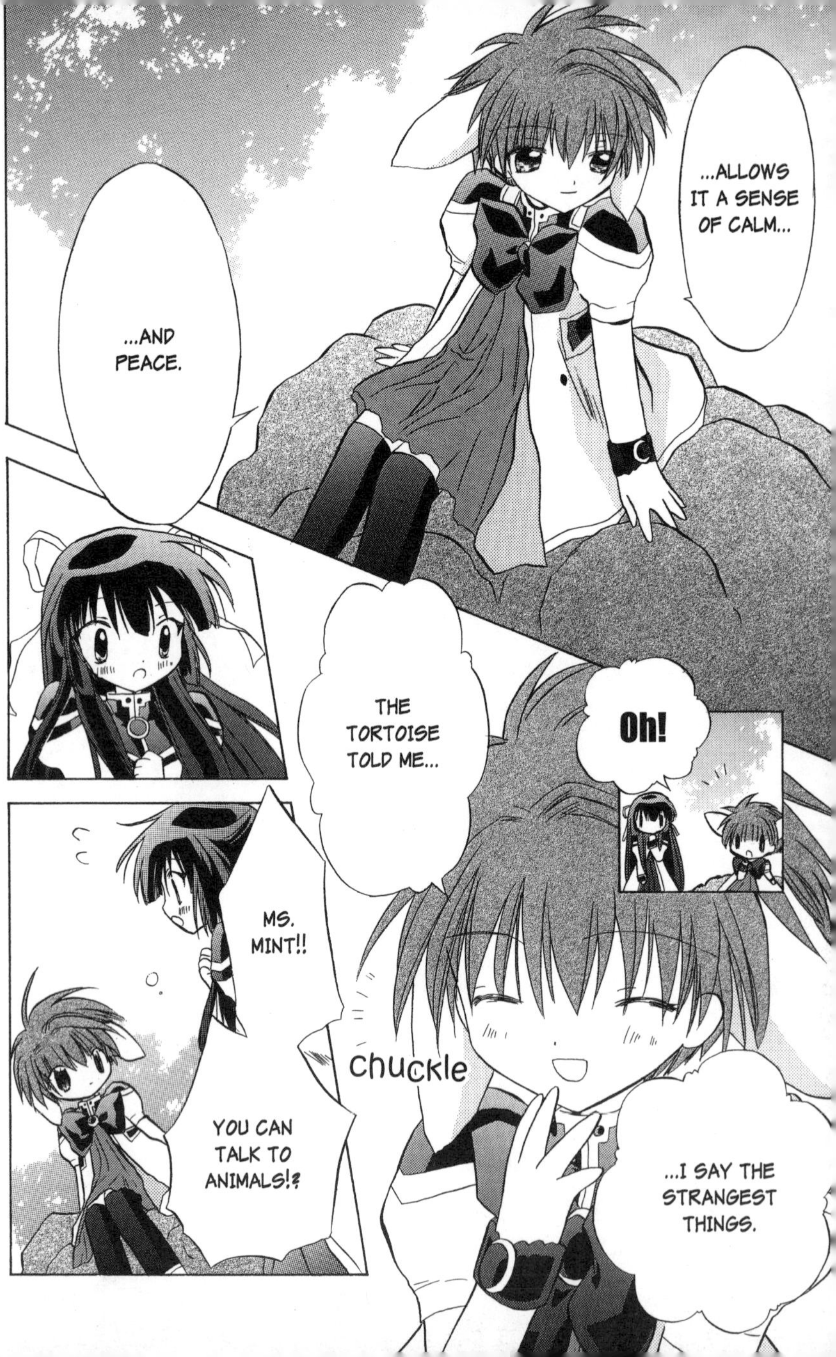

...ALLOWS IT A SENSE OF CALM...
...AND PEACE.
THE TORTOISE TOLD ME...
MS. MINT!!
YOU CAN TALK TO ANIMALS!?
Oh!
chuckle
...I SAY THE STRANGEST THINGS.

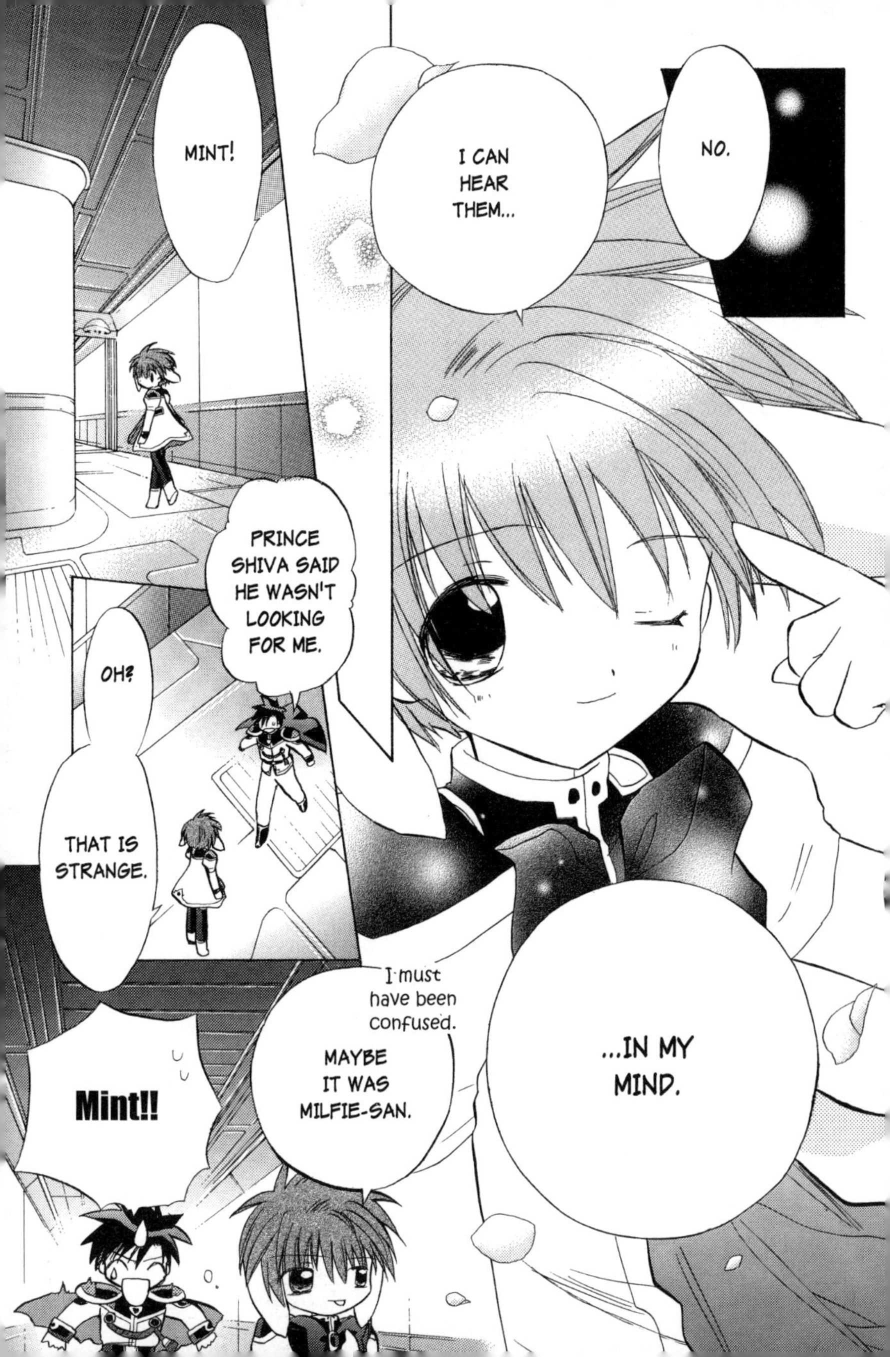
NO.
I CAN HEAR THEM...
...IN MY MIND.
MINT!
PRINCE SHIVA SAID HE WASN'T LOOKING FOR ME.
OH?
THAT IS STRANGE.
Mint!!
MAYBE IT WAS MILFIE-SAN.
I must have been confused.

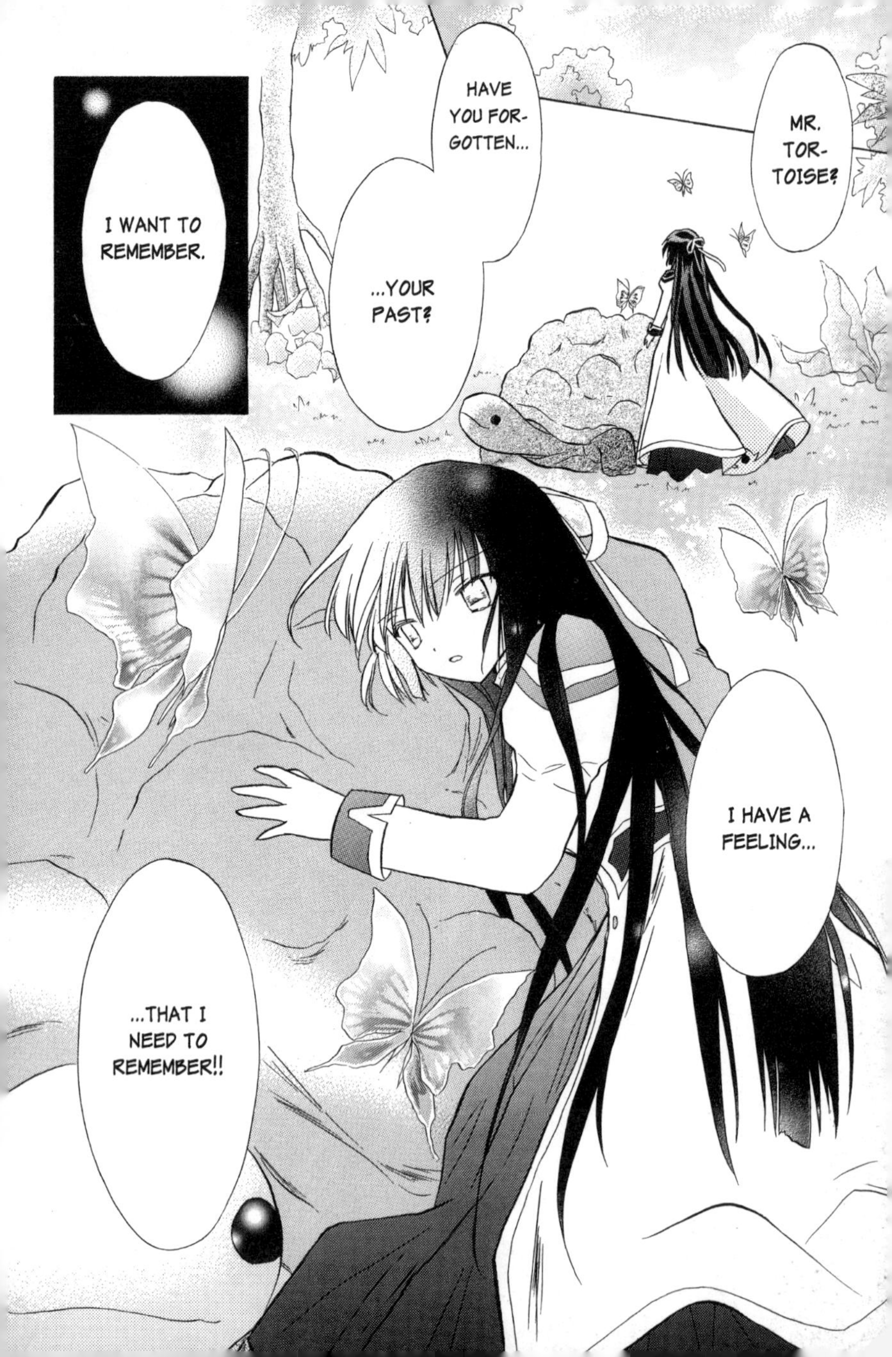
MR. TOR-TOISE?
HAVE YOU FOR-GOTTEN...
...YOUR PAST?
I WANT TO REMEMBER.
I HAVE A FEELING...
...THAT I NEED TO REMEMBER!!

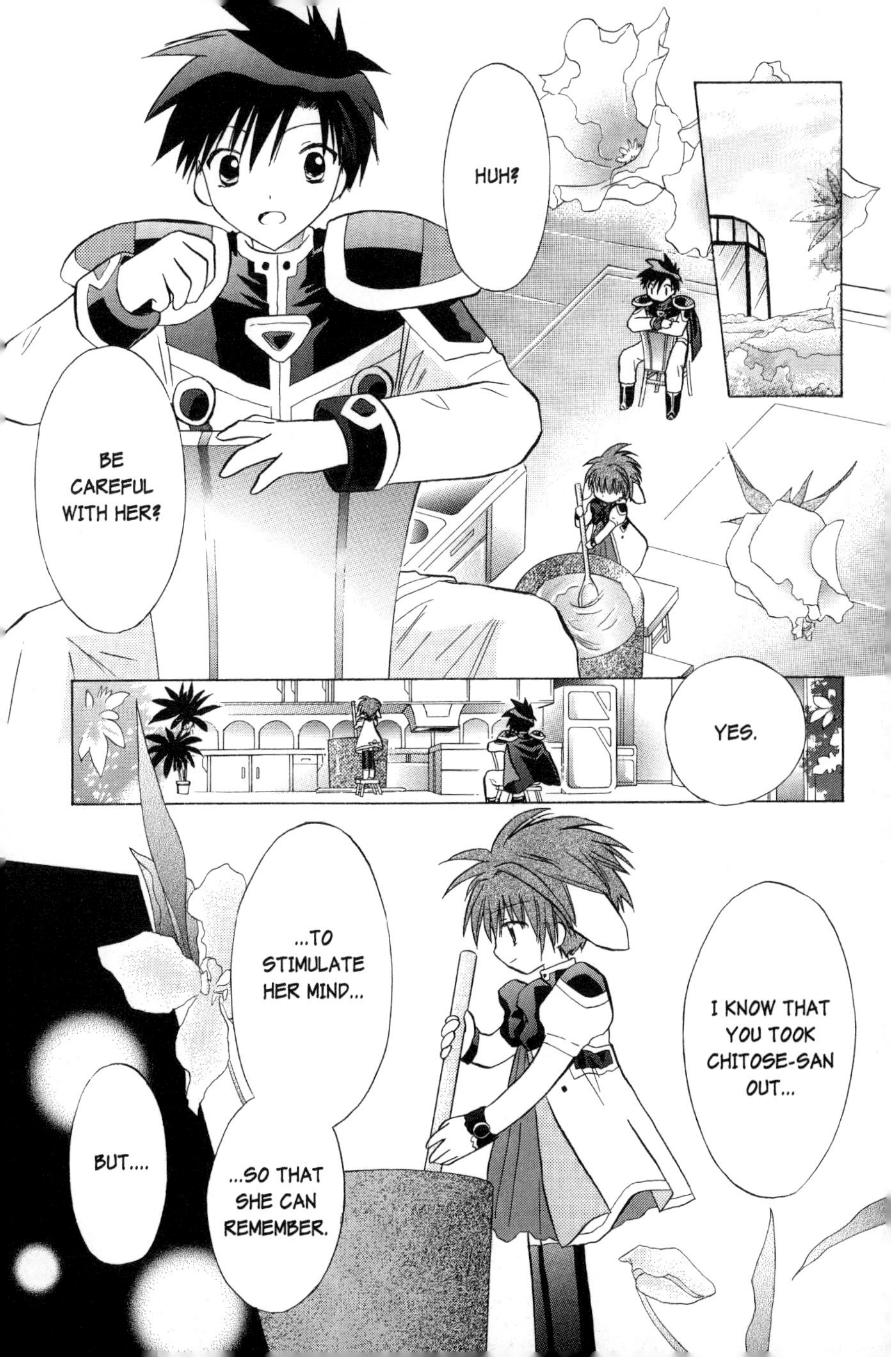
HUH?
BE CAREFUL WITH HER?
YES.
I KNOW THAT YOU TOOK CHITOSE-SAN OUT...
...TO STIMULATE HER MIND...
...SO THAT SHE CAN REMEMBER.
BUT....

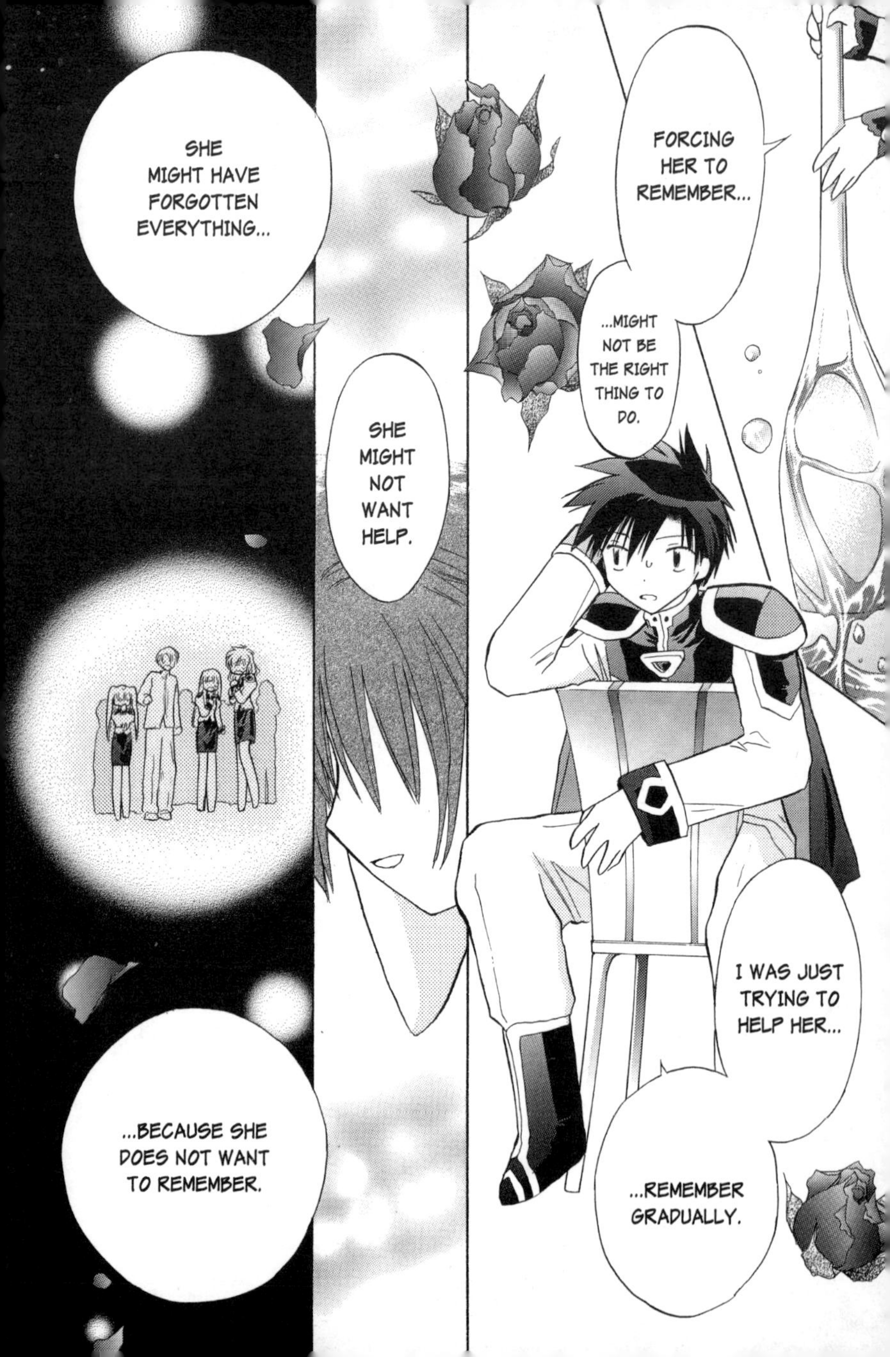
FORCING HER TO REMEMBER...
...MIGHT NOT BE THE RIGHT THING TO DO.
I WAS JUST TRYING TO HELP HER...
...REMEMBER GRADUALLY.
SHE MIGHT NOT WANT HELP.
SHE MIGHT HAVE FORGOTTEN EVERYTHING...
...BECAUSE SHE DOES NOT WANT TO REMEMBER.

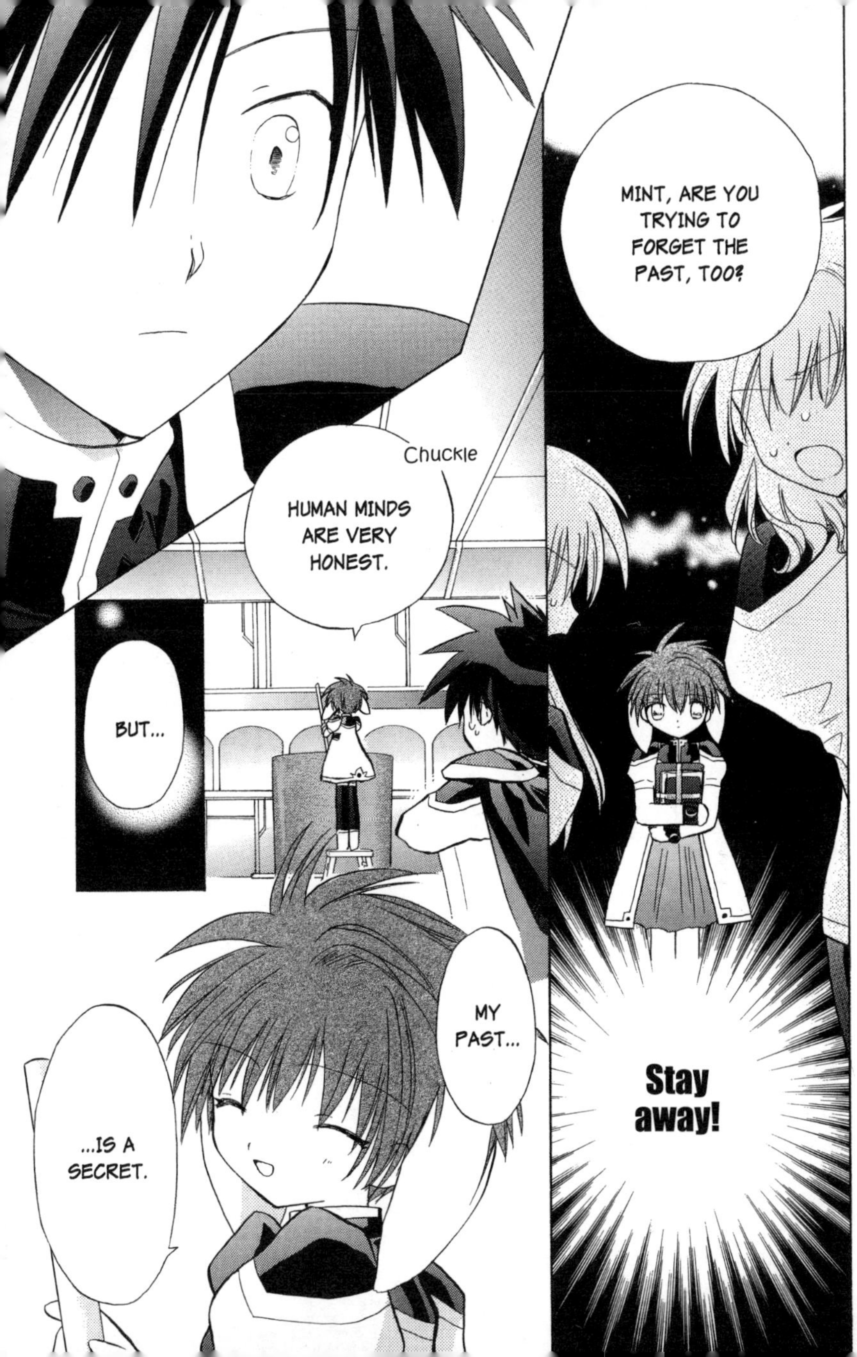
MINT, ARE YOU TRYING TO FORGET THE PAST, TOO?
Stay away!
Chuckle
HUMAN MINDS ARE VERY HONEST.
BUT...
MY PAST...
...IS A SECRET.

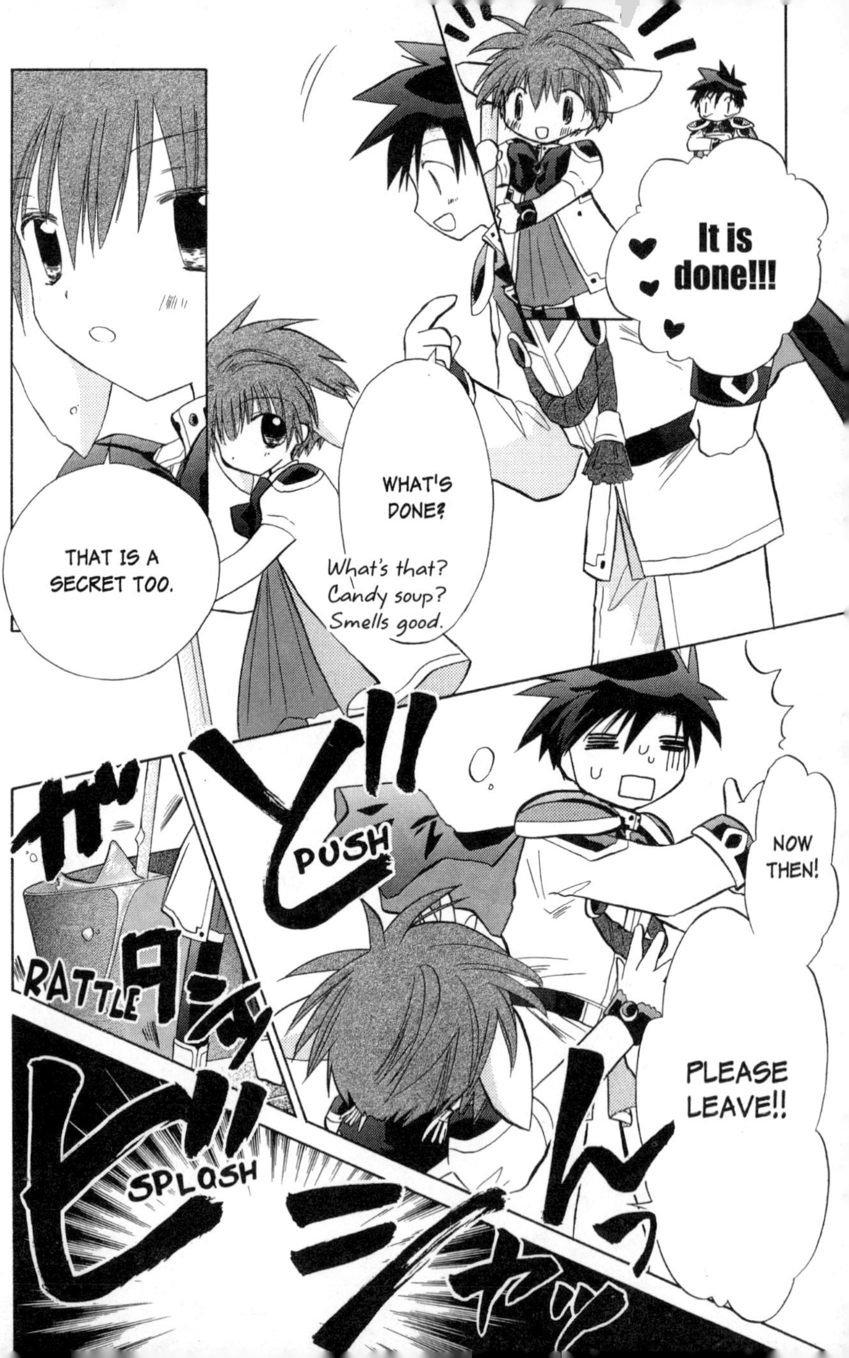
It is done!!!
WHAT'S DONE?
What's that? Candy soup? Smells good.
THAT IS A SECRET TOO.
NOW THEN!
PLEASE LEAVE!!
PUSH
RATTLE
SPLASH

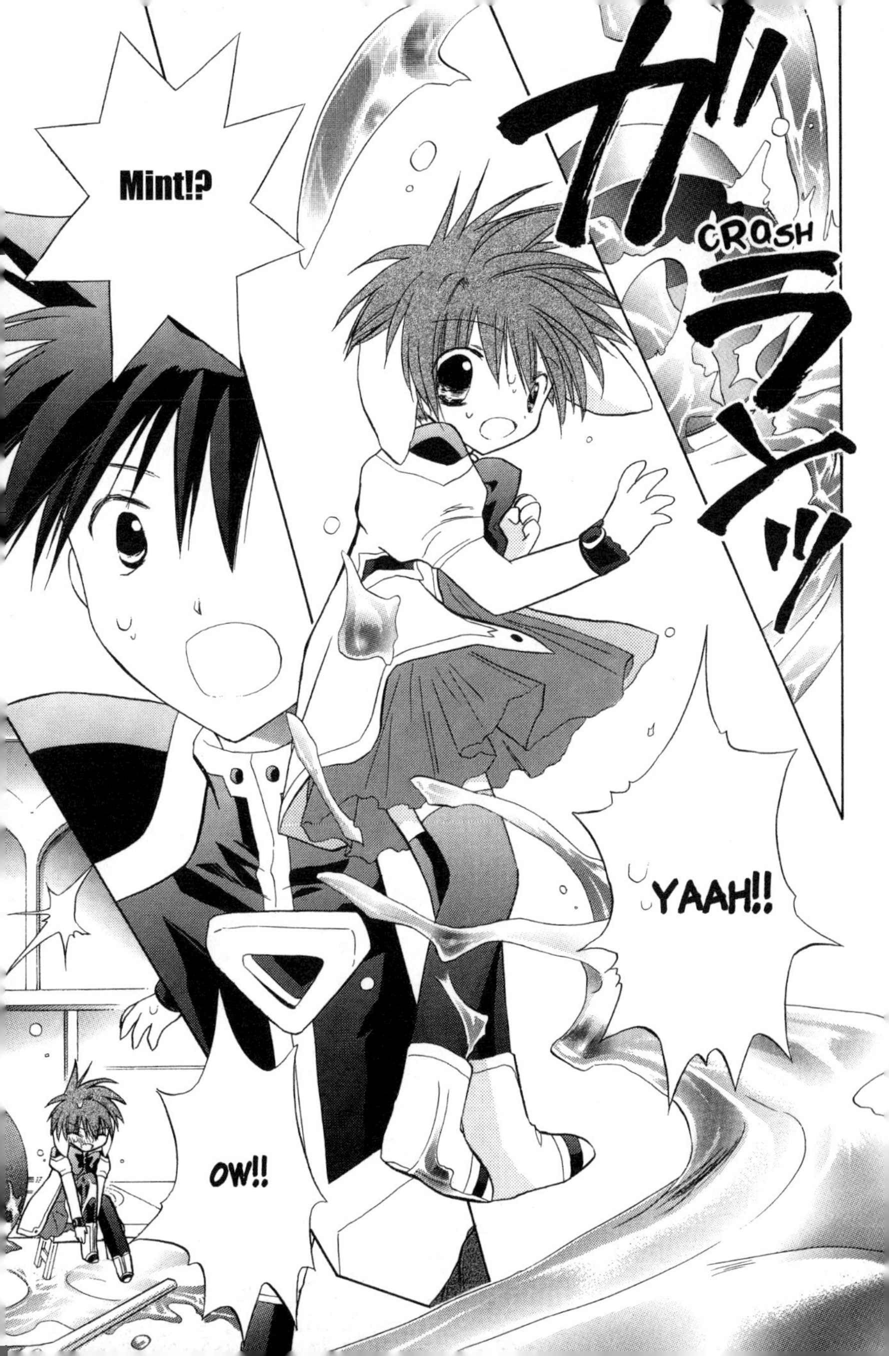
CRASH
YAAH!!
Mint!?
OW!!

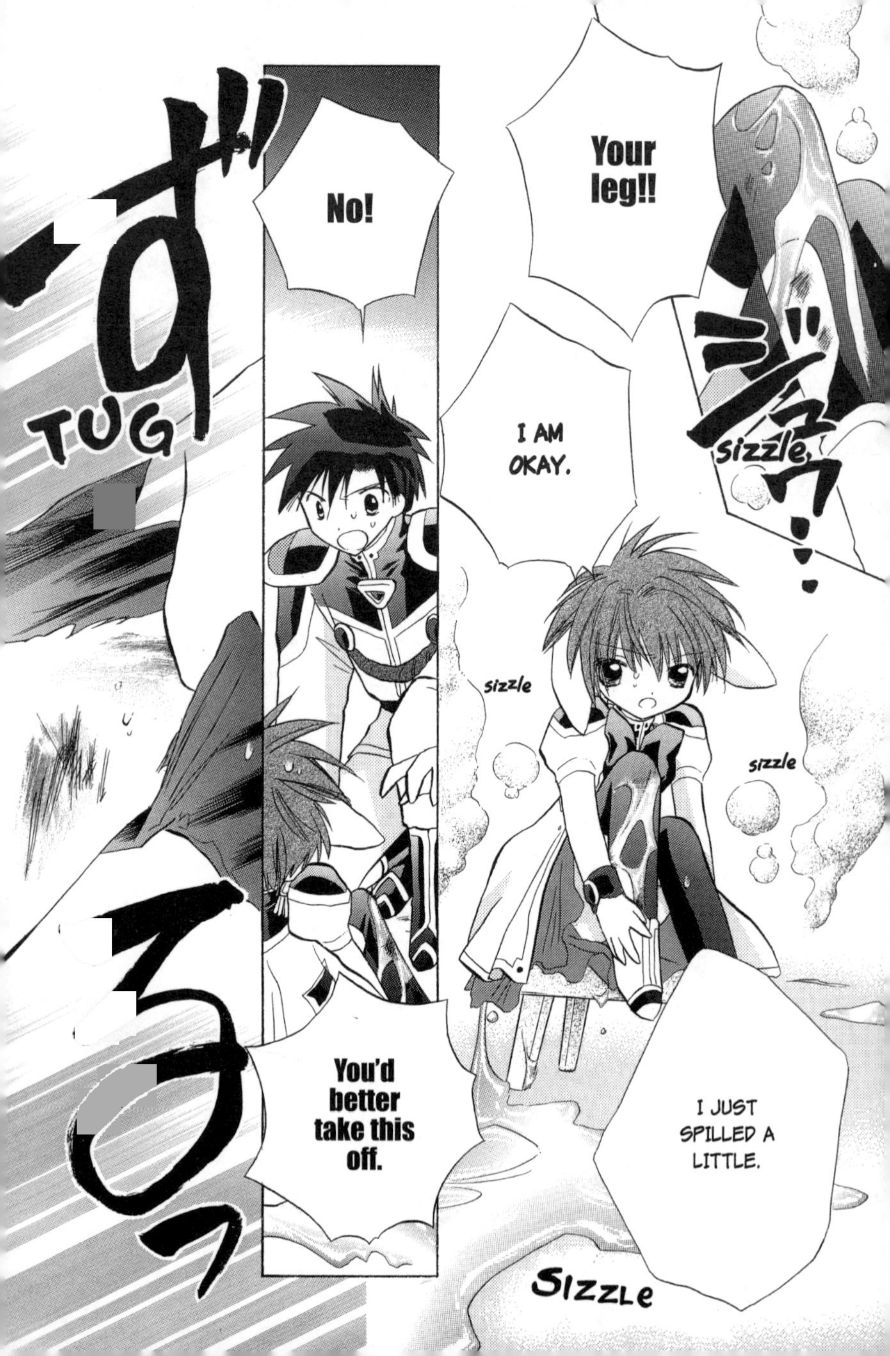

Your leg!!
sizzle
I AM OKAY.
sizzle
sizzle
I JUST SPILLED A LITTLE.
SIZZLE
No!
You'd better take this off.
TUG

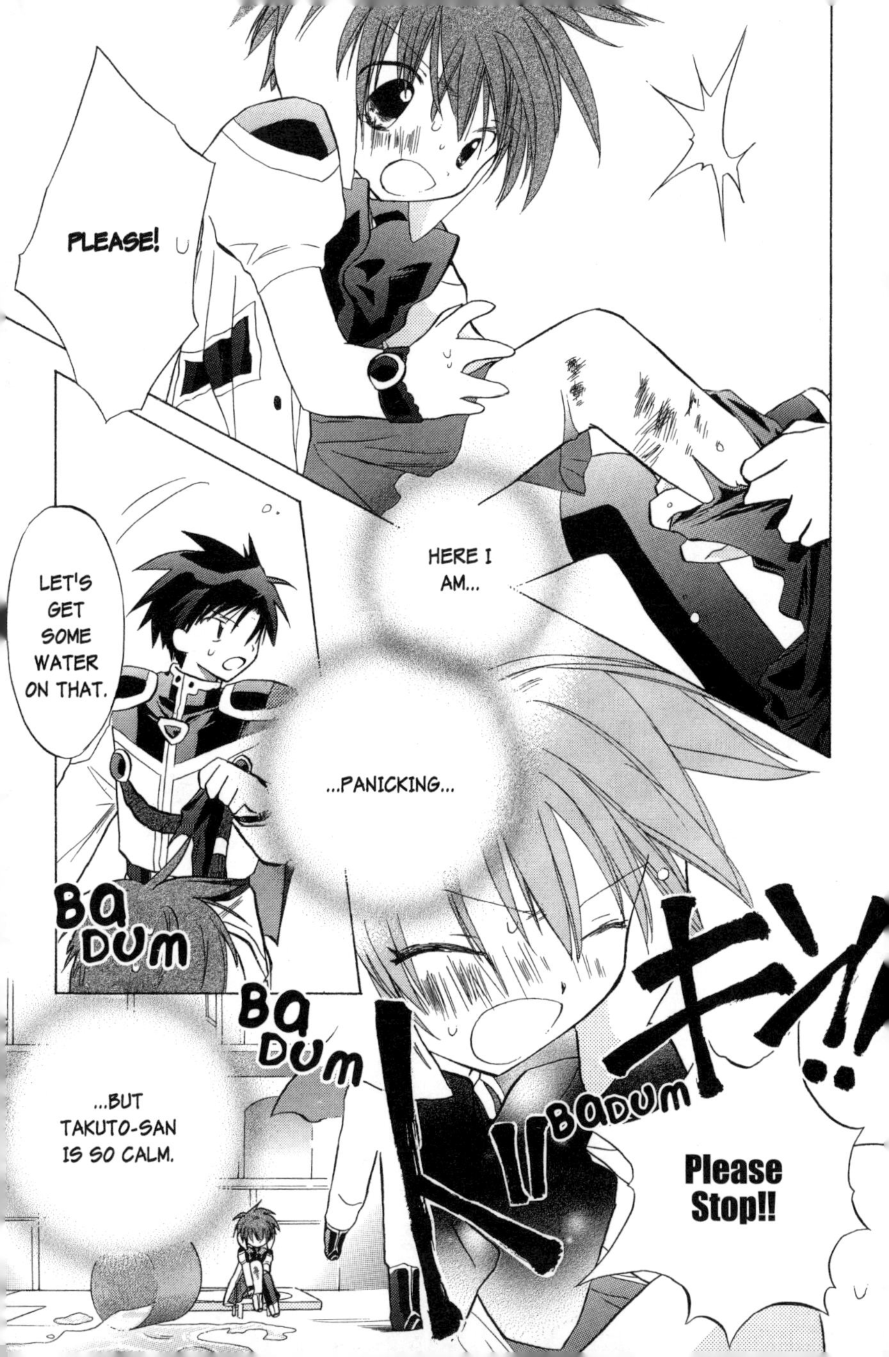
PLEASE!
HERE I AM...
...PANICKING...
LET'S GET SOME WATER ON THAT.
BA DUM
ドキッ!!
Please Stop!!
BADUM
BA DUM
...BUT TAKUTO-SAN IS SO CALM.

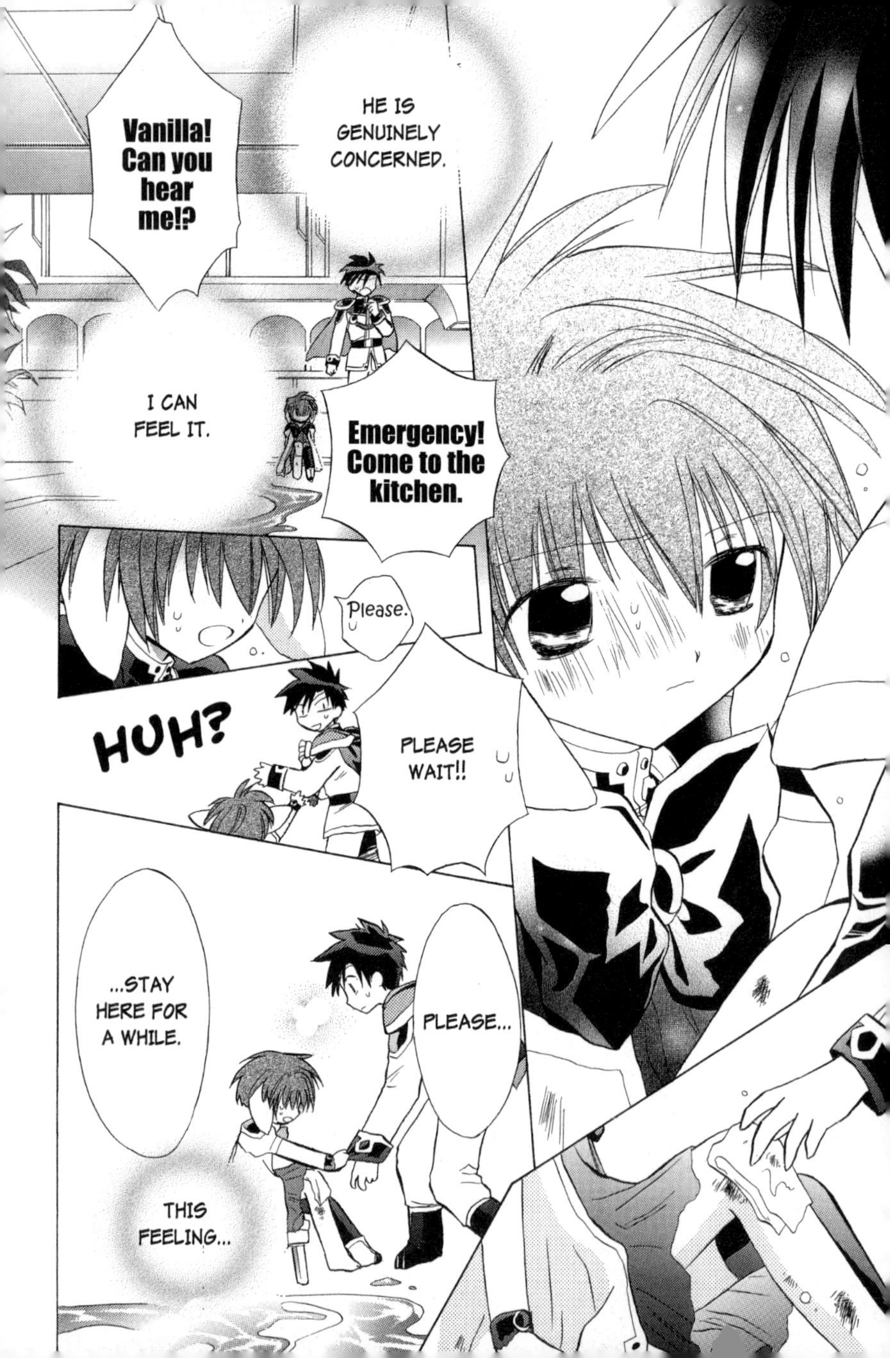
HE IS GENUINELY CONCERNED.
Vanilla! Can you hear me!?
Emergency! Come to the kitchen.
I CAN FEEL IT.
Please.
PLEASE WAIT!!
HUH?
PLEASE...
...STAY HERE FOR A WHILE.
THIS FEELING...

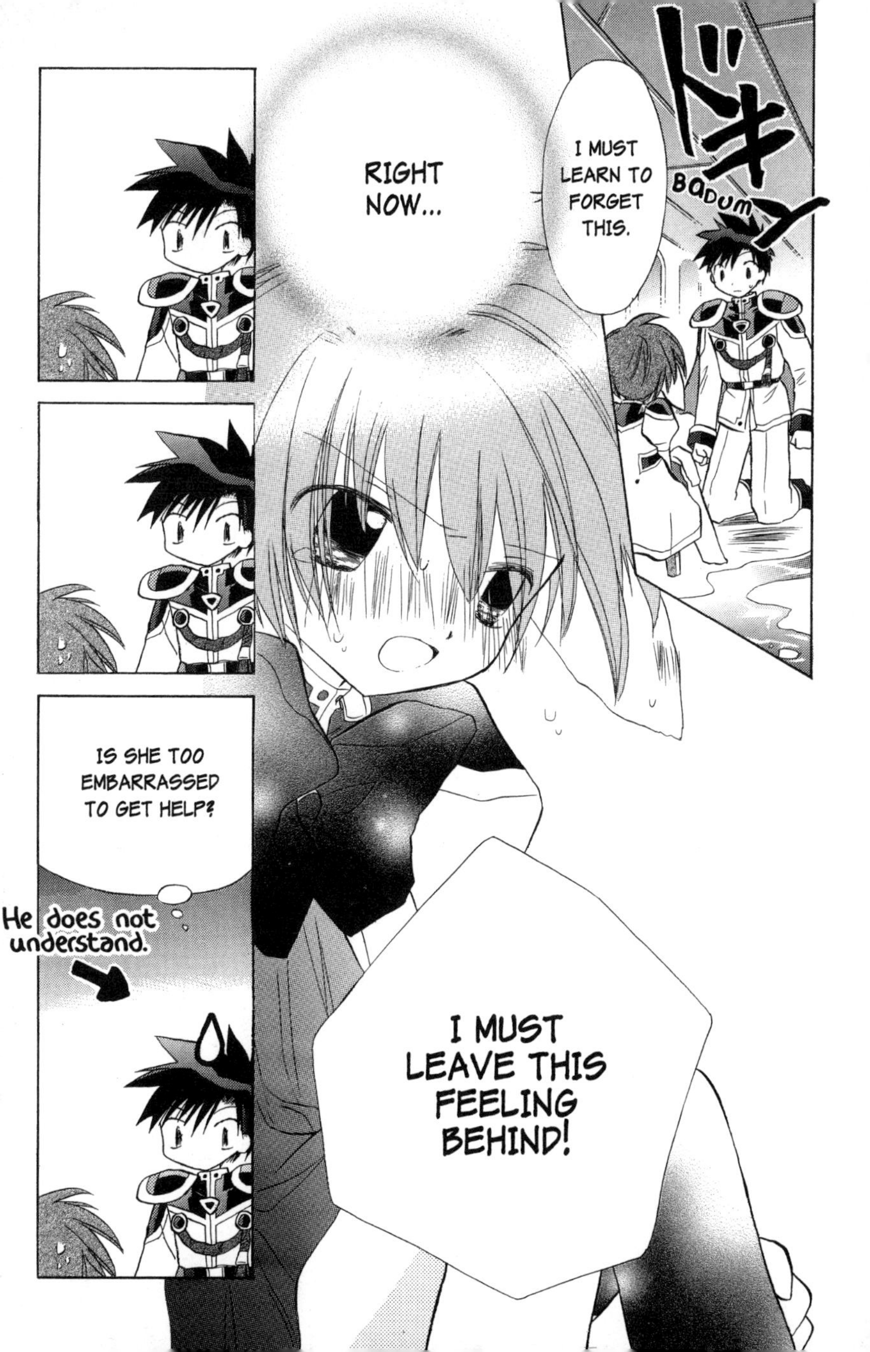
ドキン
BADUM
I MUST LEARN TO FORGET THIS.
RIGHT NOW...
I MUST LEAVE THIS FEELING BEHIND!
IS SHE TOO EMBARRASSED TO GET HELP?
He does not understand.

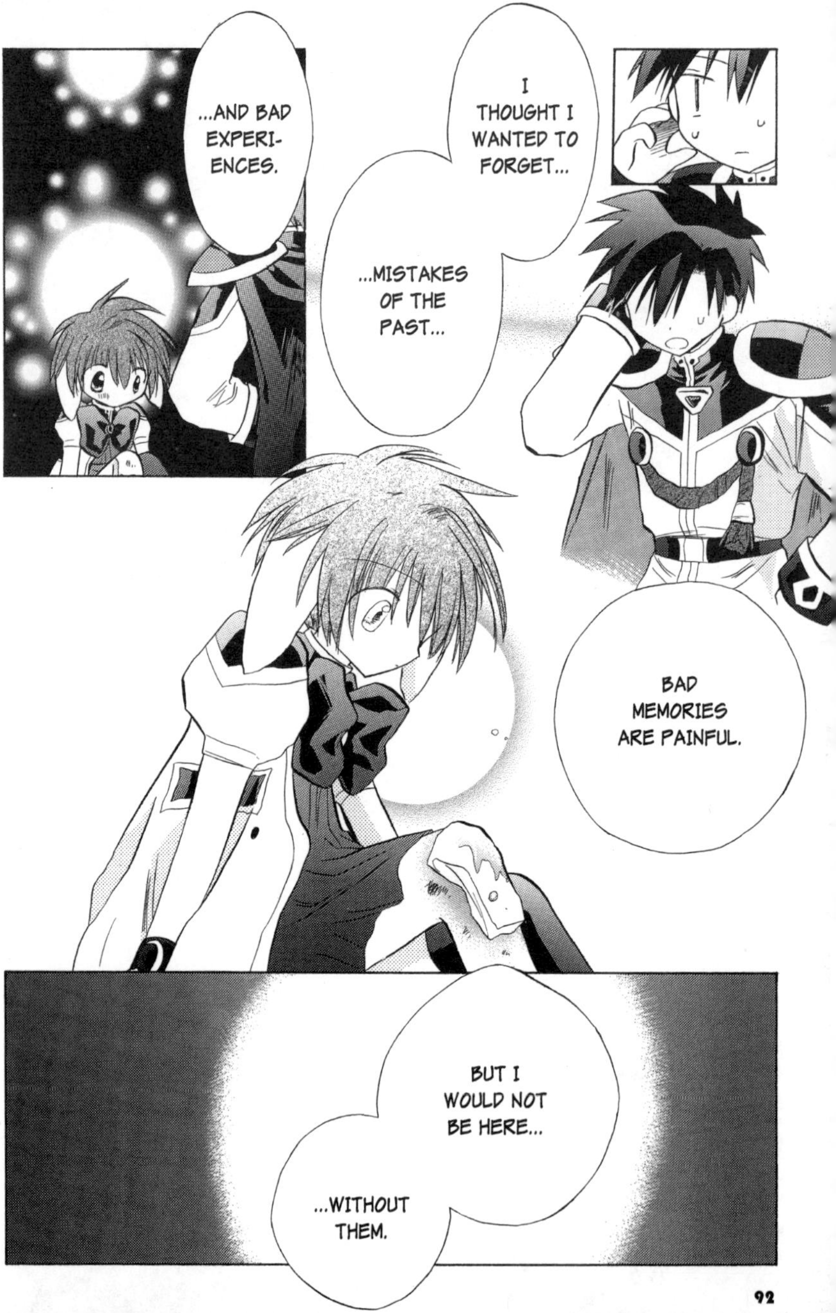
I THOUGHT I WANTED TO FORGET...
...MISTAKES OF THE PAST...
...AND BAD EXPERI-ENCES.
BAD MEMORIES ARE PAINFUL.
BUT I WOULD NOT BE HERE...
...WITHOUT THEM.

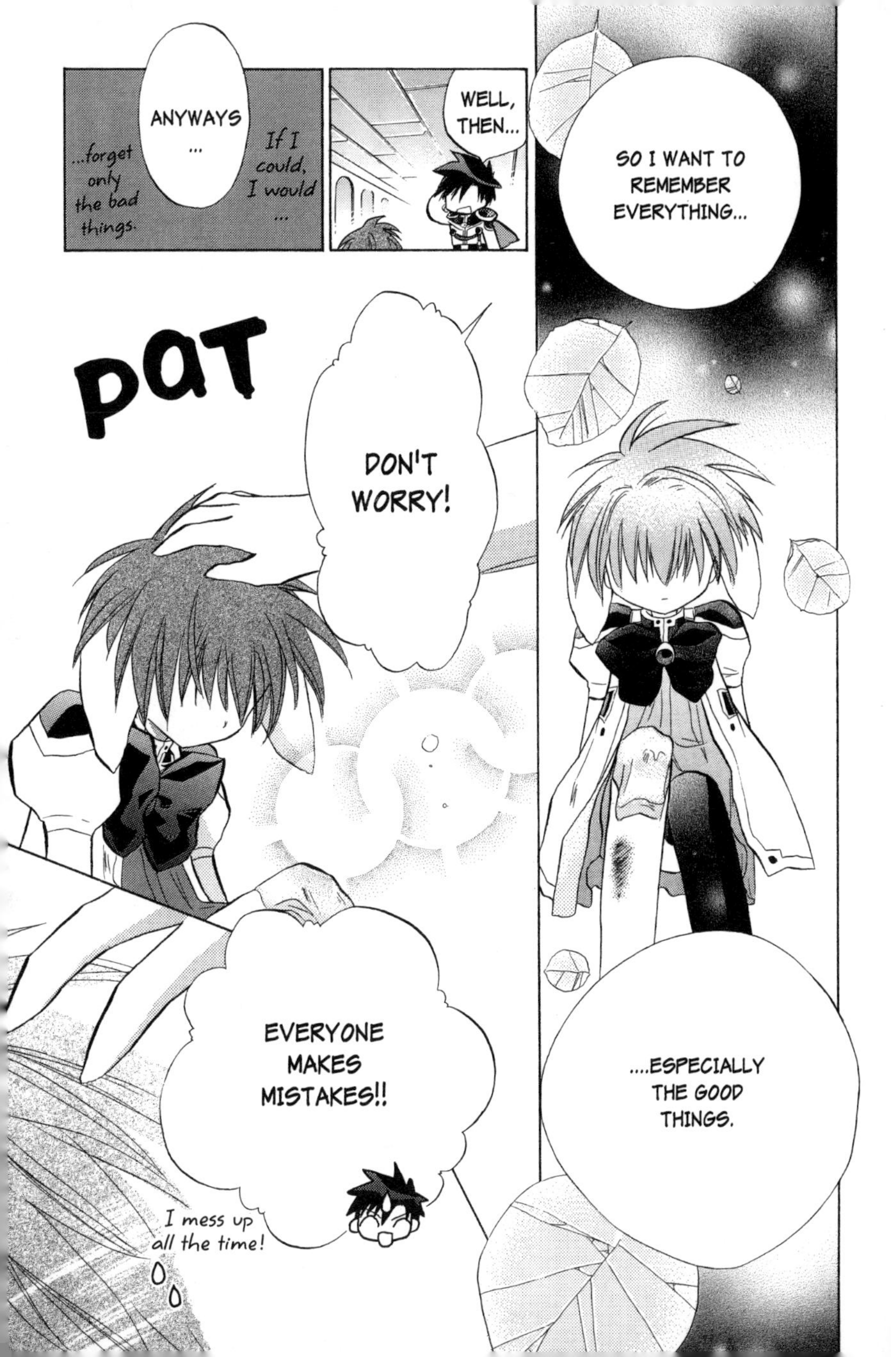
SO I WANT TO REMEMBER EVERYTHING...
....ESPECIALLY THE GOOD THINGS.
WELL, THEN...
ANYWAYS ...
If I could, I would ...
...forget only the bad things.
PAT
DON'T WORRY!
EVERYONE MAKES MISTAKES!!
I mess up all the time!

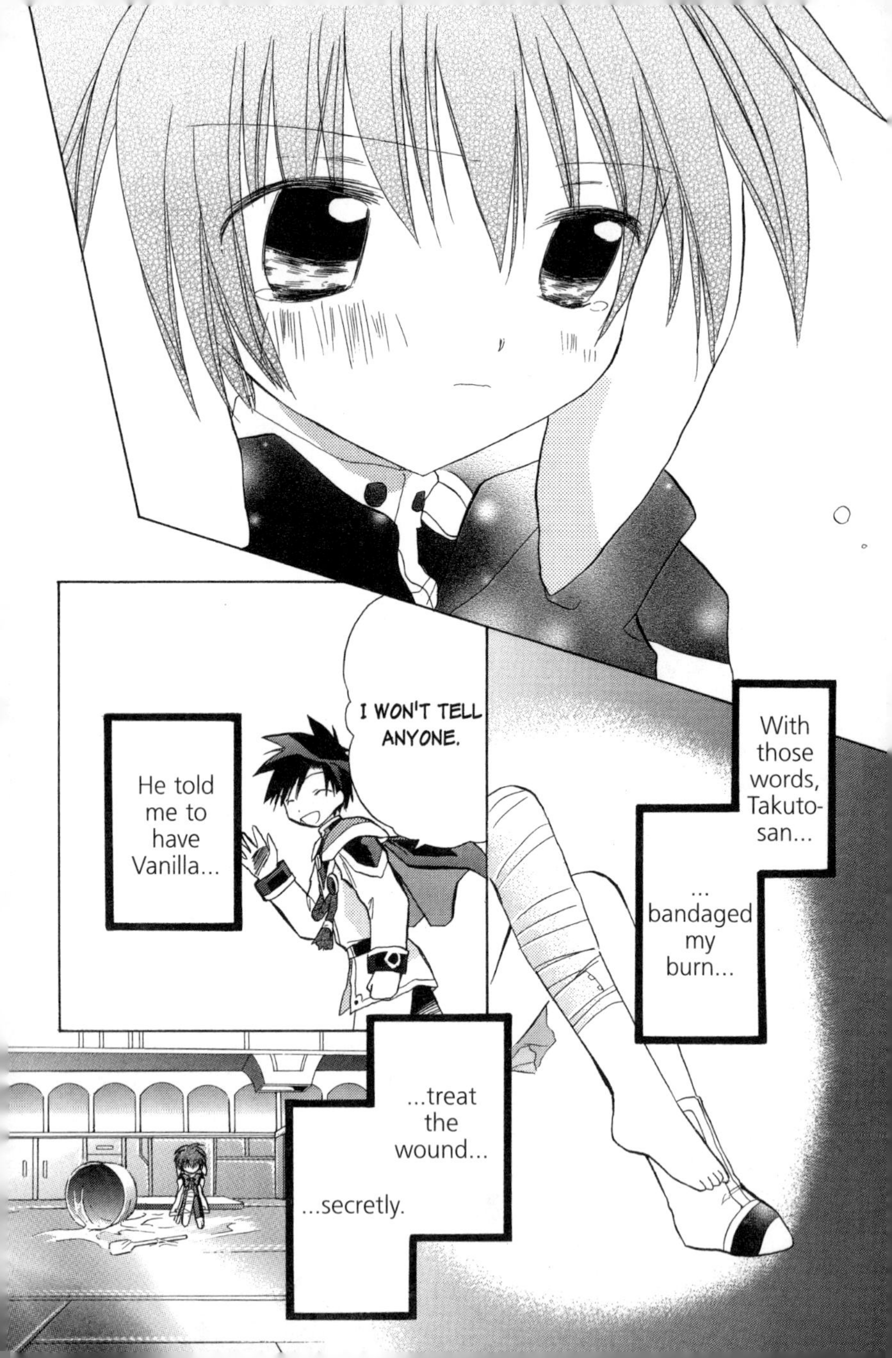

With those words, Takuto-san...
...bandaged my burn...
I WON'T TELL ANYONE.
He told me to have Vanilla...
...treat the wound...
...secretly.

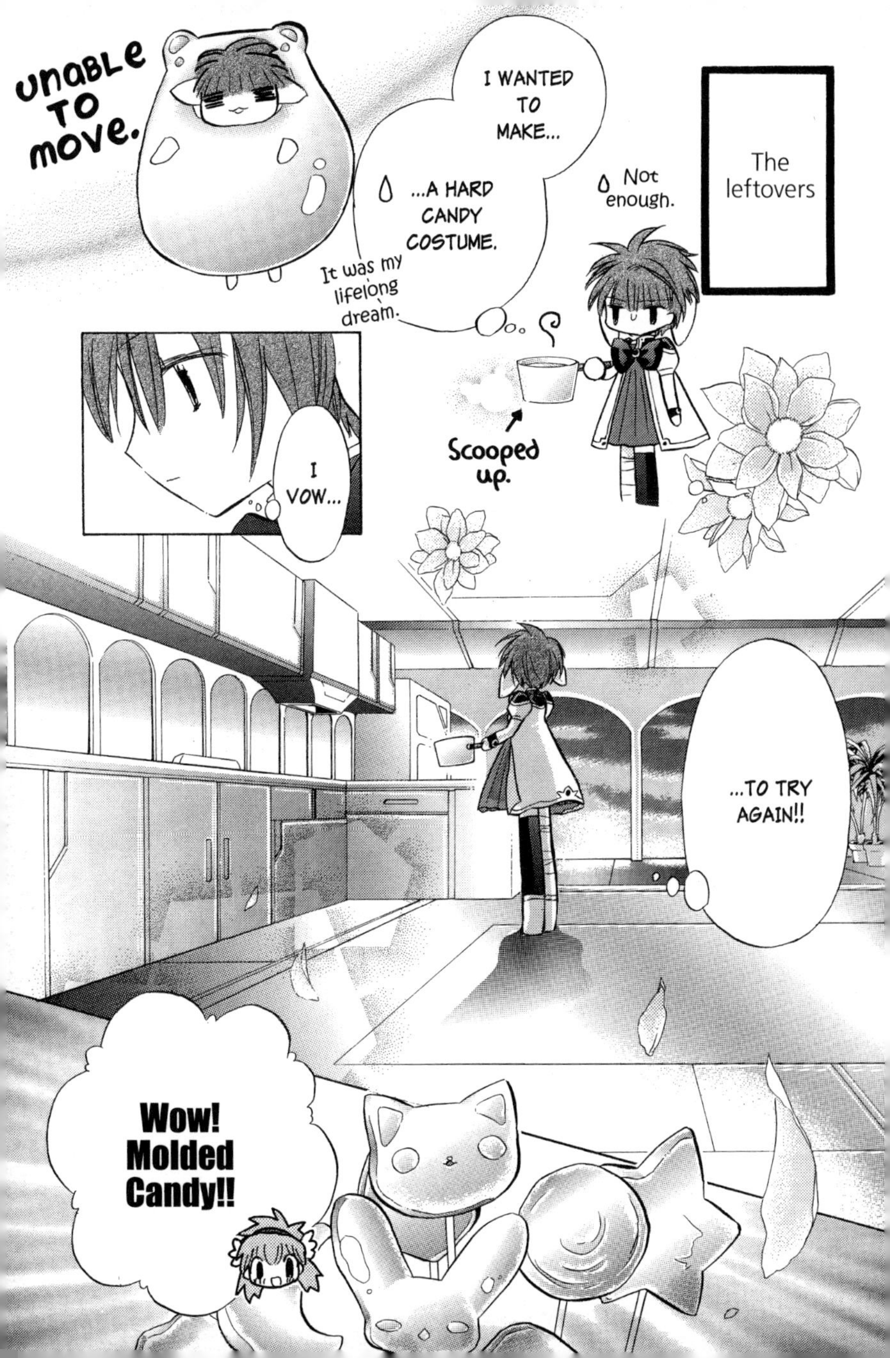

The leftovers
Not enough.
I WANTED TO MAKE...
...A HARD CANDY COSTUME.
It was my lifelong dream.
Unable to move.
Scooped up.
I VOW...
...TO TRY AGAIN!!
Wow! Molded Candy!!

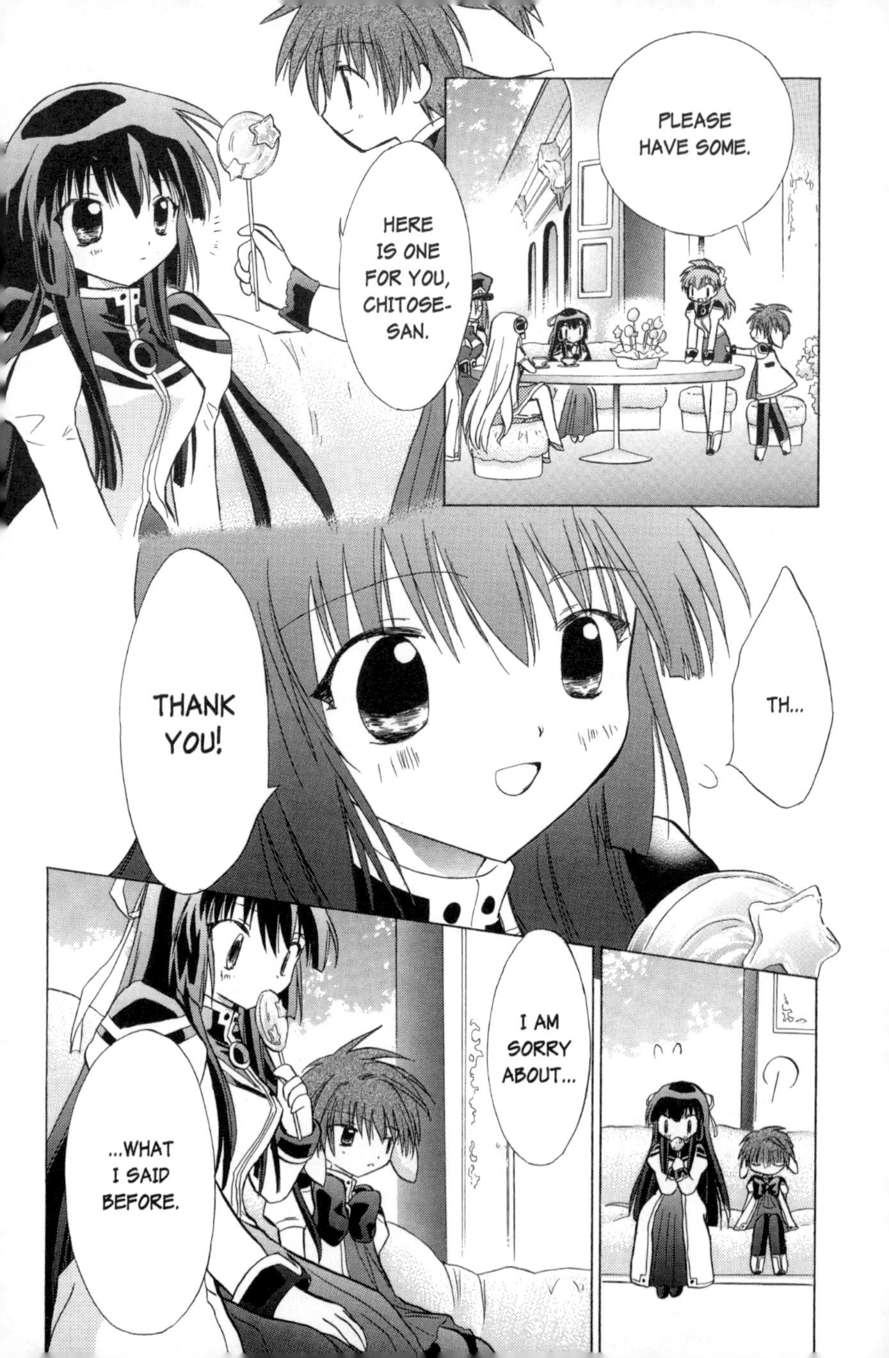
PLEASE HAVE SOME.
HERE IS ONE FOR YOU, CHITOSE-SAN.
TH...
THANK YOU!
I AM SORRY ABOUT...
...WHAT I SAID BEFORE.

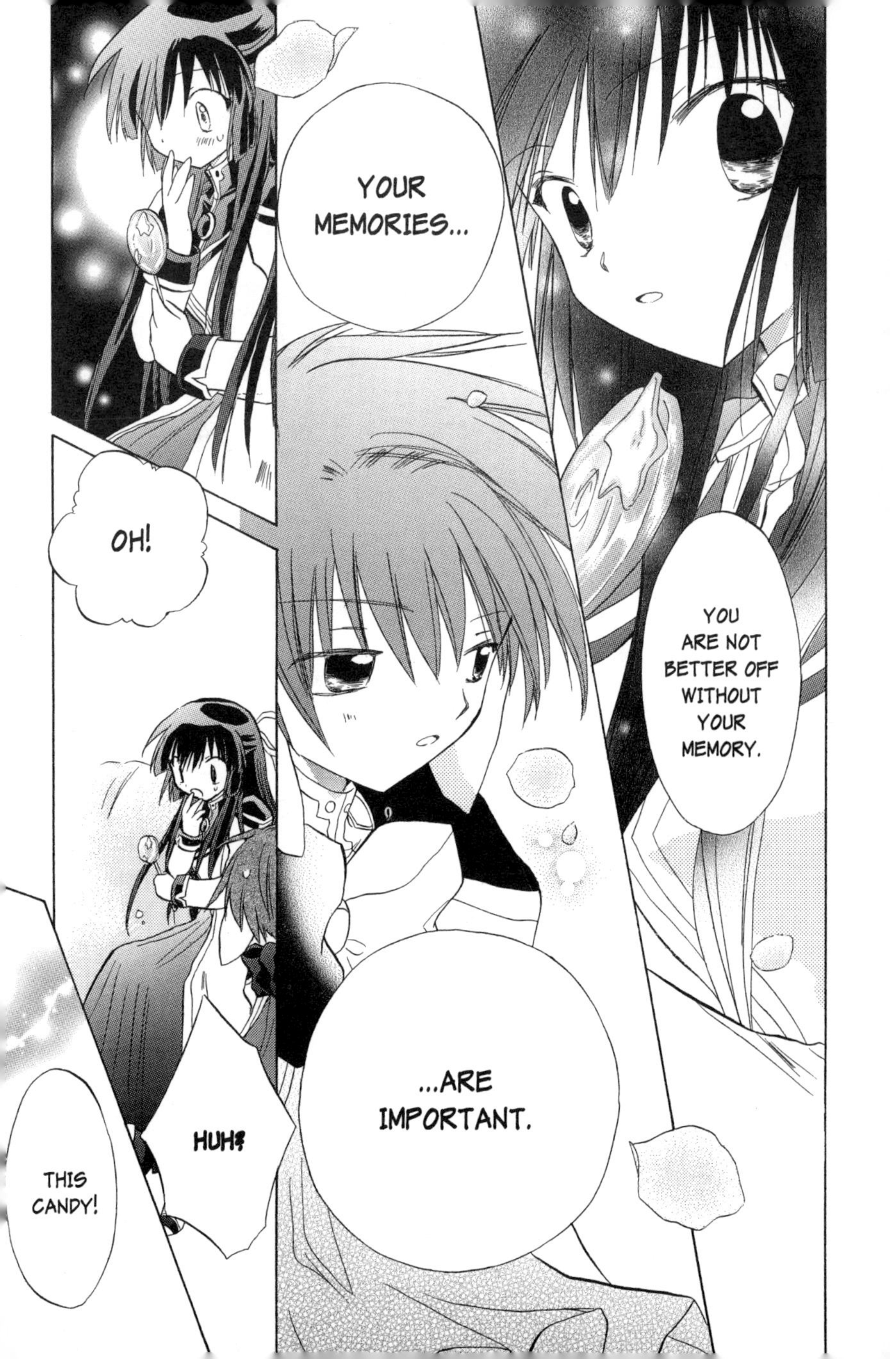
YOU ARE NOT BETTER OFF WITHOUT YOUR MEMORY.
YOUR MEMORIES...
...ARE IMPORTANT.
OH!
HUH?
THIS CANDY!

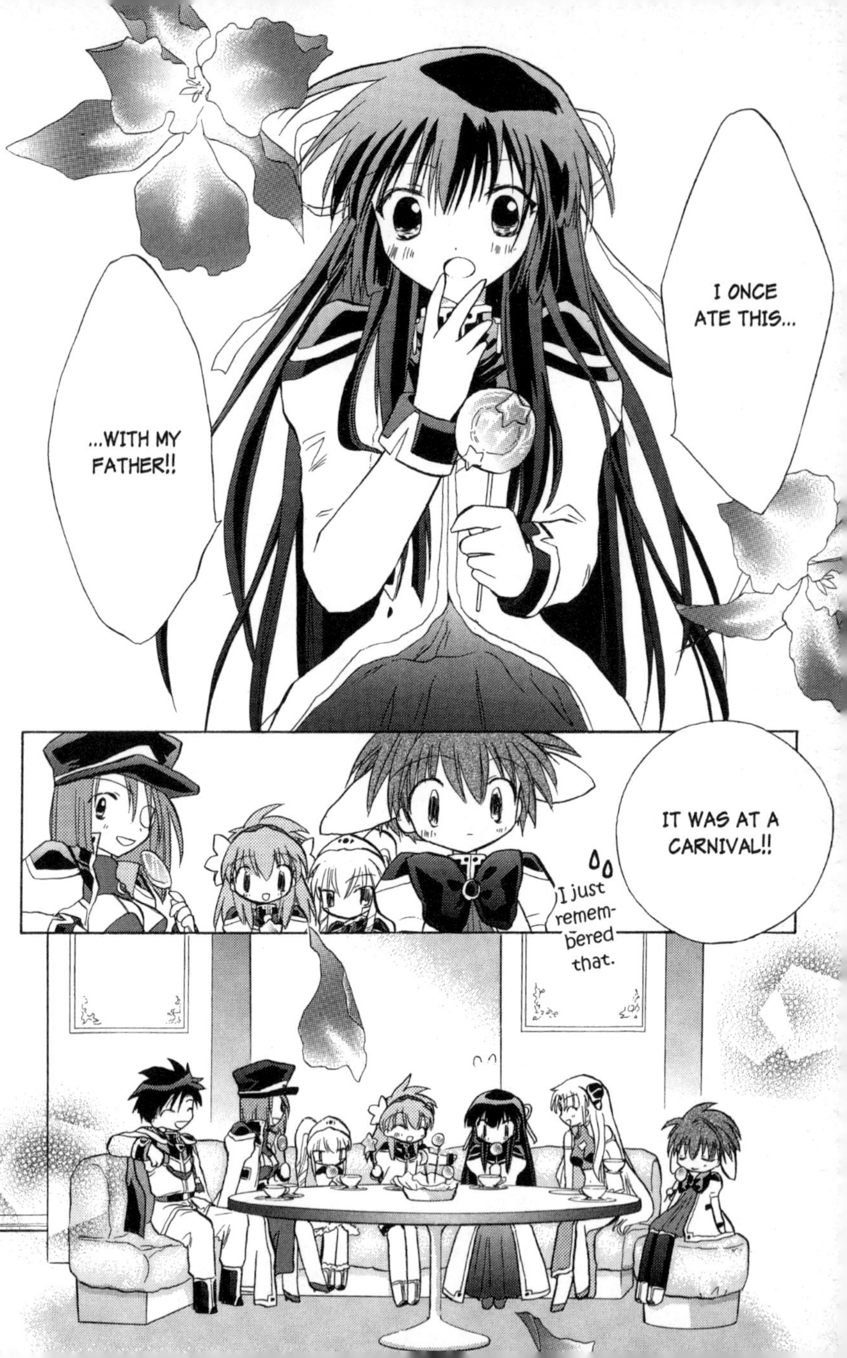

I ONCE ATE THIS...
...WITH MY FATHER!!
IT WAS AT A CARNIVAL!!
I just remem-bered that.

EPISODE 4: THE KEY OF HAPPINESS OPENS THE LOCKED HEART

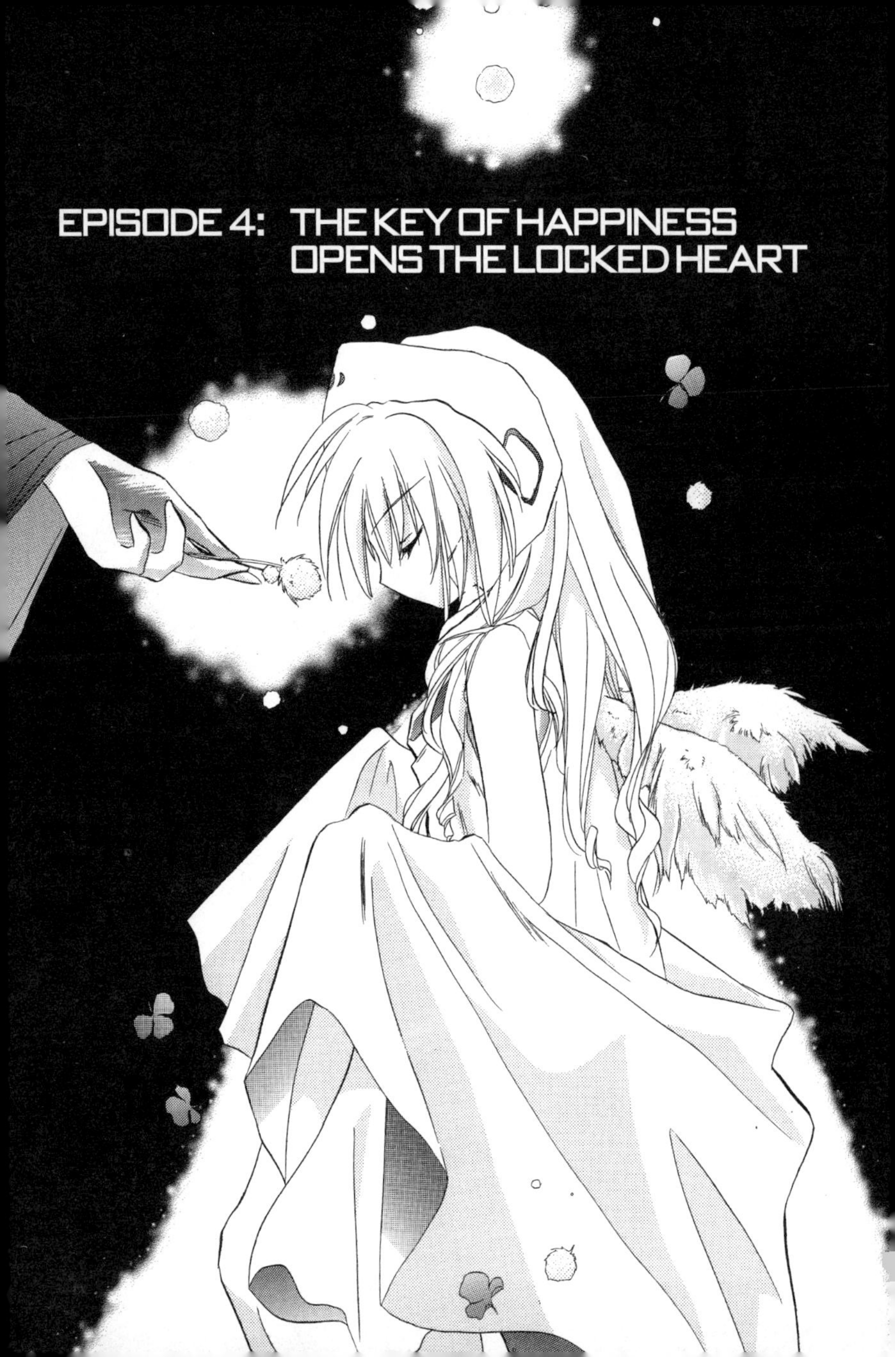

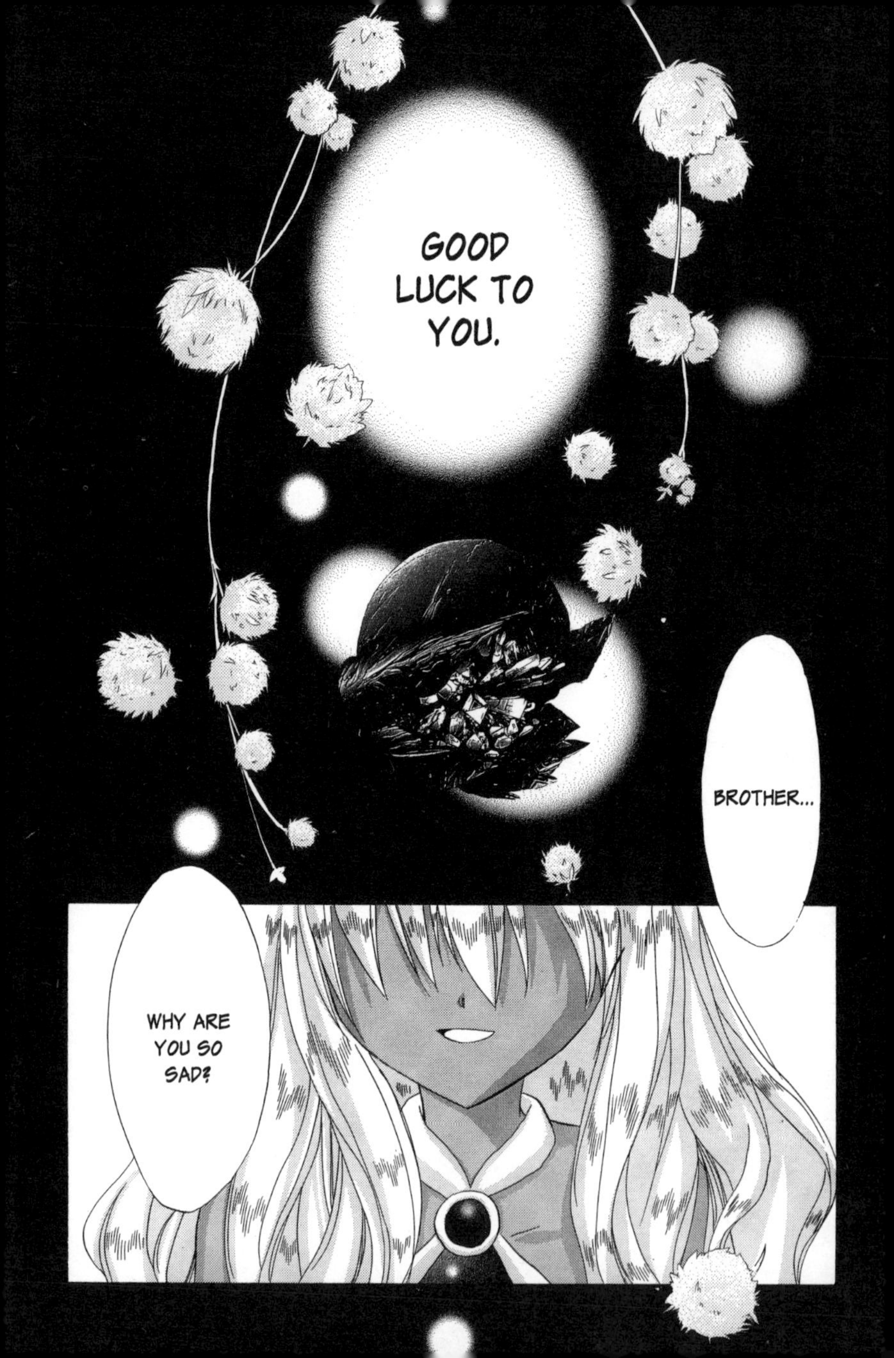
GOOD LUCK TO YOU.
BROTHER...
WHY ARE YOU SO SAD?

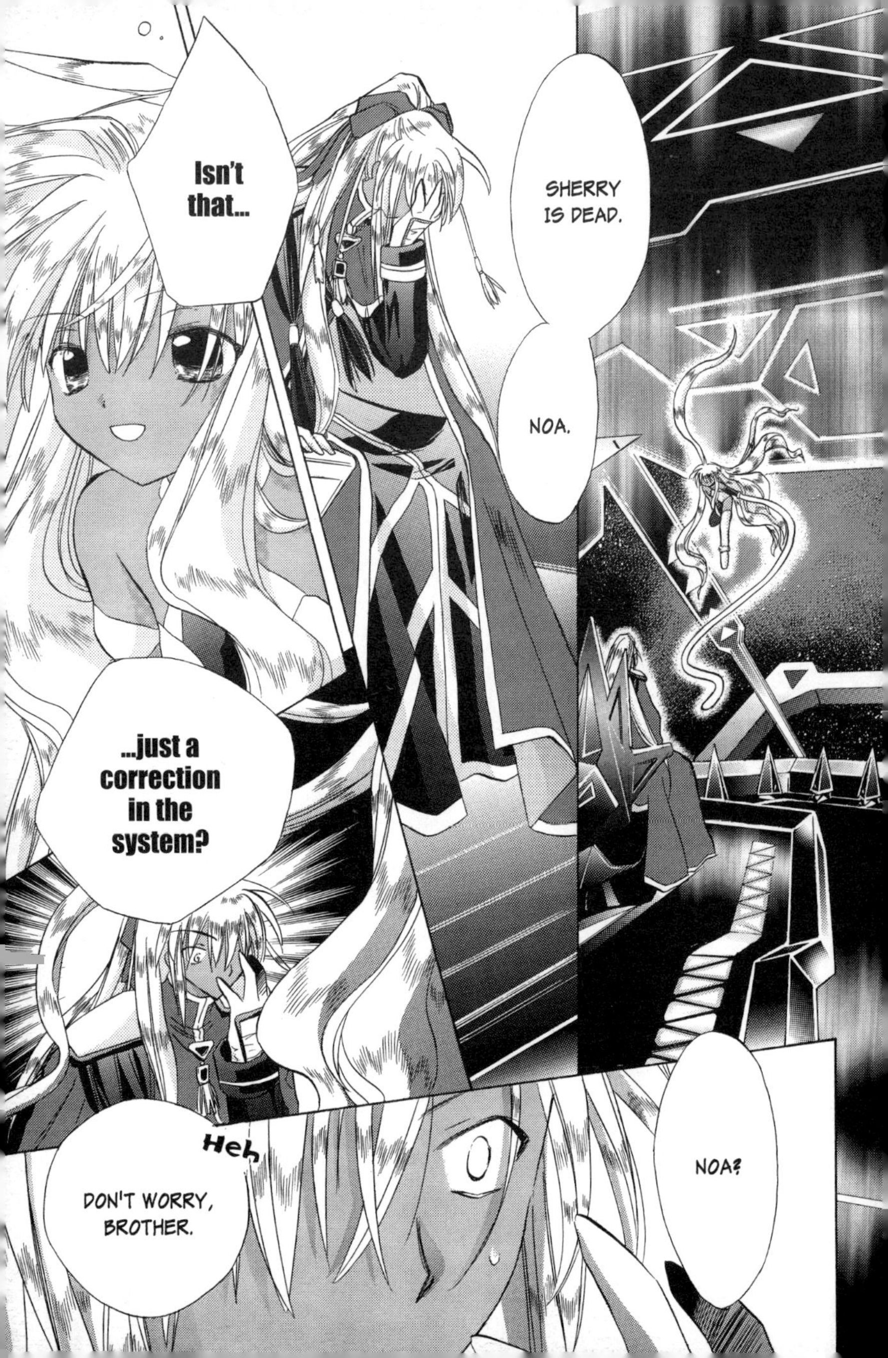
SHERRY IS DEAD.
NOA.
Isn't that...
...just a correction in the system?
NOA?
Heh
DON'T WORRY, BROTHER.

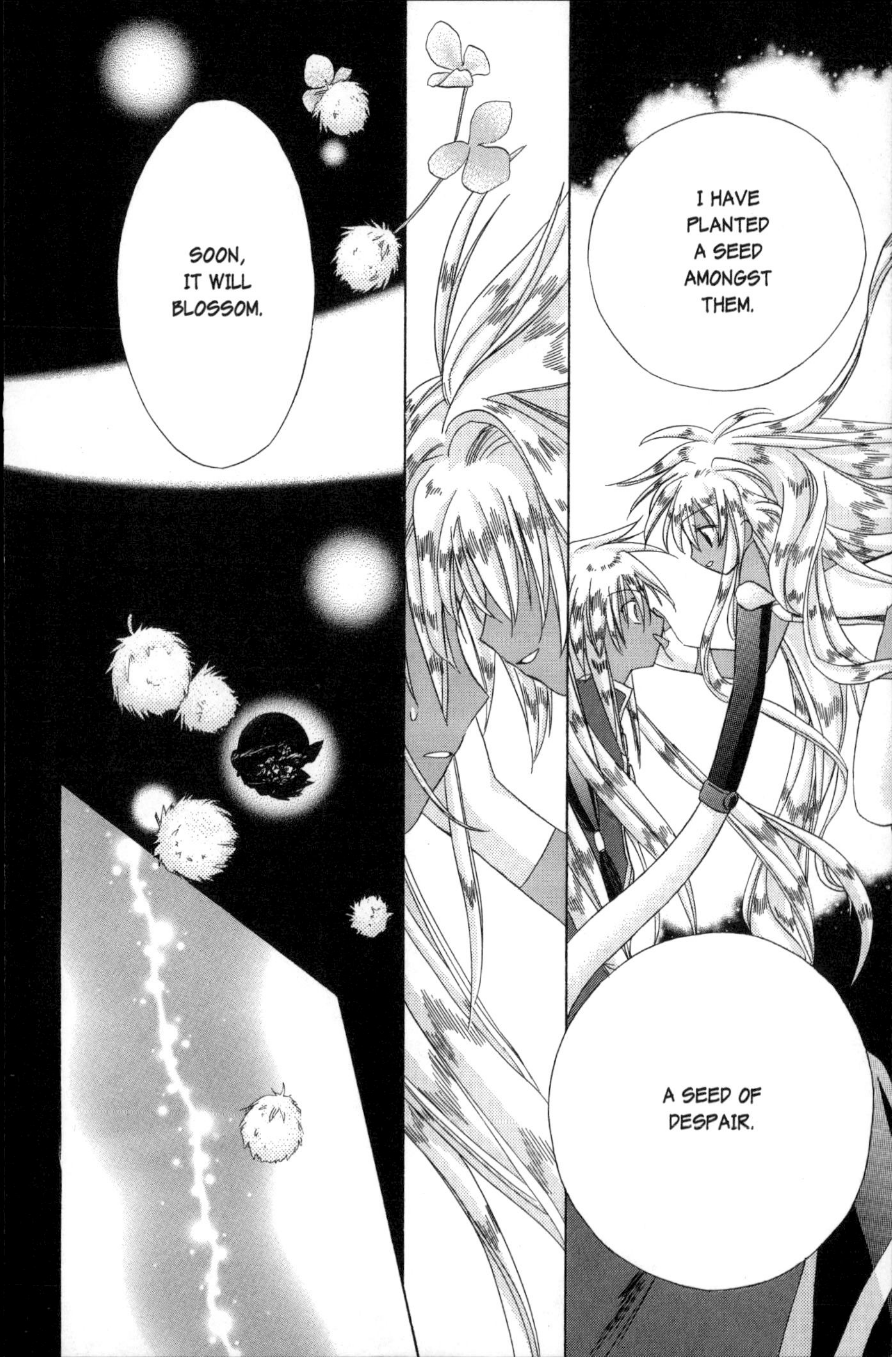
I HAVE PLANTED A SEED AMONGST THEM.
A SEED OF DESPAIR.
SOON, IT WILL BLOSSOM.

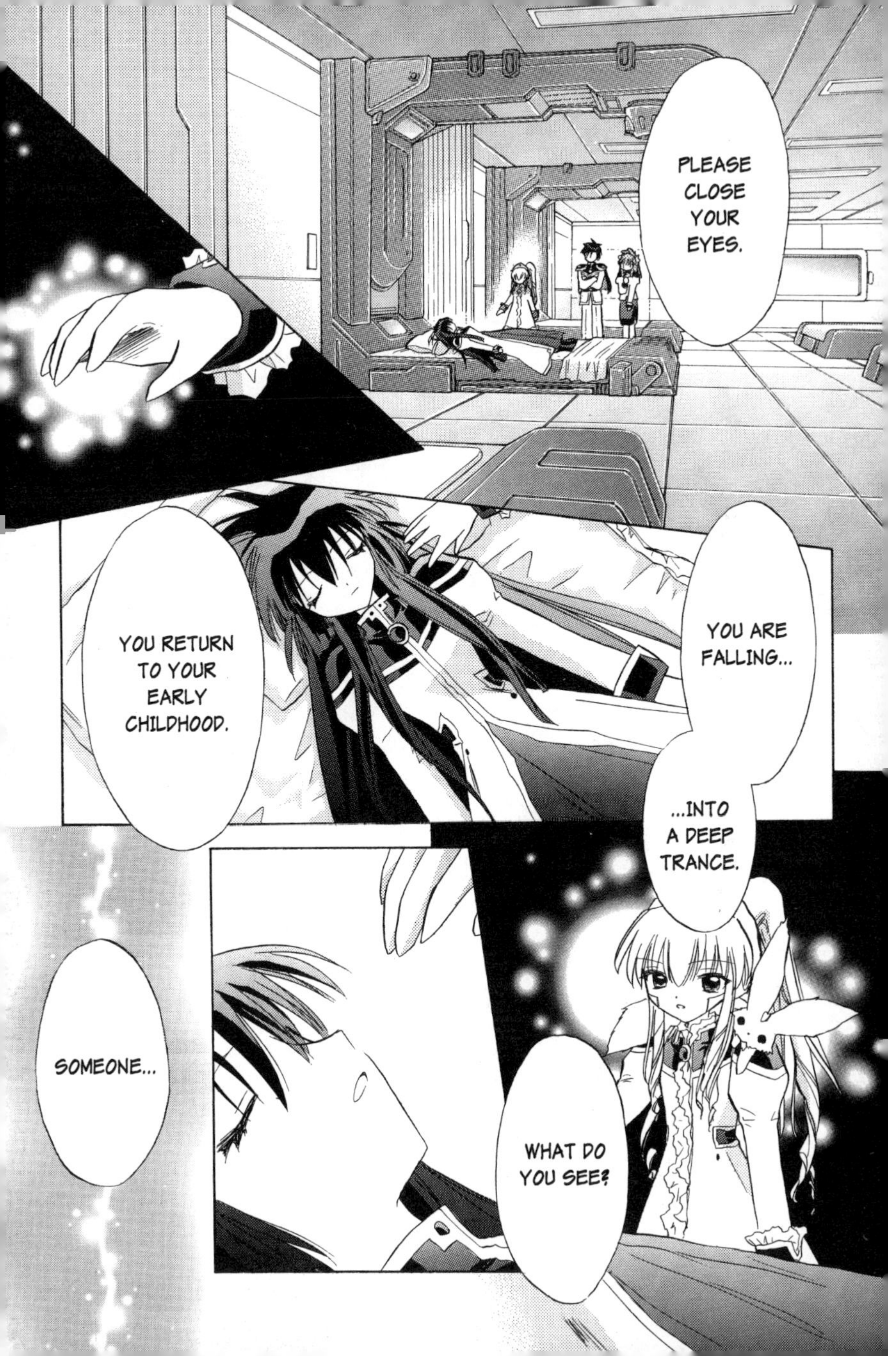
PLEASE CLOSE YOUR EYES.
YOU ARE FALLING...
...INTO A DEEP TRANCE.
YOU RETURN TO YOUR EARLY CHILDHOOD.
WHAT DO YOU SEE?
SOMEONE...

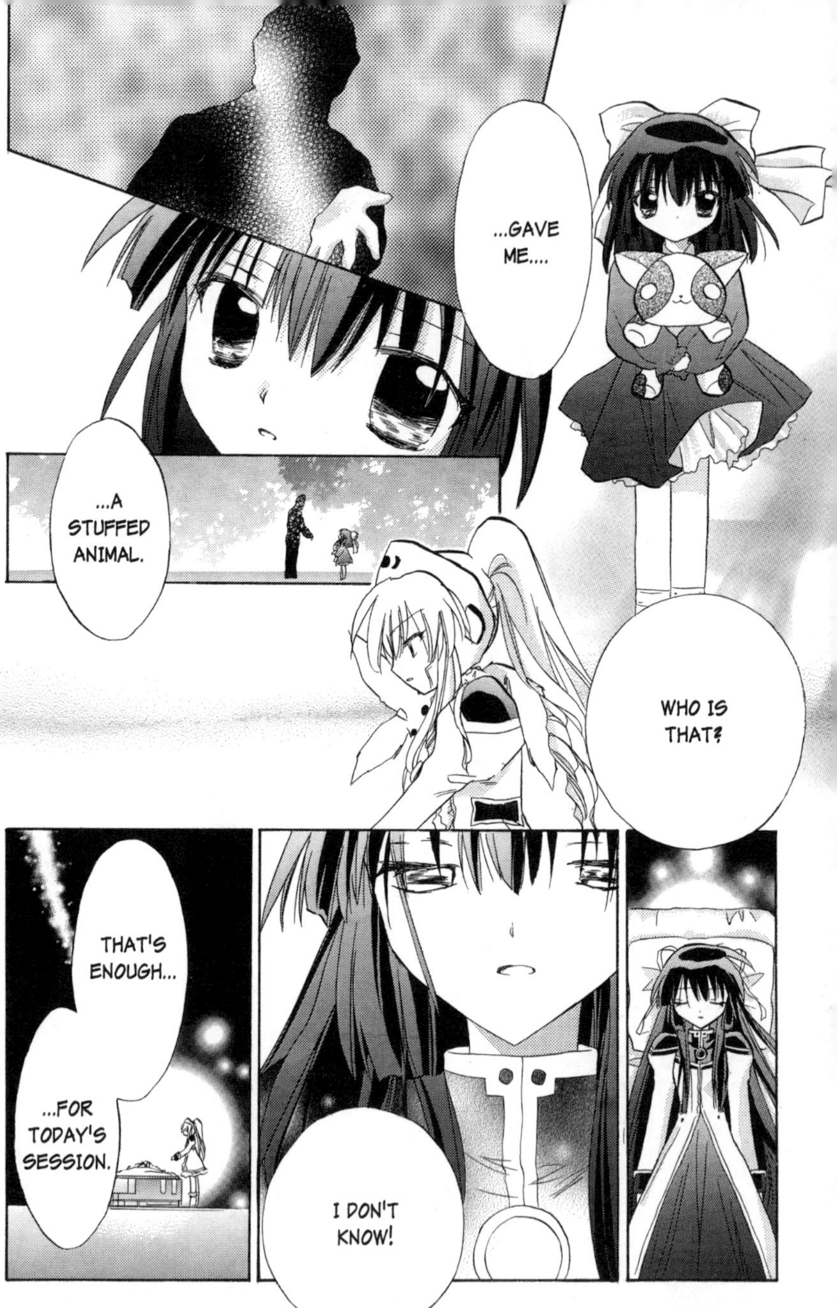
...GAVE ME....
...A STUFFED ANIMAL.
WHO IS THAT?
I DON'T KNOW!
THAT'S ENOUGH...
...FOR TODAY'S SESSION.

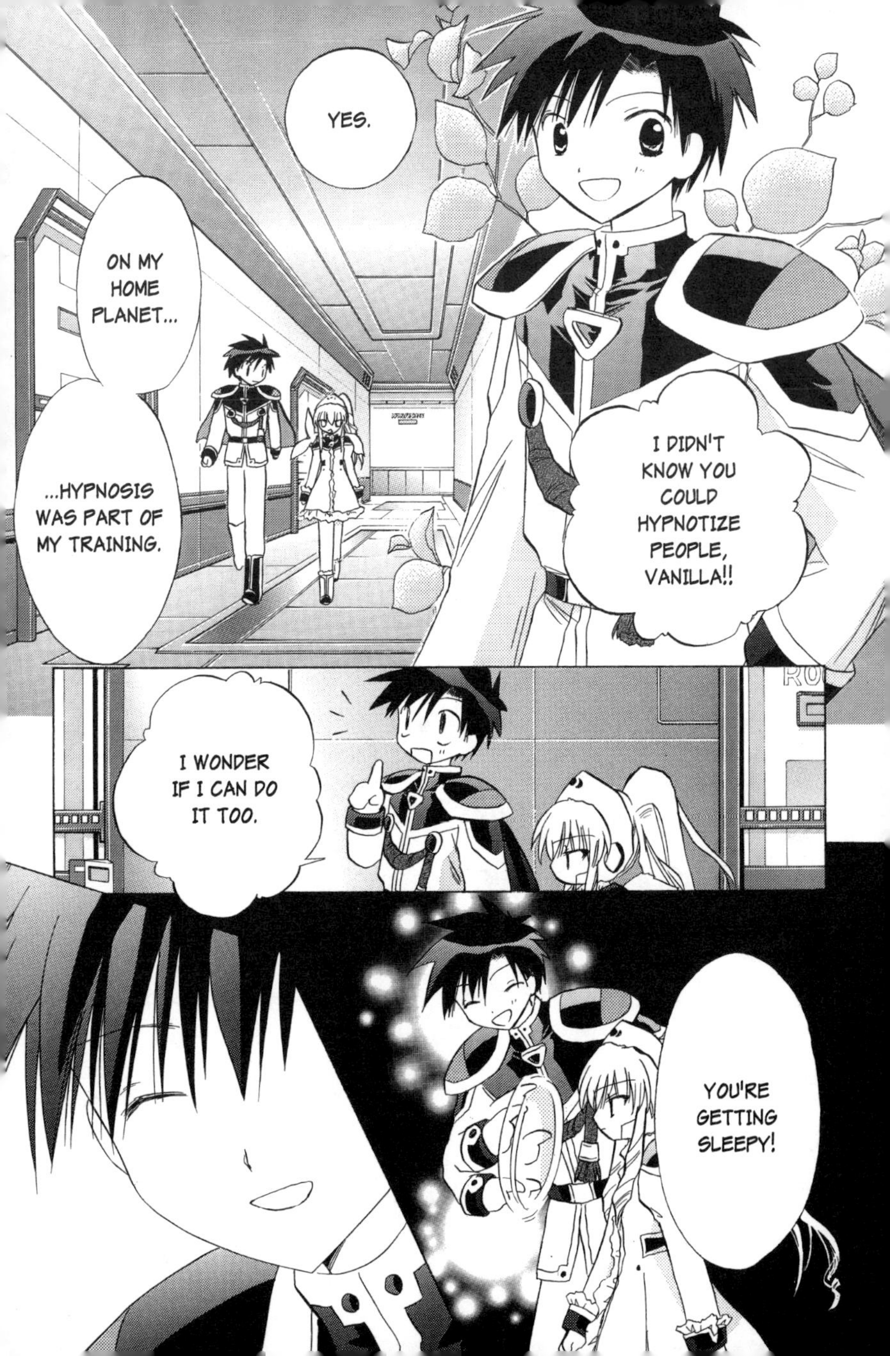
I DIDN'T KNOW YOU COULD HYPNOTIZE PEOPLE, VANILLA!!
YES.
ON MY HOME PLANET...
...HYPNOSIS WAS PART OF MY TRAINING.
I WONDER IF I CAN DO IT TOO.
YOU'RE GETTING SLEEPY!

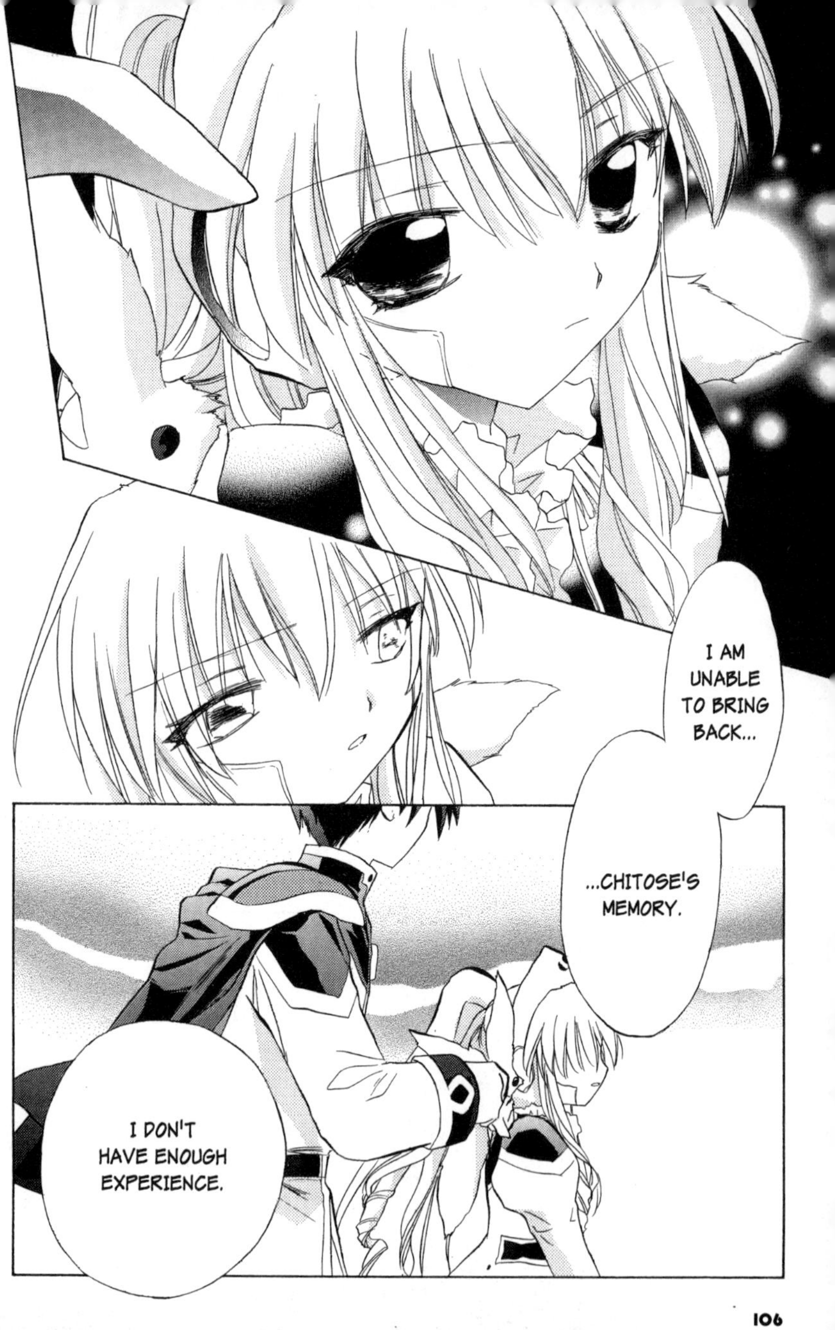
I AM UNABLE TO BRING BACK...
...CHITOSE'S MEMORY.
I DON'T HAVE ENOUGH EXPERIENCE.

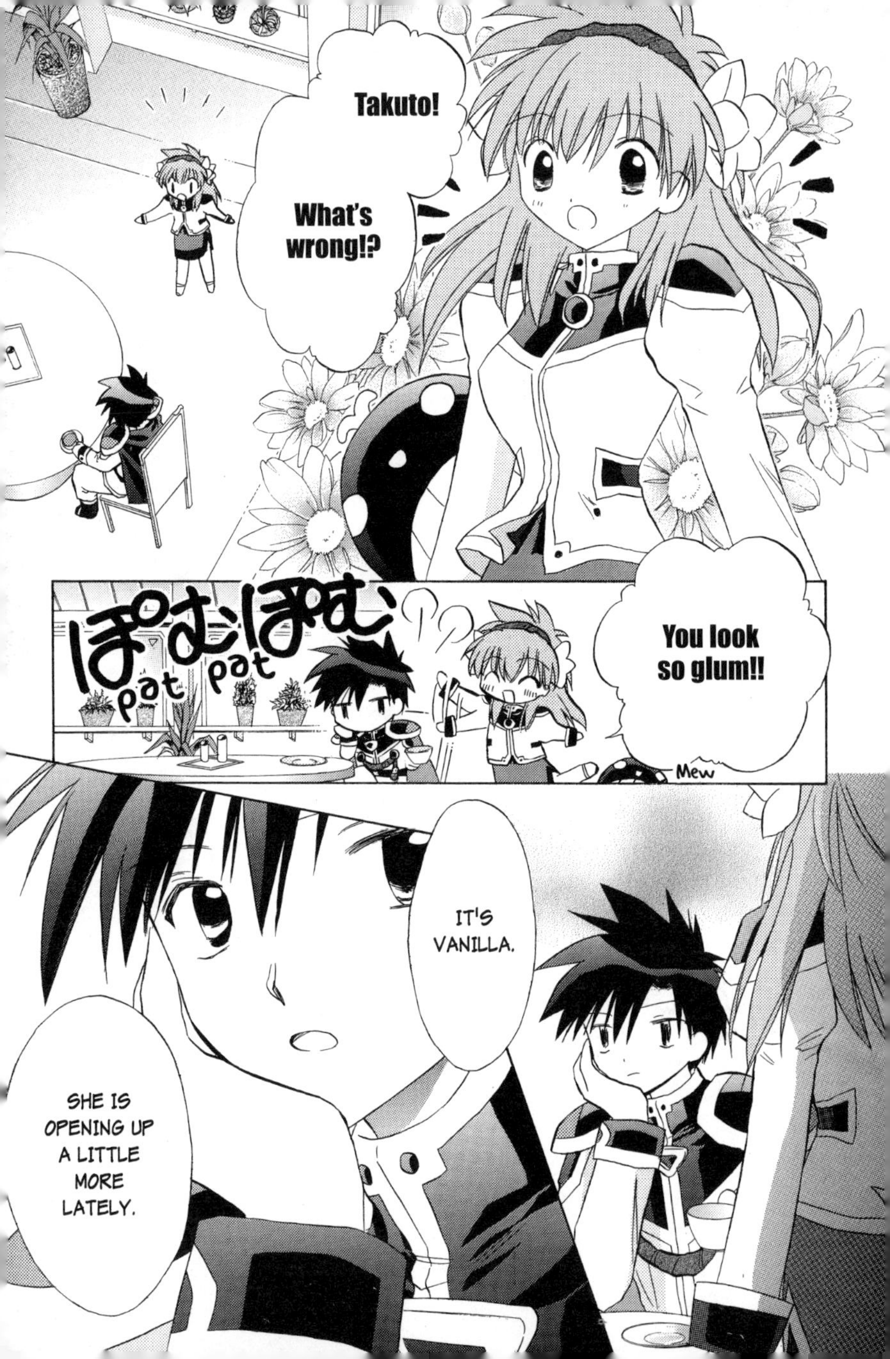
Takuto!
What's wrong!?
You look so glum!!
ぽむぽむ
pat pat
Mew
IT'S VANILLA.
SHE IS OPENING UP A LITTLE MORE LATELY.

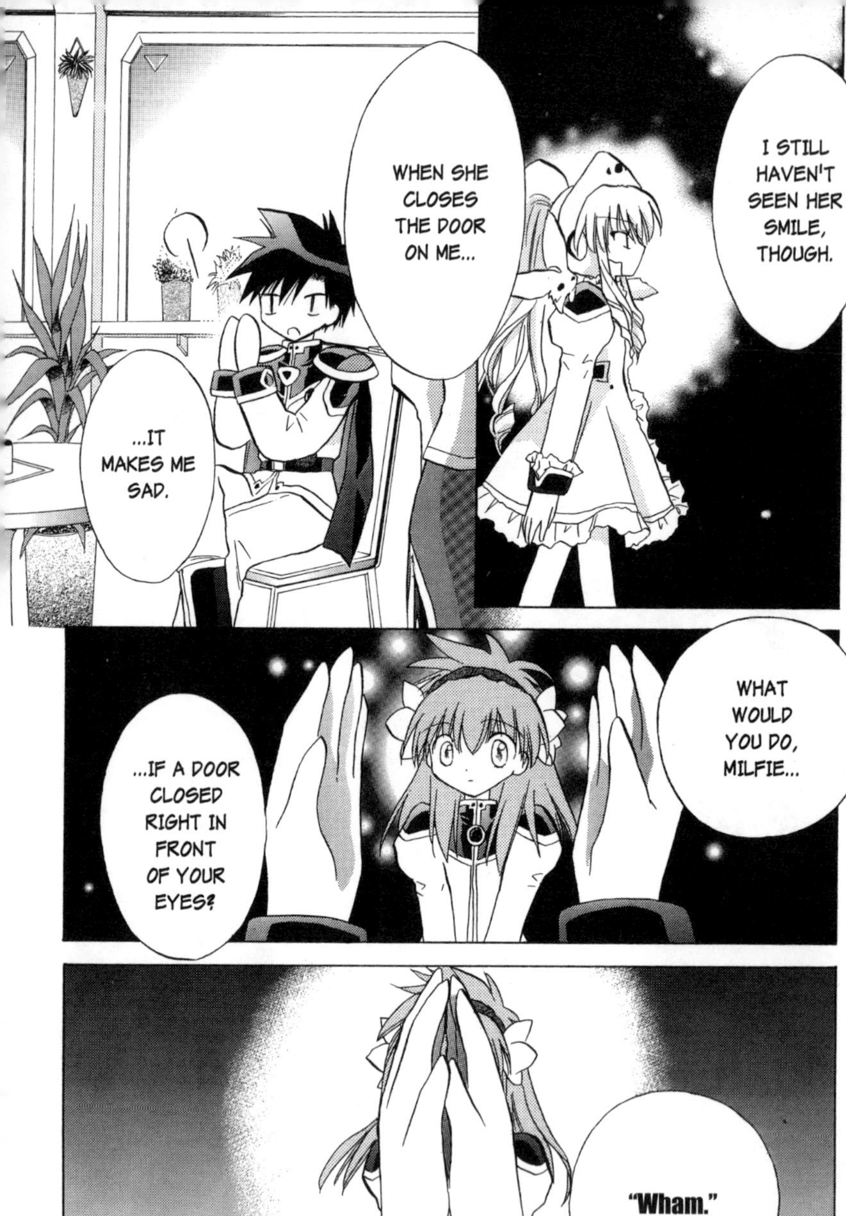
I STILL HAVEN'T SEEN HER SMILE, THOUGH.
WHEN SHE CLOSES THE DOOR ON ME...
...IT MAKES ME SAD.
WHAT WOULD YOU DO, MILFIE...
...IF A DOOR CLOSED RIGHT IN FRONT OF YOUR EYES?
"Wham."

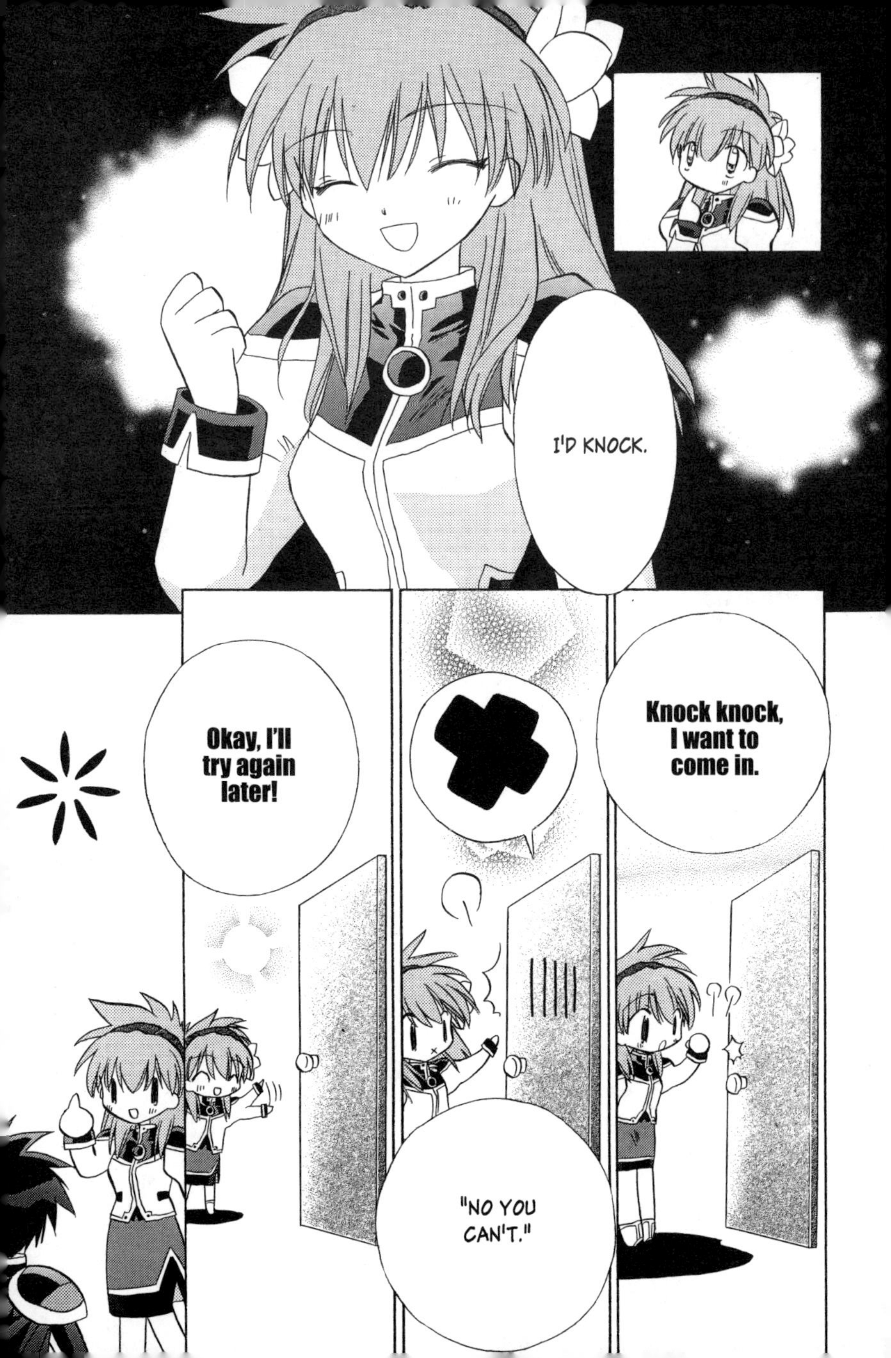
I'D KNOCK.
Knock knock, I want to come in.
"NO YOU CAN'T."
Okay, I'll try again later!

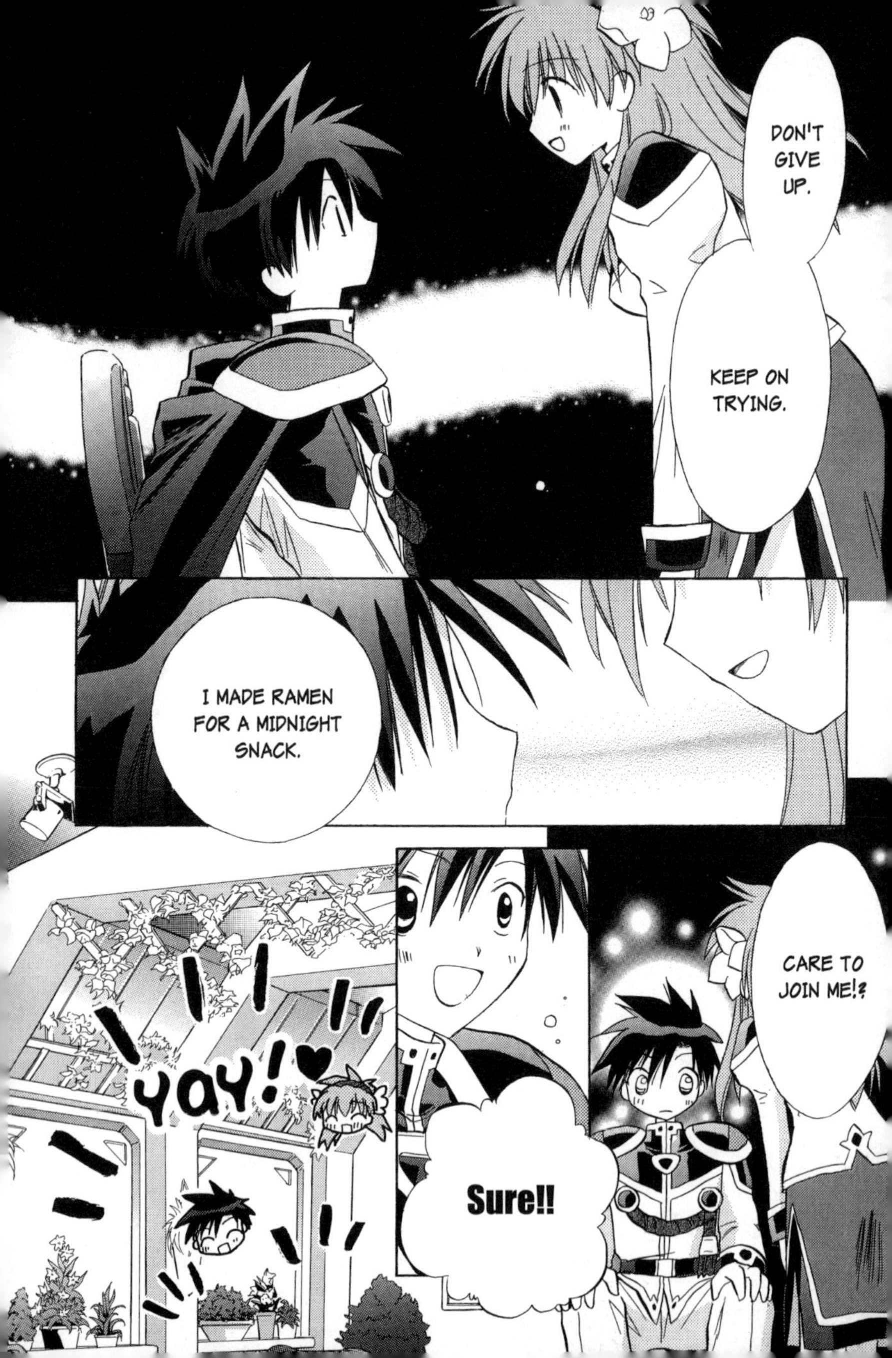
DON'T GIVE UP.
KEEP ON TRYING.
I MADE RAMEN FOR A MIDNIGHT SNACK.
CARE TO JOIN ME!?
Sure!!
YAY!

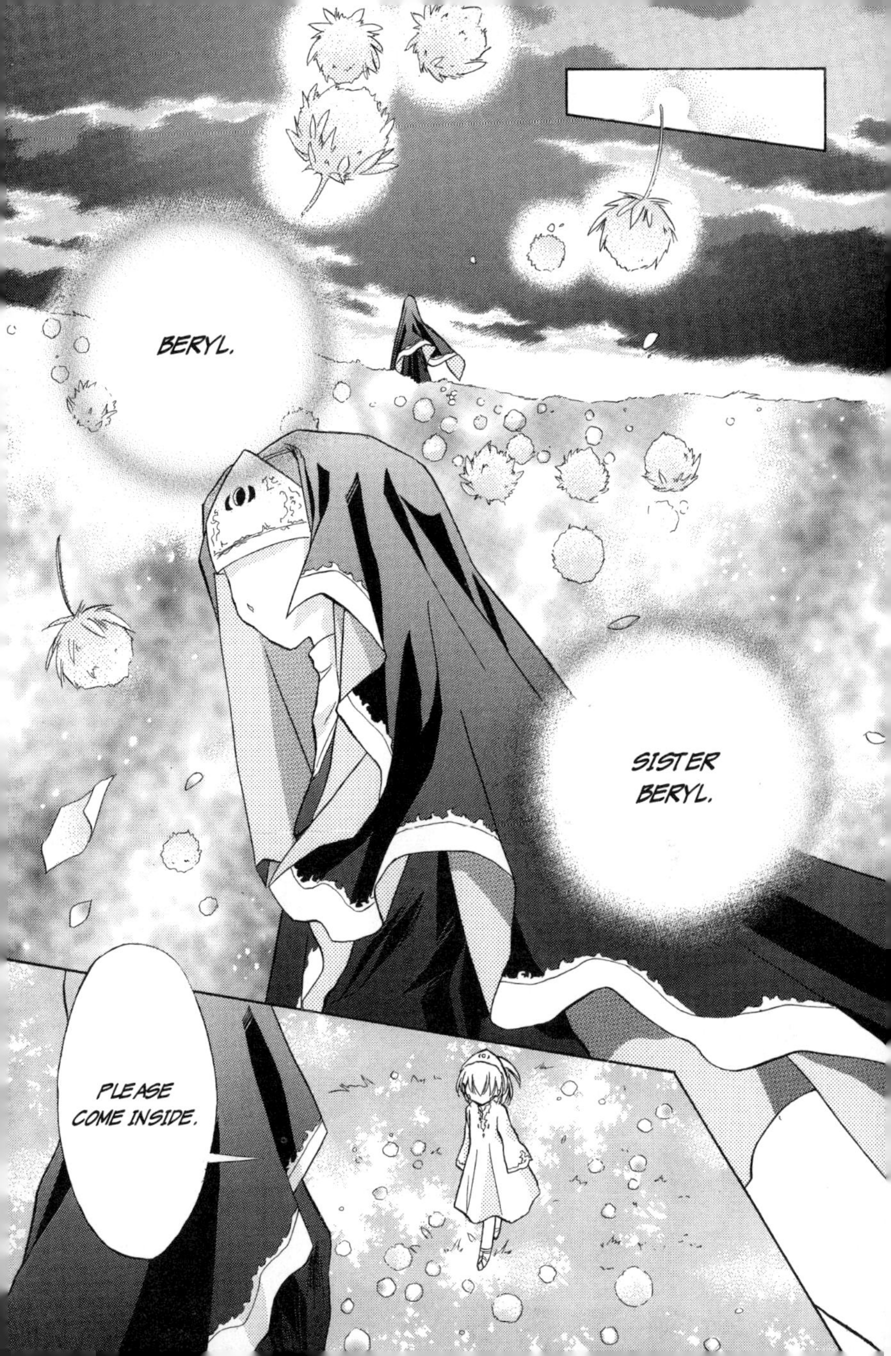
BERYL.
SISTER BERYL.
PLEASE COME INSIDE.

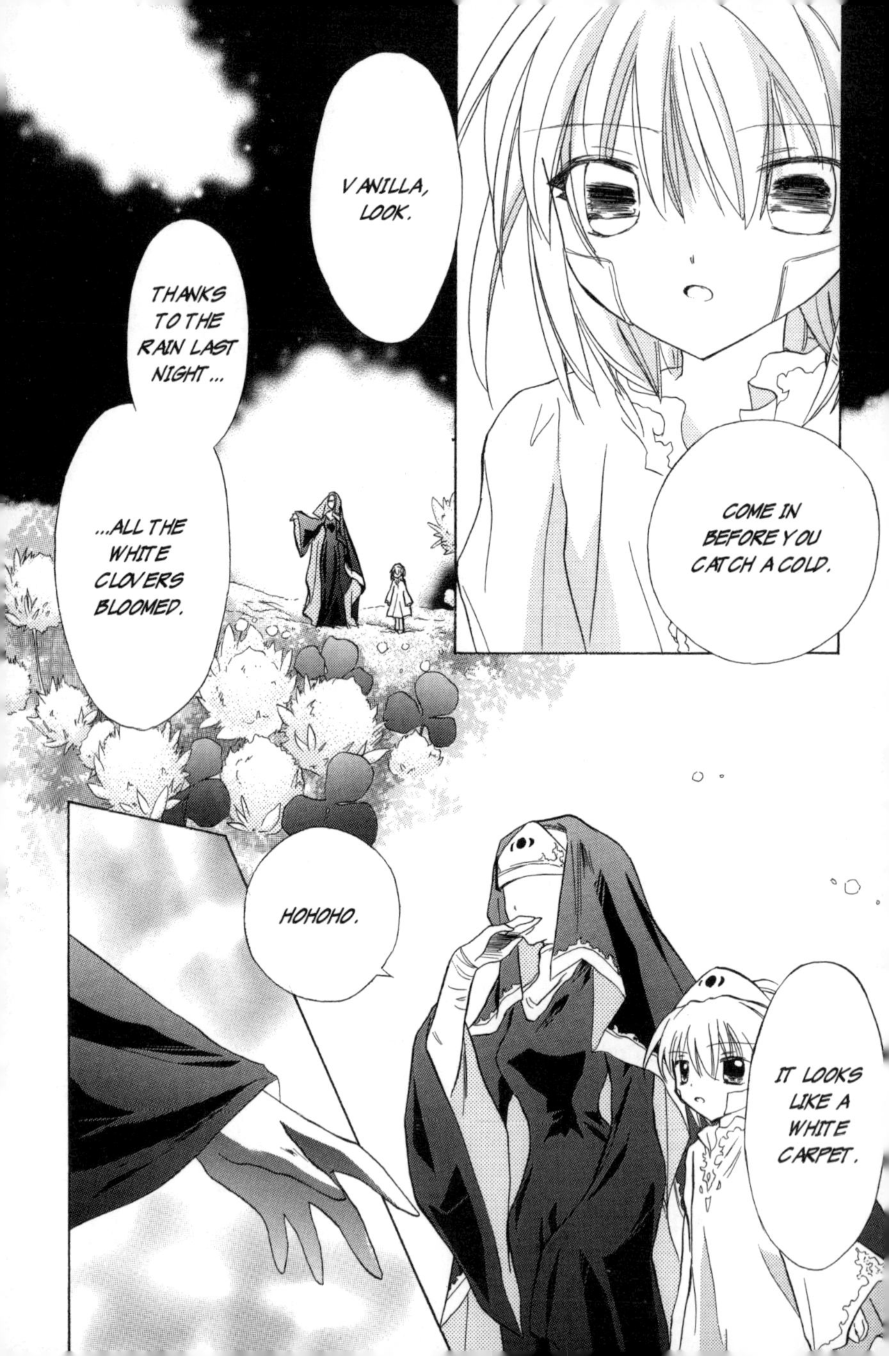
COME IN BEFORE YOU CATCH A COLD.
VANILLA, LOOK.
THANKS TO THE RAIN LAST NIGHT...
...ALL THE WHITE CLOVERS BLOOMED.
IT LOOKS LIKE A WHITE CARPET.
HOHOHO.

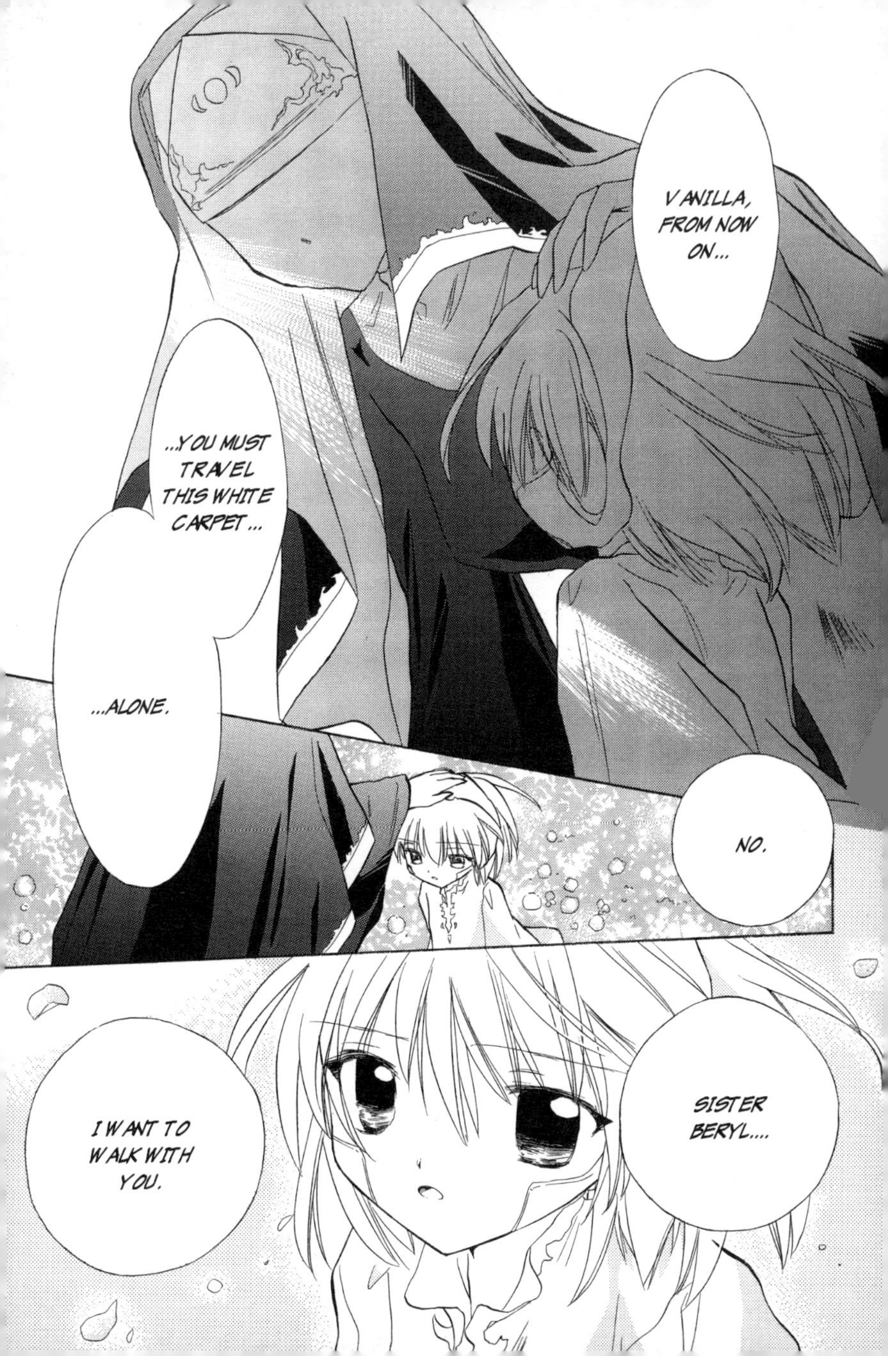
VANILLA, FROM NOW ON...
...YOU MUST TRAVEL THIS WHITE CARPET...
...ALONE.
NO.
SISTER BERYL....
I WANT TO WALK WITH YOU.

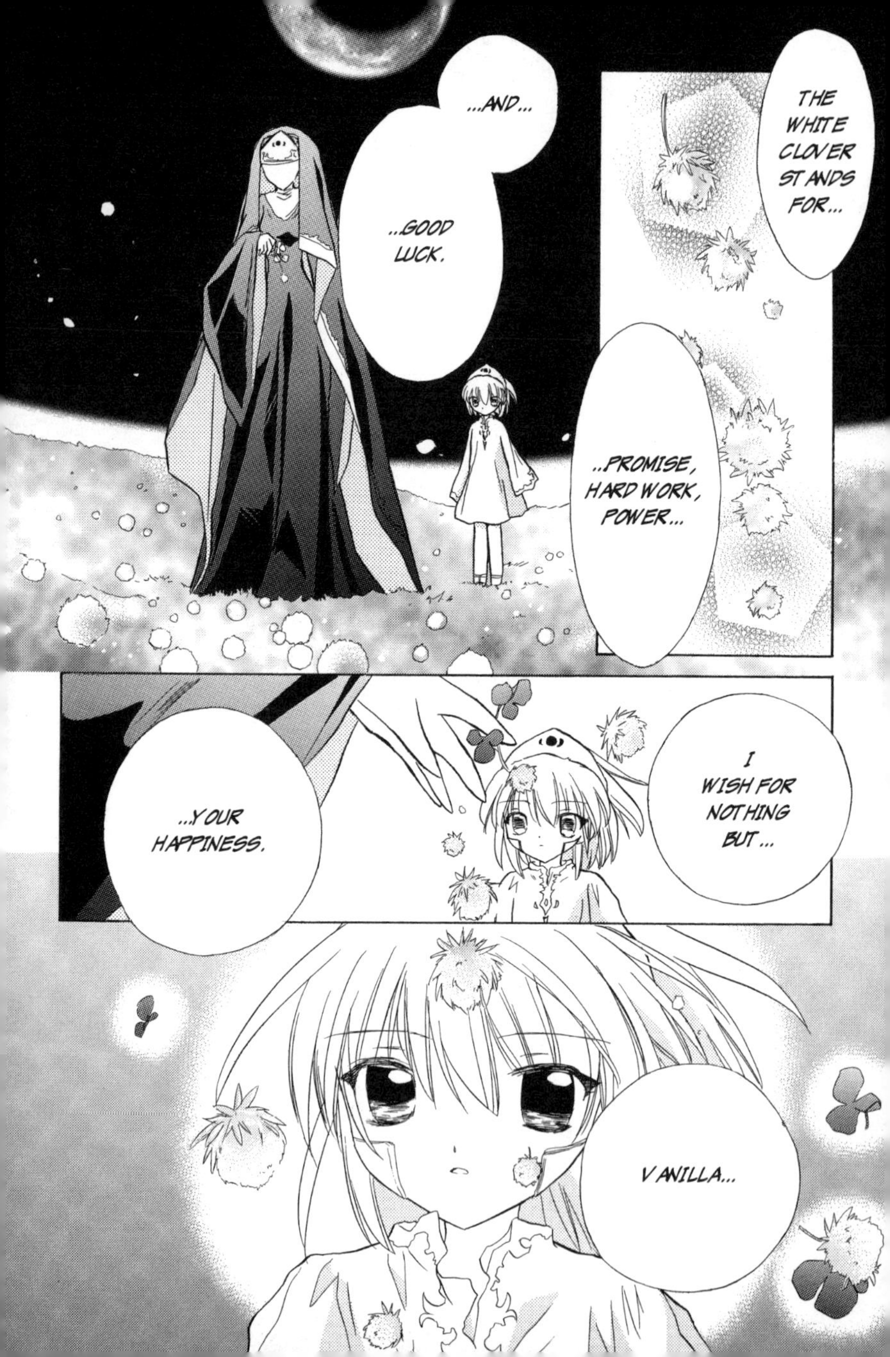
THE WHITE CLOVER STANDS FOR...
...PROMISE, HARD WORK, POWER...
...AND...
...GOOD LUCK.
I WISH FOR NOTHING BUT...
...YOUR HAPPINESS.
VANILLA...

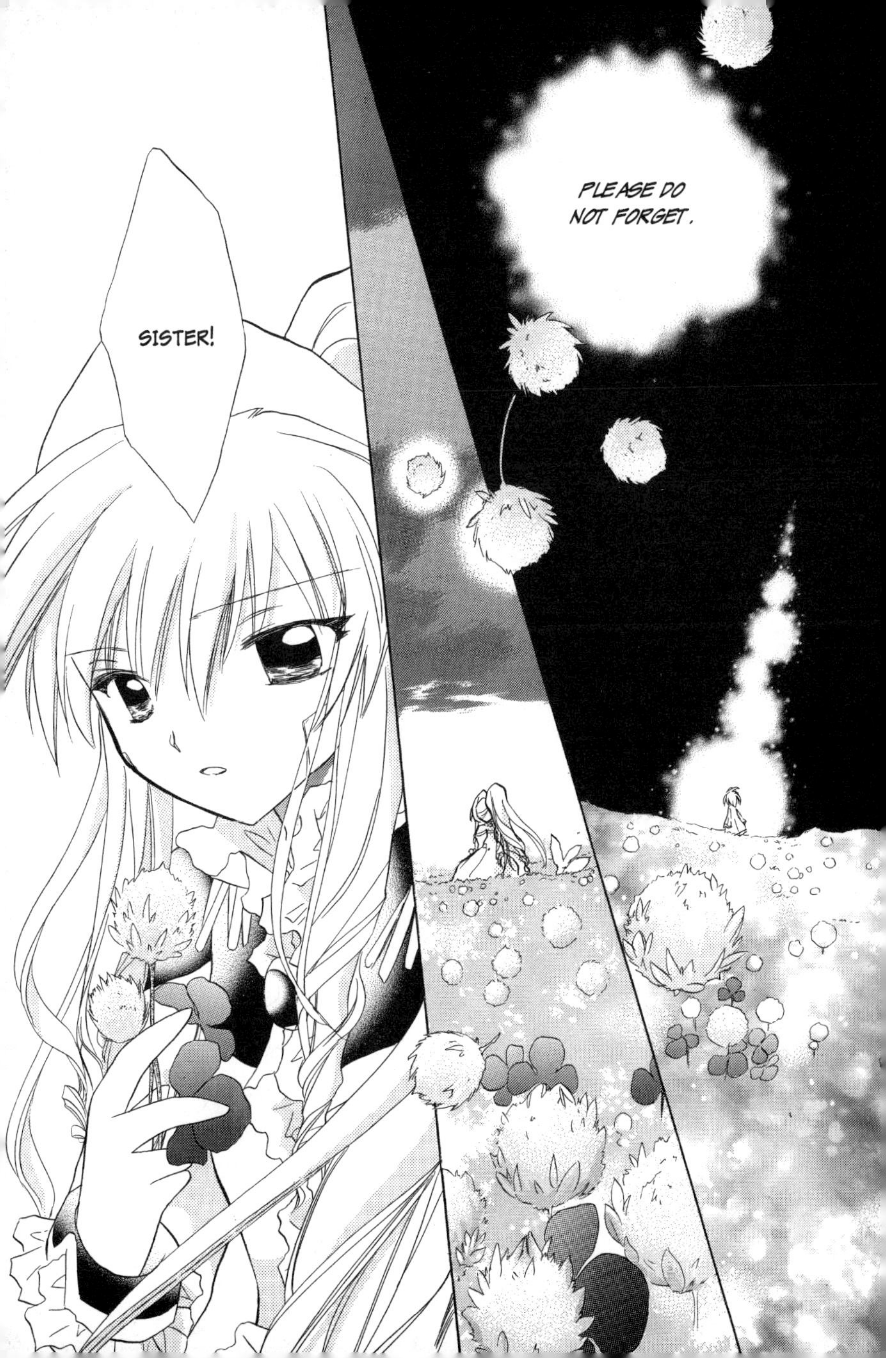
PLEASE DO NOT FORGET.
SISTER!

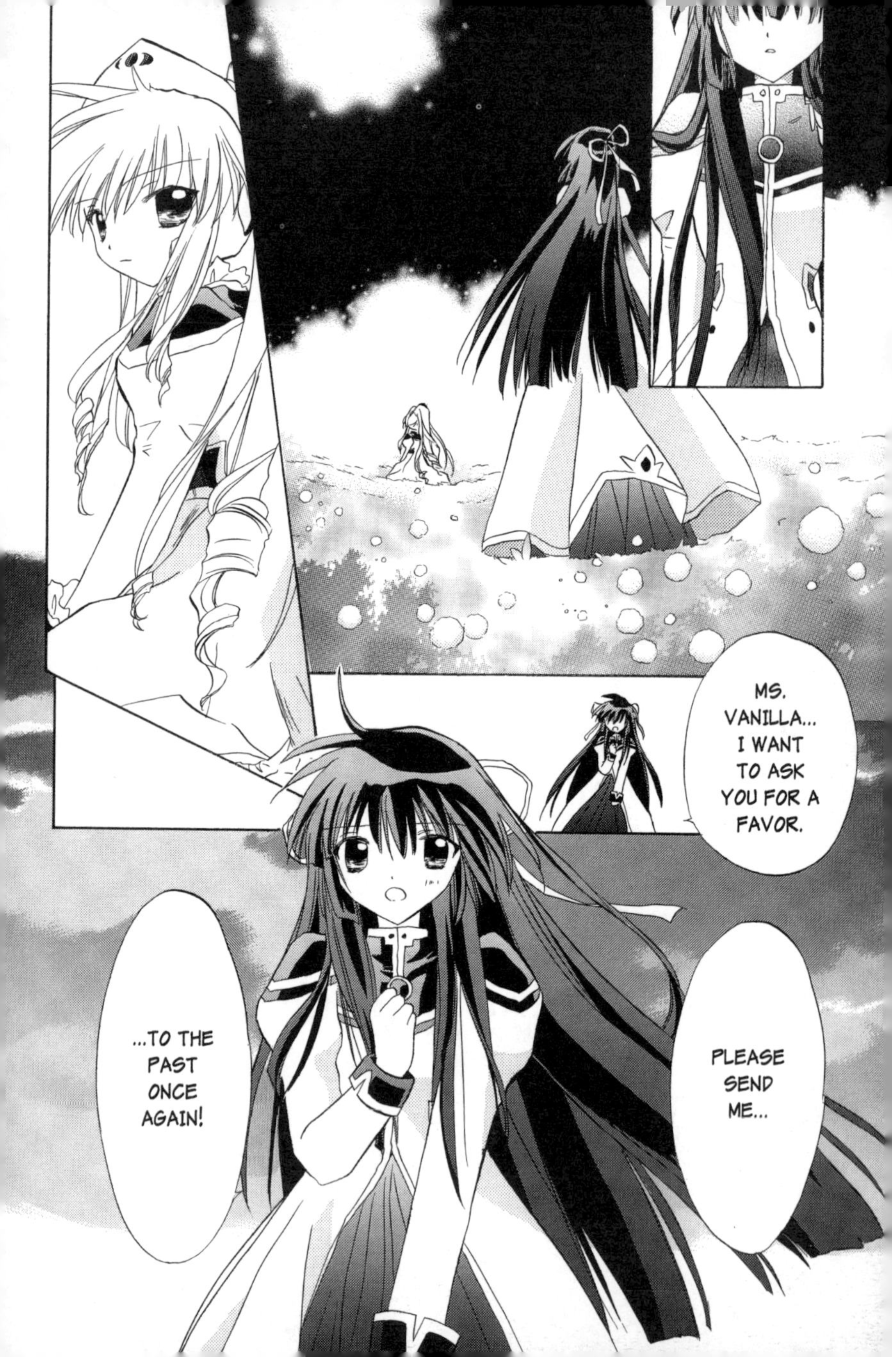
MS. VANILLA... I WANT TO ASK YOU FOR A FAVOR.
PLEASE SEND ME...
...TO THE PAST ONCE AGAIN!

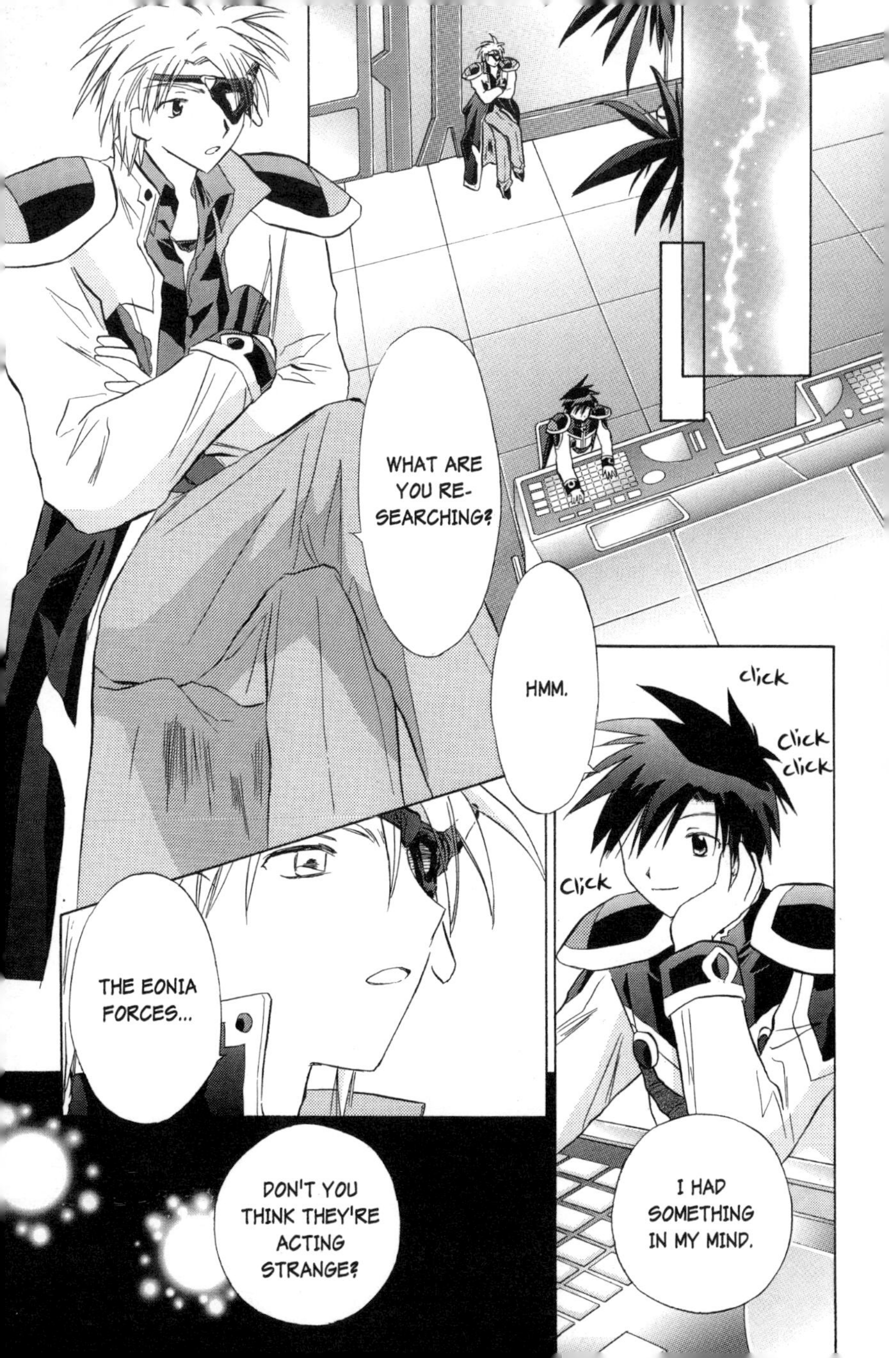
WHAT ARE YOU RE-SEARCHING?
HMM.
click
click
click
click
I HAD SOMETHING IN MY MIND.
THE EONIA FORCES...
DON'T YOU THINK THEY'RE ACTING STRANGE?

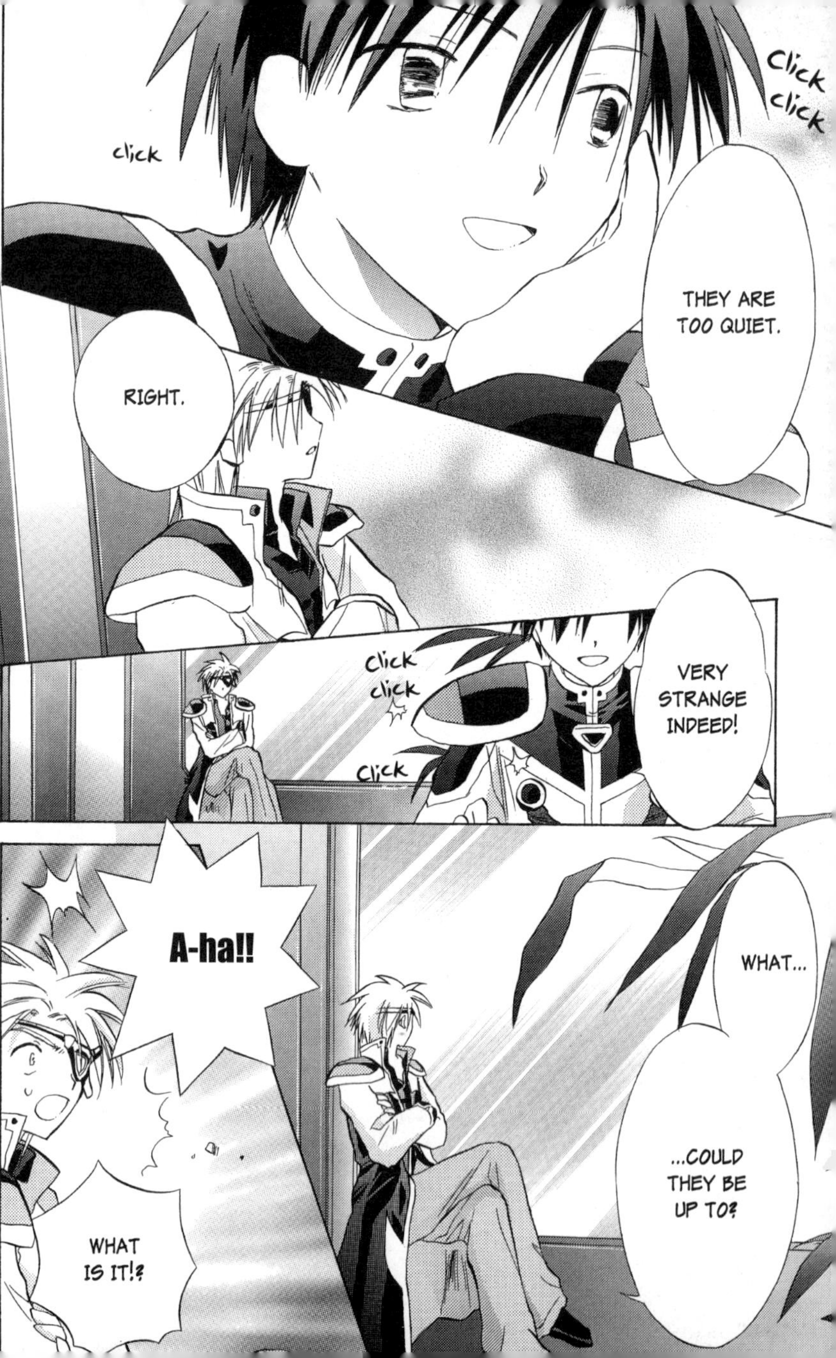
Click
click
THEY ARE TOO QUIET.
click
RIGHT.
VERY STRANGE INDEED!
Click
click
Click
WHAT...
...COULD THEY BE UP TO?
A-ha!!
WHAT IS IT!?

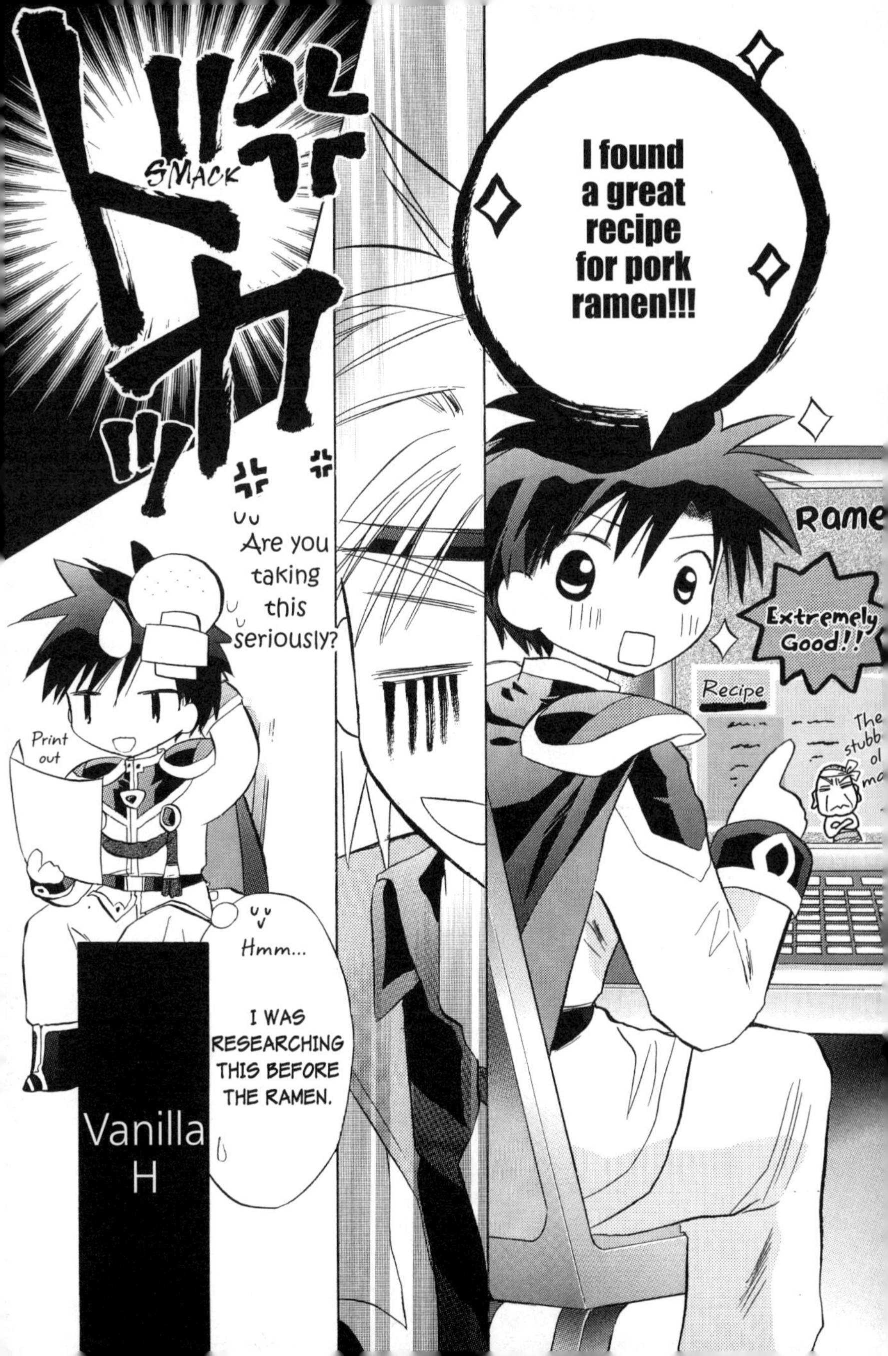
I found a great recipe for pork ramen!!!
Rame
Extremely Good!!
Recipe
The
SMACK
Are you taking this seriously?
Print out
Hmm...
I WAS RESEARCHING THIS BEFORE THE RAMEN.
Vanilla H

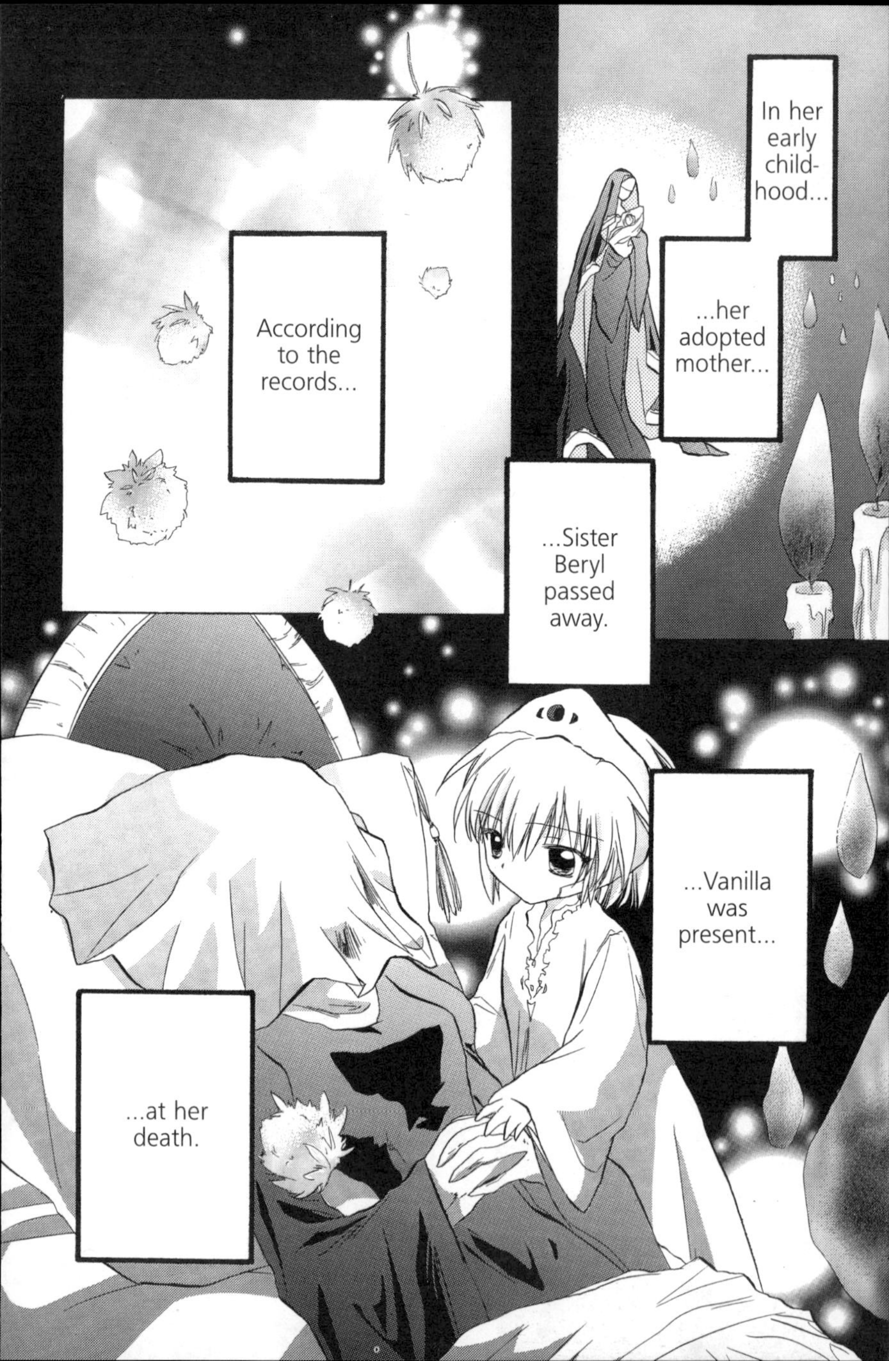
In her early childhood...
...her adopted mother...
...Sister Beryl passed away.
According to the records...
...Vanilla was present...
...at her death.

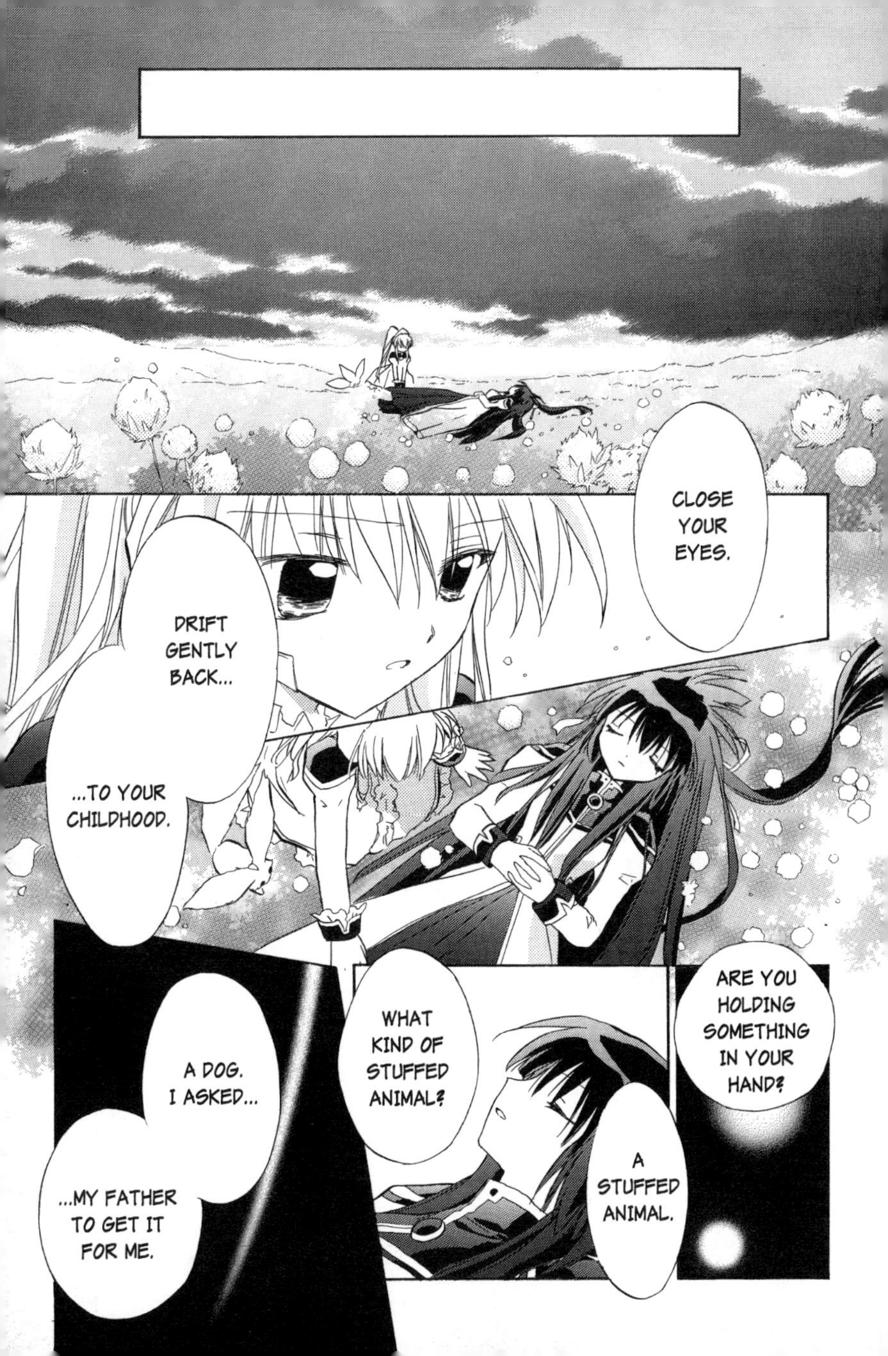

CLOSE YOUR EYES.
DRIFT GENTLY BACK...
...TO YOUR CHILDHOOD.
ARE YOU HOLDING SOMETHING IN YOUR HAND?
A STUFFED ANIMAL.
WHAT KIND OF STUFFED ANIMAL?
A DOG. I ASKED...
...MY FATHER TO GET IT FOR ME.

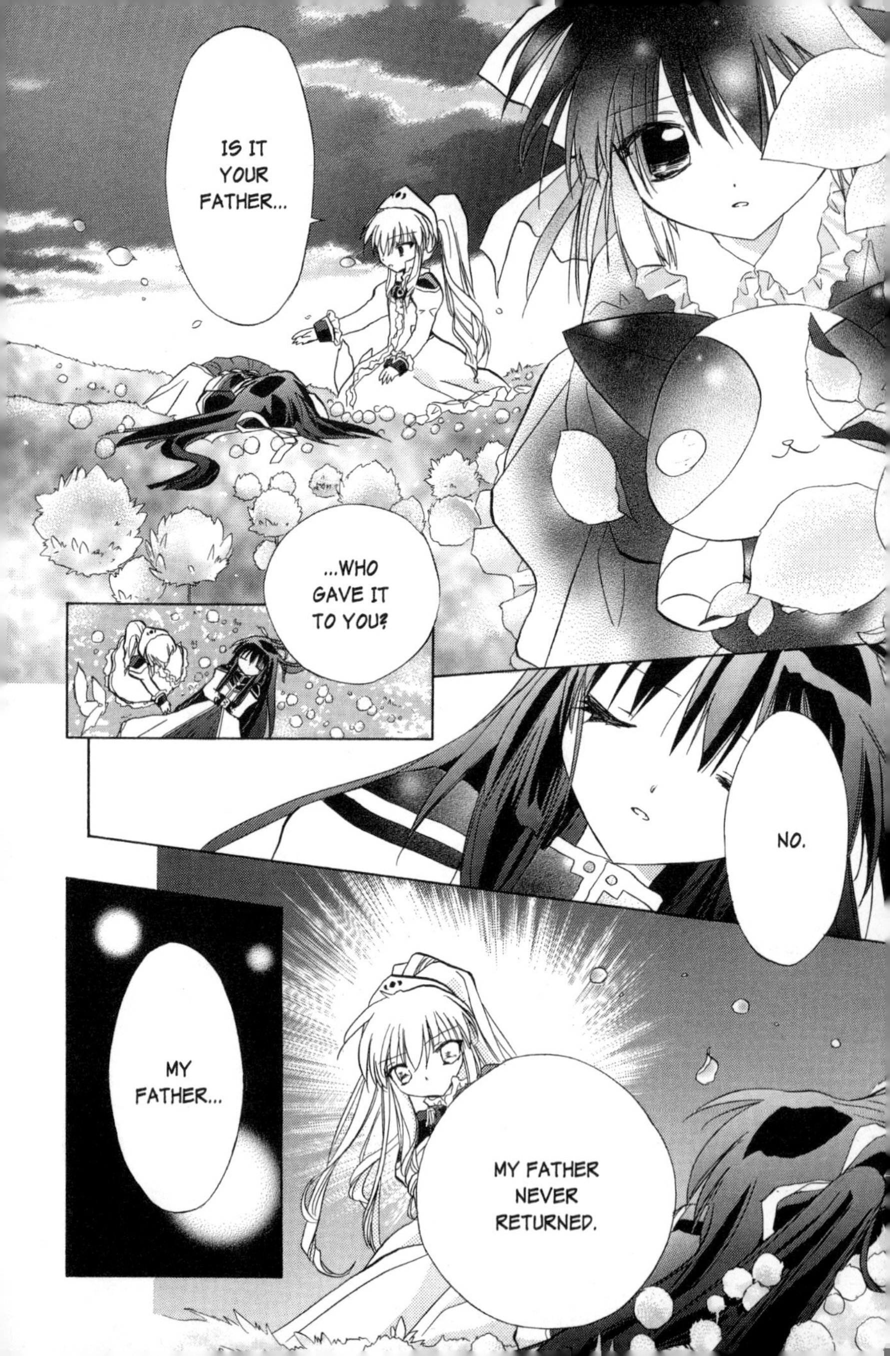
IS IT YOUR FATHER...
...WHO GAVE IT TO YOU?
NO.
MY FATHER...
MY FATHER NEVER RETURNED.

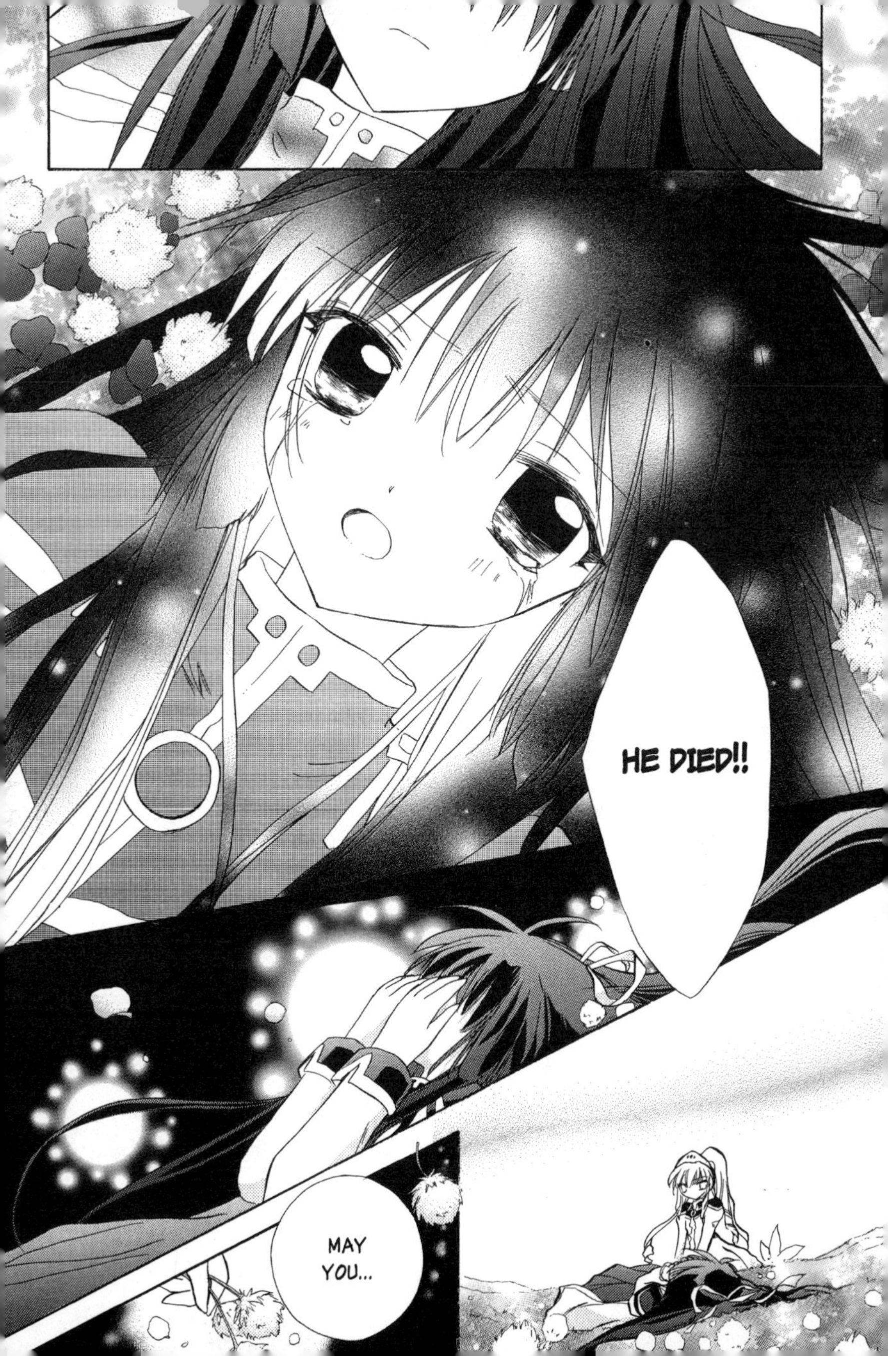
HE DIED!!
MAY YOU...

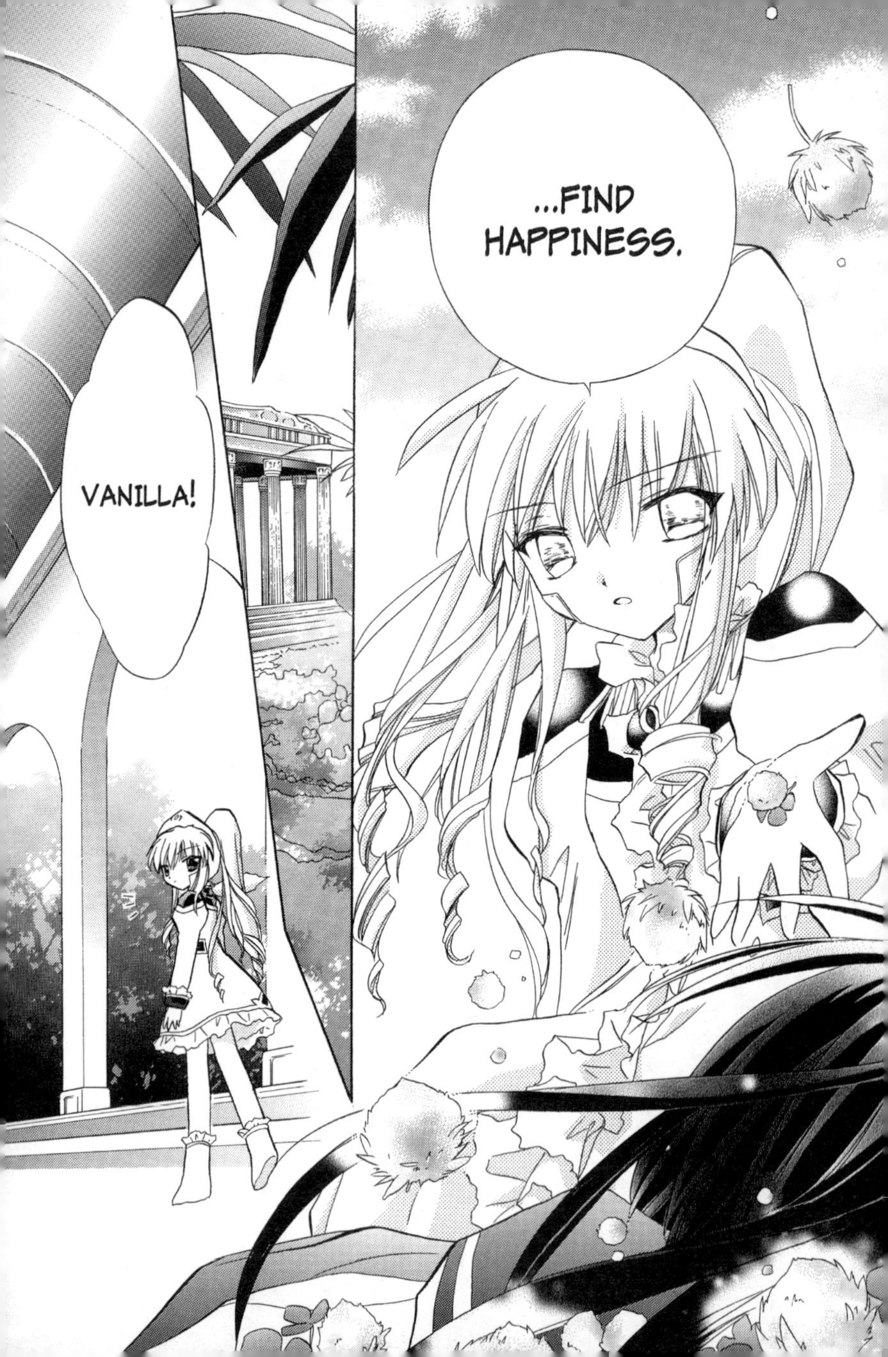
...FIND HAPPINESS.
VANILLA!

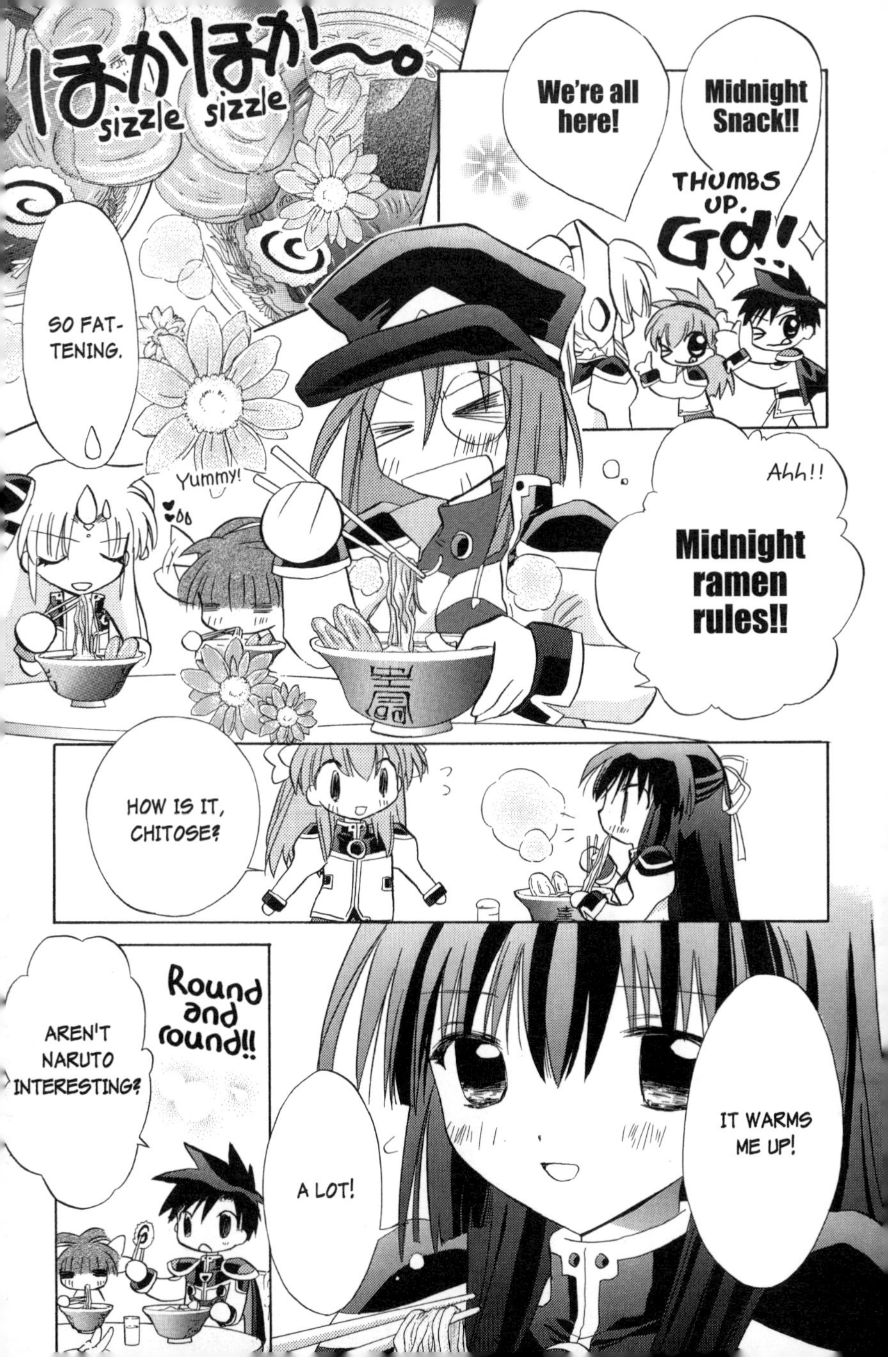
Midnight Snack!!
We're all here!
THUMBS UP. GO!!
Ahh!!
Midnight ramen rules!!
ほかほか～。
sizzle sizzle
SO FAT-TENING.
Yummy!
HOW IS IT, CHITOSE?
IT WARMS ME UP!
A LOT!
Round and round!!
AREN'T NARUTO INTERESTING?

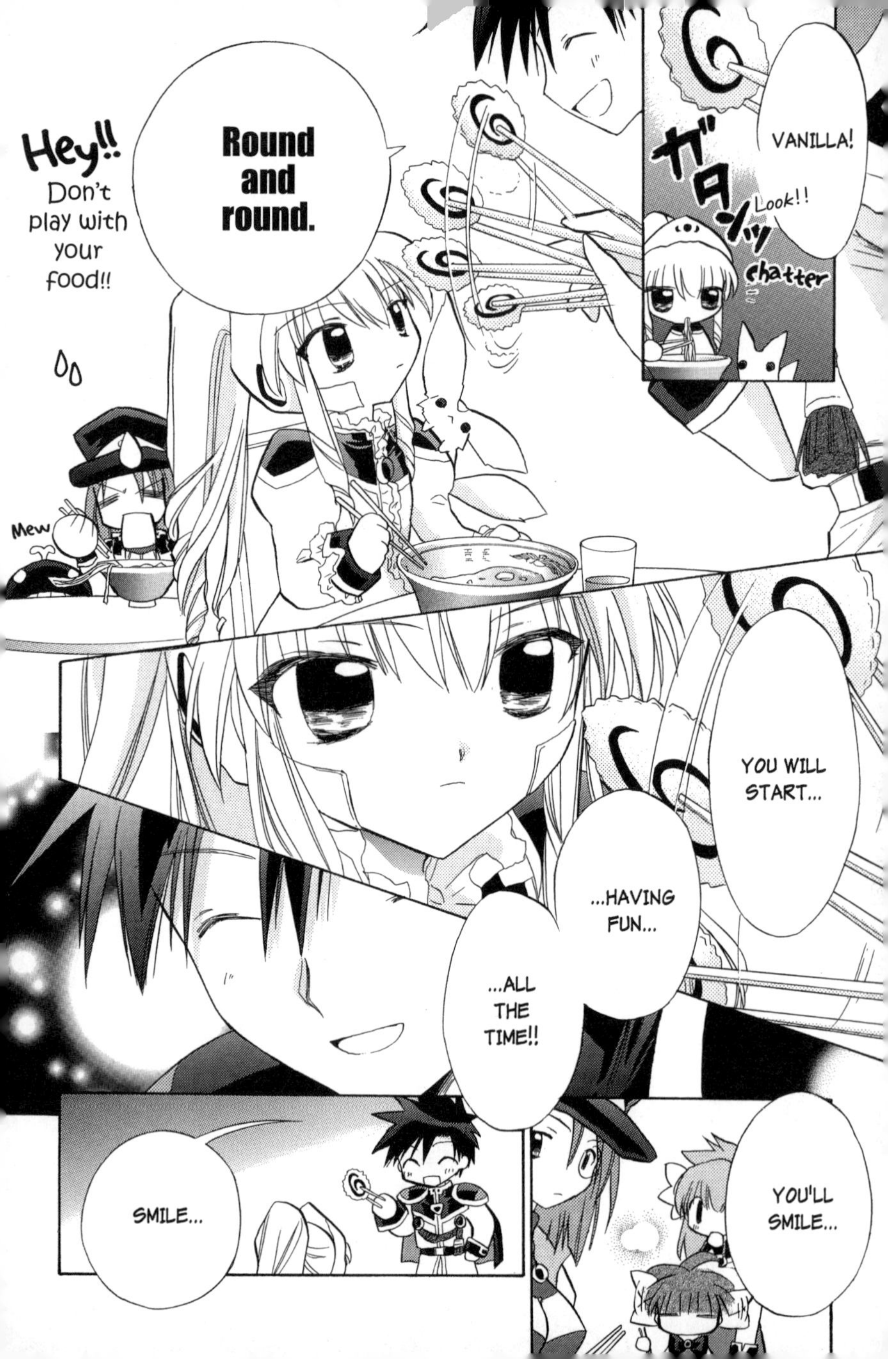

VANILLA!
Look!!
ガタッ
chatter
Round and round.
Hey!! Don't play with your food!!
Mew
YOU WILL START...
...HAVING FUN...
...ALL THE TIME!!
YOU'LL SMILE...
SMILE...

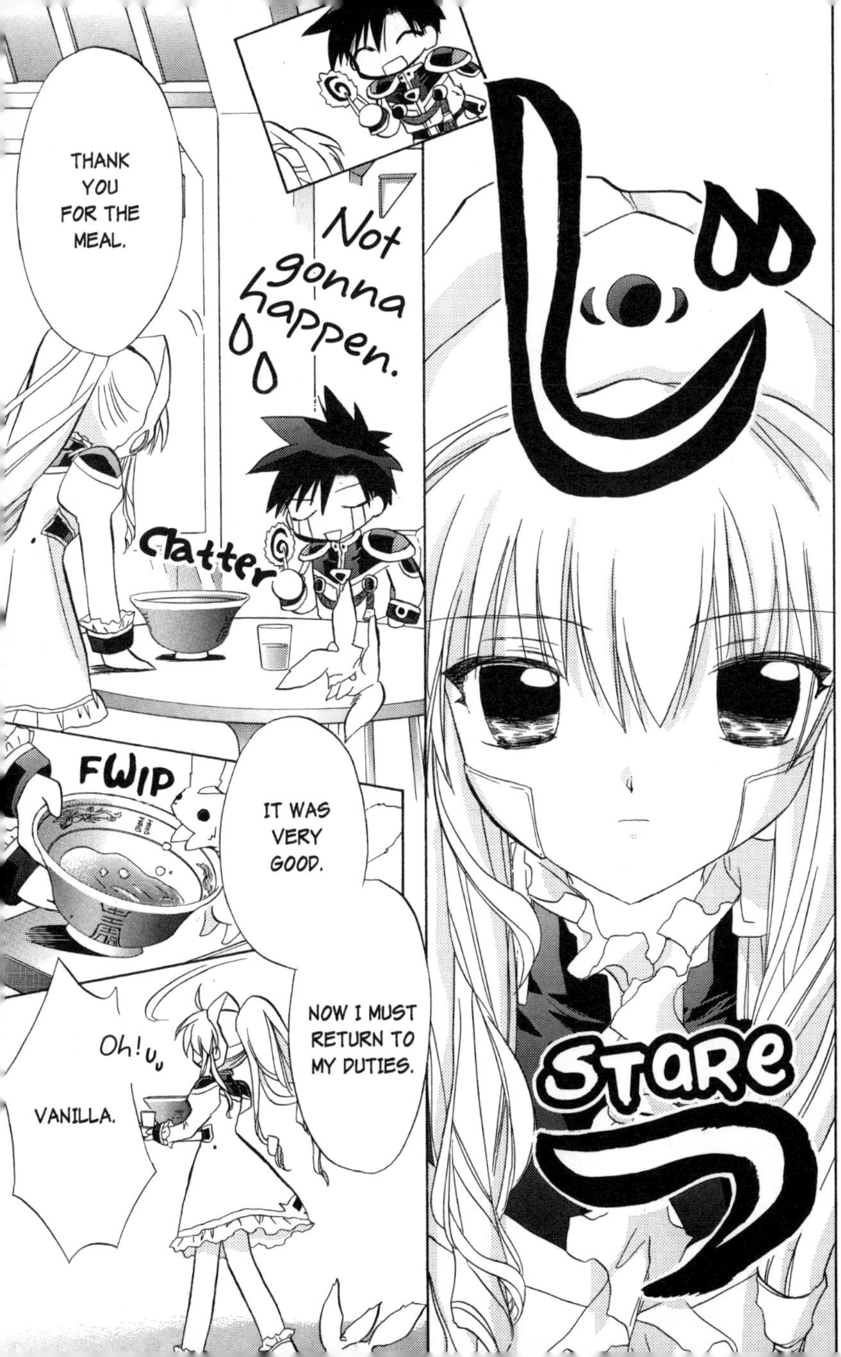
STARE
Not gonna happen.
THANK YOU FOR THE MEAL.
Clatter
IT WAS VERY GOOD.
FWIP
NOW I MUST RETURN TO MY DUTIES.
Oh!
VANILLA.

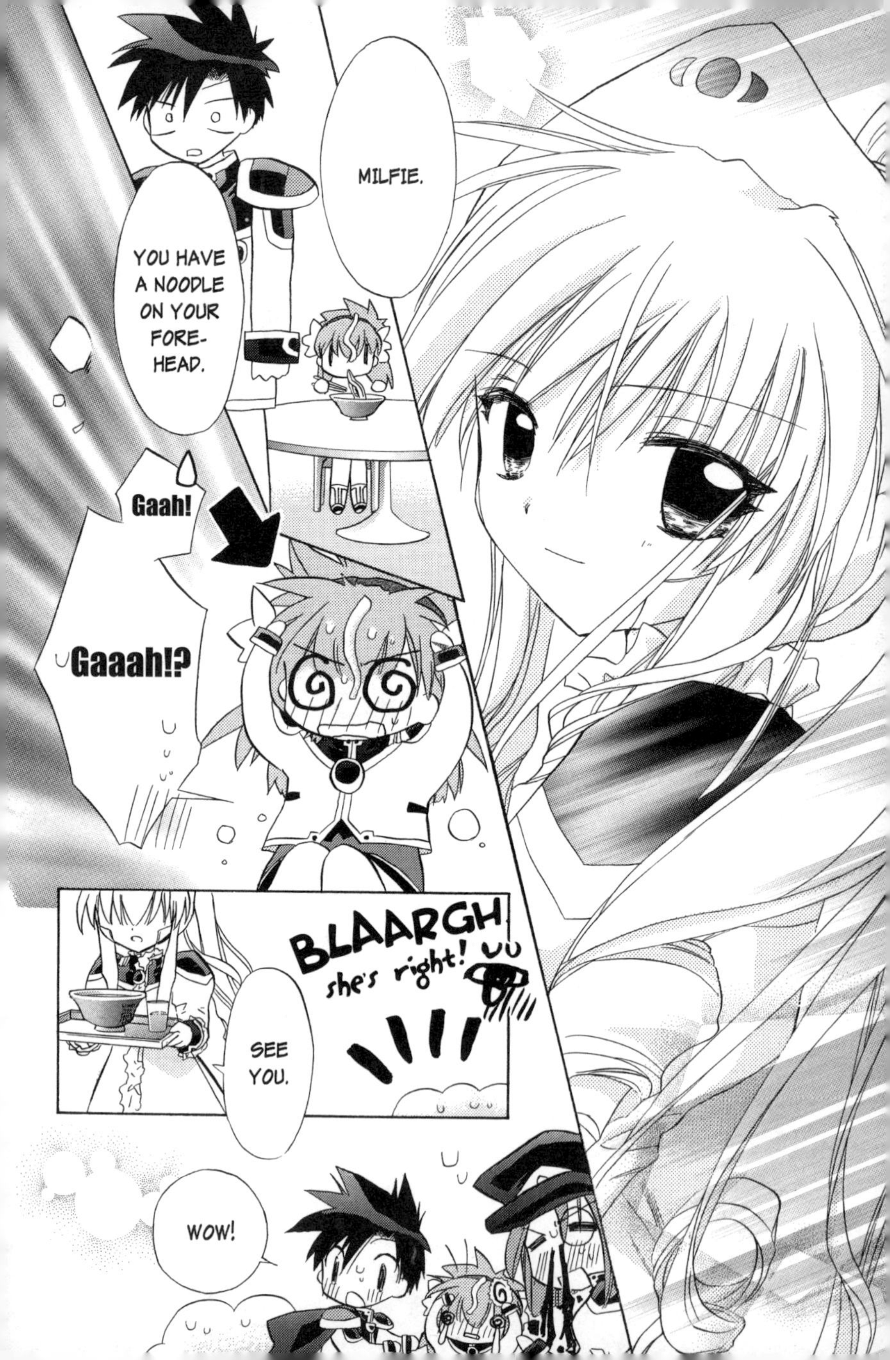

MILFIE.
YOU HAVE A NOODLE ON YOUR FORE-HEAD.
Gaah!
Gaaah!?
BLAARGH
she's right!
SEE YOU.
WOW!

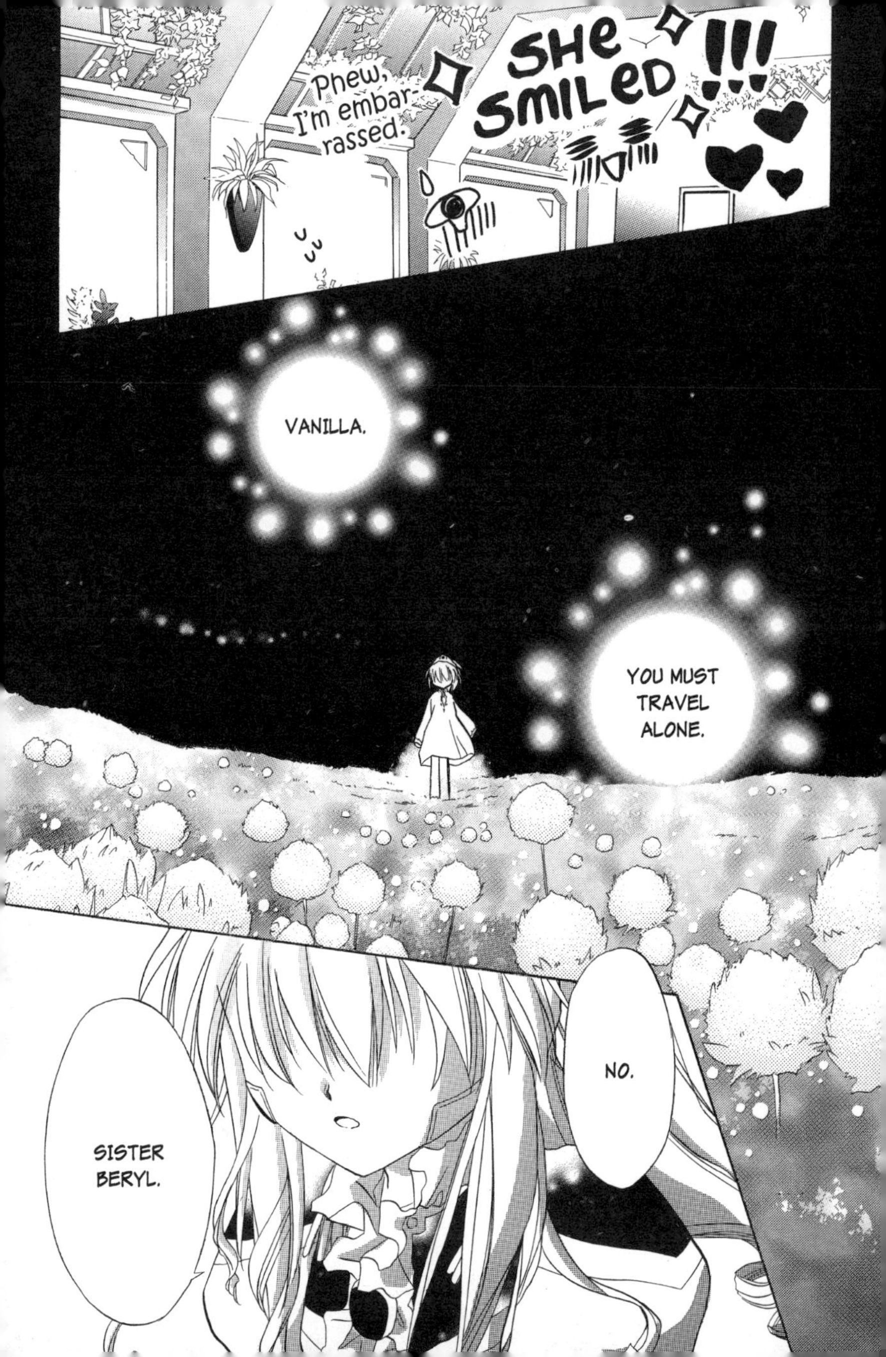
SHE SMILED!!!
Phew, I'm embarrassed.
VANILLA.
YOU MUST TRAVEL ALONE.
NO.
SISTER BERYL.

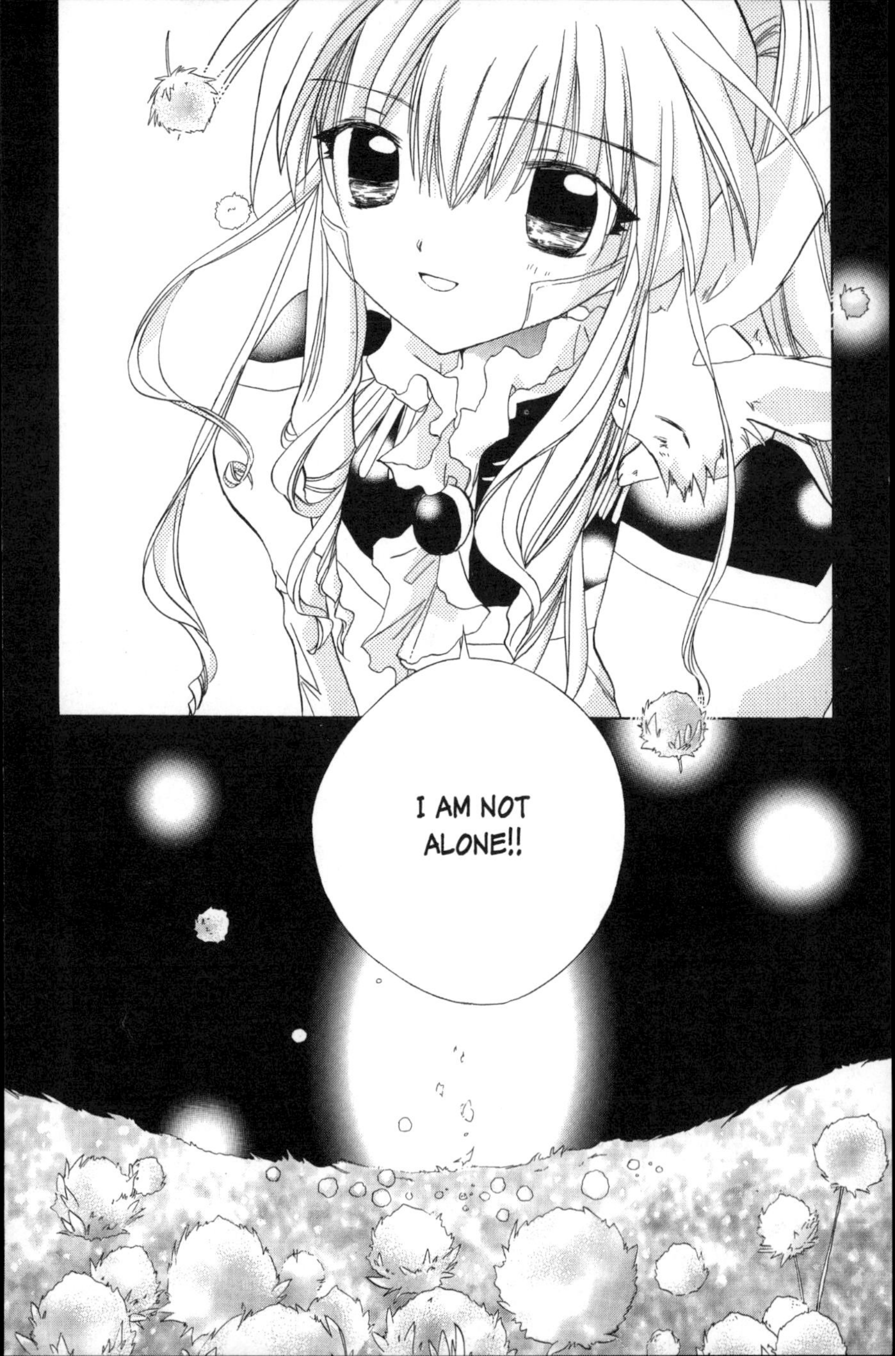
I AM NOT ALONE!!

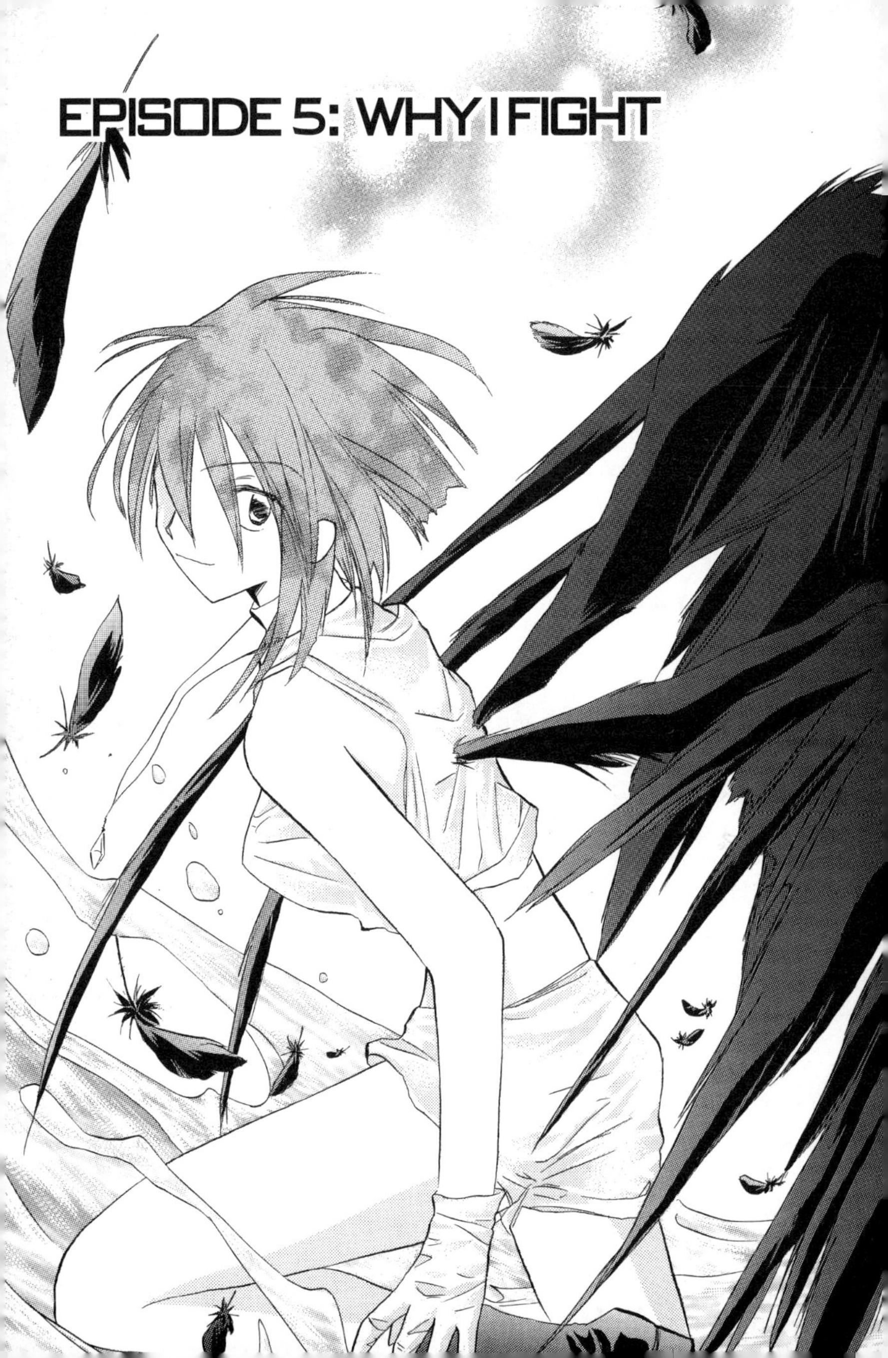
EPISODE 5: WHY I FIGHT

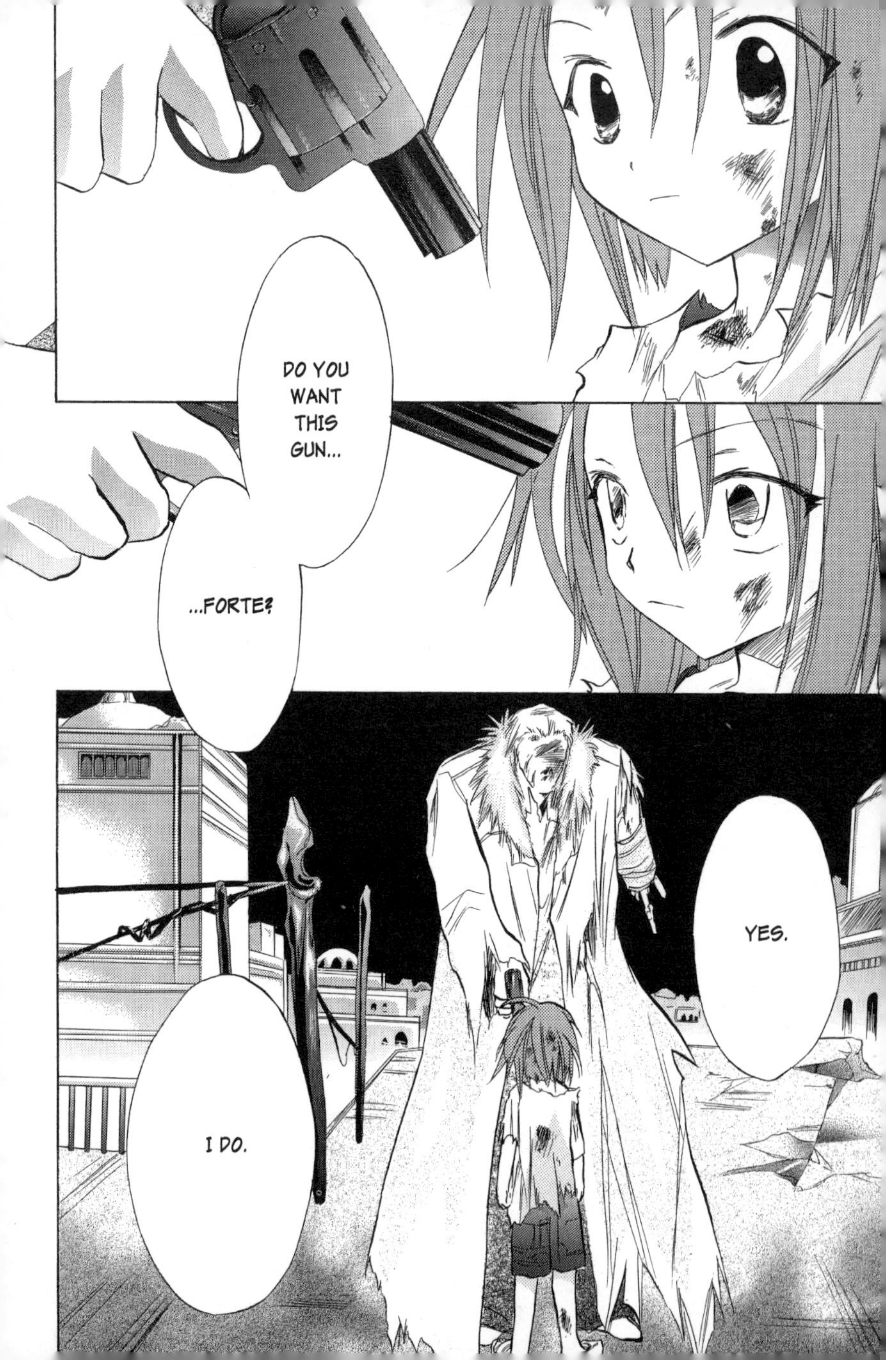
DO YOU WANT THIS GUN...
...FORTE?
YES.
I DO.

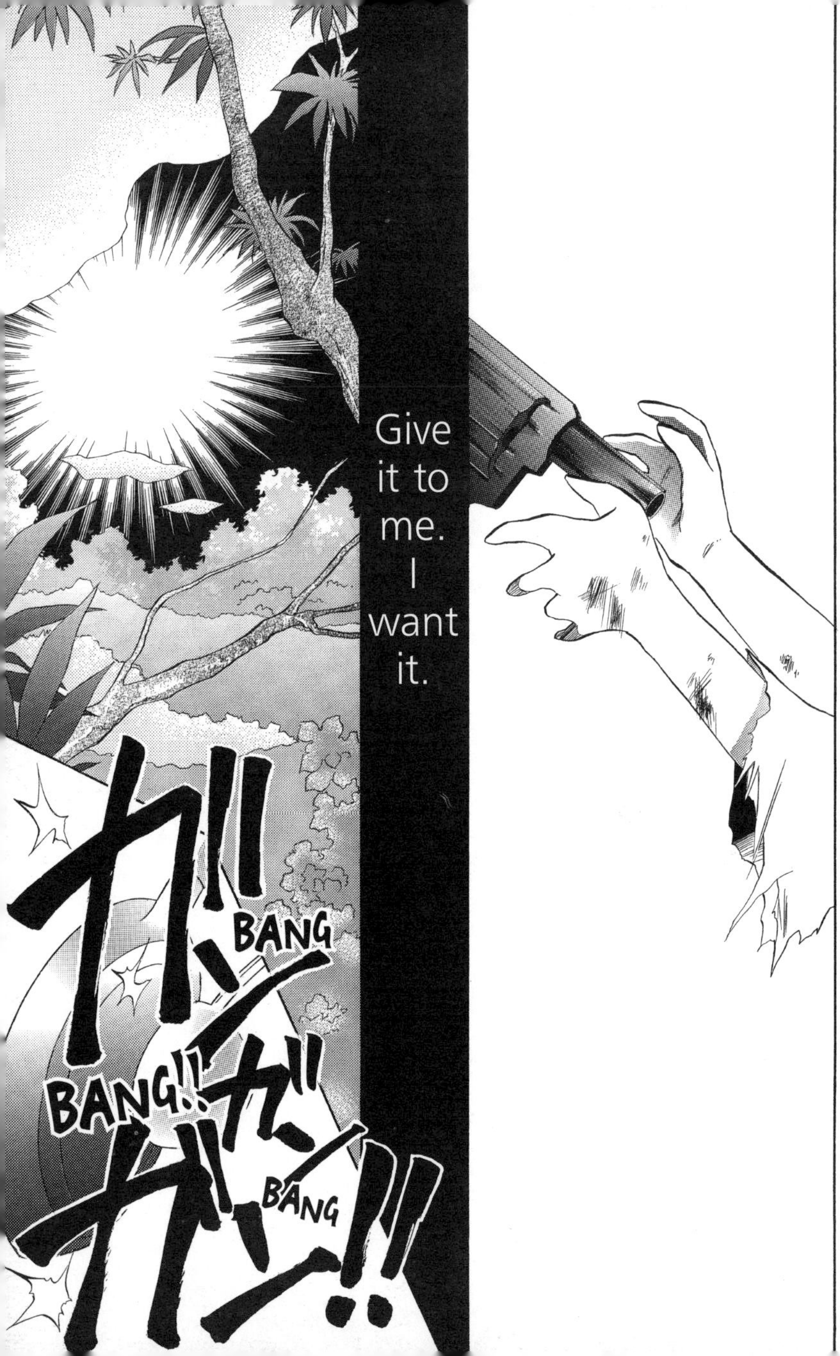
Give it to me. I want it.
BANG
BANG!!
BANG

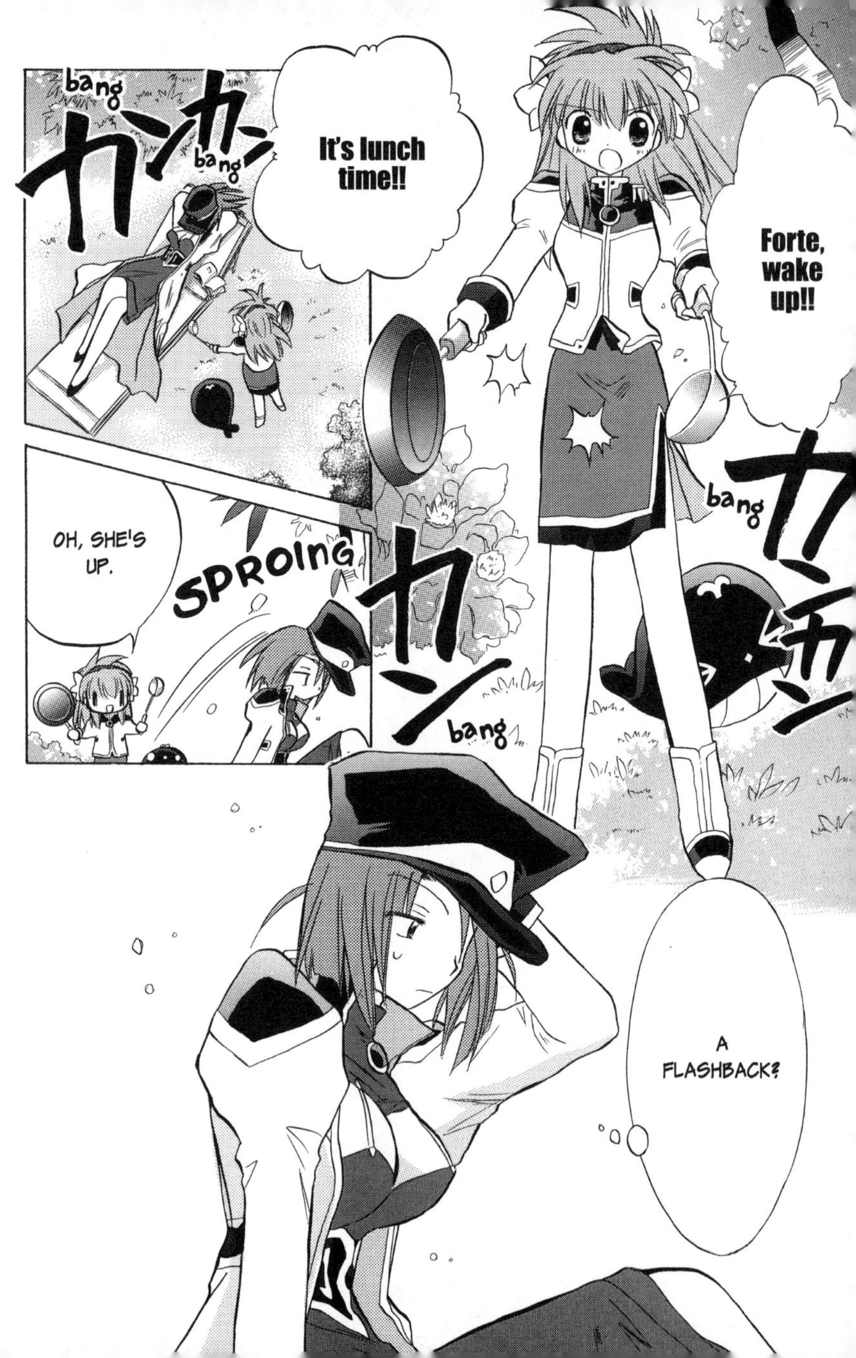
Forte, wake up!!
bang
bang
bang
It's lunch time!!
bang
SPROING
OH, SHE'S UP.
A FLASHBACK?

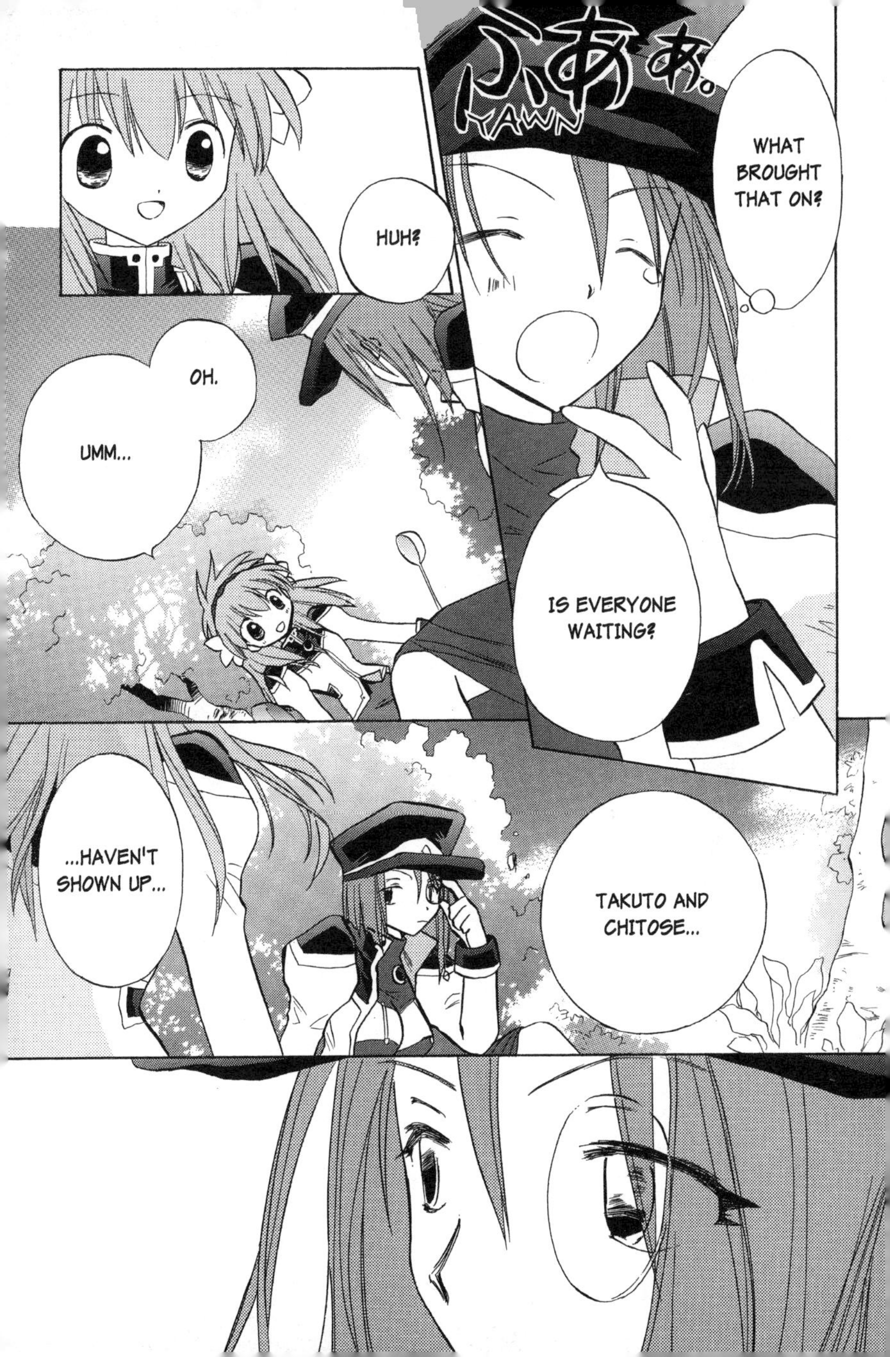
ふあぁ。
YAWN
WHAT BROUGHT THAT ON?
IS EVERYONE WAITING?
HUH?
OH.
UMM...
TAKUTO AND CHITOSE...
...HAVEN'T SHOWN UP...

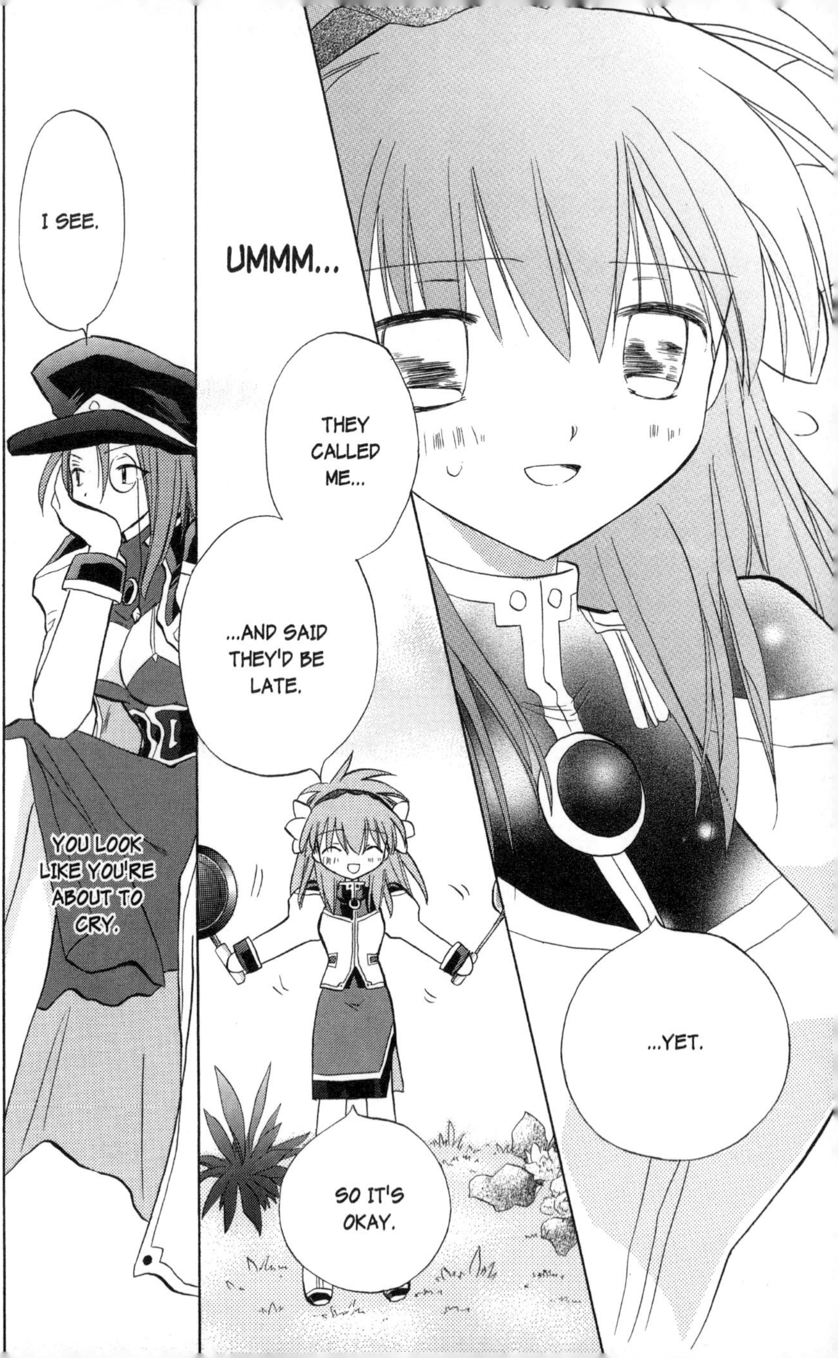
UMMM...
THEY CALLED ME...
...AND SAID THEY'D BE LATE.
...YET.
SO IT'S OKAY.
I SEE.
YOU LOOK LIKE YOU'RE ABOUT TO CRY.

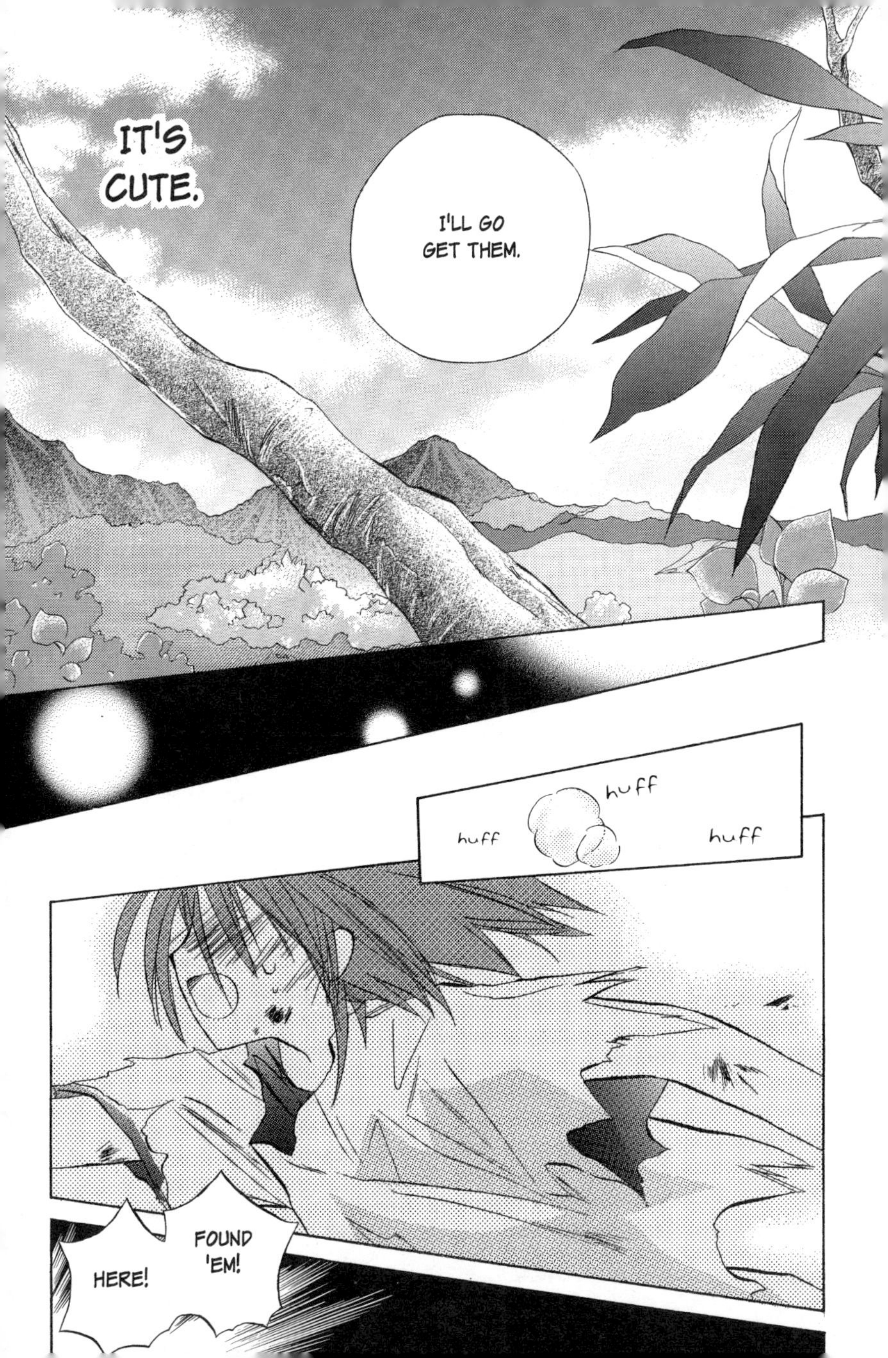
I'LL GO GET THEM.
IT'S CUTE.
huff
huff
huff
FOUND 'EM!
HERE!

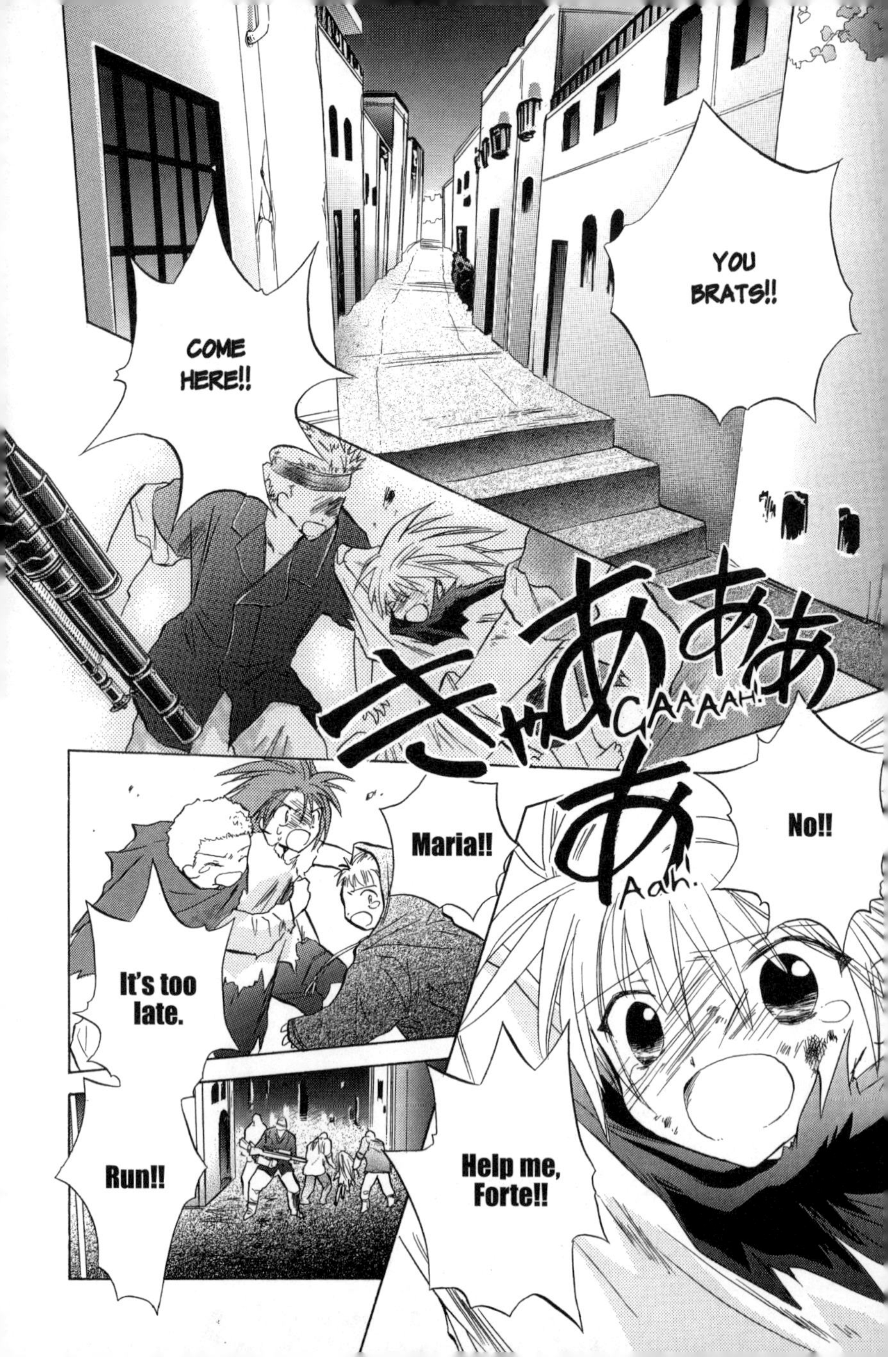
YOU BRATS!!
COME HERE!!
きゃあああ
CAAAAH!
あ
Aah.
No!!
Help me, Forte!!
Maria!!
It's too late.
Run!!

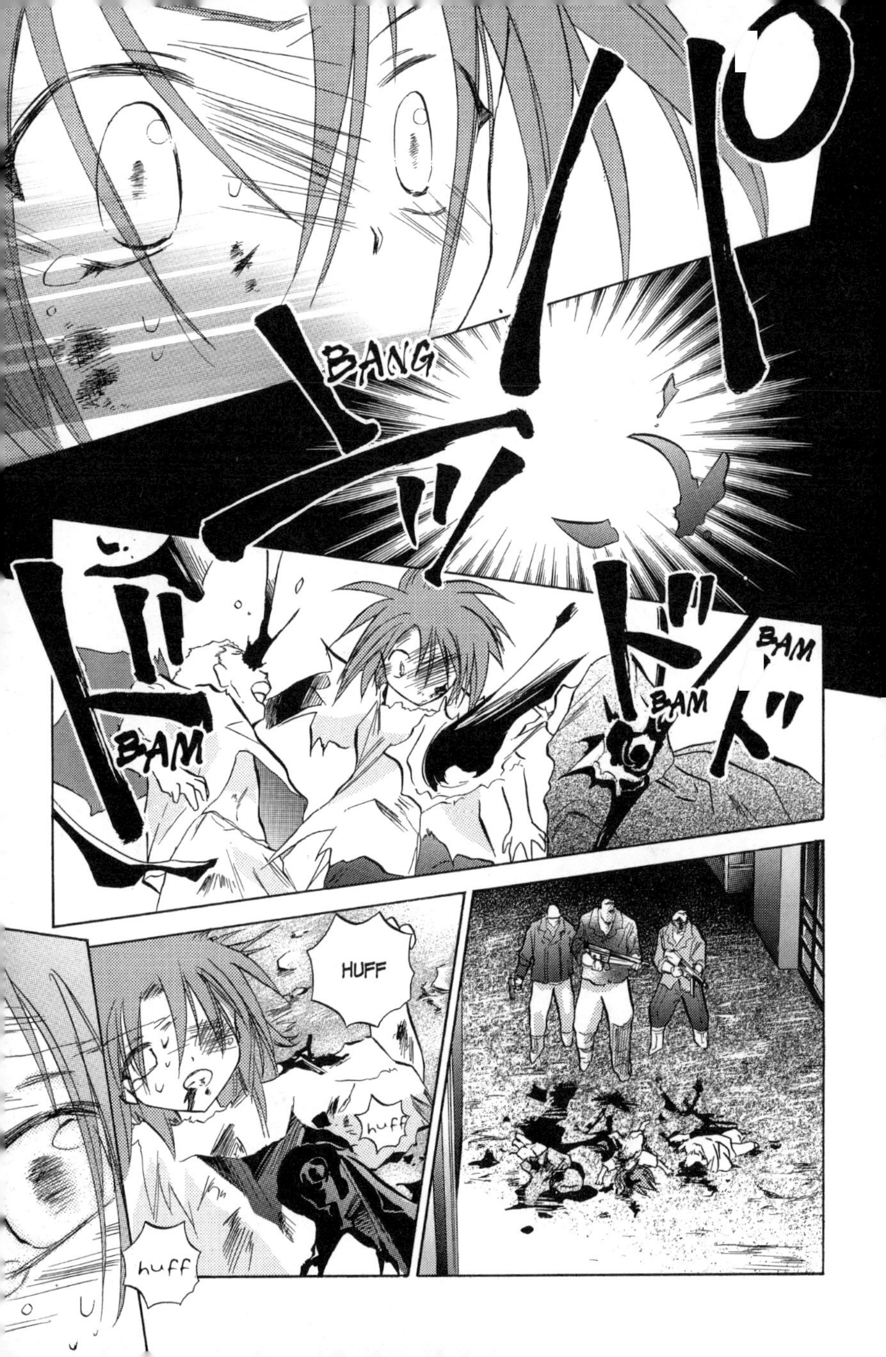
BANG
BAM
BAM
BAM
HUFF
huff
huff

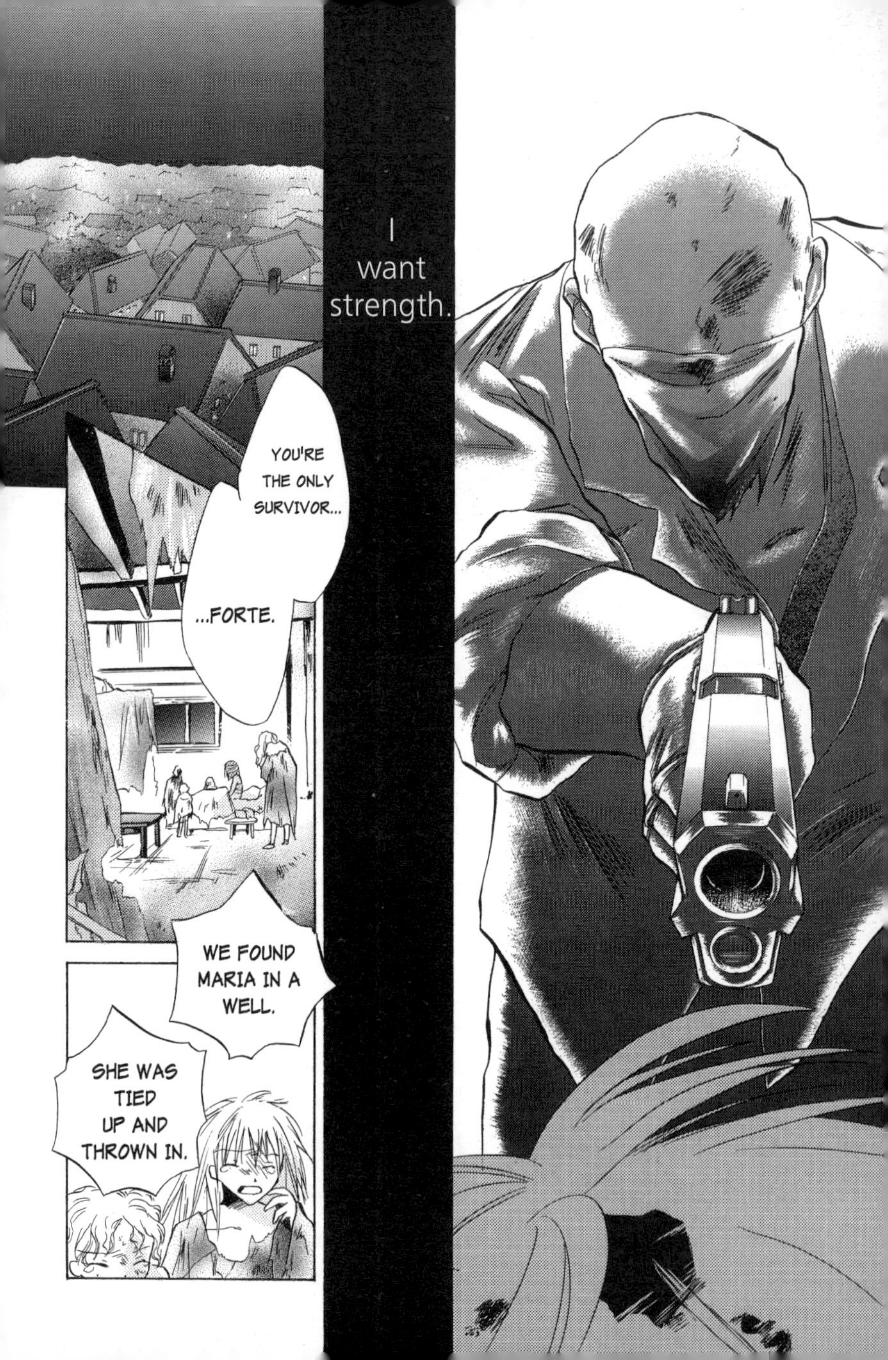
I want strength.
YOU'RE THE ONLY SURVIVOR...
...FORTE.
WE FOUND MARIA IN A WELL.
SHE WAS TIED UP AND THROWN IN.

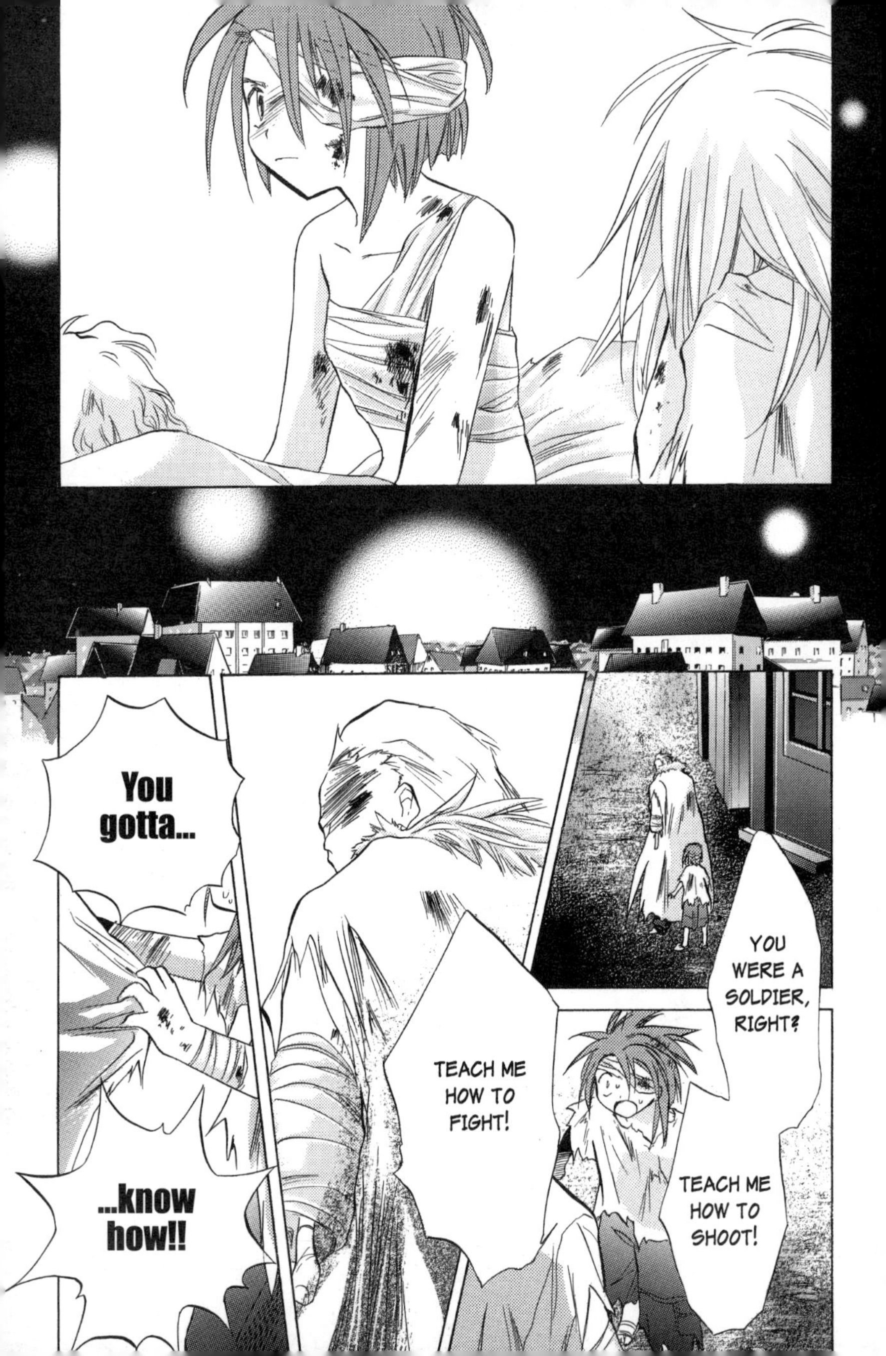
YOU WERE A SOLDIER, RIGHT?
TEACH ME HOW TO FIGHT!
TEACH ME HOW TO SHOOT!
You gotta...
...know how!!

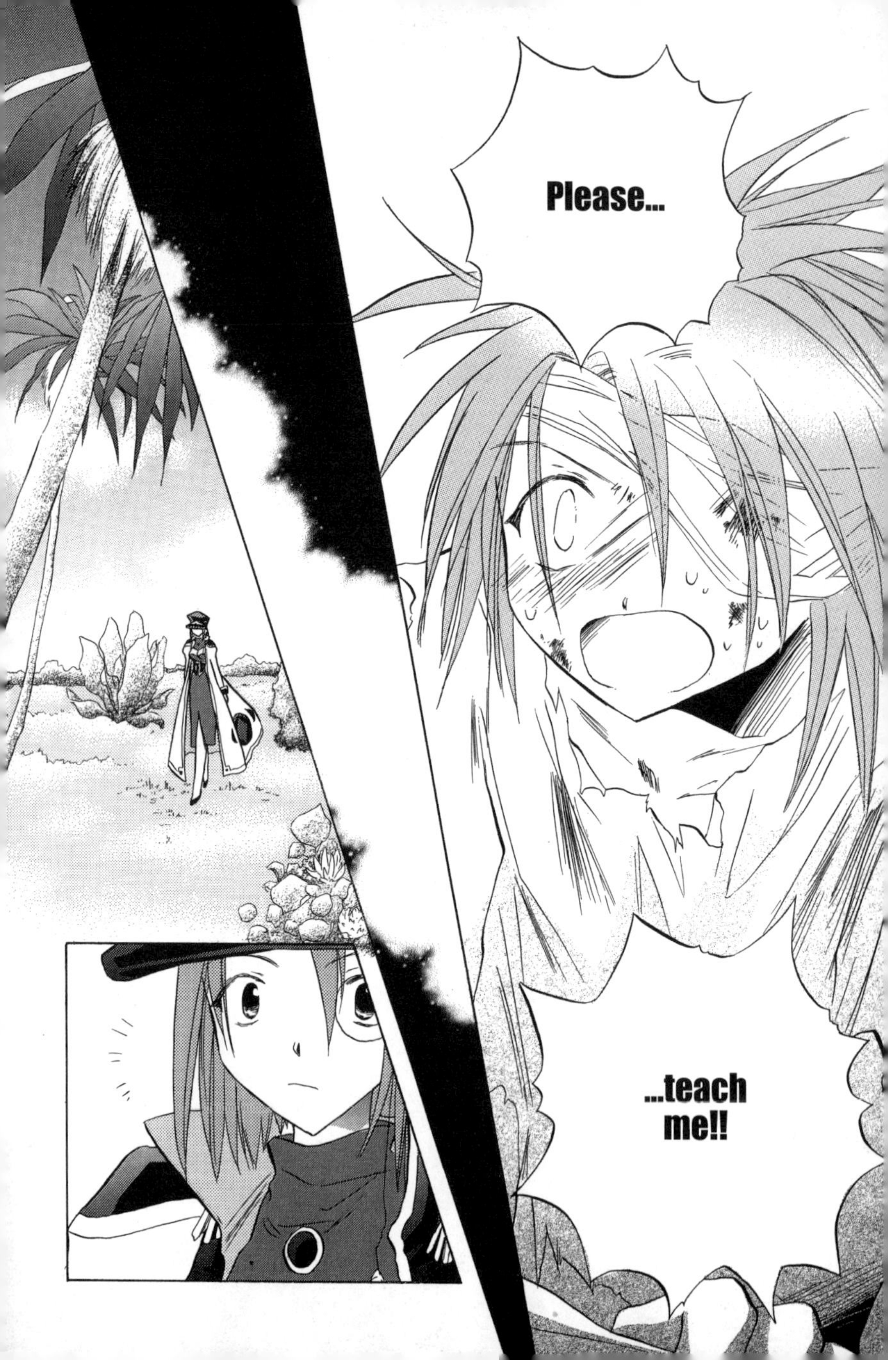
Please...
...teach me!!

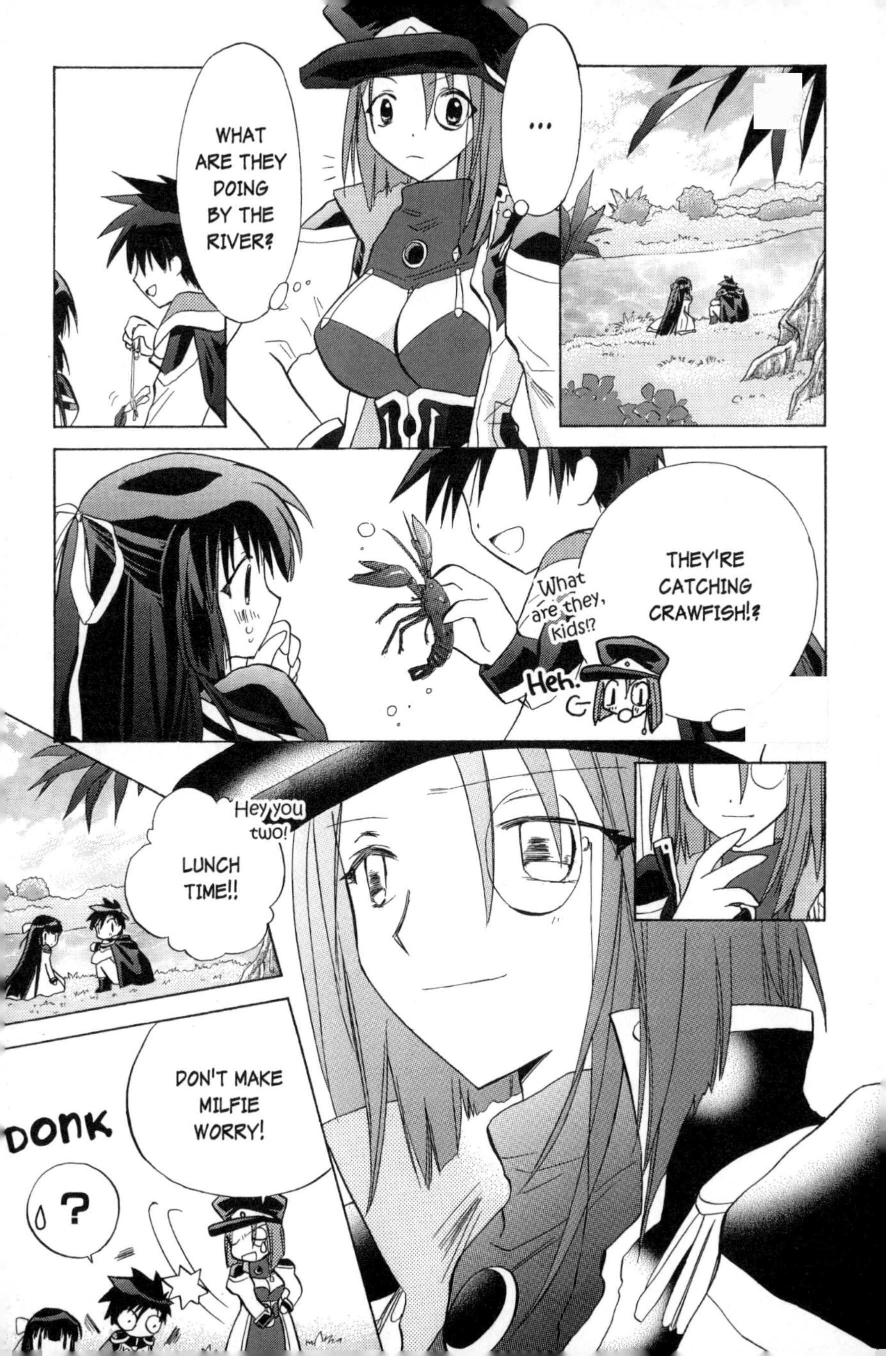
...
WHAT ARE THEY DOING BY THE RIVER?
THEY'RE CATCHING CRAWFISH!?
What are they, kids!?
Heh.
Hey you two!
LUNCH TIME!!
DON'T MAKE MILFIE WORRY!
DONK
?

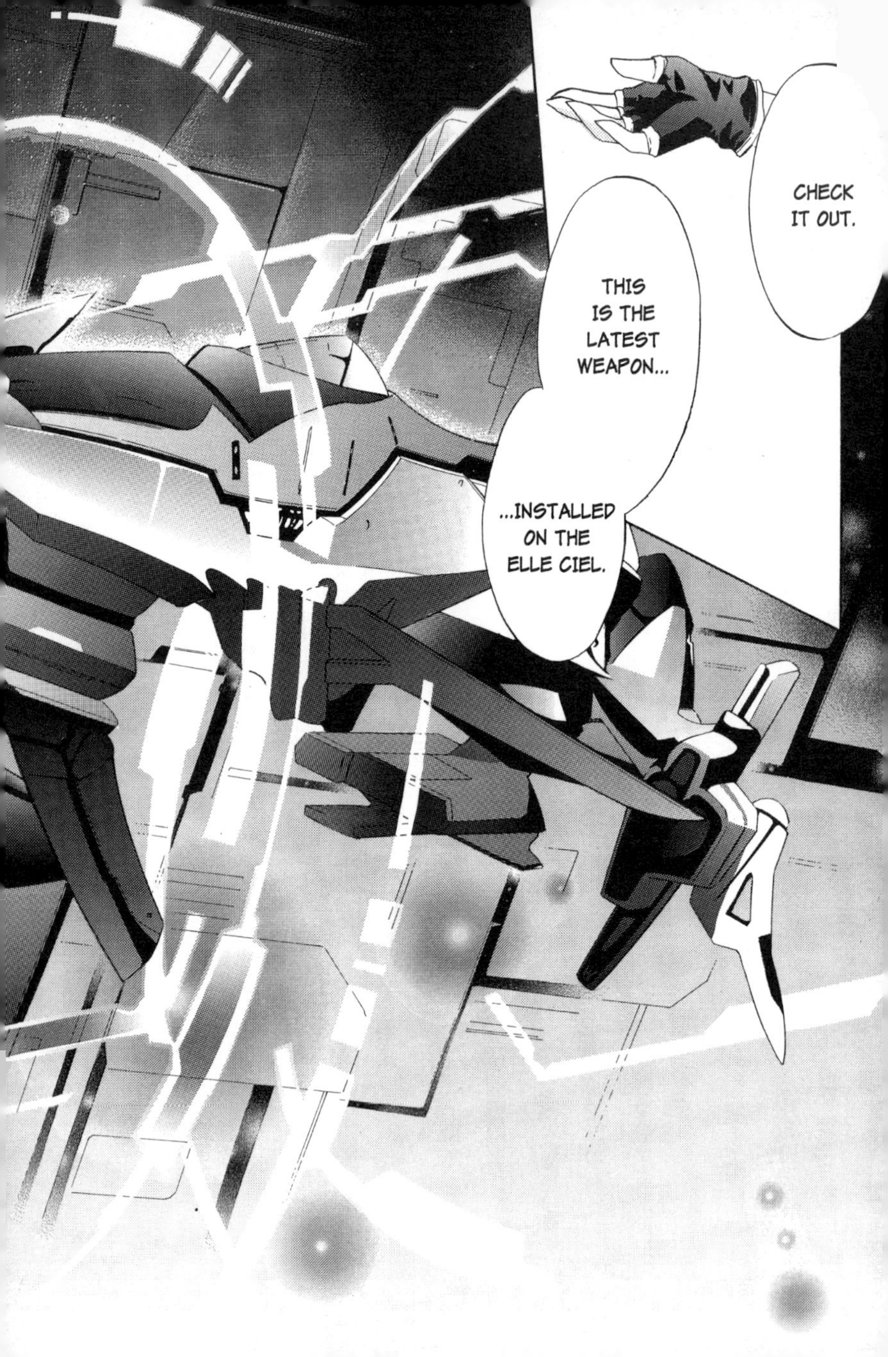
CHECK IT OUT.
THIS IS THE LATEST WEAPON...
...INSTALLED ON THE ELLE CIEL.

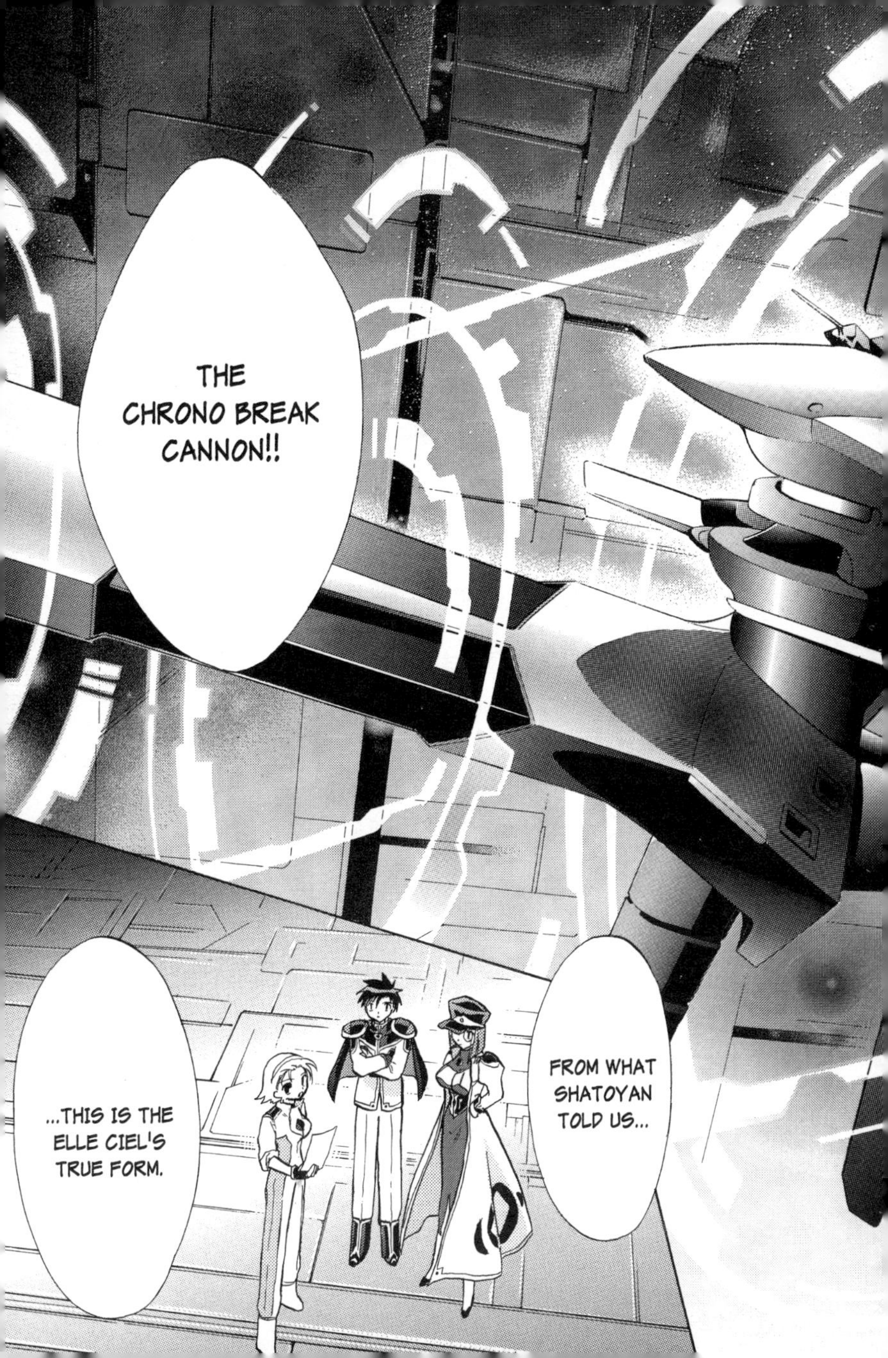
THE CHRONO BREAK CANNON!!
FROM WHAT SHATOYAN TOLD US...
...THIS IS THE ELLE CIEL'S TRUE FORM.

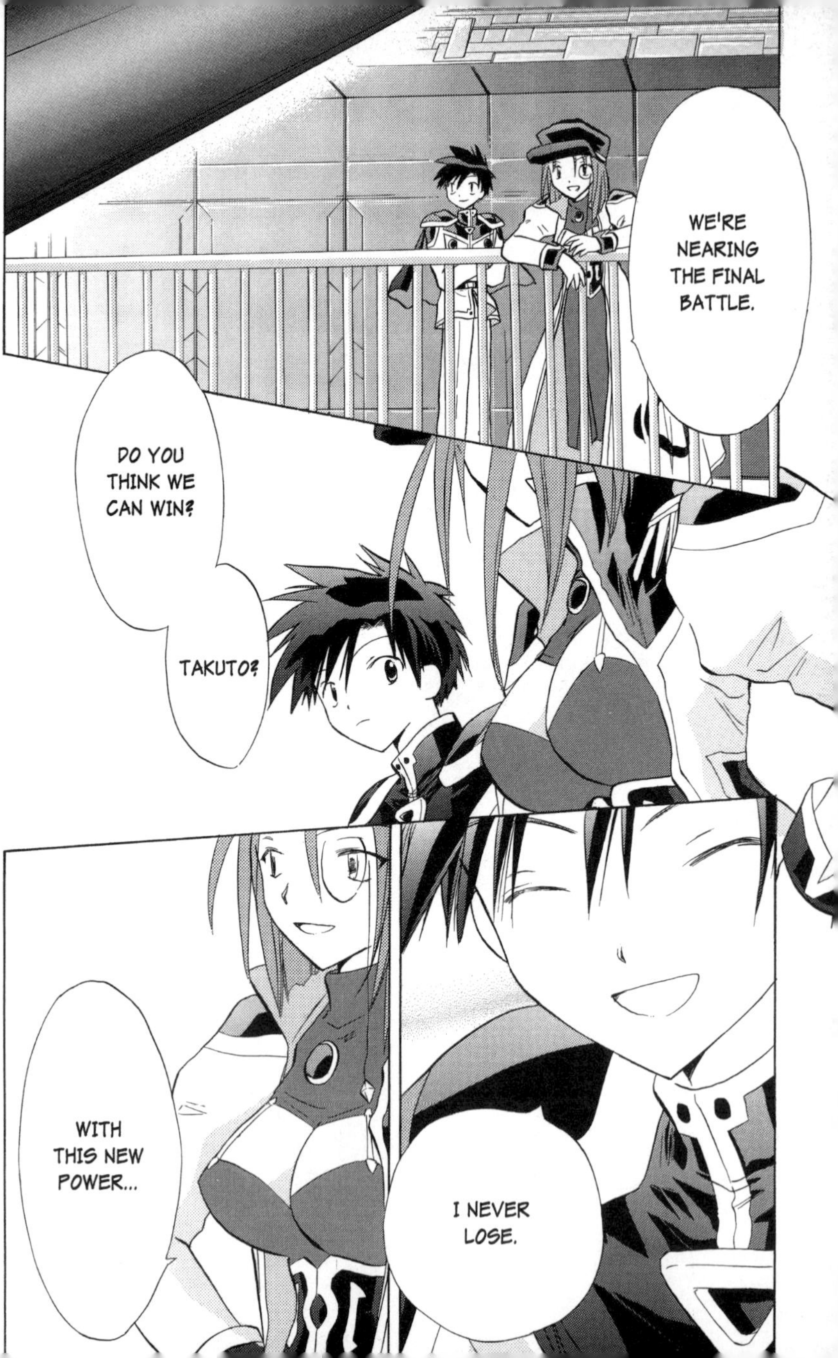
WE'RE NEARING THE FINAL BATTLE.
DO YOU THINK WE CAN WIN?
TAKUTO?
WITH THIS NEW POWER...
I NEVER LOSE.

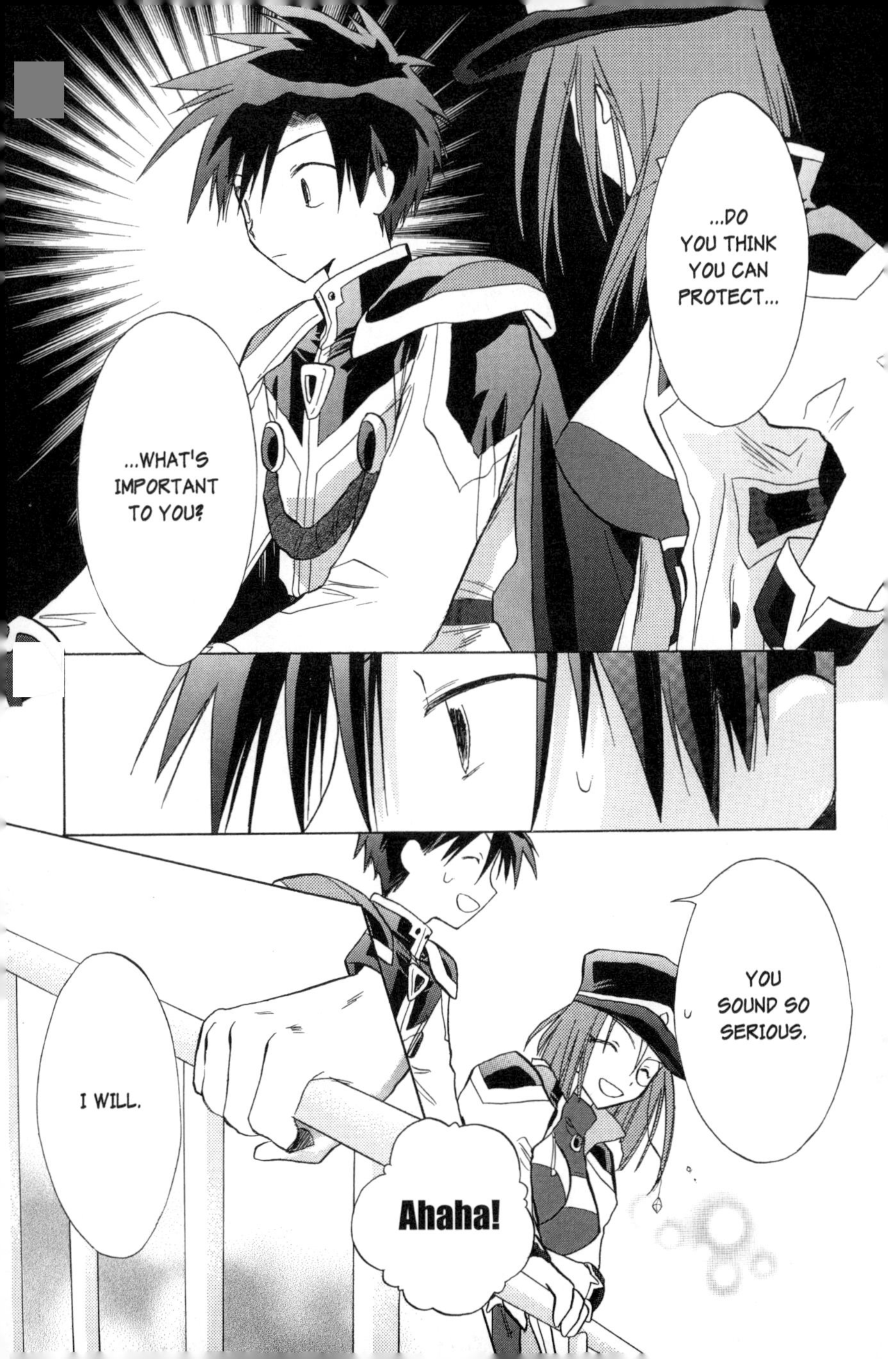
...DO YOU THINK YOU CAN PROTECT...
...WHAT'S IMPORTANT TO YOU?
YOU SOUND SO SERIOUS.
Ahaha!
I WILL.

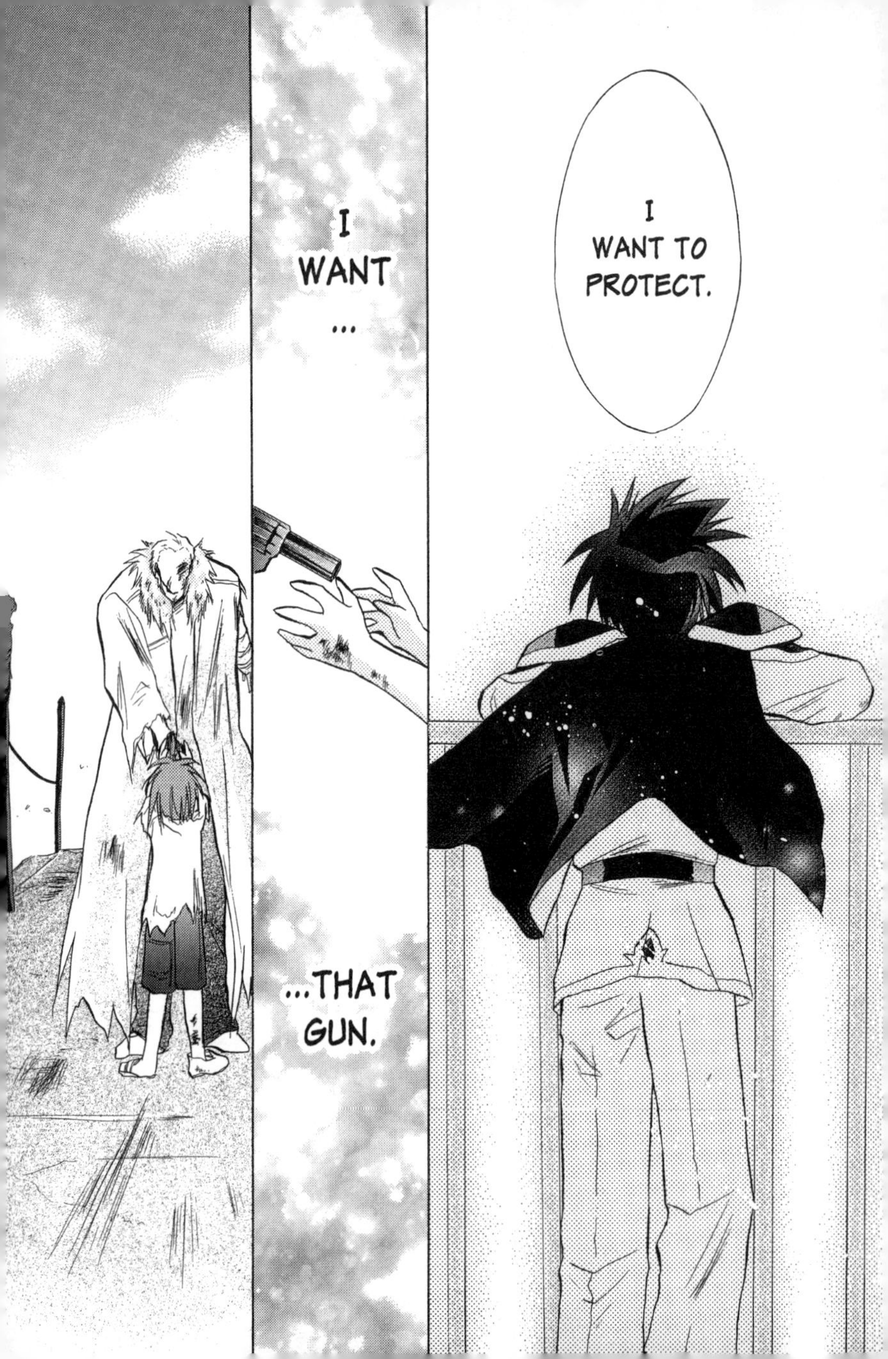
I WANT TO PROTECT.
I WANT ...
...THAT GUN.

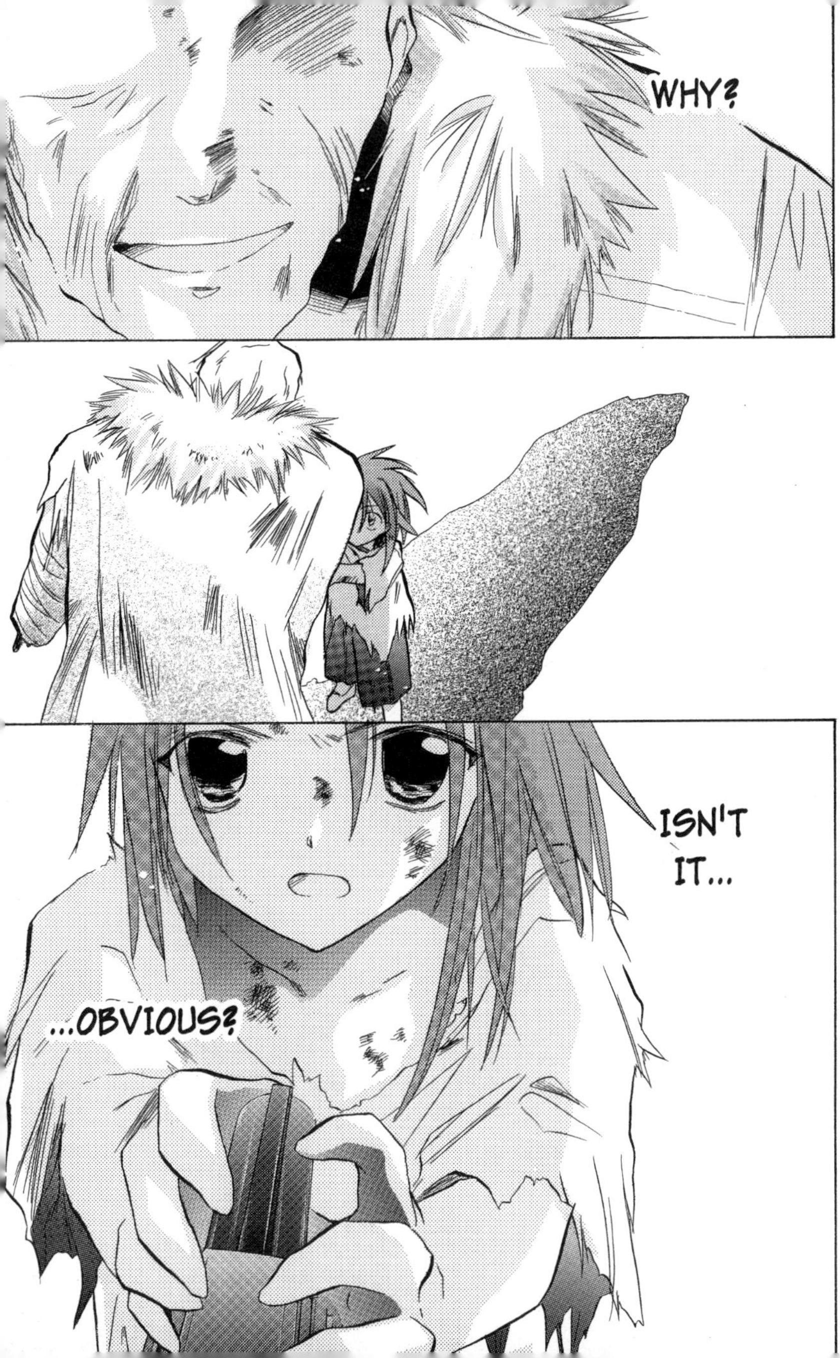
WHY?
ISN'T IT...
...OBVIOUS?

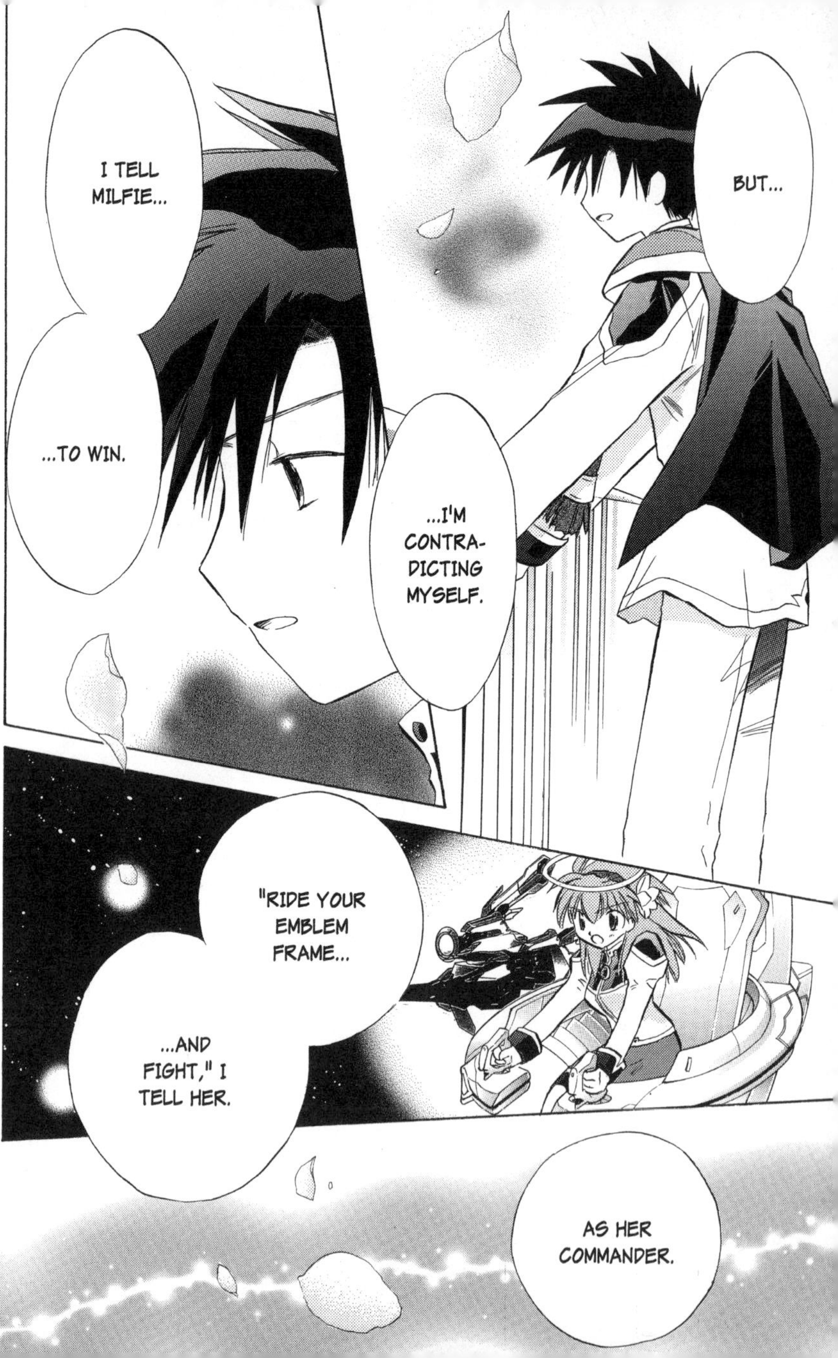
BUT...
I TELL MILFIE...
...TO WIN.
...I'M CONTRA-DICTING MYSELF.
"RIDE YOUR EMBLEM FRAME...
...AND FIGHT," I TELL HER.
AS HER COMMANDER.

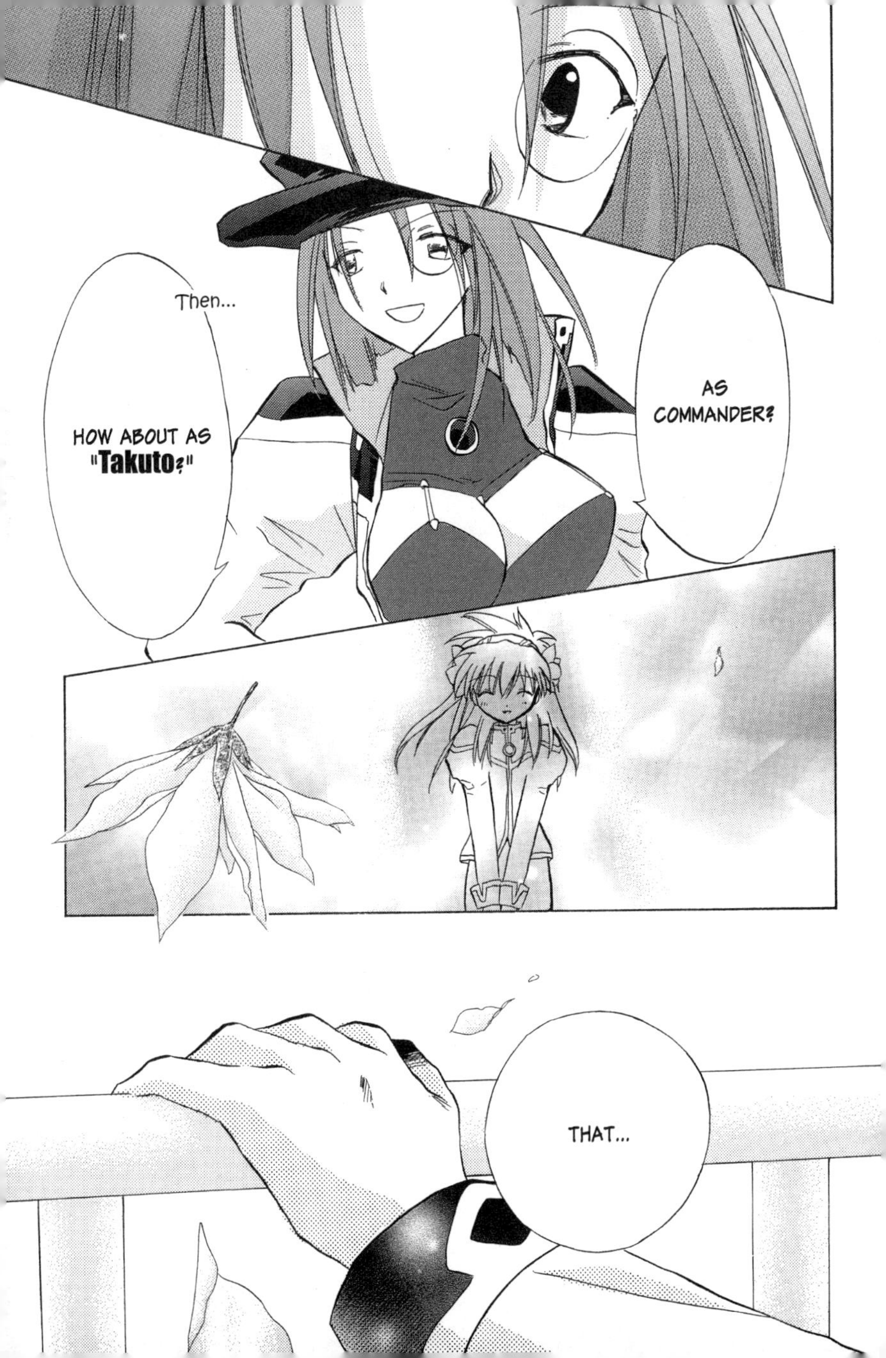
AS COMMANDER?
Then... HOW ABOUT AS "Takuto?"
THAT...

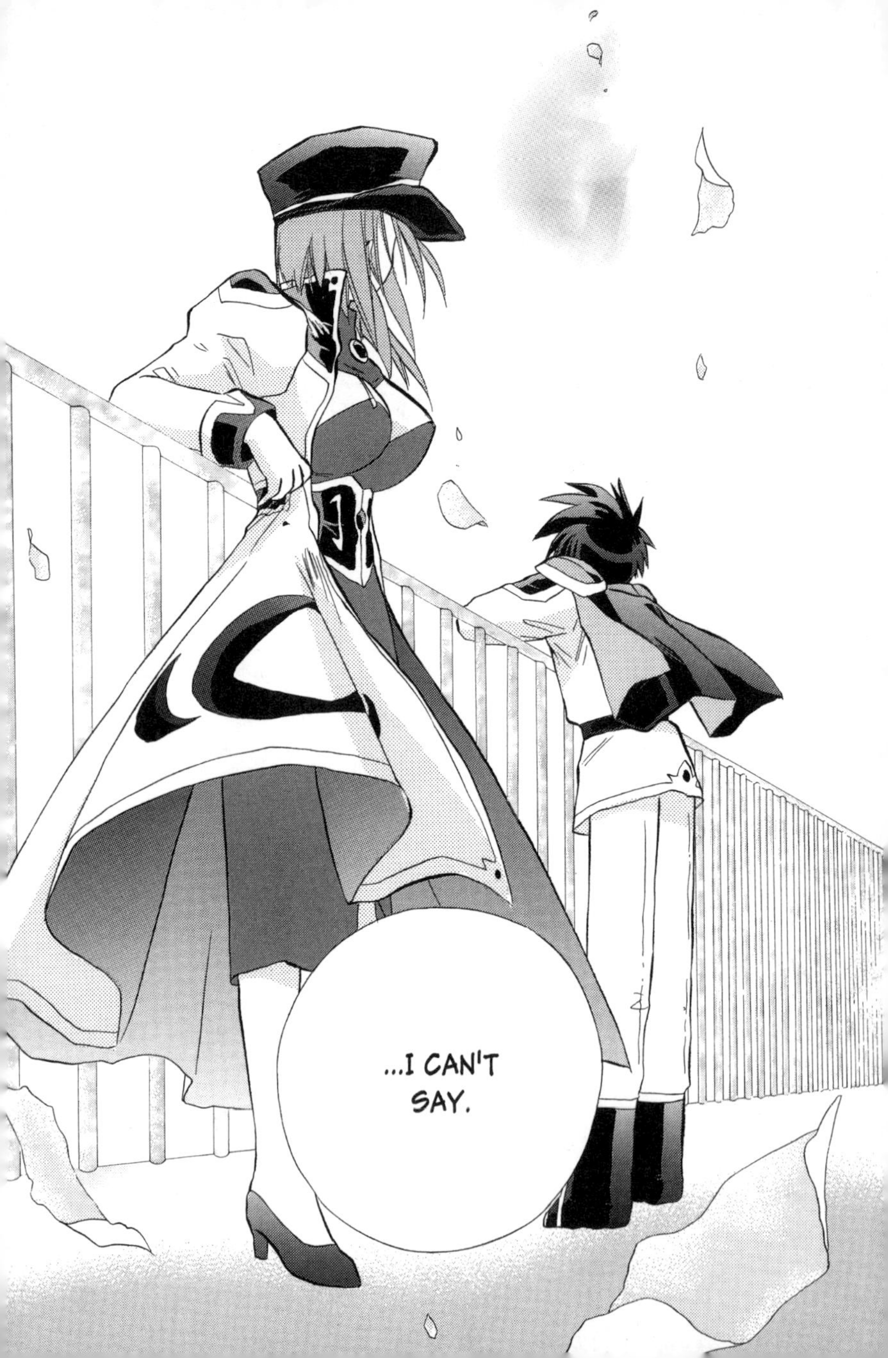
...I CAN'T SAY.

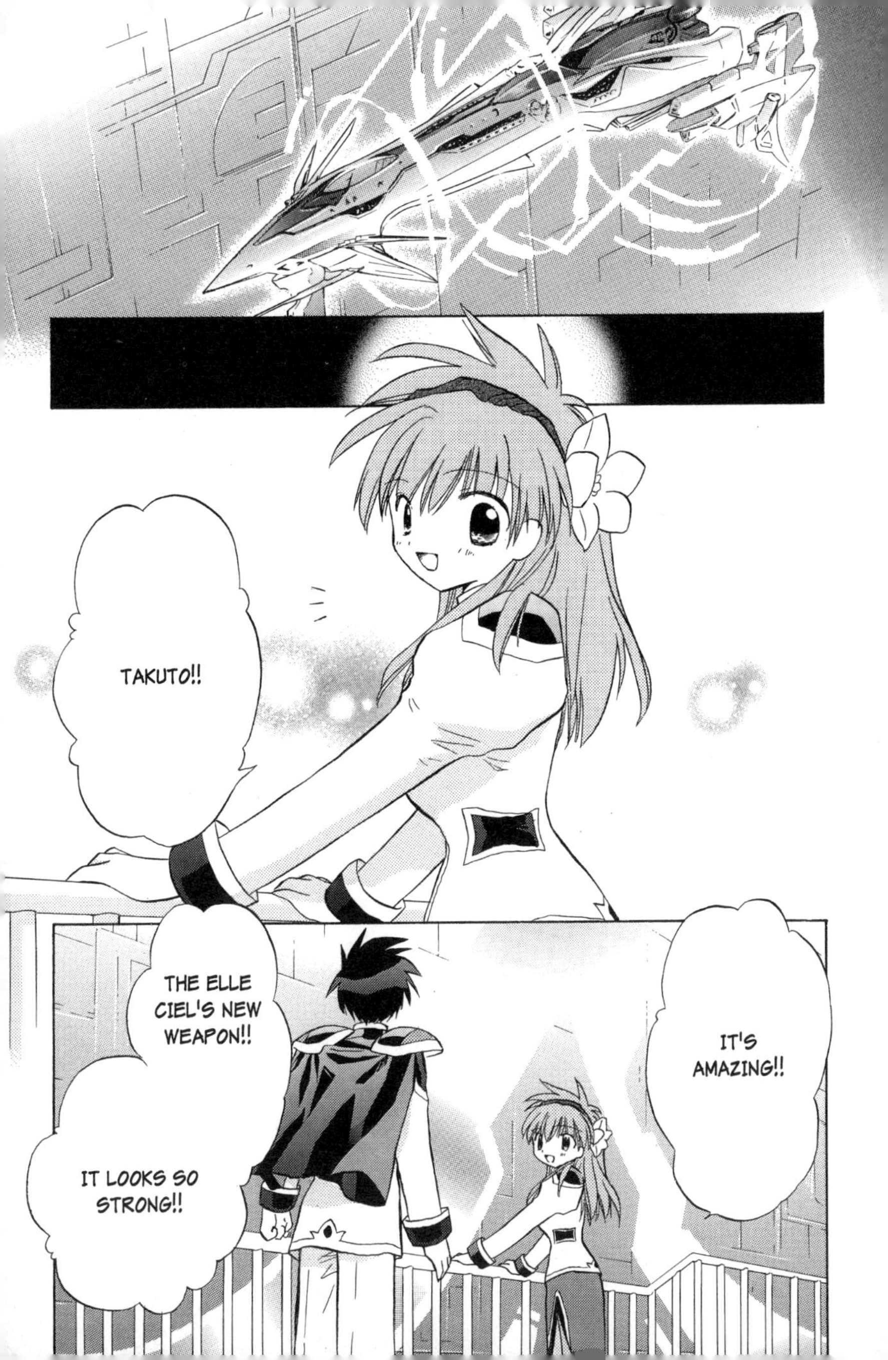
TAKUTO!!
IT'S AMAZING!!
THE ELLE CIEL'S NEW WEAPON!!
IT LOOKS SO STRONG!!

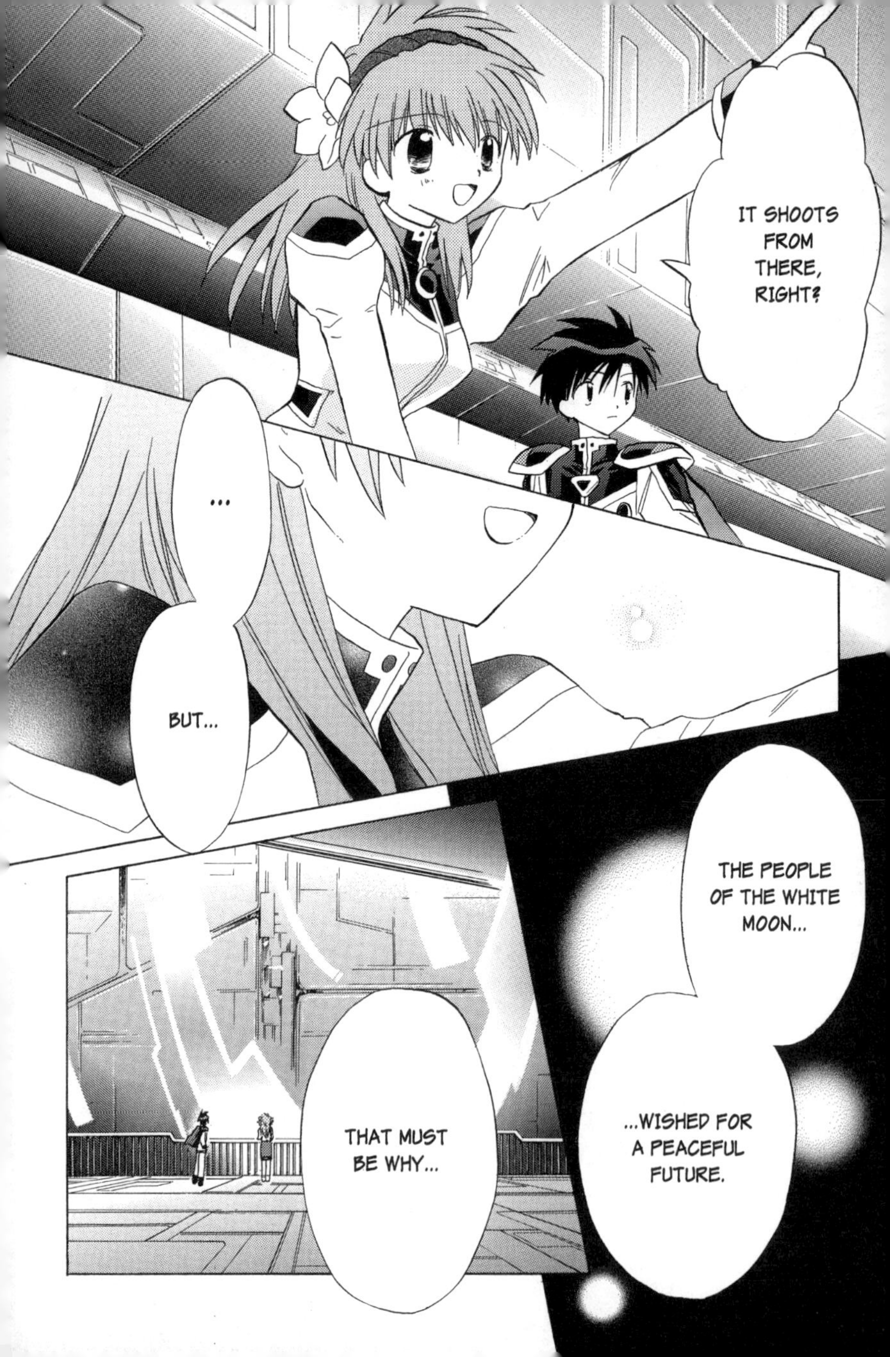
IT SHOOTS FROM THERE, RIGHT?
...
BUT...
THE PEOPLE OF THE WHITE MOON...
...WISHED FOR A PEACEFUL FUTURE.
THAT MUST BE WHY...

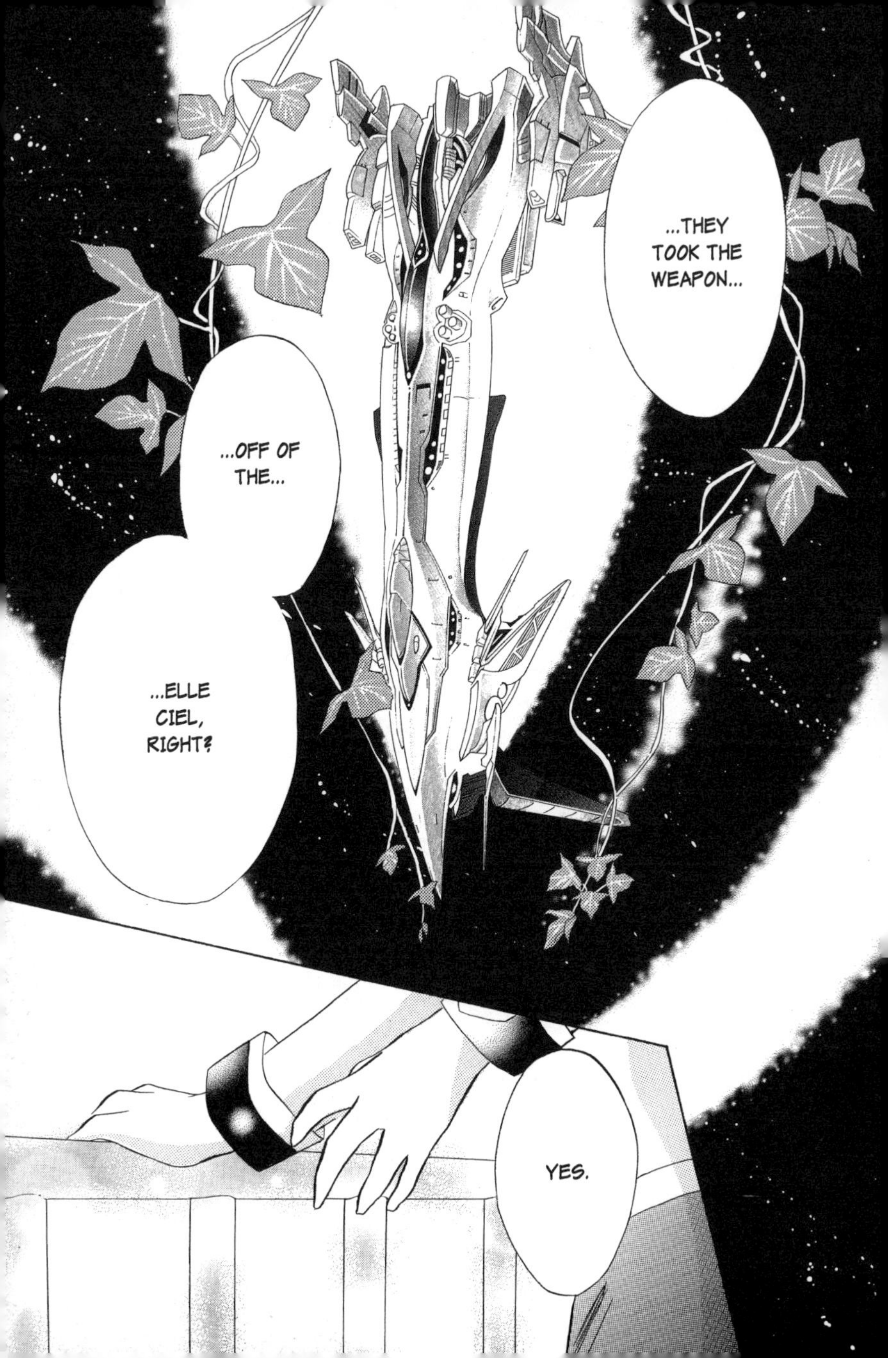
...THEY TOOK THE WEAPON...
...OFF OF THE...
...ELLE CIEL, RIGHT?
YES.

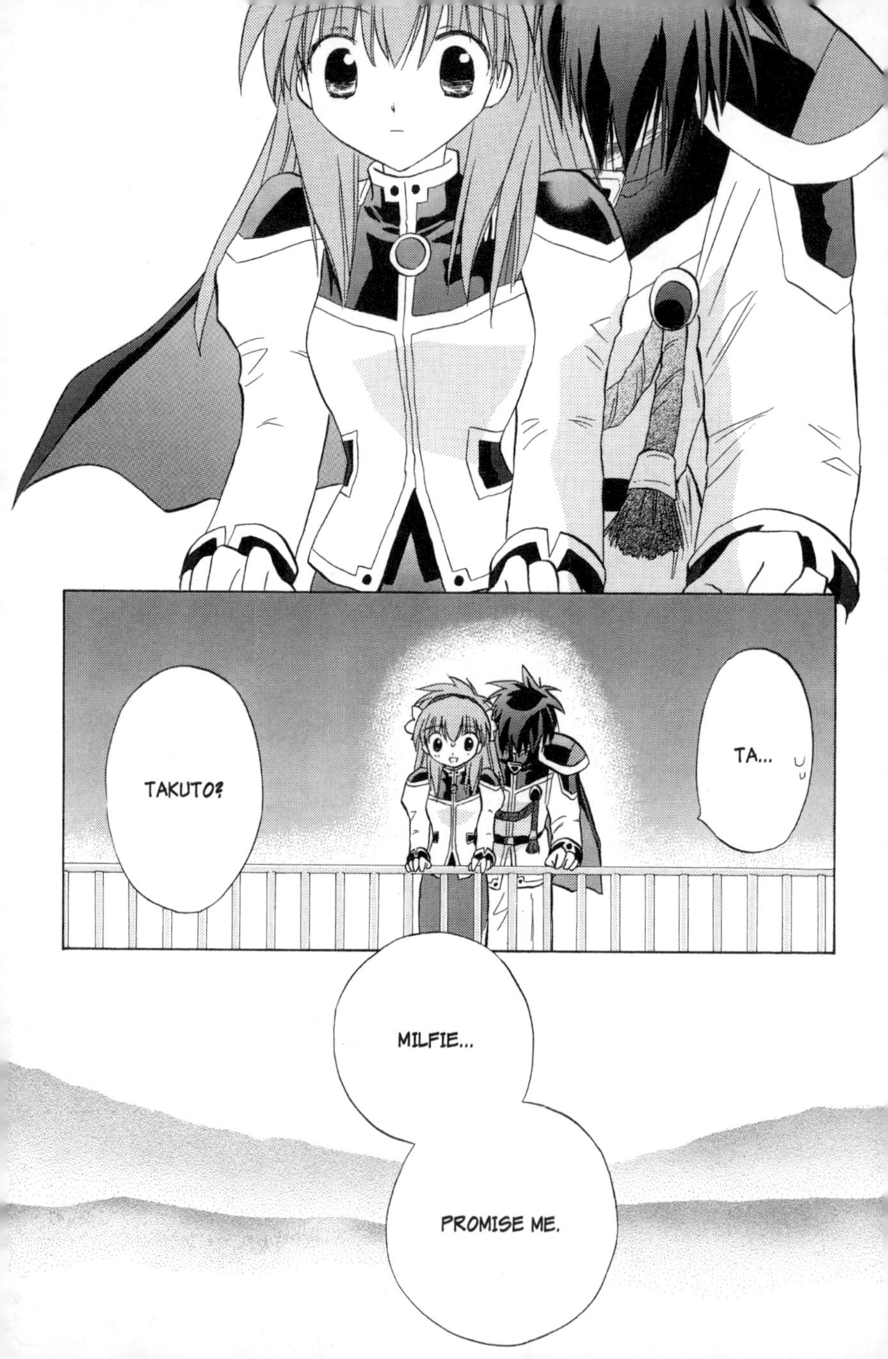
TA...
TAKUTO?
MILFIE...
PROMISE ME.

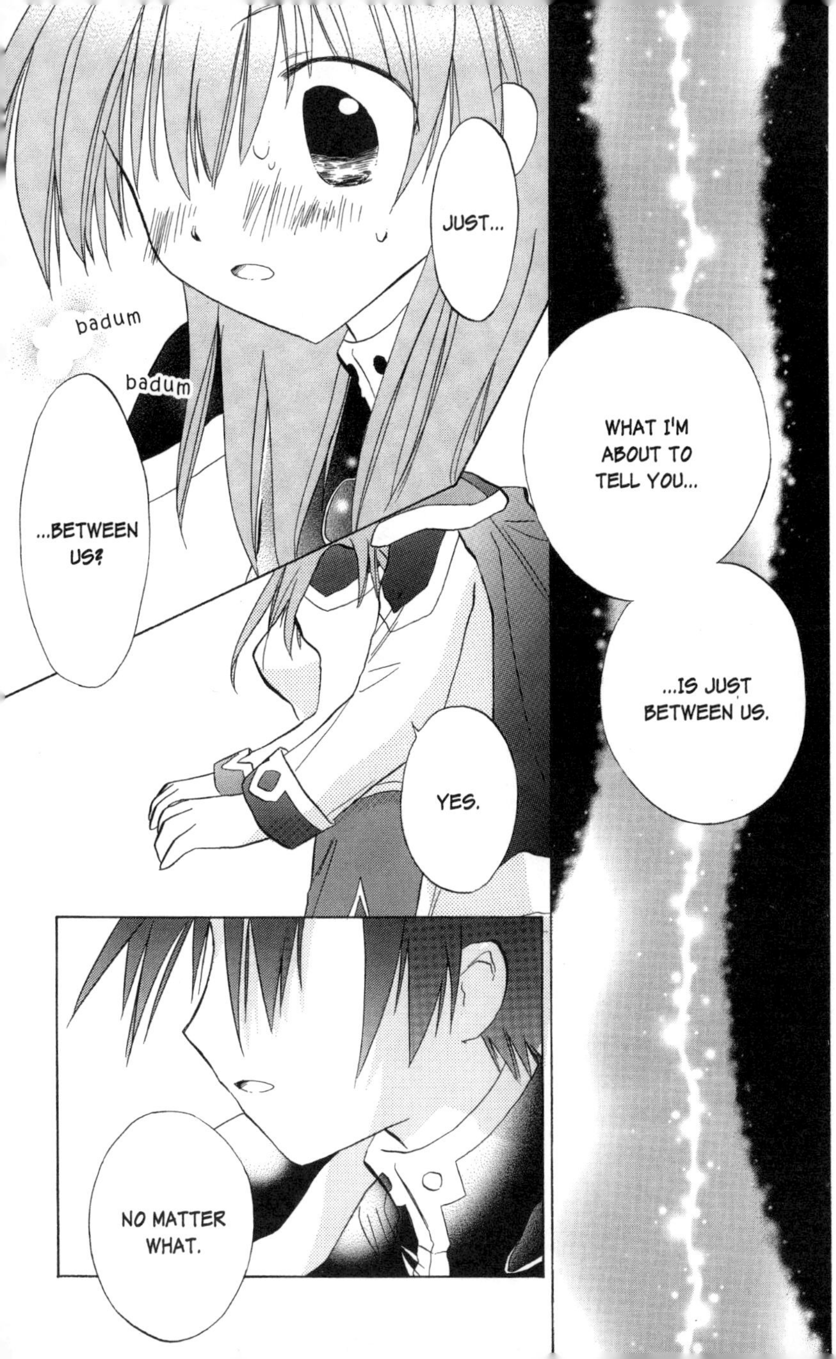
WHAT I'M ABOUT TO TELL YOU...
...IS JUST BETWEEN US.
JUST...
badum
badum
...BETWEEN US?
YES.
NO MATTER WHAT.

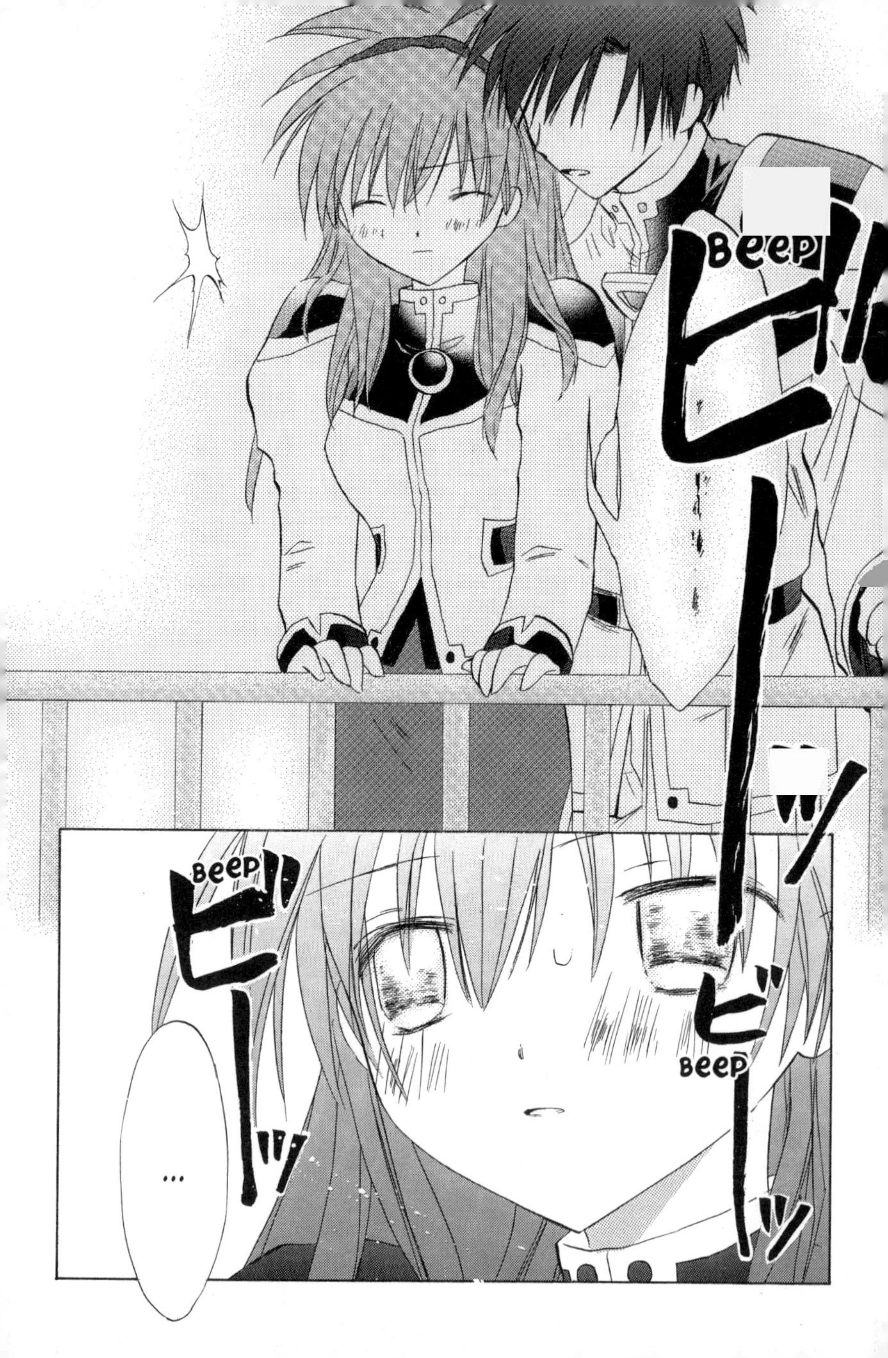

Beep
Beep
Beep
...

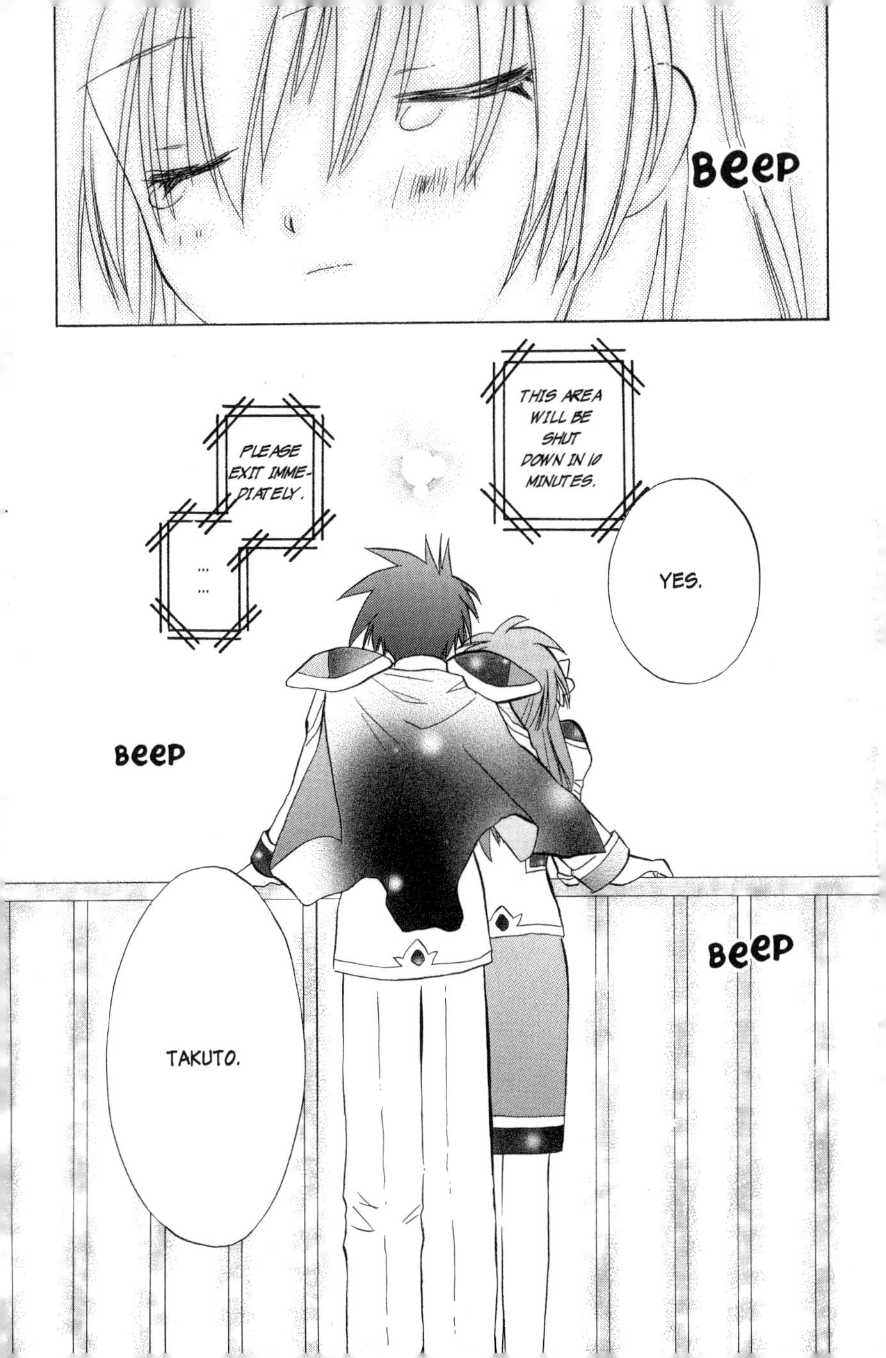
Beep
THIS AREA WILL BE SHUT DOWN IN 10 MINUTES.
YES.
PLEASE EXIT IMMEDIATELY.
... ...
Beep
Beep
TAKUTO.

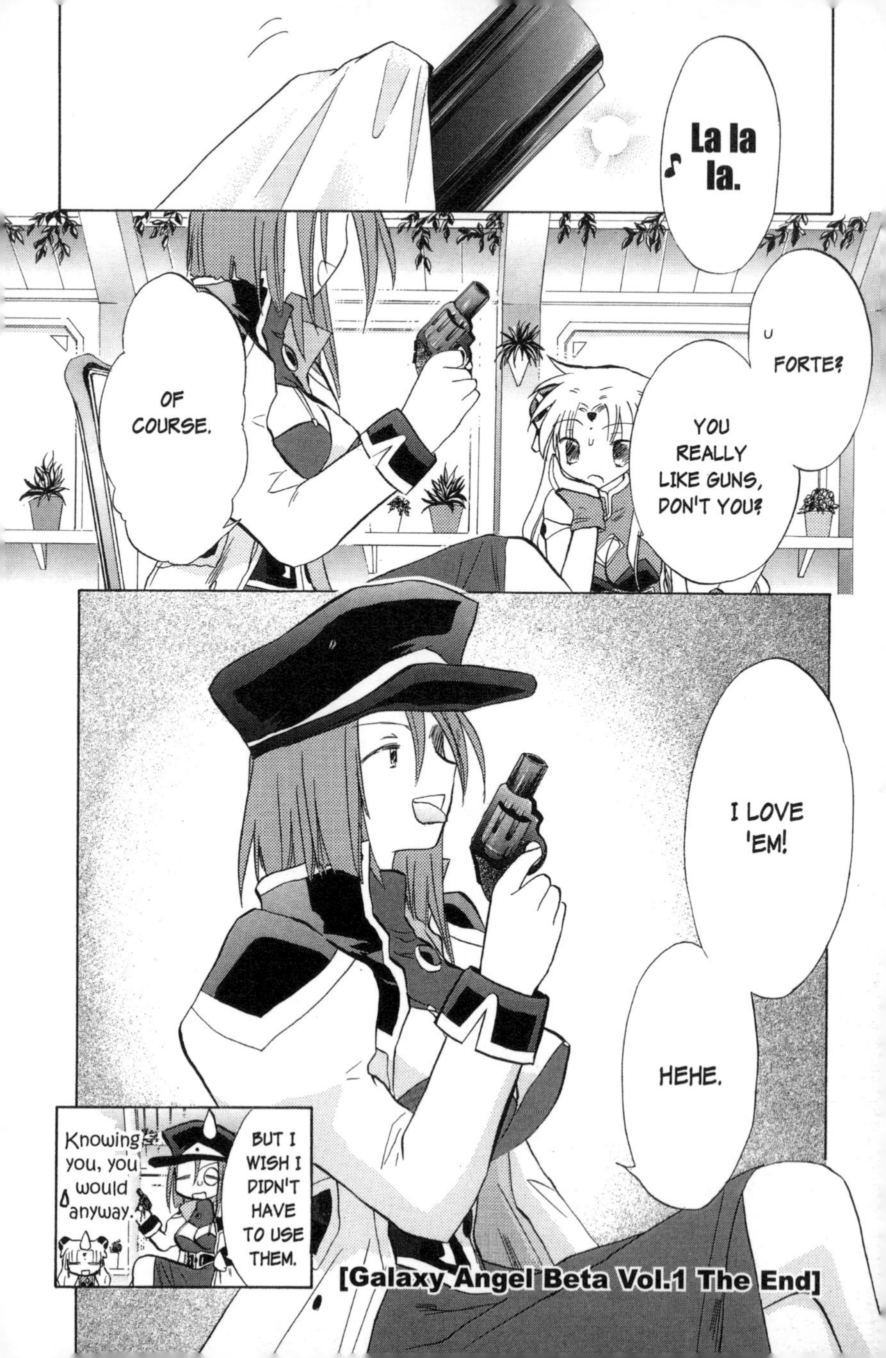
La la la.
Forte?
You really like guns, don't you?
Of course.
I love 'em!
Hehe.
But I wish I didn't have to use them.
Knowing you, you would anyway.
[Galaxy Angel Beta Vol.1 The End]

●SPECIAL THANKS●

<Resource for Spaceship, ETC>
Ikusabune

<Spaceship Design>
Kokoro Takei, Mieko Araki

<Color CGs>
Akiko Kito

●MAIN STAFF●

Mieko Araki   Kaori Sato
Mutsumi Kanei

Cooperation: Kaie Midorino

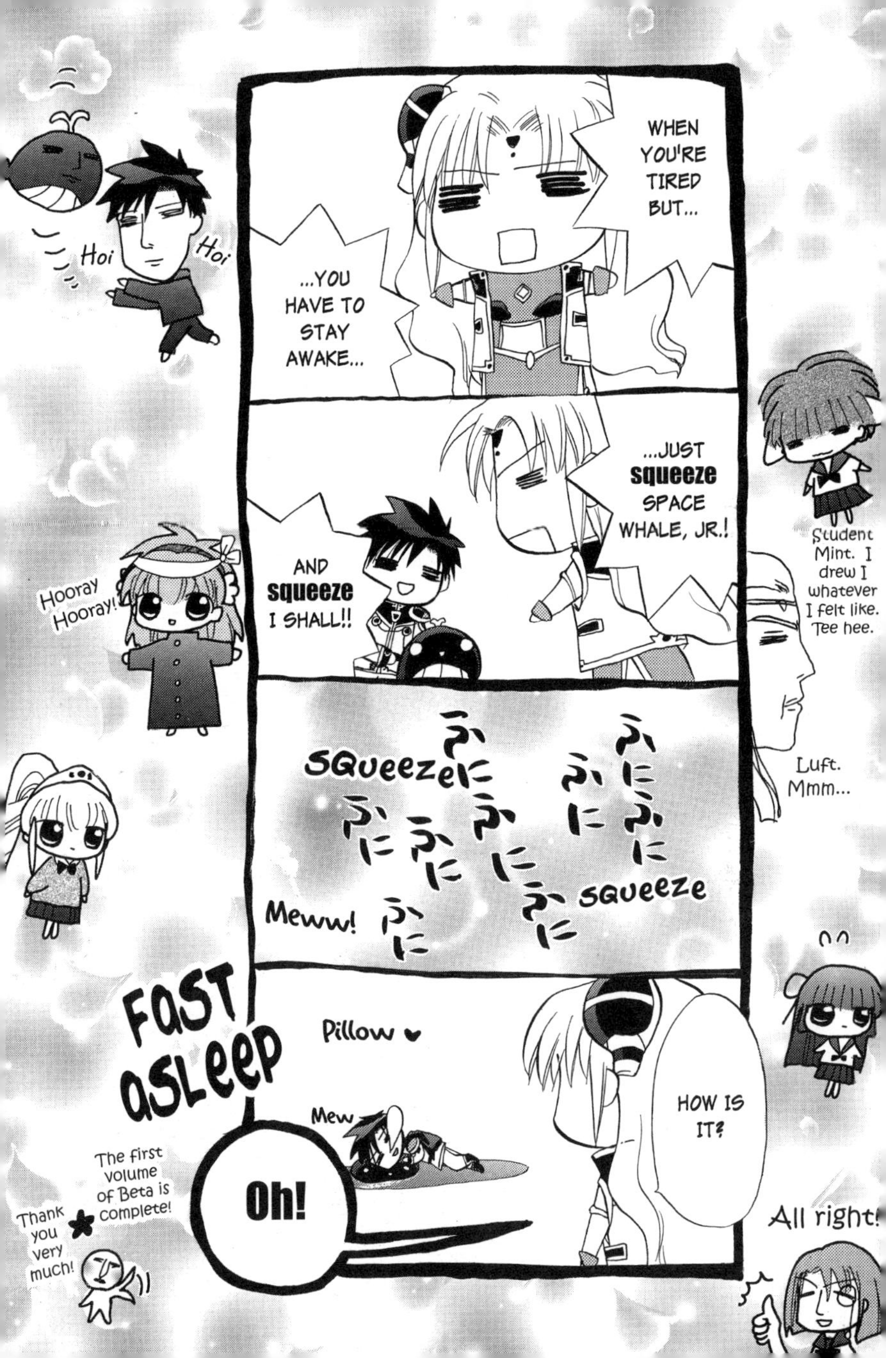

WHEN YOU'RE TIRED BUT...
...YOU HAVE TO STAY AWAKE...
...JUST squeeze SPACE WHALE, JR.!
AND squeeze I SHALL!!
ふにふにふに
ふにふに
SQueeze
ふにふにふにふに
ふにふに
SQueeze
Meww!
ふに
HOW IS IT?
Pillow
Mew
Oh!
Fast asleep
Student Mint. I drew I whatever I felt like. Tee hee.
Luft. Mmm...
All right!
Hoi
Hoi
Hooray Hooray!
The first volume of Beta is complete!
Thank you very much!

✿ I actually got married the other day. Miss Hiromi Satou and Ryoko Shintani came to sing for me. Th-thank you... (tears)

Without futher ado, here's the Broccoli News!!

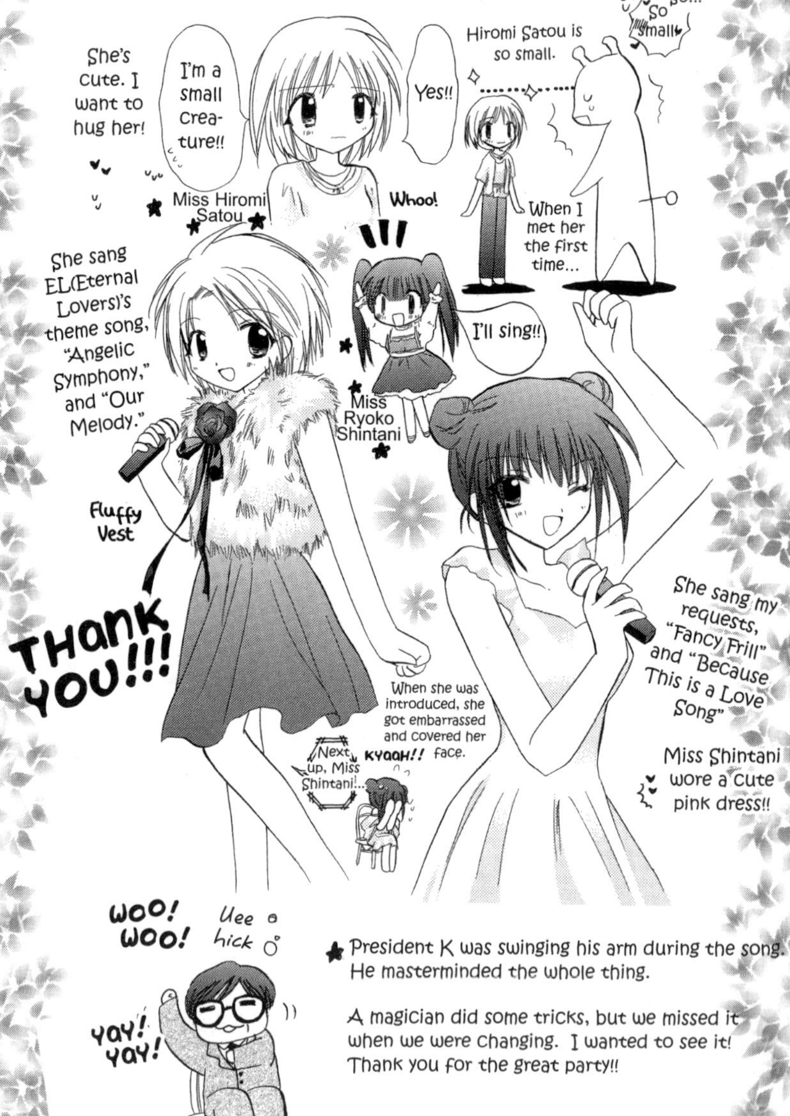

So... So small
Hiromi Satou is so small.
When I met her the first time...
Yes!!
I'm a small crea-ture!!
She's cute. I want to hug her!
Miss Hiromi Satou
Whoo!
I'll sing!!
Miss Ryoko Shintani
She sang EL(Eternal Lovers)'s theme song, "Angelic Symphony," and "Our Melody."
Fluffy Vest
THANK YOU!!!
She sang my requests, "Fancy Frill" and "Because This is a Love Song"
Miss Shintani wore a cute pink dress!!
When she was introduced, she got embarrassed and covered her face.
KYAAH!!
Next up, Miss Shintani!...
Uee hick
WOO! WOO!
YAY! YAY!

★ President K was swinging his arm during the song. He masterminded the whole thing.

A magician did some tricks, but we missed it when we were changing. I wanted to see it! Thank you for the great party!!

Everyone was happy!

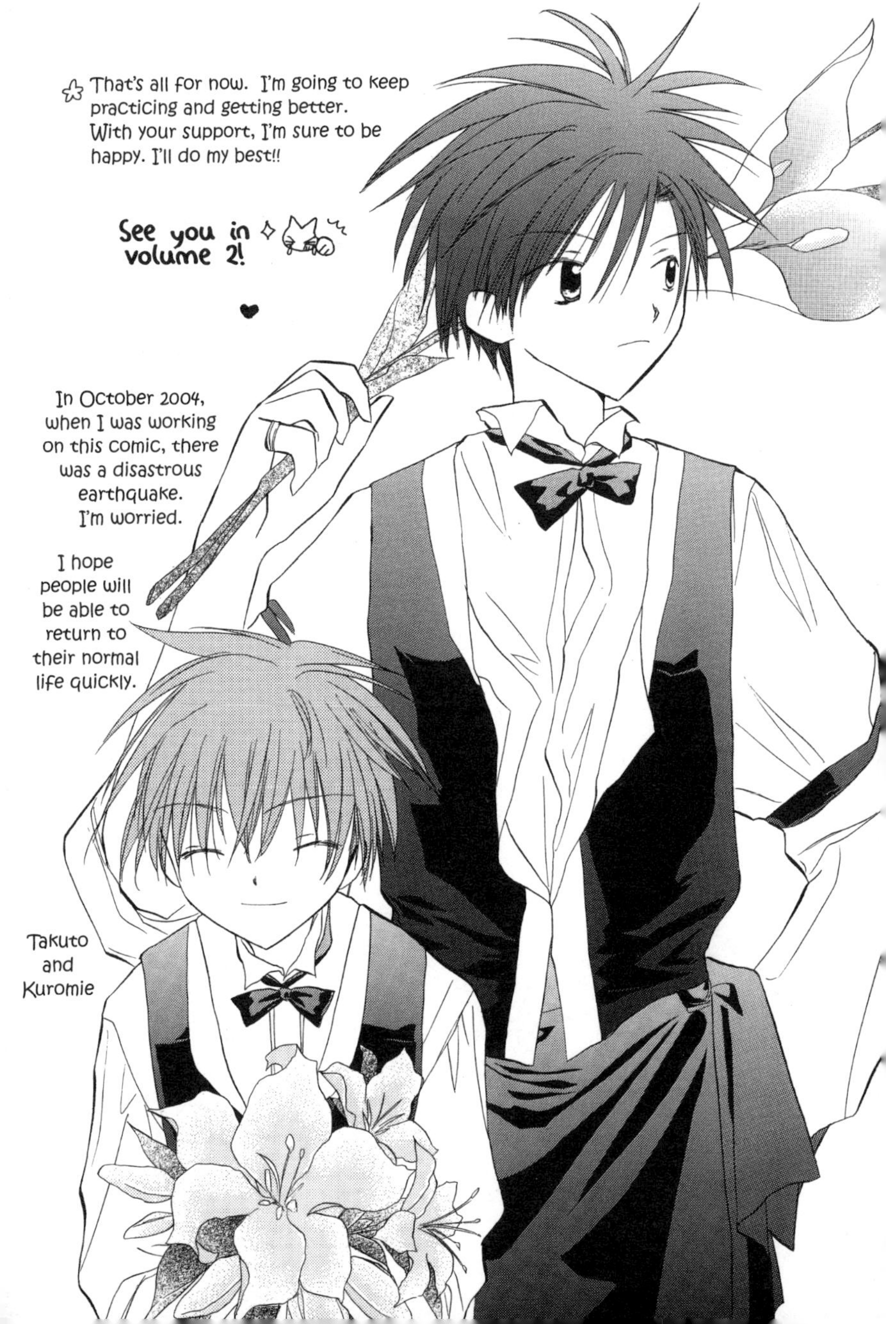
That's all for now. I'm going to keep practicing and getting better. With your support, I'm sure to be happy. I'll do my best!!
See you in volume 2!
In October 2004, when I was working on this comic, there was a disastrous earthquake. I'm worried.
I hope people will be able to return to their normal life quickly.
Takuto and Kuromie

ギャラクシーエンジェル Galaxy Angel β BETA

2

SECRETS ARE REVEALED ON THE WHITE MOON, AS FRAGMENTS OF CHITOSE'S PAST BEGIN TO SURFACE AND PRINCE SHIVA'S STORY IS FINALLY TOLD.

MEANWHILE, THE SPACE WHALE'S PICKING UP BAD VIBES, SO KUROMIE WARNS TAKUTO TO BE ON ALERT. THE ANGEL TROUPE IS UP TO SOMETHING SECRETIVE—COULD THEY BE THE SOURCE?

WITH THE DISCOVERY OF A NEW EMBLEM FRAME, THE ANGELS ARE POISED TO TAKE ON EONIA ONCE MORE. BUT WHEN HE LAUNCHES HIS ULTIMATE PLAN, HOPE BEGINS TO FADE AS THE TROUPE IS DEALT A DEVASTATING BLOW.

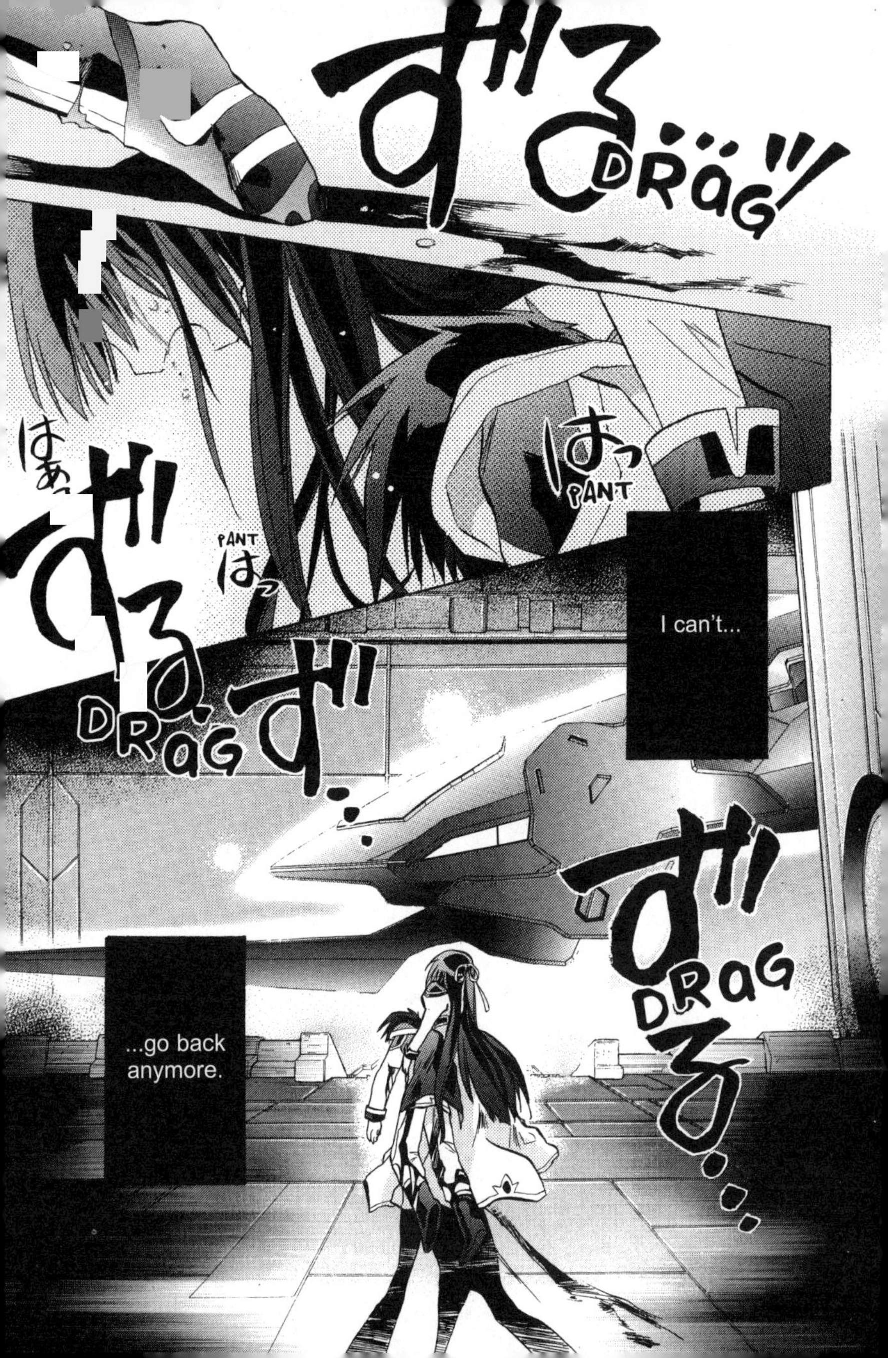
ずる
DRAG
はっ
PANT
PANT
はっ
はあっ
ずる
DRAG
I can't...
ず
ずる
DRAG
...go back anymore.

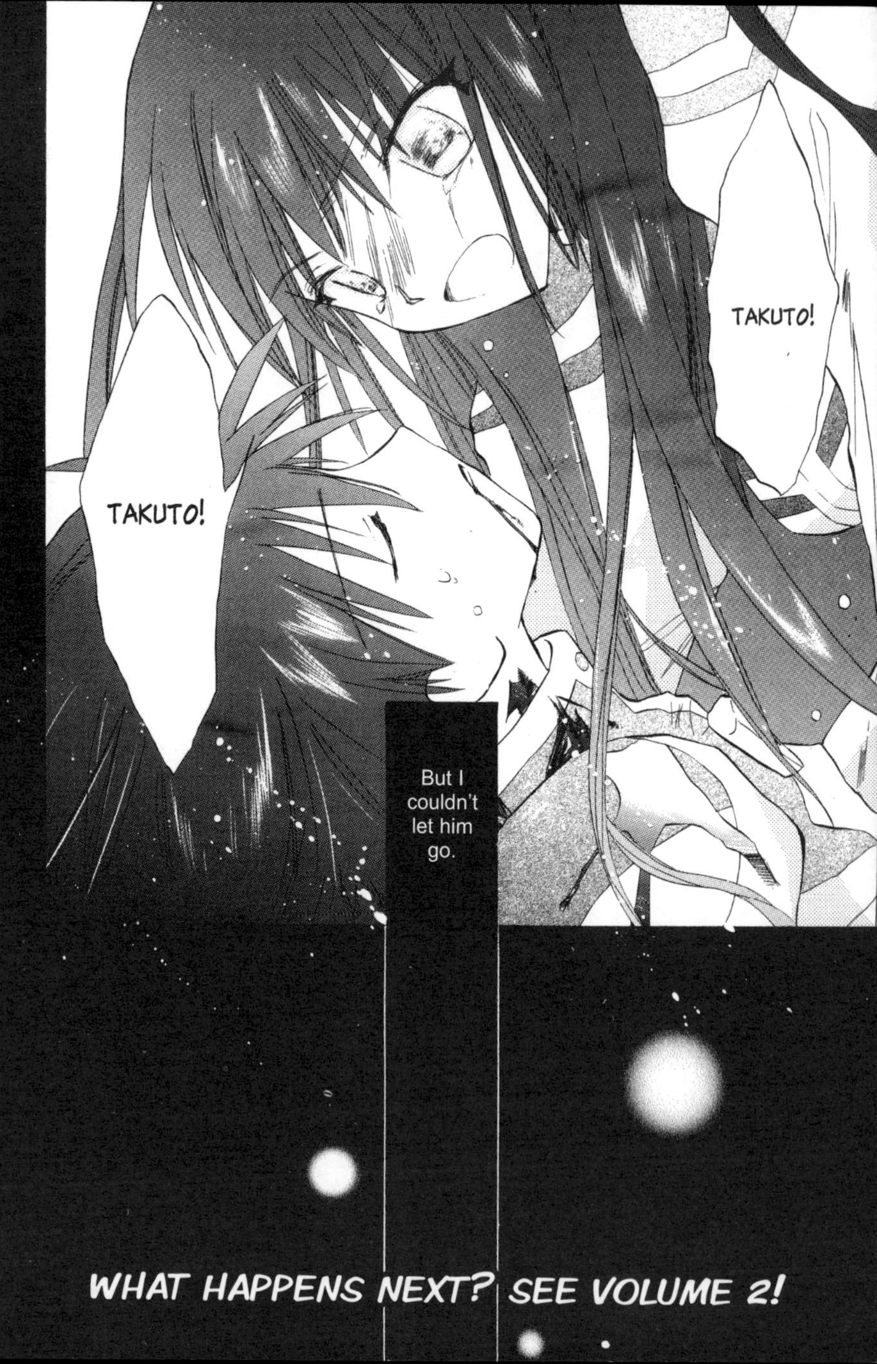
TAKUTO!
TAKUTO!
But I couldn't let him go.
WHAT HAPPENS NEXT? SEE VOLUME 2!

ギャラクシーエンジェル
Galaxy Angel™ β
BETA

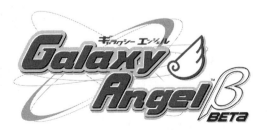

THE UNIVERSE OF GALAXY ANGEL PART 5

What is the Elle Ciel?

Title: The ceremonial ship, Elle Ciel
Property of the White Moon
Captain: Commander Takuto Meyers

The enormous vessel that is the Elle Ciel is actually a ceremonial ship with a special role. Although she is lightly armed for battle, her intended purpose is to serve the Moon Goddess, Shatoyan. So in essence the Elle Ciel is a cruising palace.

Compared to ordinary ships, its interior and facilities are extremely luxurious and offer an abundance of space. There are numerous facilities installed within the living spaces of the crew. It has a large-scale gym, a capacious dining room capable of satisfying various palates, an elegant cafeteria, a convenience store that provides the crew with everyday essentials, and also a botanical garden where one can enjoy many big trees. It also has a gigantic artificial ocean called the "Whale Room" onboard the ship. The mysterious telepathic creatures, space whales, are protected and raised there.

The Chrono String Engine, a piece of Lost Technology, is mounted in the Elle Ciel and enables the ship to go faster than the speed of light with its hyper space-time navigation mode Chrono Drive. With regards to speed, it takes it about 10 - 24 hours to get to the neighboring planets. (It takes about 10 hours to travel 1 light-year.) While in hyper space-time navigation mode, it is dangerous to come in contact with substances from space, so the ship has to choose the path with the least interstellar matter, avoiding space dust, asteroids, etc.

The Elle Ciel's role during combat

Being a ceremonial ship the Elle Ciel is quite graceful, but one cannot forget that she is also a combat vessel.

Most of the crew onboard the ship are technical experts and researchers who are studying the Lost Technology of the White Moon. They're called the "Mediums in the White Moon" and are not military personnel. It is peculiar that the actual military personnel onboard are quite few; Takuto, Lester, and the Angel Troupe are the only ones who have achieved ranks in the Transbaal Kingdom force.

The Elle Ciel's biggest role during combat is to serve as the mother ship of the five fighter ships, the Emblem Frames. The take off deck for the ships and adjacent hangar are located in the rear section of her fuselage. Because of its limited degree of armament and speed, the Elle Ciel supports the fighter ships instead of actually participating in combat. She is also able to generate a special field surrounding the ship, which is another product of Lost Technology. When the Emblem Frames come in contact with the field, it patches up any damaged fuselages and supplies energy for them within a fraction of a second.

Translation Notes

pg. 13 Mint Cosplaying - According to her character profile, Mint enjoys cosplaying, but keeps it a secret. For more information about the characters, check out GalaxyAngel.net!

pg. 15 San - A suffix; can be put after any name to indicate respect. Mint calls everyone using the "-san" suffix not only because she is one of the youngest, but because she grew up in a proper household.

pg. 49 yakitori - A Japanese dish of chicken bits grilled on skewers.

pg. 50 tsukune - A Japanese meatball of minced meat or fish mixed with vegetables. It is often served skewered and grilled as yakitori.

pg. 110 ramen - Japanese soup with long noodles. The base is usually a fish stock that can be flavored with soy sauce, miso (fermented bean paste), or other sauces. It makes an excellent midnight snack.

pg. 125 naruto - A fish cake that generally has white and pink dyed fish meat rolled into a cylinder so that it forms a spiral. It is often sliced thin and placed in ramen.

pg. 164 Hiromi Satou - An anime song singer.

pg. 164 Ryoko Shintani - The Japanese voice actor for Milfeulle in the anime. She was the winner of the Prism Palette Broccoli audition and was chosen to play the main part, Yayoi Sakuragi.

pg. 164 "Fancy Frill" and "Because This is a Love Song" - These two songs are from Ryoko Shintani's self-titled CDs.

pg. 164 Broccoli - The company who created Galaxy Angel, along with other titles such as Di Gi Charat, Aquarian Age, and Bushi Lord.

pg. 164 EL - *Galaxy Angel: Eternal Lovers* is the third Galaxy Angel videogame to be released. Featuring elements of both a dating sim and strategy RPG, it was available (in Japan) for both the PC and Playstation 2.

pg. 164 President K - President K is the president of Broccoli Japan.

ギャラクシーエンジェル Galaxy Angel β™ BETA

Illustration Gallery

CHECK OUT THESE GALAXY ANGEL SKETCHES INCLUDING COSTUME AND EARLY CHARACTER DESIGNS!

Milfeulle

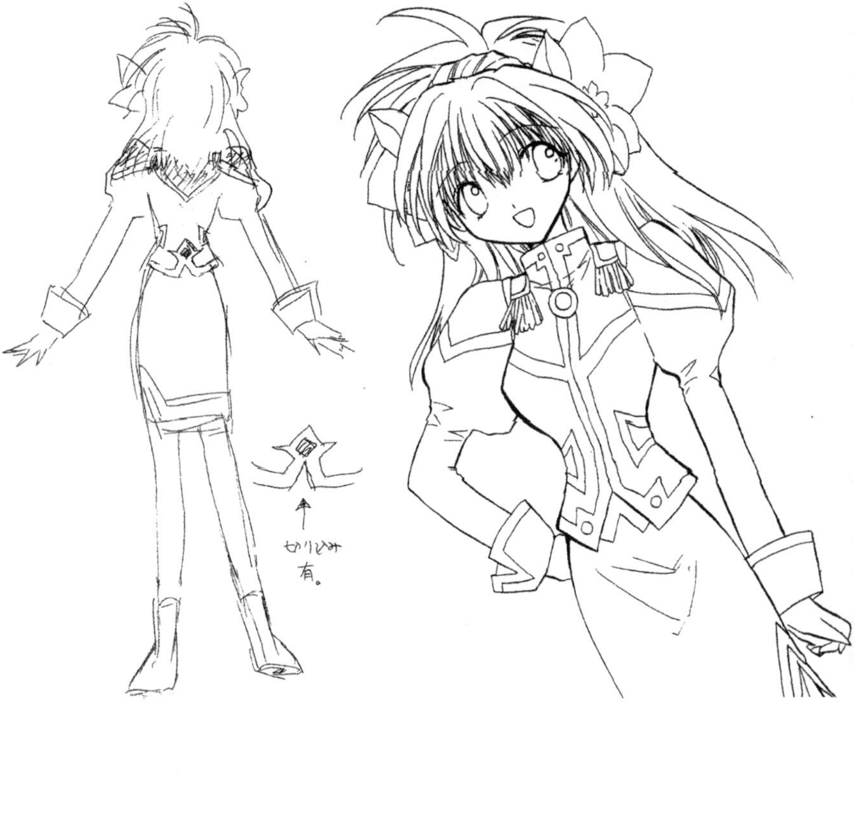
切りこみ
有。

Milfeulle

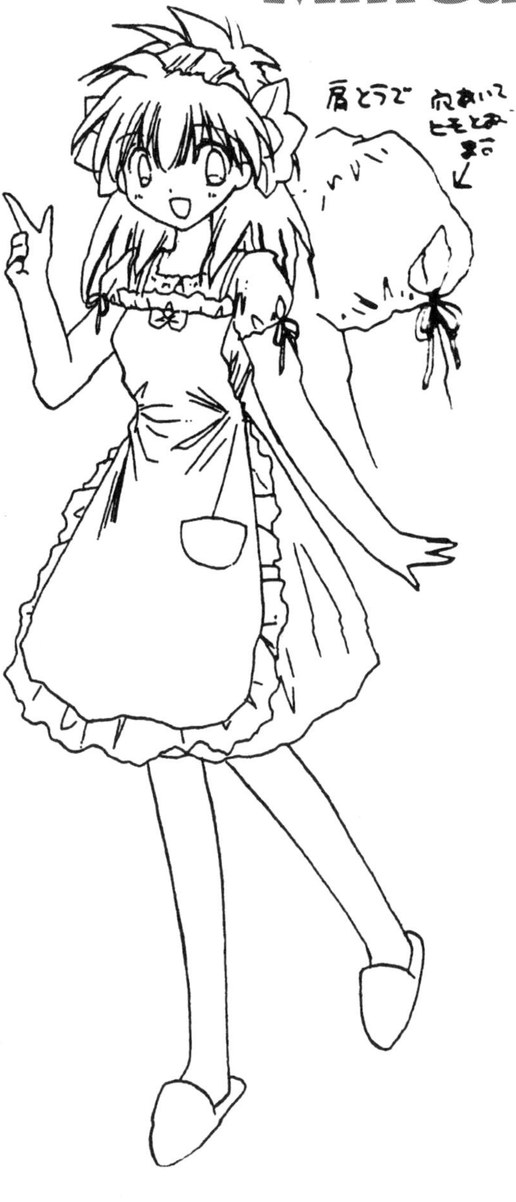
肩とうで 穴あいて
ヒモとおす

Ranpha

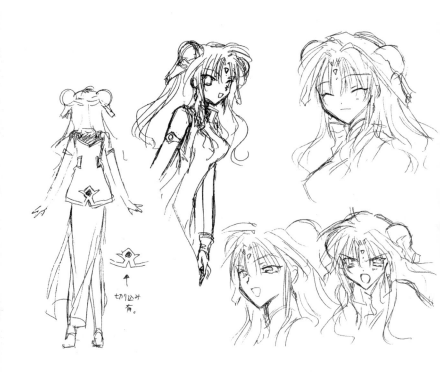

セカワ込み
有。

Ranpha

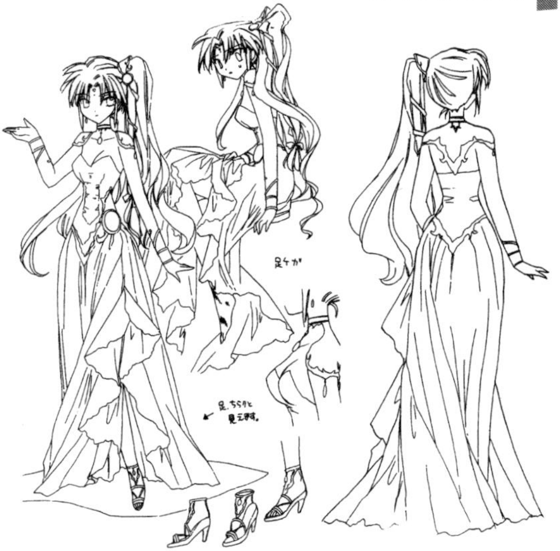
足ケガ
足、ちらりと見えます。

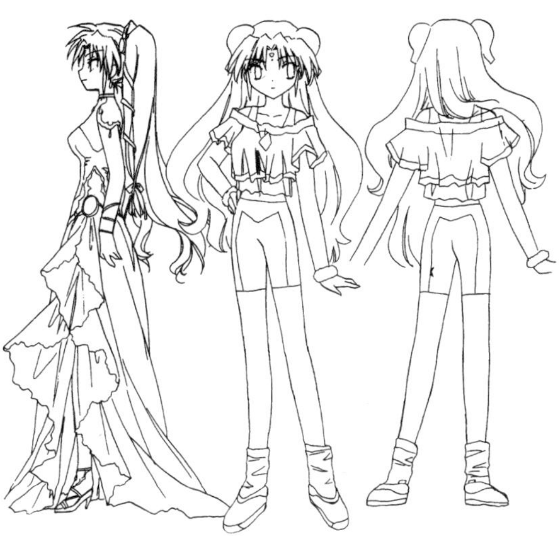

Mint

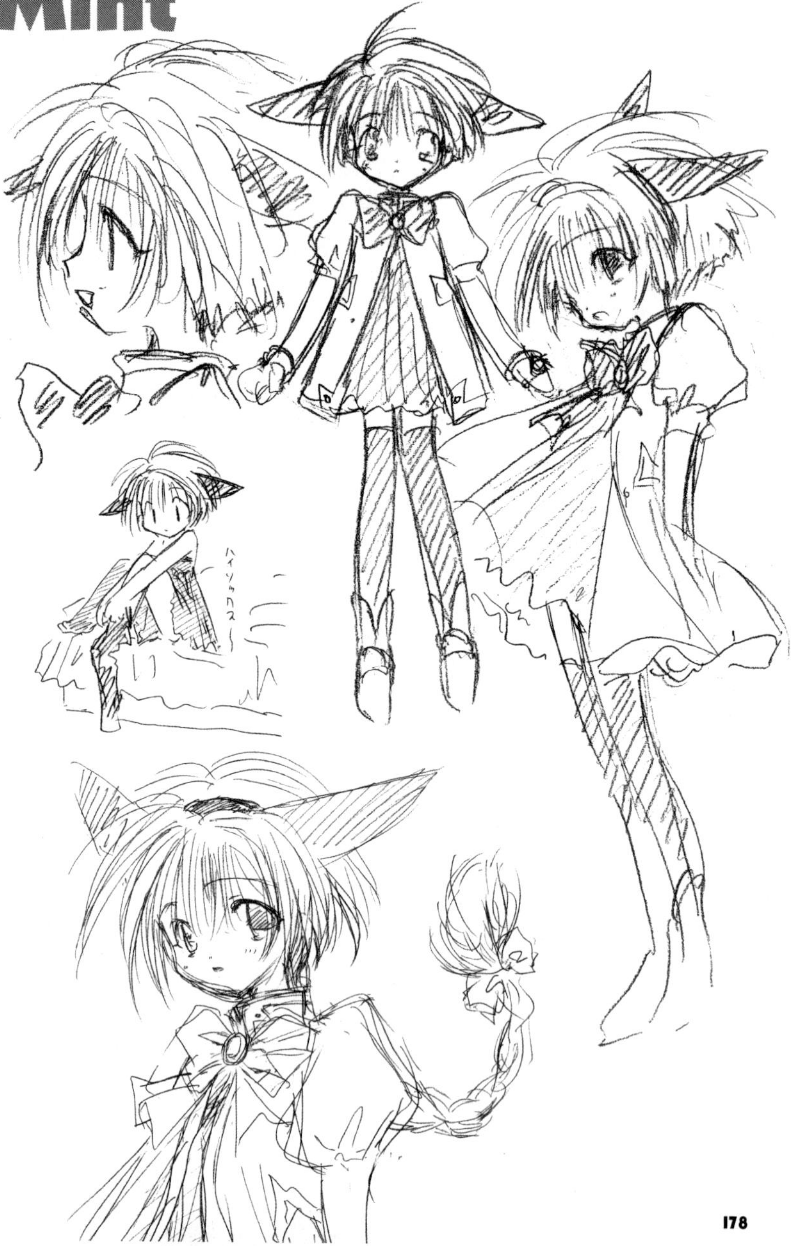
ハイソックス～

Mint

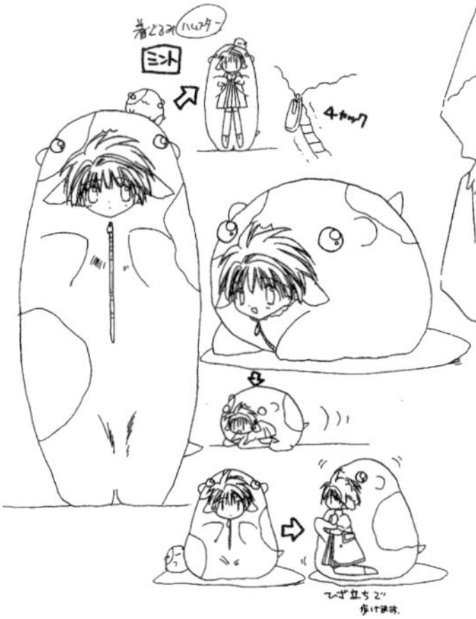
着ぐるみ ハムスター
ミント
4ーチャック
ひざ立ちで
歩けます.

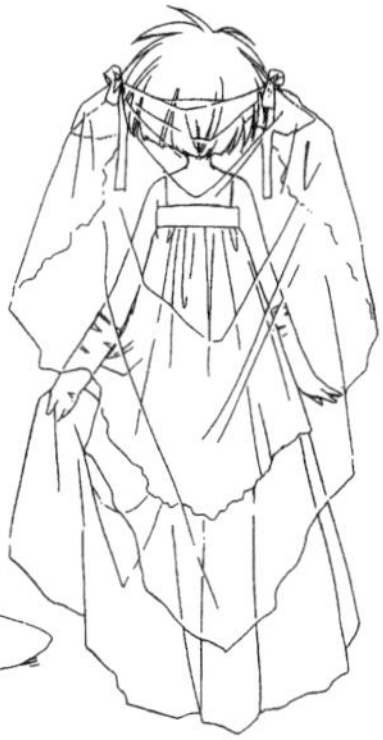

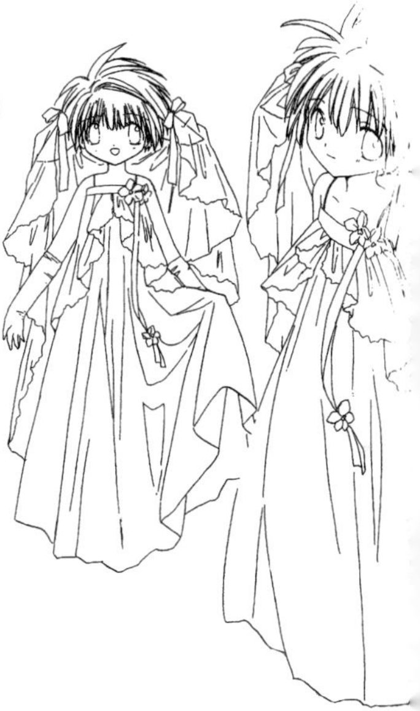

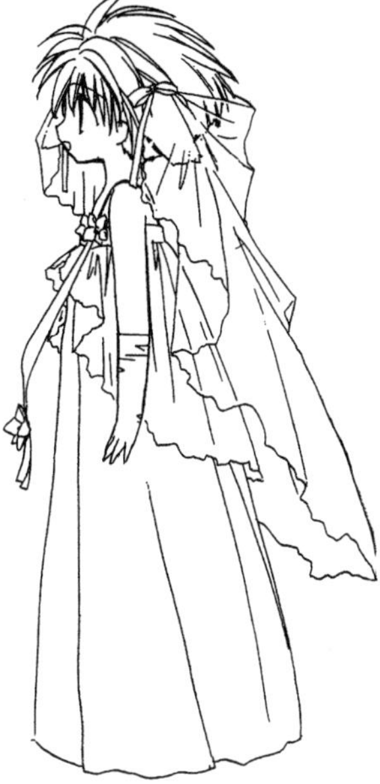

Forte

つけも.

Forte

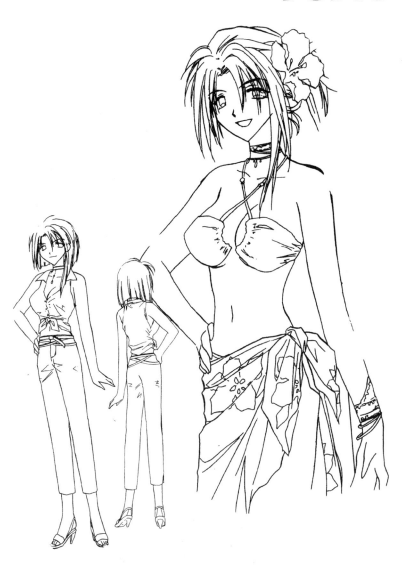

Vanilla

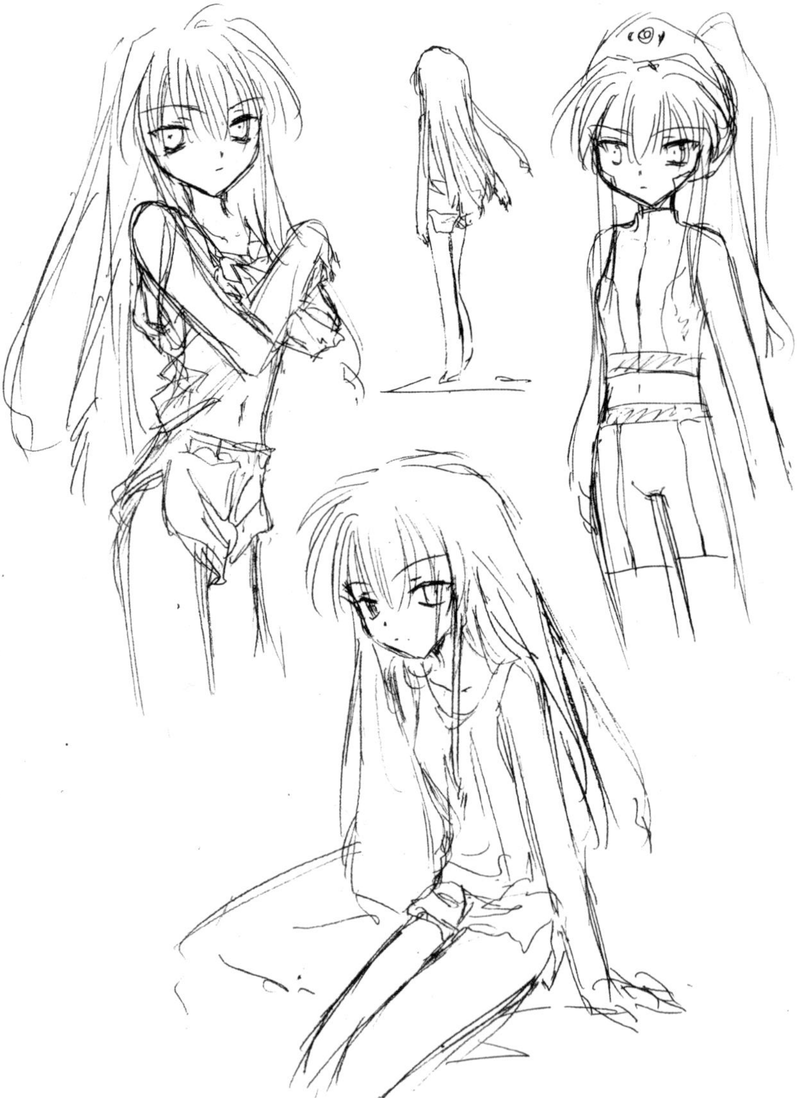

Vanilla

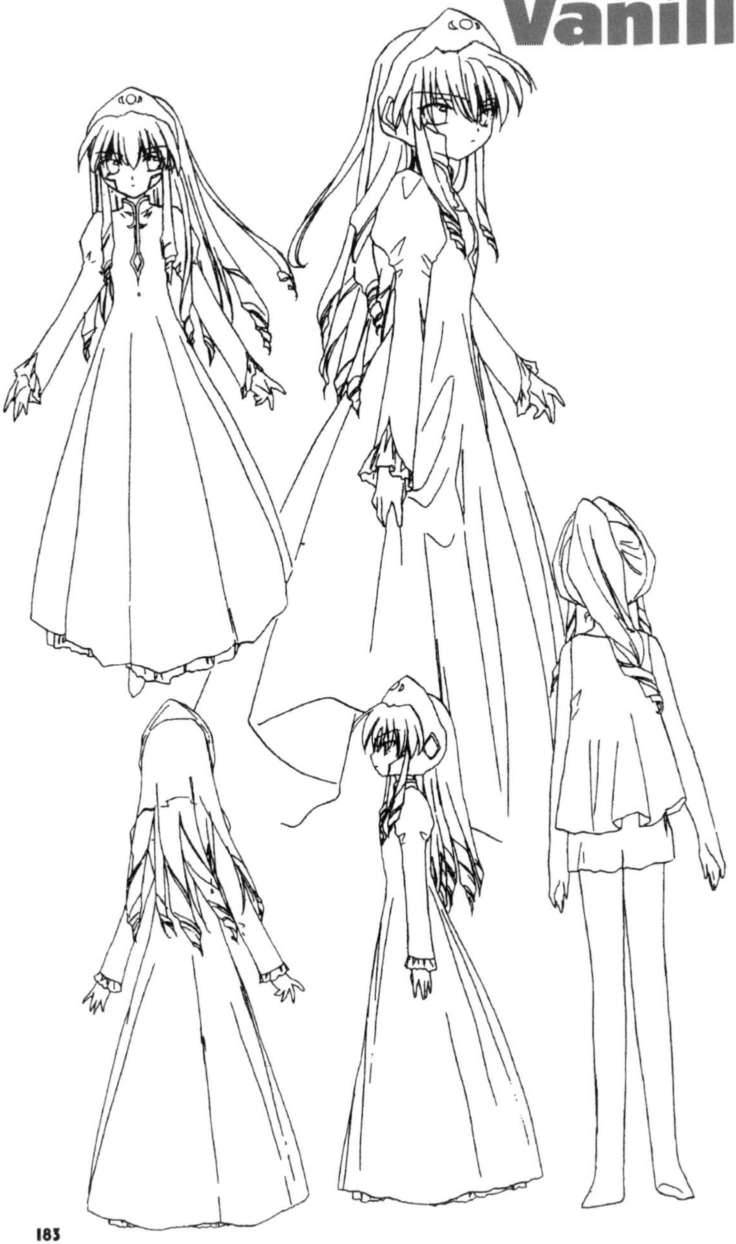

Chitose

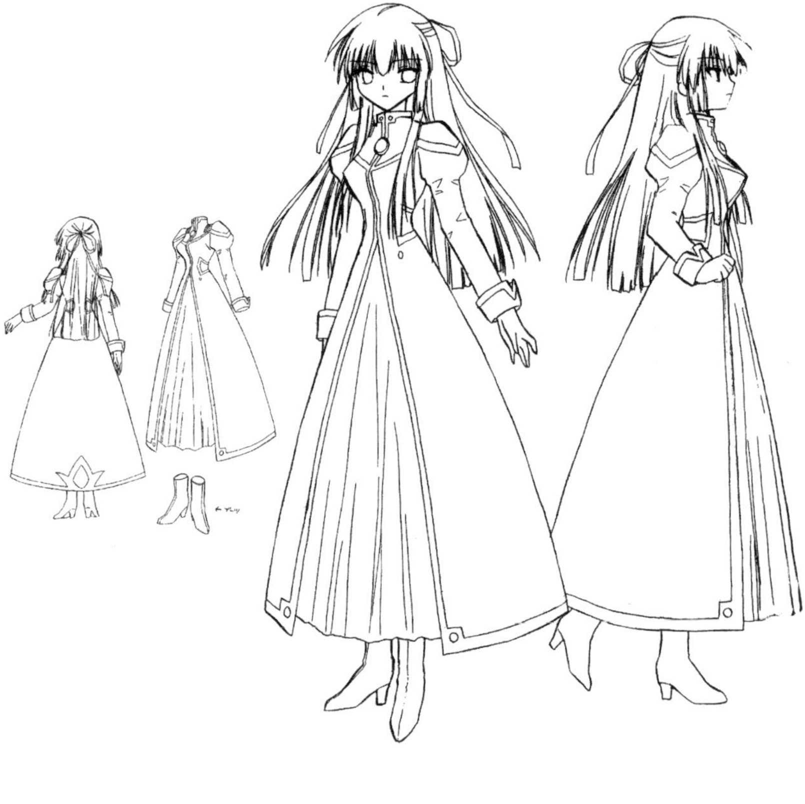

Chitose

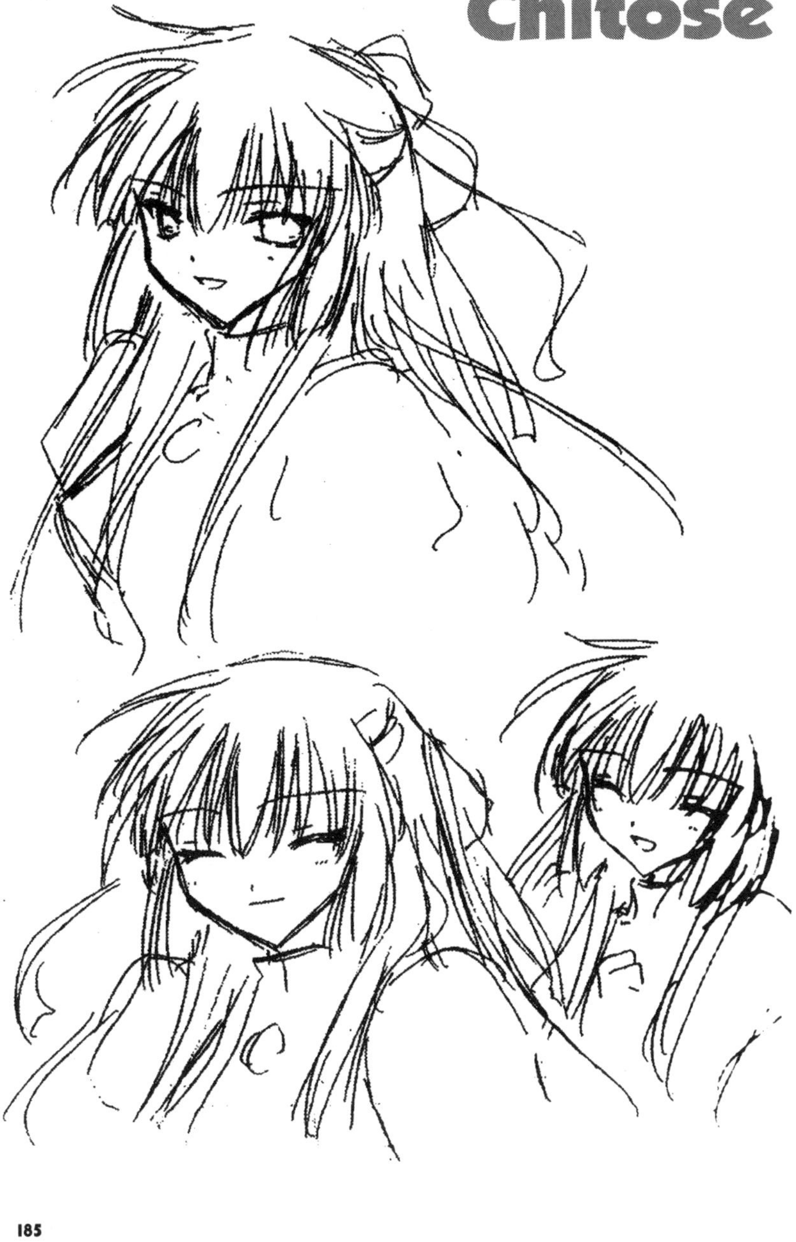

Takuto

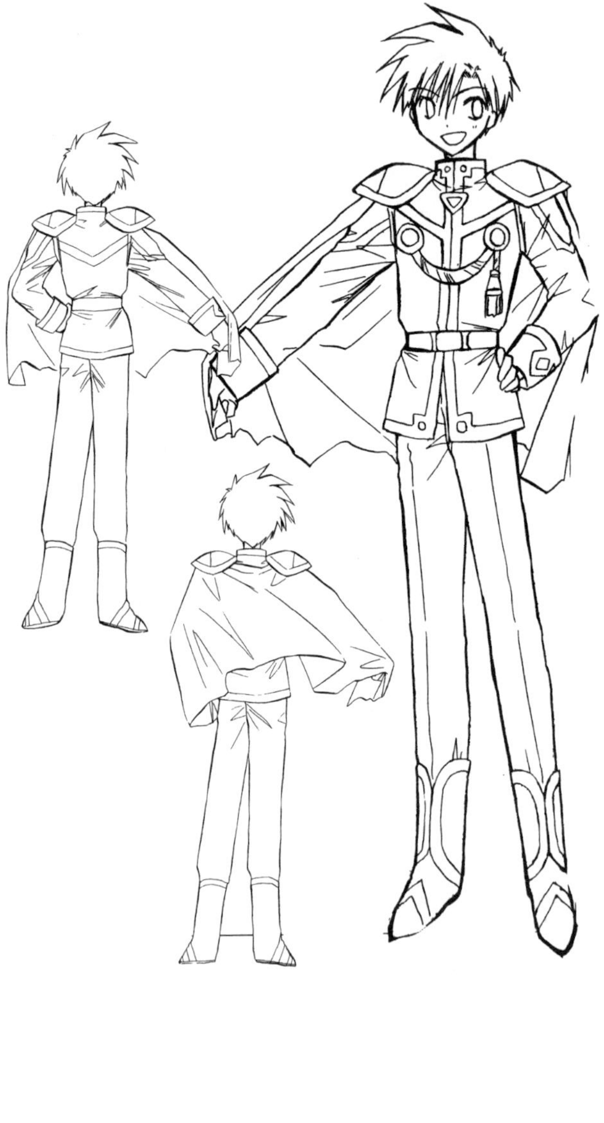

Lester

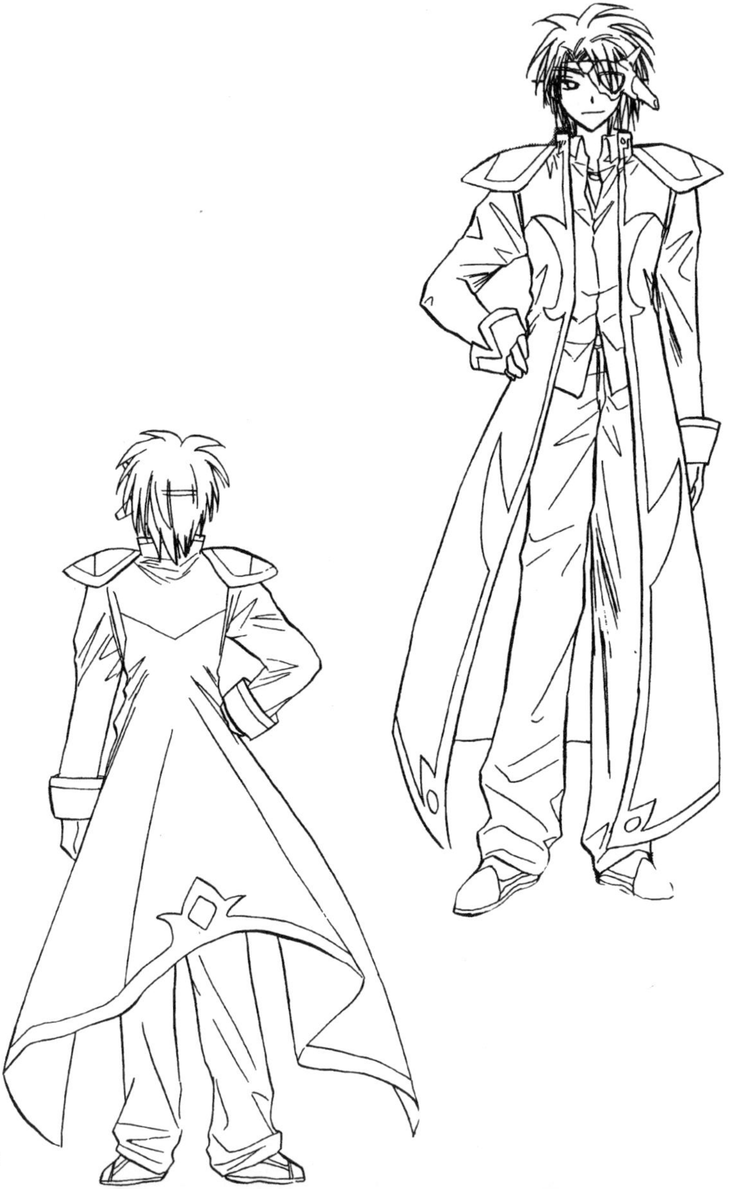

Shiva

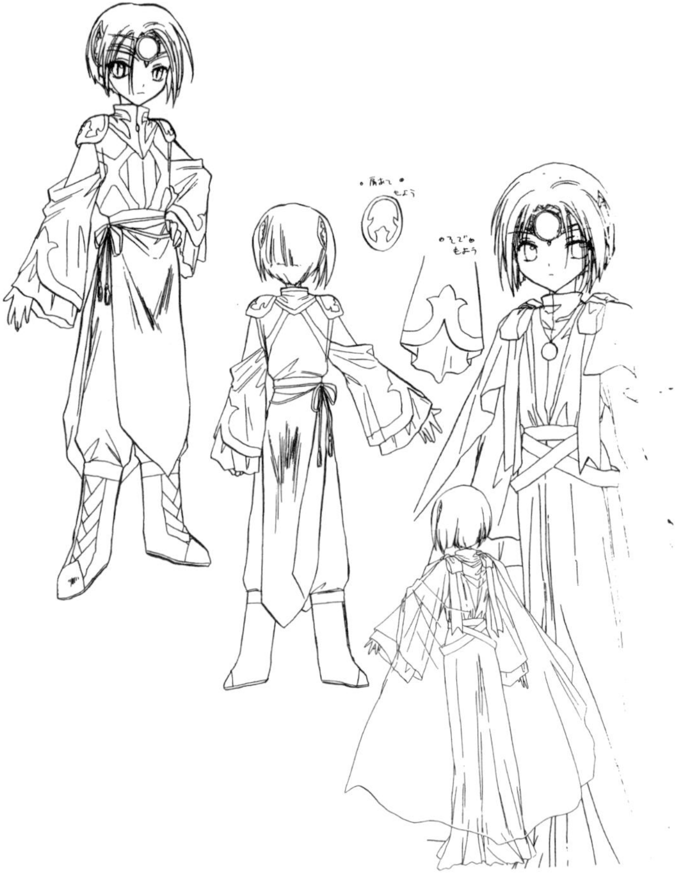

・肩あて・もよう
・そで・もよう

Shatoyan

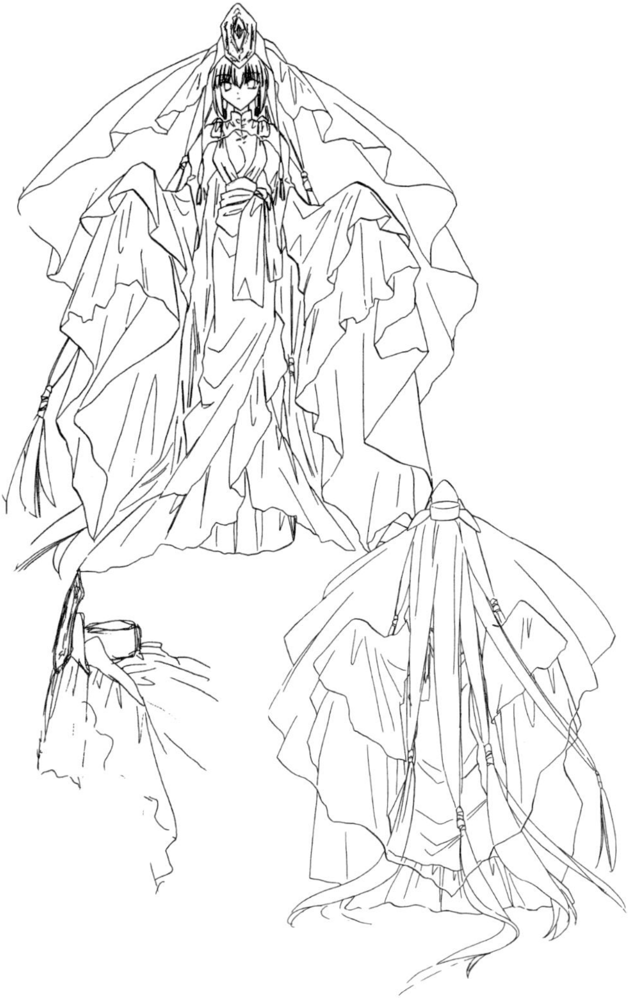

Eonia

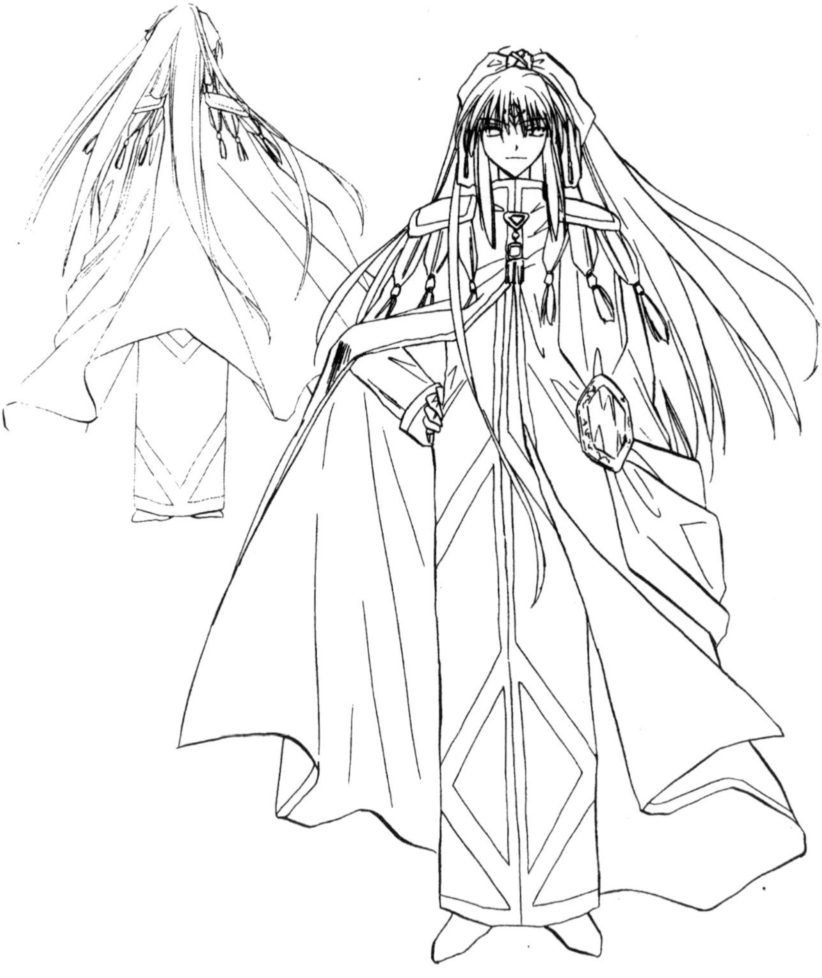

Noa

keychains

stickers

GALAXY ANGEL
ノーマッド
ステッカー
Vanilla
H
ステッカー
Forte
Stollen
ステッカー

Mint cosplay trading plush

trading pins

postcards

trading figures

6" Mint statuette

Available at your local anime store

For more information visit:
www.bro-usa.com

Galaxy Angel™ Merchandise

cell phone straps

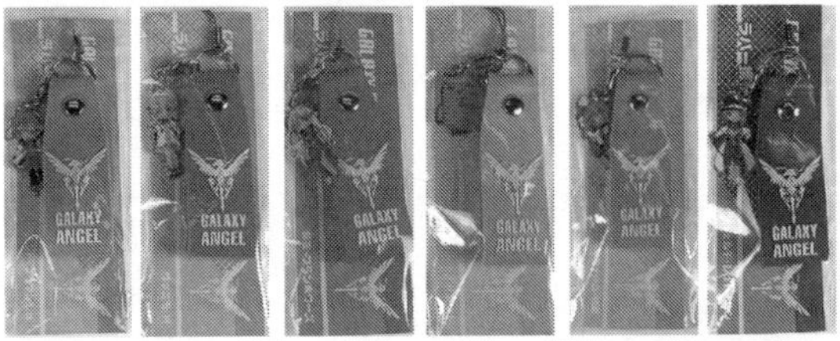

7" Milfeulle statuette

mousepads

deck cases

pencil boards

clear posters

clear stickers

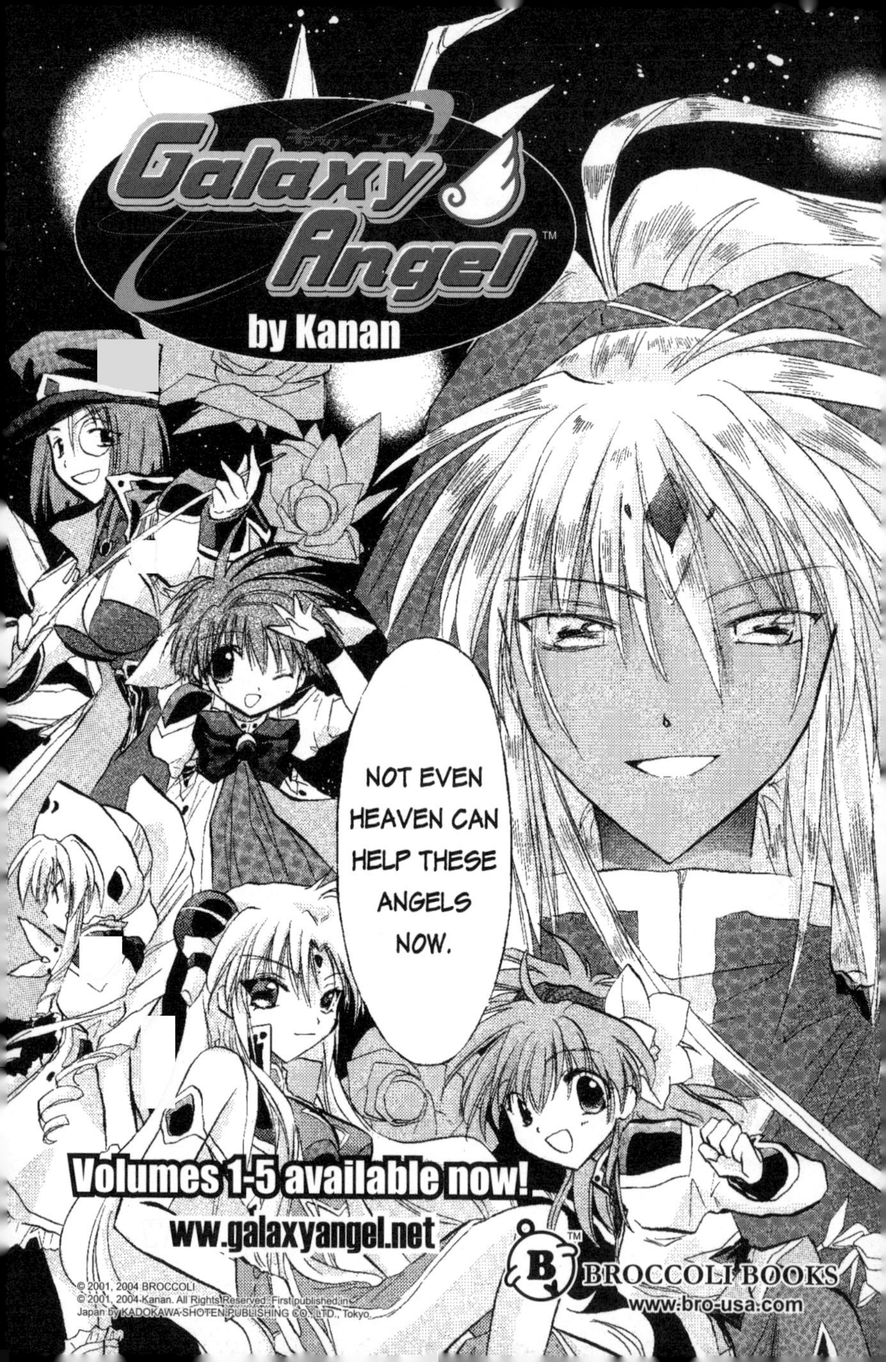

Galaxy Angel™
by Kanan
NOT EVEN HEAVEN CAN HELP THESE ANGELS NOW.
Volumes 1-5 available now!
www.galaxyangel.net
BROCCOLI BOOKS
www.bro-usa.com
© 2001, 2004 BROCCOLI
© 2001, 2004 Kanan. All Rights Reserved. First published in Japan by KADOKAWA-SHOTEN PUBLISHING CO., LTD., Tokyo.

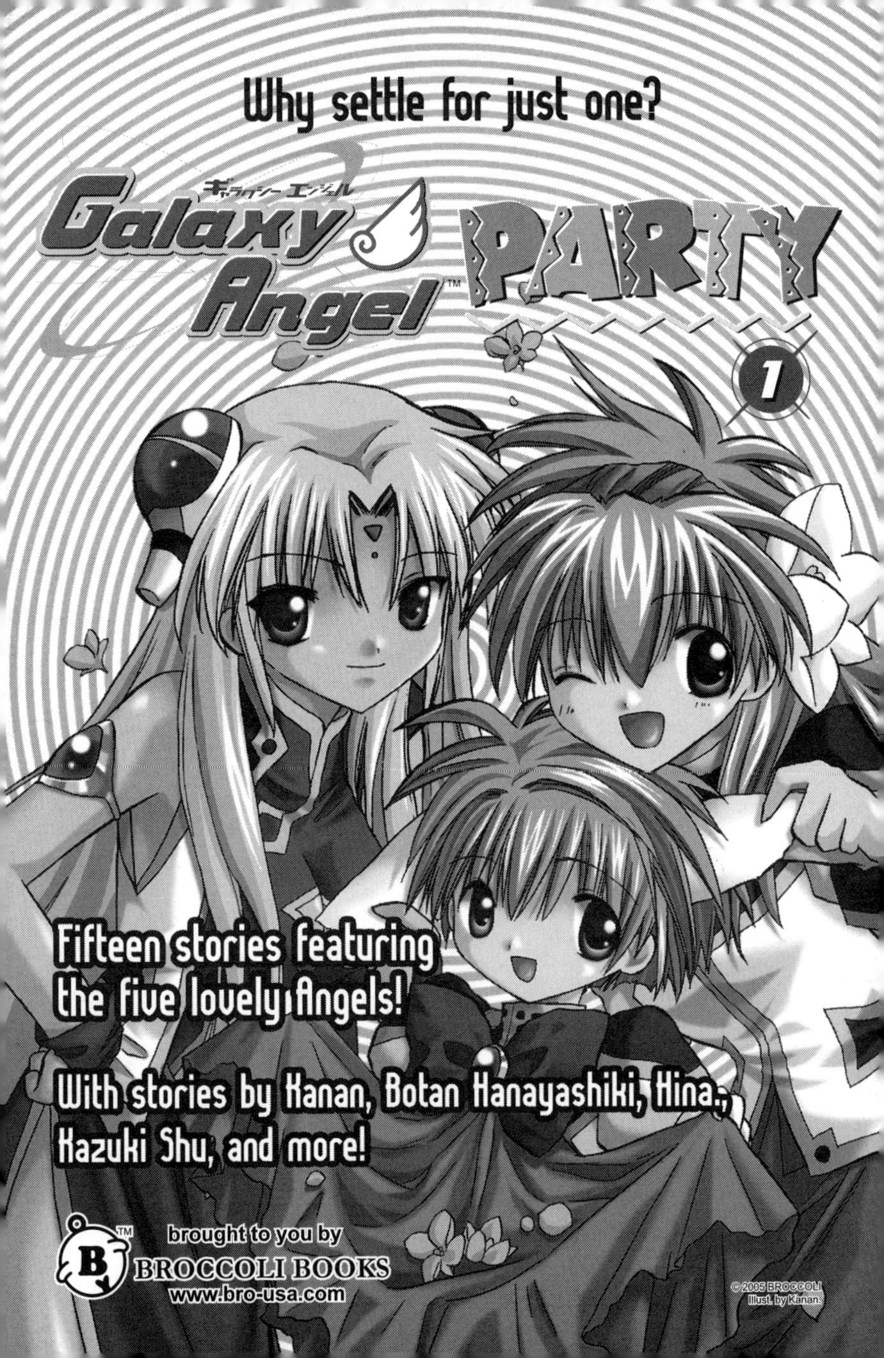
Why settle for just one?
Galaxy Angel™ PARTY 1
Fifteen stories featuring the five lovely Angels!
With stories by Kanan, Botan Hanayashiki, Hina., Kazuki Shu, and more!
brought to you by
BROCCOLI BOOKS
www.bro-usa.com
© 2005 BROCCOLI
Illust. by Kanan.

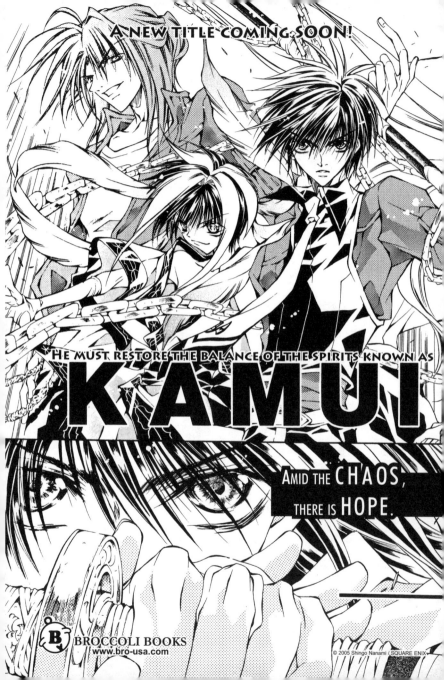

Join the celebration!

Di Gi Charat Theater - Leave it to Piyoko!, starring none other than Pyocola-sama, is coming out!

Support us, the Black Gema Gema Gang, and our mission to save Planet Analogue by buying the manga!!

Coming soon to your local bookstores!

© HINA. 2002
© BROCCOLI 2002

© 2004 BROCCOLI
First published in 2002 by Media Works Inc., Tokyo, Japan. English
translation rights arranged with Media Works Inc. through BROCCOLI Co., Ltd

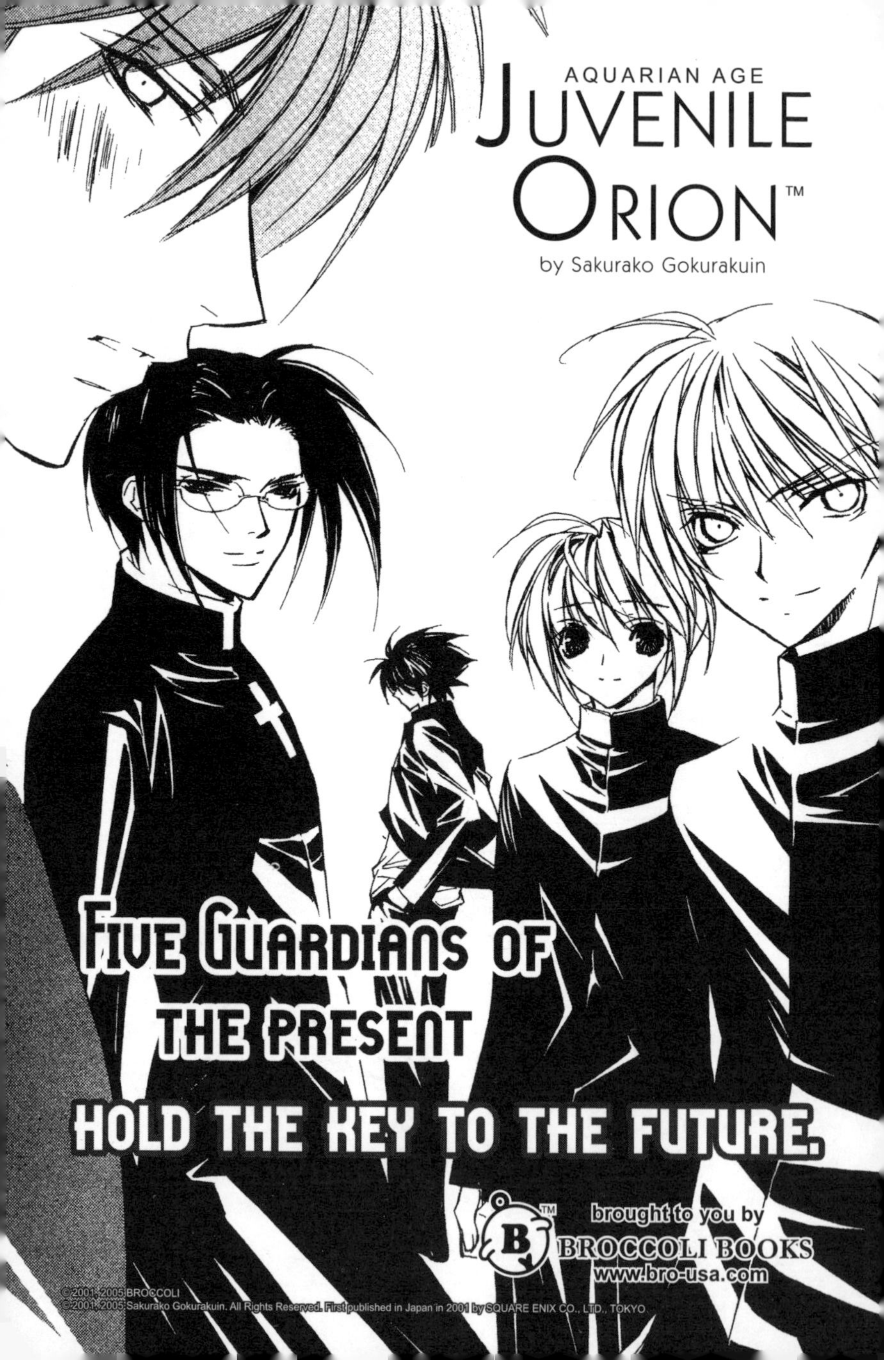
AQUARIAN AGE
JUVENILE ORION™
by Sakurako Gokurakuin
FIVE GUARDIANS OF THE PRESENT
HOLD THE KEY TO THE FUTURE.
brought to you by
BROCCOLI BOOKS
www.bro-usa.com
© 2001, 2005 BROCCOLI
© 2001, 2005 Sakurako Gokurakuin. All Rights Reserved. First published in Japan in 2001 by SQUARE ENIX CO., LTD., TOKYO.

BROCCOLI BOOKS

READ॥ POINT॥ CLICK॥

www.bro-usa.com

After reading some Broccoli Books manga, why not look for more on
the web? Check out the latest news, upcoming releases, character
profiles, synopses, manga previews, production blog and fan art!

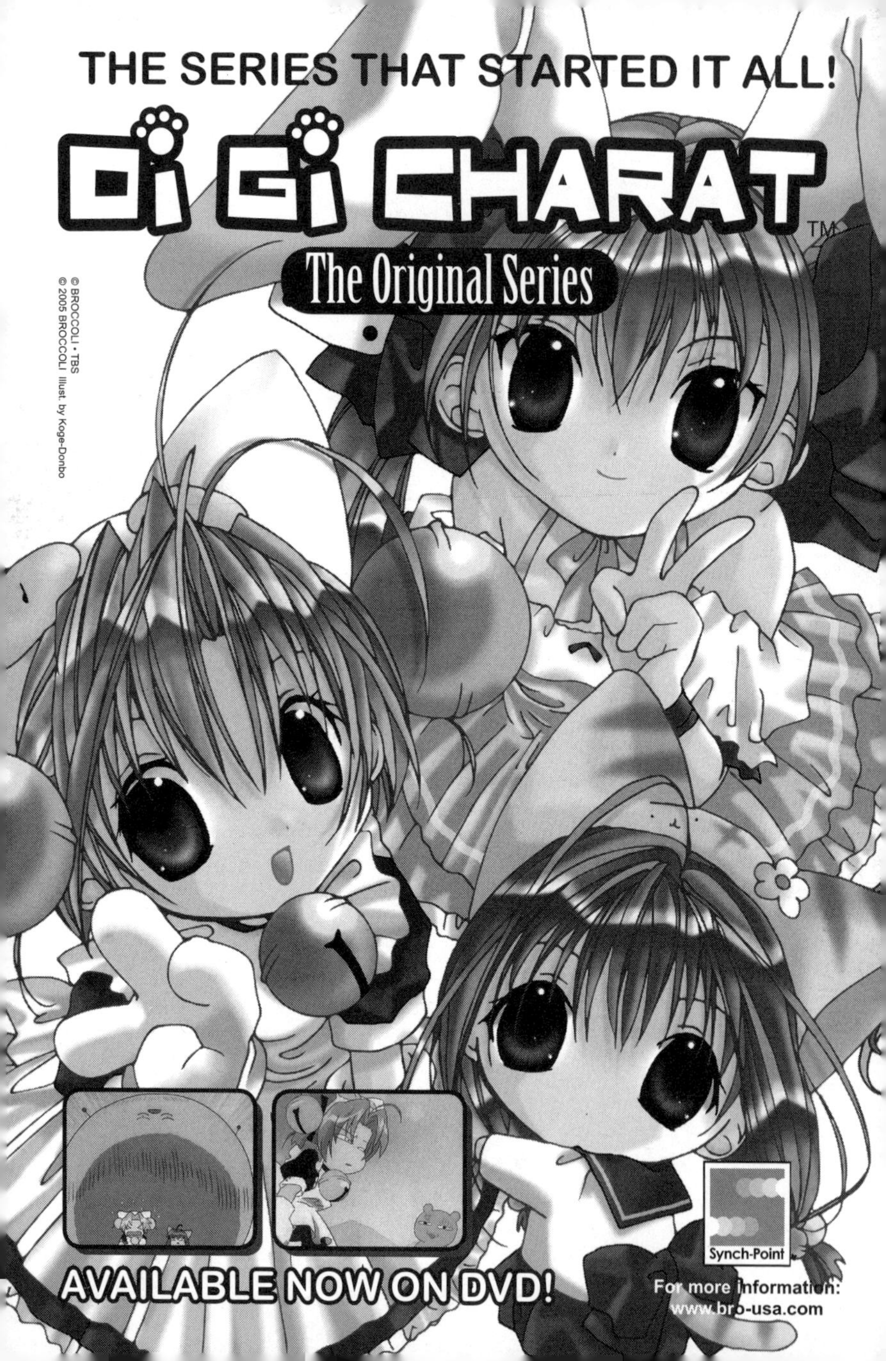
THE SERIES THAT STARTED IT ALL!
DI GI CHARAT™
The Original Series
© BROCCOLI • TBS
© 2005 BROCCOLI Illust. by Koge-Donbo
Synch-Point
AVAILABLE NOW ON DVD!
For more information:
www.bro-usa.com

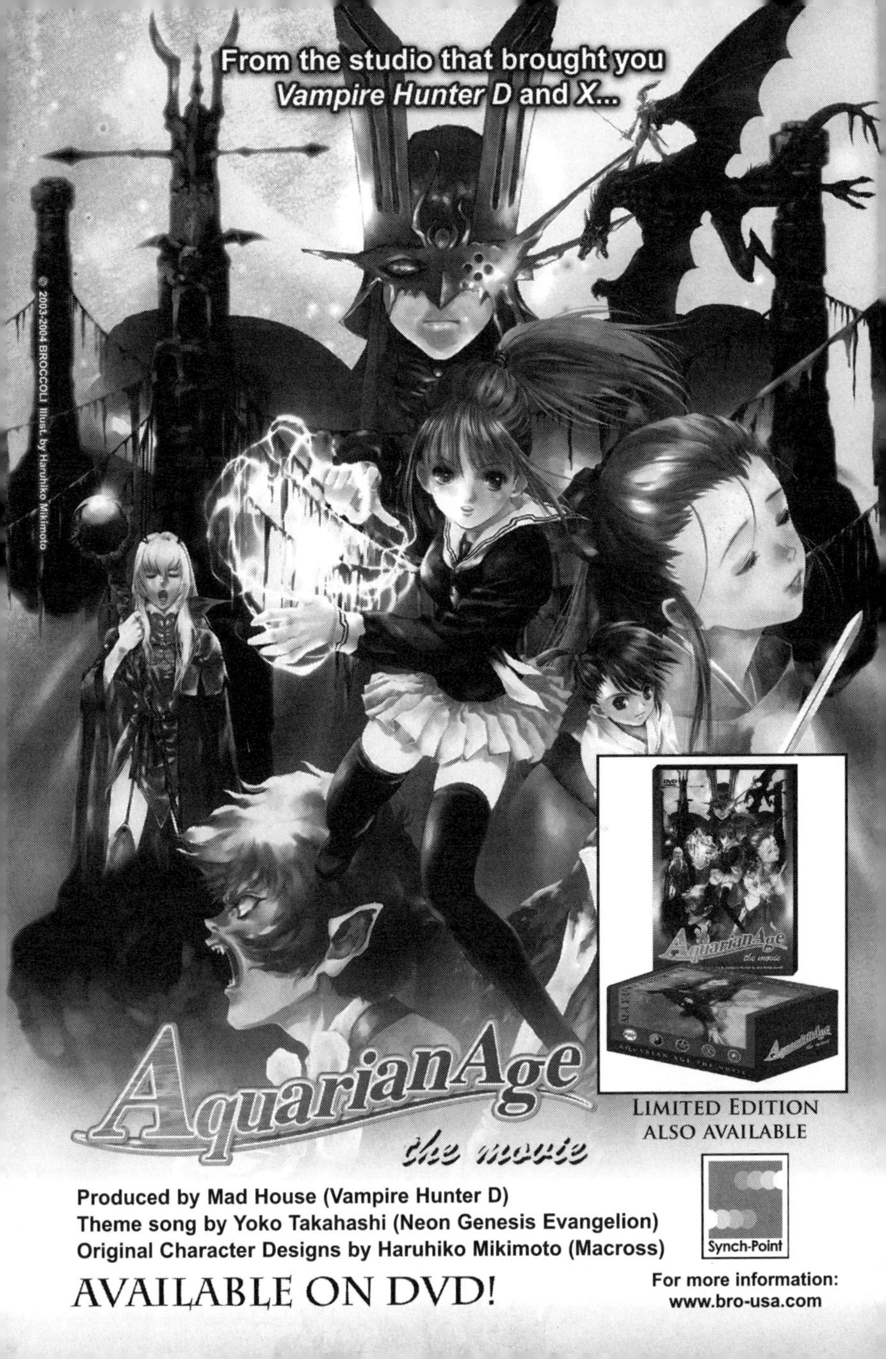
From the studio that brought you
Vampire Hunter D and *X*...
© 2003-2004 BROCCOLI Illust. by Haruhiko Mikimoto
AquarianAge
the movie
LIMITED EDITION
ALSO AVAILABLE
Produced by Mad House (Vampire Hunter D)
Theme song by Yoko Takahashi (Neon Genesis Evangelion)
Original Character Designs by Haruhiko Mikimoto (Macross)
AVAILABLE ON DVD!
Synch-Point
For more information:
www.bro-usa.com

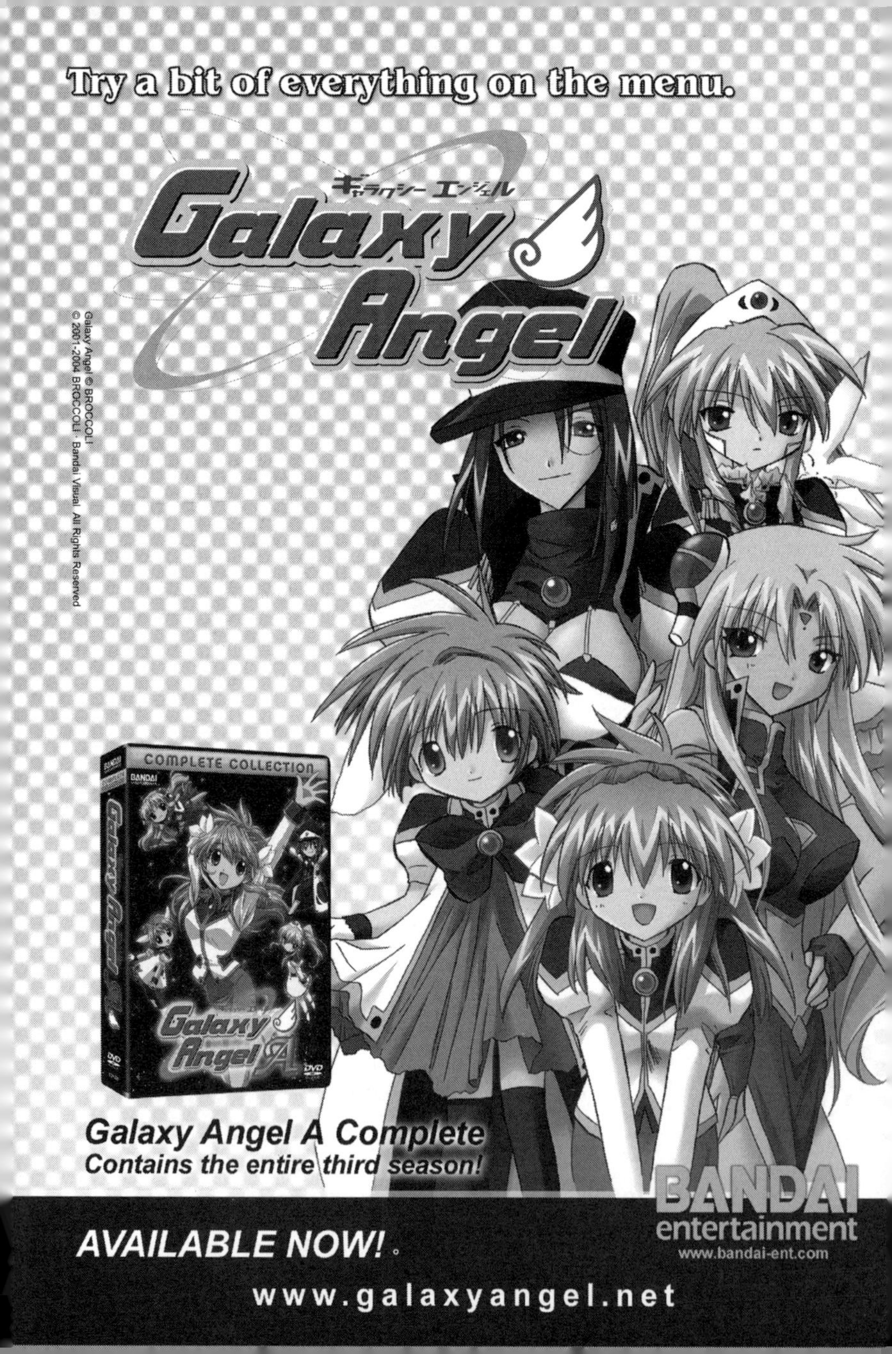
Try a bit of everything on the menu.
ギャラクシーエンジェル
Galaxy Angel
Galaxy Angel © BROCCOLI
© 2001-2004 BROCCOLI · Bandai Visual All Rights Reserved
COMPLETE COLLECTION
BANDAI
Galaxy Angel A
DVD
Galaxy Angel A Complete
Contains the entire third season!
BANDAI
entertainment
www.bandai-ent.com
AVAILABLE NOW!
www.galaxyangel.net

FIGURES WITH ATTITUDE.

STOP!
YOU'RE READING THE WRONG WAY!

This is the end of the book! In Japan, manga is generally read from right to left. All reading starts on the upper right corner, and ends on the lower left. American comics are generally read from left to right, starting on the upper left of each page. In order to preserve the true nature of the work, we printed this book in a right to left fashion. Those who are unfamiliar with manga may find this confusing at first, but once you start getting into the story, you will wonder how you ever read manga any other way!

GA

THIS QUESTIONNAIRE IS REDEEMABLE FOR:

Galaxy Angel Beta Volume 1 Dust Jacket

Broccoli Books Questionnaire

Fill out and return to Broccoli Books to receive your corresponding dust jacket!*

PLEASE MAIL THE COMPLETE FORM, ALONG WITH UNUSED UNITED STATES POSTAGE STAMPS WORTH $1.50 ENCLOSED IN THE ENVELOPE TO:**

    Broccoli International
    Attn: Broccoli Books Dust Jacket Committee
    P.O. Box 66078
    Los Angeles, CA 90066

(Please write legibly)

Name: _____

Address: _____

City, State, Zip: _____

E-mail: _____

Gender: ☐ Male ☐ Female **Age:** _____

(If you are under 13 years old, parental consent is required)

Parent/Guardian signature: _____

Occupation: _____

Where did you hear about this title?

☐ Magazine (Please specify): _____

☐ Flyer from: a store convention club other: _____

☐ Website (Please specify): _____

☐ At a store (Please specify): _____

☐ Word of Mouth

☐ Other (Please specify): _____

Where was this title purchased? (If known)
_____

Why did you buy this title?
_____
_____
_____

How would you rate the following features of this manga?

	Excellent	Good	Satisfactory	Poor
Translation	☐	☐	☐	☐
Art quality	☐	☐	☐	☐
Cover	☐	☐	☐	☐
Extra/Bonus Material	☐	☐	☐	☐

What would you like to see improved in Broccoli Books manga?

____

Would you recommend this manga to someone else? ☐ Yes ☐ No

What related products would you be interested in?

☐ Posters ☐ Apparel Other: ______________________________

Which magazines do you read on a regular basis?

____

What manga titles would you like to see in English?

____

Favorite manga titles: ______________________________

Favorite manga artists: ______________________________

What race/ethnicity do you consider yourself? (Please check one)

☐ Asian/Pacific Islander ☐ Native American/Alaskan Native

☐ Black/African American ☐ White/Caucasian

☐ Hispanic/Latino ☐ Other: ______________________________

Final comments about this manga:

____

____

____

CUT ALONG HERE

Thank you!

* While supplies last.

** For Canada residents, please send an international money order of $3.00 made out to "Broccoli International."